MW01283620

Microsoft Office Automation with Visual FoxPro

Tamar E. Granor
Della Martin

Hentzenwerke Publishing

Published by:
Hentzenwerke Publishing
980 East Circle Drive
Whitefish Bay WI 53217 USA

Hentzenwerke Publishing books are available through booksellers and directly from the publisher. Contact Hentzenwerke Publishing at:
414.332.9876
414.332.9463 (fax)
www.hentzenwerke.com
books@hentzenwerke.com

Microsoft Office Automation with Visual FoxPro
    By Tamar E. Granor and Della Martin
    Technical Editor: Ted Roche
    Copy Editor: Farion Grove

This is dedicated to the ones we love.

Our Contract with You, The Reader

In which we, the folks that make up Hentzenwerke Publishing, describe what you, the reader, can expect from this book and from us.

Hi there!

I've been writing professionally (in other words, eventually getting a paycheck for my scribbles) since 1974, and writing about software development since 1992. As an author, I've worked with a half-dozen different publishers, and corresponded with thousands of readers over the years. As a software developer and all-around geek, I've also acquired a library of more than 100 computer and software-related books.

Thus, when I donned the publisher's cap four years ago to produce the *1997 Developer's Guide,* I had some pretty good ideas of what I liked (and didn't like) from publishers, what readers liked and didn't like, and what I, as a reader, liked and didn't like.

Now, with our new titles for the spring and summer of 2000, we're entering our third season. (For those keeping track, the '97 DevGuide was our first, albeit abbreviated, season, and the batch of six "Essentials" for Visual FoxPro 6.0 in 1999 was our second.)

John Wooden, the famed UCLA basketball coach, had posited that teams aren't consistent—they're always getting better—or worse. We'd like to get better… One of my goals for this season is to build a closer relationship with you, the reader.

In order to do this, you've got to know what you should expect from us.

- You have the right to expect that your order will be processed quickly and correctly, and that your book will be delivered to you in new condition.

- You have the right to expect that the content of your book is technically accurate and up to date, that the explanations are clear, and that the layout is easy to read and follow without a lot of fluff or nonsense.

- You have the right to expect access to source code, errata, FAQs, and other information that's relevant to the book via our web site.

- You have the right to expect an electronic version of your printed book (in compiled HTML Help format) to be available via our web site.

- You have the right to expect that, if you report errors to us, your report will be responded to promptly, and that the appropriate notice will be included in the errata and/or FAQs for the book.

Naturally, there are some limits that we bump up against. There are humans involved, and they make mistakes. A book of 500 pages contains, on average, 150,000 words and several megabytes of source code. It's not possible to edit and re-edit multiple times to catch every last misspelling and typo, nor is it possible to test the source code on every permutation of development environment and operating system—and still price the book affordably.

Once printed, bindings break, ink gets smeared, signatures get missed during binding. On the delivery side, web sites go down, packages get lost in the mail.

Nonetheless, we'll make our best effort to correct these problems—once you let us know about them.

And, thus, in return, when you have a question or run into a problem, we ask that you first consult the errata and/or FAQs for your book on our web site. If you don't find the answer there, please e-mail us at books@hentzenwerke.com with as much information and detail as possible, including (1) the steps to reproduce the problem, (2) what happened, and (3) what you expected to happen, together with (4) any other relevant information.

I'd like to stress that we need you to communicate questions and problems clearly. For example…

- "Your downloads don't work" isn't enough information for us to help you. "I get a 404 error when I click on the **Download Source Code** link on www.hentzenwerke.com/book/downloads.html" is something we can help you with.

- "The code in chapter 14 caused an error" again isn't enough information. "I performed the following steps to run the source code program DisplayTest.PRG in chapter 14, and received an error that said 'Variable m.liCounter not found'" is something we can help you with.

We'll do our best to get back to you within a couple of days either with an answer, or at least an acknowledgment that we've received your inquiry and that we're working on it.

On behalf of the authors, technical editors, copy editors, layout artists, graphical artists, indexers, and all the other folks who have worked to put this book in your hands, I'd like to thank you for purchasing this book, and hope that it will prove to be a valuable addition to your technical library. Please let us know what you think about this book—we're looking forward to hearing from you.

As Groucho Marx once observed, "Outside of a dog, a book is a man's best friend. Inside of a dog, it's too dark to read."

Whil Hentzen
Hentzenwerke Publishing
May, 2000

List of Chapters

APPENDICES   417

Table of Contents

SECTION II—Automating Word   39

Chapter 4: Word Basics   41

Chapter 5: Intermediate Word   83

SECTION IV—Automating PowerPoint — 257

Chapter 10: PowerPoint Basics — 259

Chapter 11: PowerPoint Advanced Features — 297

Acknowledgements

As is true for any work of this sort, we couldn't have written this book without the help of many people. We'll start with shared thanks to the people who contributed in one way or another to the content of the book, then finish with our more personal thank yous.

Our technical editor, Ted Roche, tested tons of examples, asked hard questions, caught us when we got sloppy, and generally did the things technical editors are supposed to do. But he really did much more because he's the one who first showed Tamar how elegant Automation could be and got her hooked on it. Without Ted, this book would never have existed.

Whil Hentzen has been a friend for much longer than he's been a publishing magnate. Thanks for once again providing an outlet for people who just need to put words on pages.

Lots of people answered our questions as we tried to understand how Office worked. Many of them are Microsoft MVPs for the help they give others. Our thanks to Chris Woodman, Bob Buckland, Brian Reilly, Rolf Keller, Jessie Louise McClennan, Mike Sherrill, and Steven Stern. Special thanks to Cindy Meister, who reviewed some of the Word material in an earlier form, as well as answering tons of questions. Our apologies to anyone we missed.

A couple of people provided more than just answers. Rick Strahl allowed us to include GetConstants.EXE, an application that extracts the constants from a type library, in the Developer Download files available at www.hentzenwerke.com. See Chapter 2, "The Office Servers," for more information.

John V. Petersen introduced us to VFPCOM.DLL, which provides two-way communication between VFP and Automation servers (see Chapter 13, "Inter-Office Communication"), and wrote a special DLL that makes it work with PowerPoint. John's DLL is included in the Developer Download files. Robert Green of Microsoft also provided some of the information we needed to include VFPCOM.DLL.

Sometimes, the biggest help comes not from answering our questions, but from providing ideas and opportunities. In 1995, Brian Jones approached Della with his ideas for an Office Automation component of the famous JFAST program. Della's been writing Automation code ever since. Thanks to Brian's ideas and the ability to implement them in such a long-lived project, Della has the knowledge and experience to document for others in this book.

Over the years, far too many people in the FoxPro community have helped us out for us to begin to list them all here. You know who you are, and we appreciate all your help. However, special thanks to Mac Rubel, who helped formulate some of these ideas very early in the process, and Dan Freeman, who taught Tamar an awful lot about spelunking in the Office object models.

Many people in a number of different product groups at Microsoft have participated in bringing Automation to the point that it's a viable technology. We don't know their names, but we sure do appreciate their work.

By the time you write the third book, your family gets kind of used to it and starts wondering if it's an addiction of some sort. (It is.) Thanks once again to my husband, Marshal, who makes it all possible, and my sons, Solomon and Nathaniel, who make it worthwhile.

To my extended family and friends, your willingness to let me babble on about my work is always appreciated, as is the change of pace from it you provide.

Thanks as always to the crew at Advisor Media, and my other friends and colleagues in the professional community.

—Tamar

Because this is my first book, my family is just getting used to this, and, thanks to Tamar's influence, they're assuming this is going to become a way of life. (I hope so.) My husband, Mike, has been a terrific source of encouragement, inspiration, and support. My daughter, Kelsey, and my son, Kerry, have been wonderfully patient, hearing me say many, many times, "We'll do that later, honey. Mommy's writing her book, now."

Thanks to my Mom and Dad, for all their love and immense support. My extended family deserves a lot of credit for putting up with my laptop at a number of family gatherings.

There are so many others of you to thank. Many thanks to the CompuServe FoxGang, for all the confidence and knowledge you've helped me build. Thank you so much to my co-workers at the Systems Development Institute at the University of Tennessee, and especially the entire JFAST team. And to all the friends and acquaintances I've met on-line and at DevCons, thanks for your encouragement.

Tamar, Ted, and Whil: a special thanks to you for inviting me to collaborate with you, and make my dream of writing a book come true.

—della

About the Authors

Tamar E. Granor

Tamar E. Granor, Ph.D., has developed and enhanced numerous FoxPro and Visual FoxPro applications for businesses and other organizations. She served as Editor of *FoxPro Advisor* magazine from 1994 to 2000, and is co-author of the magazine's popular *Advisor Answers* column.

With Ted Roche, Tamar is co-author of the *Hacker's Guide to Visual FoxPro 6.0* (Hentzenwerke Publishing, www.hentzenwerke.com), one of the most widely recommended Visual FoxPro books ever, and its predecessor, the *Hacker's Guide to Visual FoxPro 3.0* (Addison-Wesley).

Tamar is a Microsoft Certified Professional and a Microsoft Support Most Valuable Professional. Tamar speaks frequently about Visual FoxPro at conferences and user groups in North America and Europe. She served as Technical Content Manager for the 1997–1999 Visual FoxPro DevCons and as part of the coordination team for the Visual FoxPro Excellence Awards.

Tamar earned her doctorate in Computer and Information Science at the University of Pennsylvania, where her research focused on implementation of user interfaces. Tamar lives in suburban Philadelphia with her husband and two teenage sons. E-mail: tamar_granor@compuserve.com.

Della Martin

Della Martin has worked on some of the most unusual FoxPro and Visual FoxPro applications. She got her start writing a recruiting database for Duke Basketball while attending Duke University. She majored in both Design and History.

Continuing in the line of non-traditional database applications, Della worked for Woolpert, an architectural and engineering firm, where she specialized in GIS work for such diverse applications as water distribution systems, military master planning, oil well evacuation plans, and facility management programs. She moved on to the University of Tennessee to work on a military logistics application, JFAST, perhaps the most well known VFP application in the world. At nearly every DevCon since 1994, attendees have seen this cutting-edge application, which includes sophisticated briefing and analysis tools developed by Della using Automation with many Microsoft products. Since Della's recent move to North Carolina, she is still consulting for the University of Tennessee, as well as other clients.

Della has written for *FoxPro Advisor* magazine, and served as a judge for the 1998 and 1999 Visual FoxPro Excellence Awards. She has spoken at various conferences, including the American Water Works Association Computer Specialty Conferences, and was a panelist at the 1996 Microsoft Developers Conference. Della lives in Cary, North Carolina, with her husband and two school-age children. E-mail: dellamartin@aol.com.

Ted Roche

Ted Roche develops commercial applications using Microsoft Visual Studio, Microsoft Back Office, and other best-of-breed tools. He is a Director of Development at Blackstone

Incorporated, a Microsoft Certified Solution Provider based in Waltham, Massachusetts. He is co-author of the critically acclaimed *Hacker's Guide to Visual FoxPro 6.0* (Hentzenwerke Publishing, www.hentzenwerke.com), contributor to numerous magazine articles, and a frequent speaker at FoxPro conferences worldwide. Ted is an MCSD, MCSE, and MVP. E-mail: troche@bstone.com, phone: (781) 663-7423.

How to Download the Files

There are two sets of files that accompany this book. The first is the source code referenced throughout the text, and noted by the spider web icon; the second is the e-book version of this book—the compiled HTML Help (.CHM) file. Here's how to get them.

Both the source code and the CHM file are available for download from the Hentzenwerke web site. In order to do so, follow these instructions:

1. Point your web browser to www.hentzenwerke.com.

2. Look for the link that says "Download Source Code & .CHM Files." (The text for this link may change over time—if it does, look for a link that references Books or Downloads.)

3. A page describing the download process will appear. This page has two sections:

Section 1: If you were issued a username/password from Hentzenwerke Publishing, you can enter them into this page.

Section 2: If you did not receive a username/password from Hentzenwerke Publishing, don't worry! Just enter your e-mail alias and look for the question about your book. Note that you'll need your book when you answer the question.

4. A page that lists the hyperlinks for the appropriate downloads will appear.

Note that the .CHM file is covered by the same copyright laws as the printed book. Reproduction and/or distribution of the .CHM file is against the law.

If you have questions or problems, the fastest way to get a response is to e-mail us at books@hentzenwerke.com.

Introduction

What is this book? Why do you need it? How do you use it?

This book grew out of another book. In 1995, when FoxPro grew into Visual FoxPro, Tamar, together with Ted Roche, the technical editor of this book, wrote a book called *Hacker's Guide to Visual FoxPro 3.0* (Addison-Wesley). The bulk of that book, nearly 700 of its 900-some pages, was an alphabetic reference to every command, function, property, event, method, and system variable in Visual FoxPro. Oddly enough, Tamar and Ted didn't just sit down and create a single Word document starting from "A" and working their way through to "Z." In fact, about 600 documents went into that section of the book.

When the writing was done and the smoke cleared, Ted had a brilliant idea. (Actually, he had the idea well before the writing was done.) VFP 3 was the first version of the product to support Automation. He wrote some code to take those 600 documents and put them together in the right order to create the reference section of the Hacker's Guide.

In 1998, Tamar and Ted were at it again with an updated and expanded version called *Hacker's Guide to Visual FoxPro 6.0* (Hentzenwerke). This time, Tamar took on the task of assembling the book while Ted used Automation to turn the whole thing into an HTML Help file. With the new material from VFP 5 and 6, there weren't 600 documents involved; there were more than 800.

In addition, changes in the way the book was managed meant that, before producing the final version, a lot of clean-up work had to be done. For example, Microsoft had changed the name of the product during the beta process. (Visual FoxPro 98 became Visual FoxPro 6.) The copy editor had done a wonderful job of finding inconsistencies in terminology, catching things like "textbox" vs. "text box," but some sections edited early in the process needed to be corrected. The biggest issue of all came very late in the game when a decision was made to make the book 8.5" x 11" instead of 7" x 9"—this meant that margins had to be changed, tables had to be resized, and many other changes were needed to every one of those 800+ documents.

Handling all of these changes by hand would have taken months and the book would have been hopelessly late. Automation to the rescue. Tamar wrote VFP code to open each document in Word, do the necessary processing, and save it as a new document. After all the processing was done, an updated version of Ted's original assembly code created the reference section.

Along the way, while falling in love with Automation, Tamar beat her head against the wall regularly. Brute force was the order of the day. The Word documentation was helpful, as were the people on CompuServe's MSWord forum. But nowhere was there a real resource for someone writing Automation code like this, especially someone writing it from Visual FoxPro.

Meanwhile, back at the ranch

While Tamar and Ted were having adventures with books, Della was working on perhaps the best-known FoxPro application in the world. The Joint Flow and Analysis System for Transportation (JFAST) is a logistics application written for the US Department of Defense. It aids in planning the movement of people and materiel—give it a long list of what you need (from tanks to troops to canteens), along with where it is now, where it needs to be, and when it needs to get there, and it produces a detailed schedule to load the people and materiel onto ships and aircraft to get it to its destination. (That sentence is far too bald a statement of what JFAST does. Watching this application in action is an astonishing experience.)

Della's portion of the tool creates reports and briefings that explain the recommended plan. Automation is used to produce PowerPoint briefings, suitable for presenting the plan to high ranking generals, and even the Commander In Chief. Automation is also used to generate a Word document that analyzes the strengths and weakness of the plan. Other modules were developed to automate Microsoft Project and Microsoft Schedule+ to provide still more analytical views.

This all came about when Brian Jones, the genius behind JFAST (and its project manager), came to Della's office with an idea. He knew it was possible to take data from FoxPro tables and put it into another program and that Automation (actually, DDE was the reigning technology at the time) was key. He described what he wanted, and Della set off to accomplish her mission.

First came AutoBrief, the automated briefing system. The idea is that the user can select a series of slides from a master list, and push the Start button. AutoBrief generates slides based on the current data in the FoxPro tables. In AutoBrief's infancy, Office 95 was the current version. Documentation on the Office object models was sparse; as for example code, what example code? Even VB examples were hard to come by. But with a lot of perseverance, Della managed to conquer the PowerPoint object and the Excel model as well—Excel is used to generate the many graphs that are needed in the presentation.

Then came AutoAnalysis, which produces a Word document containing lists, tables, charts, and even verbal analysis. Again, using limited documentation, Della's code produces a very professional document at the touch of a button, including table of contents, index, headers, footers, lists, and Excel graphs and DataMaps. At least Word and Excel had a macro recorder, making it much easier to learn the object model; PowerPoint 95 didn't have a macro recorder at all. (See Chapter 2, "The Office Servers," to find out just how useful the macro recorders are.)

Then Office 97 shipped. The entire object model for Excel, Word, and PowerPoint was radically changed. The change was for the better because each application's object model was *much* more consistent with the other Office applications (that is, had better polymorphism). Regardless of how wonderful the changes were, though, the code was still broken. Big time. It was then that Della realized the value of writing wrapper code. Big time. Fortunately, the wrapper code was a little easier to write, since Office 97 had much better documentation, in both quantity and quality. Error handling became an issue, as more and more users relied heavily on this Automation feature, illustrating the need to check for broken registries, improper installations of Office, and other gotchas that FoxPro developers aren't used to checking.

Della's been developing Automation code in FoxPro on a daily basis since 1995. She still wishes for a good Automation resource for the FoxPro developer. So she jumped at the chance to write this book.

What is this book?

In this book, we'll try to save you from the pain we've already been through. We'll do it in a couple of ways. First, we'll share the key pieces of automating the Office applications, the things we think pretty much anyone working with them needs to know. In fact, we think most of this is relevant whether you're automating Office from Visual FoxPro, Visual Basic, Visual C++, or Visual SquidPro.

Second, we'll tell you everything we know about how to find out more about the Office Automation servers. We'll share our tricks for figuring out which object you need to talk to, what method to call, and which property really matters.

Third, we'll tell you what tripped us up. We'll tell you about the methods that seemed intuitively obvious to us, but in reality, were just the wrong thing.

Versions

This book was written with Visual FoxPro 6.0 (actually VFP 6.0 Service Pack 3, but it applies to the original version as well) and with Microsoft Office 2000. Almost everything here applies as well to Office 97. When there are serious version differences, you'll find an icon in the text to warn you.

On the VFP side, it's a little trickier. Automation worked quite well in VFP 5, and the chances are good that almost everything here works there, too, but we haven't tested most of it there. As we're writing this book, we hope to see early betas for the next version of Visual FoxPro soon. Everything in our past experience tells us that all of this will work there, too, and in fact will work better, that is, that any problems we might have in VFP 6 are likely to get fixed in VFP 7 (or whatever they decide to call it).

Using the examples

Because we're FoxPro programmers, and because every other book on the market uses Visual Basic for examples, the examples in this book are written in VFP. What's amazing, though, is that you have to really look at the code examples to realize that. In this brave new world of Automation and interoperability, VFP code and VB code don't look as different as they used to. But more about that later.

The major examples in this book use the TasTrade database that comes with Visual FoxPro. If you've worked with another Microsoft product (say, Access), you may find the actual data familiar. That's because it is—VFP's TasTrade data is pretty much the same as Access's Northwinds database. There are some differences, but the customers, employees, and data within look pretty similar.

In VFP 6 and later, the system variable _SAMPLES points to the directory where sample programs and data were installed. The examples in this book use this variable to find the TasTrade data. To install the sample data, you must perform the MSDN portion of the VFP installation, which also installs the Help file.

If you're using an earlier version of VFP, replace references to _SAMPLES with HOME()+"\SAMPLES\". In those versions, the samples were installed as part of the main VFP installation. No MSDN installation was needed.

Most of the in-line examples throughout the book assume that you have already created the appropriate Automation server and stored a reference to it in a variable. In the first chapter that addresses each of the servers, we show you how to do so and introduce the variable that we use for that server (for example, oWord for Word). After that, we assume the existence of the variable and that it has a valid reference. If you're working through the examples from the Command Window as you read, you should find this assumption quite comfortable.

For larger examples, we had to make a choice. In real applications, you almost always want to open the Automation server, do what needs to be done, and close the server. In that situation, you can use a local variable to hold the reference to the server. For our purposes, however, we usually want the server to stay open and accessible following the example so that you can examine the results and reference the server from the Command Window. However, we didn't want to leave multiple instances of the servers running, abandoned and using your system resources. So most of the examples that are included in the Developer Downloads clear any variables that might be references to Automation objects, and then create a public variable to reference the server. We do not recommend using this technique in your applications.

Section I
Getting Started

Chapter 1
Introducing Automation

Automation is the latest and most successful in a series of attempts at inter-application communication. It lets one application boss another around.

Once upon a time, every application stood alone. If it needed to do something, it had to do it all by itself. There was no alternative because each application took control of the computer when it ran. That was, more or less, "a long time ago in a galaxy far, far away."

Since those long ago days of DOS, many schemes have been attempted to allow applications to cooperate with each other. Each successive attempt has been an improvement upon the one that preceded it. (Well, most of them have been improvements, anyway.) Automation is the latest and greatest in the never-ending quest for applications that do one thing well and communicate with other applications that do something else well.

If all you have is a hammer, does that make everything a nail?

When you're really familiar with a product, it's tempting to use it for all your needs. Many people have been doing that with their favorite applications for years. We know people who do their word processing in Quattro Pro and others who do "database processing" with mail merge in Word.

Certainly it's true of FoxPro programmers. Need a number cruncher? Write it in FoxPro. Need a word processor? Write it in FoxPro. Need a file manager? Write it in FoxPro. That we can do so many diverse things is a testament to FoxPro's strength and versatility. But using our hammer (FoxPro) to do it doesn't make all those tasks nails.

Both users' needs and applications' capabilities are growing. While it made sense to write a simple word processor for editing customer notes in FoxPro/DOS in 1994, it doesn't make sense to do so in Visual FoxPro 6.0 in 2000. There are too many alternatives out there that can just be plugged into a VFP app.

A brief history of Automation

In the beginning, there was DDE, *Dynamic Data Exchange*. DDE was Windows' first attempt at allowing applications to communicate directly with each other. (Before that, of course, applications could communicate by sharing data through common file formats and the Clipboard.) With DDE, a document could be linked from a client application into a document in a server application. The server exposed one or more "topics" that it could make available; the client could then ask to "discuss" any of those topics. A number of applications still offer DDE.

OLE, the successor to DDE, incorporated several approaches to inter-application communication. The service that gives OLE its acronym, though, is the ability to put a document from one application (the server) inside a document from another (the client). You can *link* the server document to the client document so that the client document gets updated when the server document is changed. Alternatively, you can *embed* the server document in the client document, which makes a copy of the server document, breaking its ties with the original. These two choices led to the name *Object Linking and Embedding*. (Microsoft has actually disavowed that version of the name. As far as it's concerned, OLE is just OLE, but we find it easier to remember its meaning.)

Over time, OLE was extended to support *in-place editing*, which allows objects from one application to be both viewed and edited in another. When the user decides to edit the linked object, the client application's menu is replaced by or supplemented with items from the server application's menu. The user can edit the server document as needed and then return to the client application, at which point the original menus and toolbars return.

The frosting on the OLE cake, though, is Automation, which was introduced in OLE 2.0. With Automation, commands can be issued in one application and sent to another. They're written in standard object code, using the appropriate syntax for the host language (the one issuing them, which in our case is FoxPro). Think of Automation as one application grabbing a megaphone and telling another one what to do. The number of applications that work with Automation, either as the application holding the megaphone or as the application listening on the other end, is increasing all the time.

OLE or ActiveX or COM or what?

Since all of this comes from Microsoft, it goes without saying that the names of things have changed over time. When Automation was first introduced, it was called "OLE Automation." Then "OLE" was changed to "ActiveX," and OLE Automation became, briefly, ActiveX Automation. Ultimately, Microsoft dropped "ActiveX" from the name, and this technology became known as simply "Automation."

The technology that holds the whole thing together is COM (Component Object Model or Common Object Model, depending on the phase of the moon), which specifies ways for applications to work together. The COM umbrella incorporates the OLE/ActiveX techniques and even provides hooks into operating system objects, many of which also work with Automation.

The latest, hottest version of all this is DCOM (for Distributed COM), which allows COM to work across multiple machines. With DCOM, Automation can involve applications running on two different machines.

Putting Automation to work

Two applications are involved in any Automation session. The application that's in charge (issuing the orders) is called the *Automation client* (or just *client*). The application that's being manipulated is the *Automation server* (or just *server*). The client addresses an instance of the server as if it were any other object, reading and setting properties and calling methods. This simple technique means that a Visual FoxPro application (the client) can address anything from the Office applications to Windows' file system to Lotus Notes to all kinds of other things. In fact, VFP itself can be used as an Automation server.

To get started, the client creates an instance of the server application. (See the various "Basics" chapters in the product-specific sections of this book for details on how to do so for each of the Office applications.) Internally, when a client attempts to instantiate a server,

Windows goes off to the registry and says, "Help! Somebody wants to create such-and-such server." The registry looks up the server by name and then finds out what program it is and where that program is stored. Windows executes the program in question (assuming it finds such an entry in the registry and finds the specified program where it's supposed to be). It then returns a reference to the newly executing program to the client, which hangs on to it so it can find it again later.

Obviously, there are lots of places along the way where something can go wrong. The server name might not be found in the registry, the program might not be found where it's supposed to be, there may not be sufficient system resources to start the program, and so on and so forth. If anything goes wrong, an error is raised and the server fails to start. (See Chapter 14, "Handling Automation Errors," for ideas about what to do when that happens.)

However, if all goes well, the client has a reference to the server and can start ordering the server around. It's like being in a restaurant once the waiter has introduced himself. You know his name, and you know what he looks like, so you can call him over when you need him, and you can start telling him what to do. Except for one thing. You don't know what's on the menu. You can make some educated guesses based on what the place looks like. For an application, that corresponds to guesswork based on which application it is and what you know it does. But to use the restaurant efficiently, you need the menu. To work with the application server efficiently, you need to know what it can do. Chapter 2, "The Office Servers," examines how to find the menu for an application server.

Where do you go from here?

The remaining chapters in Section I take a look at the Office servers generally and at VFP's commands and functions for writing Automation code. Chapter 2 shows how to explore the Office servers to find out what they can do and how they do it. Chapter 3, "Visual FoxPro as an Automation Client," examines FoxPro's role as an Automation client.

Sections II through V each focus on one of the Office applications. Word, Excel, and PowerPoint have a lot in common, so those three sections are structured in a fairly similar manner, each starting with a "Basics" chapter and then branching out into more advanced topics for that application. Outlook has its own outlook on the world. (We don't discuss Access in this book because automating Access from Visual FoxPro didn't seem like a pressing need, though it is possible.)

It's also important to realize that to automate any application, you must first be familiar with that application. This book does explain how various features of the Office applications work before showing how to automate them, but it also assumes that you've used them before. If you've never opened PowerPoint and worked with it interactively, you'll find Section IV pretty tough going, for example. Spend some time as an end user before you try to program it. We'll return to this theme over and over because it's an important one.

Section VI covers an assortment of advanced topics. First, we look at the construction of documents involving multiple Office servers, including tasks like putting charts from Excel into PowerPoint presentations or Word documents. Chapter 14 covers handling Automation errors. Your existing error handler probably can't manage these for you because they don't happen inside FoxPro. Finally, in Chapter 15, "Wrapping Up the Servers," we show why it's a good idea to write wrapper classes for the Automation servers—among other things, it protects you when a new version of Office changes the Automation interface.

Chapter 2
The Office Servers

Learning about the Office servers is a challenging task, but there are a variety of approaches, tools, and resources available. Certain features of the Office applications, like collections, are common to all of them—mastering them up front will pay off fast.

Microsoft Office incorporates a whole bunch of applications and applets, but the main reason people buy and use it are the big two: Word and Excel. Along with them come a couple of others that are used by an increasing number of people who may not have planned to do so initially—PowerPoint and Outlook.

Word is an incredibly powerful word processor. It provides users with the ability to create anything from a simple note to complex reports and legal documents, and everything in between.

Excel is a sophisticated spreadsheet program. It includes integrated graphing capabilities and has a significant collection of built-in financial, statistical, and mathematical functions.

PowerPoint builds and displays presentations. Like the other applications, its abilities range from simple to complex—it offers everything from straightforward slides with a few bullet points and some text to full multimedia shows.

Outlook is harder to describe because it has a little of everything. For some, it's simply a mail client. For others, it's a calendar and to-do list. It also incorporates an address book, a journal, a notebook, and lots of opportunities to customize.

Exploring the Office servers

All of the Office applications share a programming language—Visual Basic for Applications, or VBA. For Automation developers, having a shared programming language isn't as impressive as it sounds because, while each Office application uses the same syntax and commands, that's only helpful if you're actually writing in that programming language. For Automation, you're not. You're writing in the language of the client application—the one controlling the Automation process.

On the other hand, for a variety of reasons, it's very handy to be able to read VBA when you're writing Automation code. Since we're all programmers here, that's not a big problem. But there are a couple of peculiarities about VBA (from the FoxPro developer's perspective, anyway) that make it hard to read for those who are unfamiliar with it. We'll look at each of these issues as we dig into the Office servers.

To use the Office servers, then, the key issue is finding out what methods and properties they have and determining the parameters to pass to their methods. There are three main approaches to take. In most cases, you'll need to combine all three to get what you need. Beyond those, there are a couple of other ways you can learn about Automation and then test out what you've learned.

Read the fine manual (RTFM)

Each of the Office servers has a Help file that documents its members. The method of getting to that Help file varies with the application. In the big three—Word, Excel, and PowerPoint—you can access it from the main Help menu for the application. On the Contents page, go down almost to the bottom. In Word and Excel 2000, look for "Programming Information" just above the bottom of the Contents list. In PowerPoint 2000, the entry to find is "Microsoft PowerPoint Visual Basic Reference," also near the bottom of the Contents list. In all three cases, you can open the specified item to see a list of Automation topics. Outlook's Automation Help is well hidden. You have to open the "Advanced Customization" topic to find "Microsoft Outlook Visual Basic Reference."

 Getting to the Help files is a little different in Office 97. You start out the same way in Word, Excel, and PowerPoint—by choosing the Contents page from Help and scrolling down to the bottom. Then, in all three, look for "Microsoft X Visual Basic Reference," where X is the product you're using. When you choose that item, it opens to reveal "Visual Basic Reference." Choosing that item opens a new Help window that contains just the Automation Help for that product. Getting to Visual Basic Help for Outlook 97 is extremely complex. The steps are spelled out in the main Help file—search for "Visual Basic." Understand, though, that VBA is not the primary programming language for Outlook 97, and automating it with VBA is trickier in some ways than automating the other Office 97 products.

If you can't find the appropriate item in the Help contents, it means you didn't install the VBA Help file with the application. To do so, you have to choose Custom installation. The standard installation doesn't include these files. (In Office 97, the standard installation was called "complete," but it wasn't.) You can install the VBA Help files at any time by running Setup again. In Office 2000, you do so by choosing Visual Basic Help from Office Tools. (By default, the VBA Help files are set to install on first use. If you know you're planning to do Automation work, we suggest that you go ahead and install them on your hard drive in the first place. The whole set of four [Word, Excel, PowerPoint, and Outlook] for Office 2000 is less than 5 MB.)

By this point, you may have noticed that getting to the VBA portion of the Help can be something of a pain. In Office 2000, VBA Help is integrated into the regular Help and doesn't open a separate window, so working within it is difficult, too. In Office 97, once you get to VBA Help, it's way too easy to close it—just hit ESC and it's gone.

Fortunately, there's an easy alternative here. Although accessible from within the main Help file for its respective application, the VBA Help for each Office application actually lives in a separate file. In Office 97, the filename is in the form VBAapp8.HLP, where "app" is some form of the application name. For Office 2000, it's VBAapp9.CHM, because the Office 2000 applications use HTML Help; that's why you can't close Help with ESC anymore. Given all of these difficulties in getting to VBA Help, we strongly recommend that you create shortcuts on your desktop for each of the Help files you're likely to use. Then, they're only a double-click away.

For the most part, the upgrade from Office 97 to Office 2000 is either positive or neutral. We also like HTML Help in general. In fact, the electronic version of this book uses HTML Help. However, the Office 2000 Help files, including the VBA Help files, are far less useful than their Office 97 equivalents. In Office 97, Help files had three pages: Contents, Index, and Find. Index featured an alphabetic list of terms from the Help file (like the index of a book), while Find provided full-text searching. For the VBA Help files, the Index page offered a quick way to go directly to any object, property, or method.

Office 2000 Help files have only two pages: Contents and Search. The team at Microsoft merged the Index and Find pages to create a single Search page, which offers full-text search without the real-time component of the Find page. There is no way to move quickly to a keyword. We suspect that there are some good usability arguments for the new search mechanism in the Help files for the main products. End users probably find this approach more productive. However, we cannot understand how programmers can be expected to use the VBA Help files productively without an index. (The best substitute for the Index page is the separate alphabetical lists of Objects, Properties and Methods on the Contents page. While we kept the VBA Help files on the Index page in Office 97, in Office 2000, we tend to keep it set to the Contents page.)

Each of the VBA Help files includes a diagram of the object model for that product. The model is "live"—when you click on it, you either move to another level of the diagram or to the appropriate entry in Help. **Figure 1** shows the top level of the Word object model diagram.

The Help entries for objects include small pieces of the object model diagram as well—clicking on these also jumps to the indicated entries. **Figure 2** shows the entry for the Documents collection in the Word VBA Help file. The dotted box that says "Multiple Objects" has been clicked, bringing up a dialog box of objects contained in the Document object.

Despite the difficulties in getting directly to a particular item in Office 2000 Help (a task that was incredibly easy in Office 97), the VBA Help files are generally clear and correct. If you know what you're looking for, you can find it there. The real challenge, then, is to figure out what you're looking for.

Let the server write the code

Word, Excel, and PowerPoint have macro recorders that let you turn user actions into VBA code. (Outlook supports macros, but unfortunately it doesn't include a macro recorder.)

So one way to figure out how to automate something is to record a macro to do it, and then examine the macro.

From the menu, choose Tools|Macro|Record New Macro to start recording. Give the macro a name (preferably a meaningful one, so you can find it again and so you'll know what it is when you come across it six months from now). Then interactively perform the operation you want to automate. When you're done, click on the Stop Recording button on the Macro toolbar (which appears automatically when you start recording).

Microsoft Word Objects

See Also

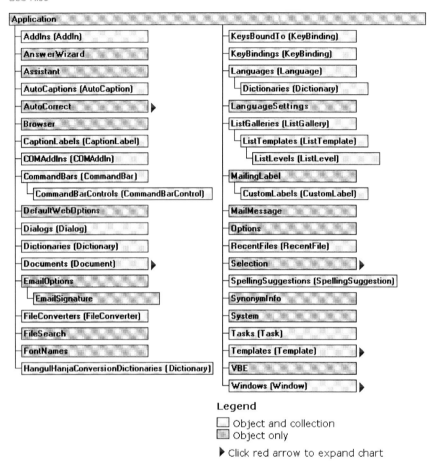

Figure 1. The Word object model diagram. The Help file for each Office product contains a diagram of the object model for that product. Clicking on one of the rectangles takes you to the Help entry for that object. Clicking an arrow takes you to another level in the object model diagram.

To look at the recorded macro, choose Tools|Macro|Macros from the menu; that opens the Macros dialog shown in **Figure 3**. Highlight the macro you just created (see, you need to know the name already), and then choose Edit. This brings you into the Visual Basic Editor (VBE)—**Figure 4** shows the highlighted macro from Figure 3 as it appears in the VBE. This particular macro was recorded in Word. (You can also get to the VBE by choosing Tools|Macro|Visual Basic Editor, or by pressing Alt-F11.)

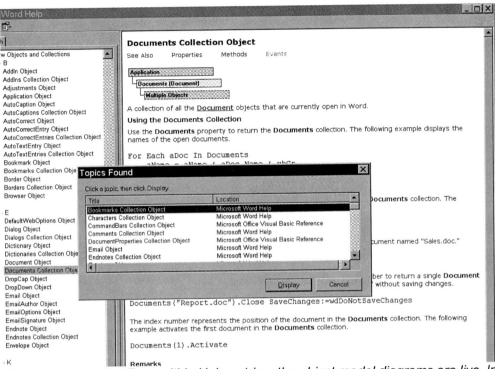

Figure 2. *Live Help. Even within Help entries, the object model diagrams are live. In this case, clicking on the "Multiple Objects" rectangle calls up a dialog that lists other objects contained in the Document object.*

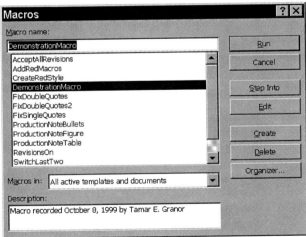

Figure 3. *The Macros dialog. This dialog lists all the macros you've recorded or otherwise stored in an Office application. It's one entry point to the Visual Basic Editor.*

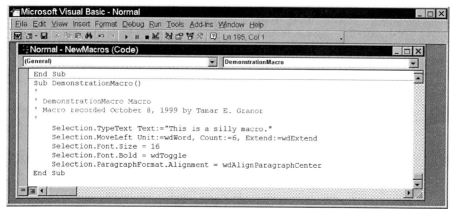

Figure 4. *Viewing macros. Editing a macro takes you to the Visual Basic Editor. At first glance, the code may seem mysterious, but just a few tricks can decode it.*

Converting a VBA macro to VFP code is harder than it should be for several reasons. The macro shown in Figure 4 demonstrates all of them. Consider this line of Word VBA code as you read the following sections. The line moves the insertion point (the vertical bar that determines where the next character is inserted) six words to the left, highlighting the words in the process:

```
Selection.MoveLeft Unit:=wdWord, Count:=6, Extend:=wdExtend
```

Default objects

First, unlike VFP, VBA makes some assumptions about what object you're talking to. In the preceding line, Selection translates to VFP's This.Selection, which represents the current selection (highlighted area) of the Word instance.

In each Office application, certain objects are considered default objects in the VBA environment. Your code won't be treated so kindly—you need to be explicit about what object you're addressing. The code you send to the Automation server must be addressed to the correct object.

Named parameters

VBA allows methods to use what are called *named parameters*. In the example code line, the method called is MoveLeft. Three parameters are passed, each in the following form:

```
parameter name := parameter value
```

This syntax allows VBA programmers to include only the parameters they need and not worry about the order of the parameters. Since some VBA methods have a dozen or more parameters, this is a very handy option.

However, VFP doesn't support named parameters; you must specify parameters in the proper order. Fortunately, the Help files show the parameters in their required order. (That wasn't true in versions of Office before Office 97; Help for many methods showed the parameters out of order, and finding the correct order was extremely difficult.)

When translating from VBA to VFP, add parentheses around the list of parameters, and delete the parameter names and ":=" symbols. Check Help (or the Object Browser, discussed later in this chapter) to determine the correct order and number of parameters. Usually, the macro recorder puts the parameters in the correct order; however, some parameters may be omitted, as named parameters allow VBA developers to leave out any parameters that are to take the default value. Be sure to check Help for omitted values. Also check to ensure that the macro recorder really did put them in the proper order; occasionally it doesn't.

Defined constants

The first parameter in the example line shows the third problem that occurs in translating VBA to VFP. It specifies that a parameter called Unit should have the value wdWord. But what is wdWord? It's one of thousands of defined constants available in Word's version of VBA. (It turns out that wdWord is 2.)

The VBA Help files don't supply the values of defined constants. In fact, Help uses them exclusively and doesn't show their actual values anywhere (ditto for the macro recorder). (Outlook is the exception here. It has a Help topic titled "Microsoft Outlook Constants" that includes a complete list.) To find out what wdWord and all of the others stand for, use the Object Browser available through the Visual Basic Editor. (See the section "Take me for a browse" later in this chapter.)

 If there was ever a reason to use header files, VBA constants is it. However, to build the header file, you need to find the values of the constants. Rick Strahl of West Wind Technologies has created a freeware tool that reads a COM type library, extracts the constants, and creates a Visual FoxPro header file. The tool, called GetConstants, is included in the Developer Download files available at www.hentzenwerke.com and can also be downloaded from Rick's site (www.west-wind.com). The Developer Download files also include header files for each of the Office applications.

We do *not* recommend using these files as is in your Automation work. The number of constants contained in them is mind-boggling. The smallest set is for Outlook—it contains 251 constant definitions. Word's file is nearly 10 times that size, with more than 2,400 constants defined. On one of our test machines, saving a form with no controls, but pointing to the full Word constant definition file as its Include file, took more than five seconds. (By contrast, on the same machine, saving a totally empty form took well under a second.)

However, having the complete set of constants at your disposal is very handy. You can cut and paste from them to create header files appropriate to the tasks you're doing. Rick's tool also makes it easy to keep your header files up-to-date as Microsoft adds new constants.

Macro recorder tips

Before moving on to the Object Browser, there are a couple of things worth noting about the macro recorder and the Visual Basic Editor. First, be aware that the macro recorder doesn't always produce the *best* code for a task. The code it produces gives you an idea of what can be done, but there are often better ways to accomplish the same task.

The macro recorder is focused on interactive users. While it doesn't just record the user's keystrokes, neither does it have the intelligence to figure out the task at hand and put together a complete, logical program to do it. Lines and lines of code are generated. A good deal of the time, several lines of code can be replaced with a single method call. Other times, many lines of code are generated that set every possible property for an object. Perhaps 15 properties are set when you only changed one. Many times, you won't need to set all of them. However, when you're trying to figure out which properties need to be set, be sure to consider that many users change the application's defaults, so don't assume anything!

Second, the Visual Basic Editor has a feature called IntelliSense that makes writing code there easier. When you type an object name and a period (like "oRange."), an appropriate list of properties and methods appears. When you choose a method from the list (use Tab to choose without ending the line), a list of parameters for that method appears like a ToolTip to guide you. As you enter parameters, your position in the parameter list is highlighted to keep you on track. This can be very handy when you're trying to figure out what parameters to pass to a method. Unfortunately, at this writing, Visual FoxPro doesn't natively support IntelliSense (though early demos of VFP 7 include it). Write the code in the VBE, and cut and paste it into VFP.

Take me for a browse

One of the most powerful tools available for figuring out Automation code is the Object Browser (see **Figure 5**). It lets you drill into the various objects in the hierarchy to determine their properties and methods, see the parameters for methods, determine the values of constants, and more.

The easiest way to find out about a specific item is to type it into the search dropdown, then press Enter or click the Find (binoculars) button. The middle pane fills with potential matches. Choose one to learn more about it in the main section of the Browser underneath. The left pane is filled with the properties, methods, collections, and constants. The right pane describes what's available for the highlighted item in the left pane. In Figure 5, the Object Browser has been used to determine the value of the constant wdWord. In the bottom-most pane, you can see that it's a constant with a value of 2.

The Object Browser is also useful for moving around the object hierarchy to get a feel for what the various objects can do. **Figure 6** shows the Object Browser with Excel's objects rather than Word's (the Visual Basic Editor was opened from Excel). The members of Excel's Workbook object are shown in the right pane. The PrintOut method is highlighted, so the very bottom panel shows its (complex) calling syntax. The advantage of this approach over Help is that the Object Browser actually looks at the type library, so the list it shows is more likely to be correct than Help. Even better, the Object Browser and Help can work together. Press F1 in the Browser, and Help opens to the highlighted item.

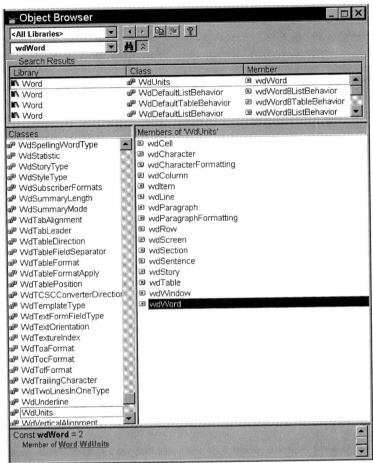

Figure 5. *The Object Browser. This powerful tool lets you drill down into objects, find out constant values, and determine parameters. Here it shows that wdWord is a constant, is a member of a group of constants called WdUnits, and has a value of 2.*

The Browser is also useful for exploring the object hierarchy itself. **Figure 7** shows the PowerPoint version of the Object Browser (this time, the VBE was opened from PowerPoint). The Presentation object's members are shown in the right pane. The Slides property is highlighted. In the bottom pane, we learn that Slides is a reference to a Slides collection. Clicking on the underlined Slides takes us to the Slides collection, shown in **Figure 8**.

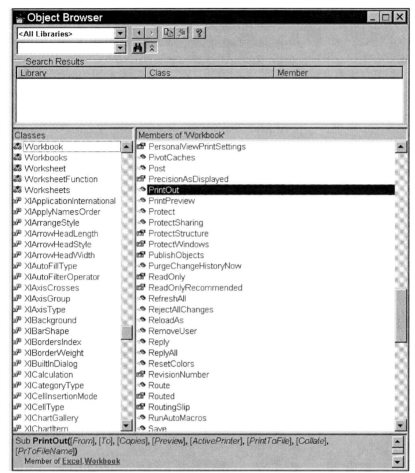

Figure 6. *Using the Object Browser to determine parameters. When a method is highlighted, the bottom pane shows the calling syntax. Since the Browser gets its information directly from the server, it can't be wrong.*

What does the Browser browse?

For Figure 6, we commented that the Object Browser had been opened from inside Excel. That wasn't really necessary. You can use the Object Browser from any of the Office tools to open and explore any registered type library. You can even look at the objects from multiple type libraries at the same time.

To open a type library so the Object Browser can display its contents, choose Tools|References in the Visual Basic Editor. The dialog shown in **Figure 9** is displayed. Check the libraries you want to add to the Object Browser, and then choose OK. (Be aware that, if you're actually writing code in the VBE, referencing type libraries in this way has consequences for your projects. So be careful what you actually save.)

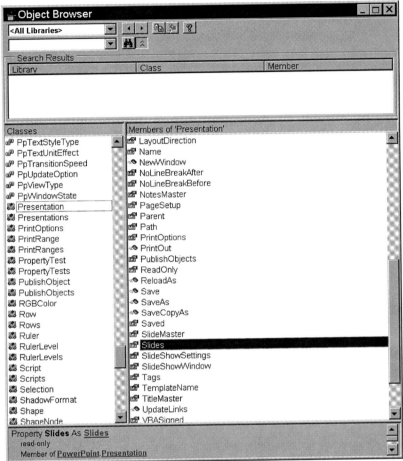

Figure 7. *Exploring the object model. When an item is underlined in the bottom pane, you can click on it and change your focus in the Browser. Click on Slides, underlined here, to change to the display shown in Figure 8.*

Within the Object Browser, you determine whether you see information from one type library or all of them with the drop-down list in the top left-hand corner. There's no way to choose a varied subset of the open libraries, however—your choice is all or one.

At your command

The Visual FoxPro Command Window is another powerful tool for learning about Automation servers. Once you've read what Help has to say and looked it up in the Object Browser, sometimes you just need to try it. That's where the Command Window comes in.

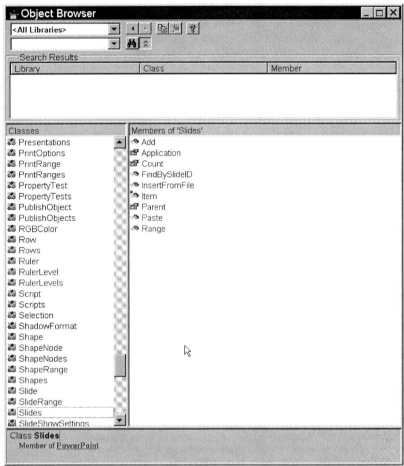

Figure 8. *The Slides collection. Clicking on the reference to the Slides collection shown in Figure 7 produces this display in the Object Browser. The Browser makes it easy to explore the relationships among objects in the hierarchy.*

Just as it does in every other aspect of working in VFP, the Command Window lets you try things and see what happens without the overhead of building entire applications or setting up complex scenarios. Create a reference to the appropriate server and try the sequence of commands one by one, observing the results as you go.

You can query the value of a property with ? (assuming the value is printable) or execute a method. Even the VFP Debugger can be used in a limited way. The limit is that properties of COM objects are visible in the Debugger only after they've been accessed from VFP. You can't just drill down into COM objects in the Debugger the way you can into VFP's own objects. Too bad.

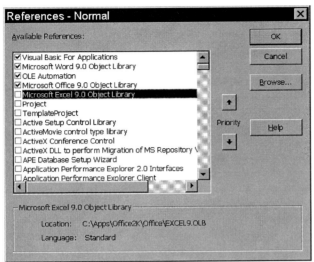

Figure 9. Adding type libraries. You can examine all kinds of type libraries using Office's Object Browser.

We've found it very useful to keep the Command Window visible as we write code. Some commands, particularly those with lots of specified named parameters (and lots more omitted parameters), can be particularly gruesome to get right. Try them in the Command Window, and when they're finally correct, cut and paste them into your code. One big drawback: the Command Window doesn't do #DEFINEs. Either set a variable in the Command Window, or use the corresponding values (remembering to change them to #DEFINEd constants when you paste into your code).

You may find that you get a lot more out of this book if you "work along" in the code. You'll see that we've provided the values for each of the constants in #DEFINE statements at the top of the code. While a #DEFINE line by itself does you no good in the Command Window, cutting and pasting an entire section from the HTML Help version of this book into the Command Window, and then right-clicking and selecting Execute runs the code correctly.

Another really cool piece is that you can move back and forth between doing things interactively and doing them with Automation. That is, when you have an instance of a server available from the Command Window and visible, you can switch over to the server application and work with it interactively, then come back to VFP and check the values of properties that were just set by your action, or execute a method, or set some other properties.

While trying to understand how a particular feature works, we often try something from the Command Window, then switch over to the server application to see the result, then hit Ctrl-Z (Undo) in the server to reverse that action before we go back to VFP and try a different parameter or value or approach. Perhaps more than any other, this ability drives home the reality that Automation really is just one more way to do the same things a user can do interactively.

We encourage you to explore the servers in the Command Window. It really helps to see instantly just what that line of code does (or it becomes an instant approach to finding a syntax error, which is still very helpful, but not nearly as much fun to watch).

On-line and print resources

There are a number of references available for the Office servers besides their respective Help files. Microsoft Press offers a *Visual Basic Programmer's Guide* for both Office 2000 and Office 97. Each is available both in book form and on-line. Since Microsoft is in the habit of rearranging its web site regularly, the best way to find the on-line versions is to search microsoft.com for "Visual Basic Programmer's Guide."

The VBA Help files are also available in printed form. If you'd rather work with a paper copy, you can order them from Microsoft Press. Look for the *Office Language Reference* (or the *Language Reference* for the individual application you're interested in). The *Language Reference* guides are available on the Microsoft web site, too, in case you find yourself stuck somewhere without the Help file.

Microsoft's web site for Office development is located at msdn.microsoft.com/officedev/ (at least it was at the time of this writing). Check it out for official support, technical articles, bug fixes, and so forth, as well as pointers to other useful sites.

Once you become comfortable enough reading VBA code, the various Office and Visual Basic magazines and journals can be useful resources. Take a look at *Microsoft Office & Visual Basic for Applications Developers* (www.OfficeVBA.com) and *Woody's Office Watch* (www.woodyswatch.com) for starters. Also, a new journal from Advisor Media, *Advisor Expert: Microsoft Outlook and Exchange*, looks like it will cover Outlook automation (www.Advisor.com). The major FoxPro magazines, *FoxPro Advisor* (www.Advisor.com) and *FoxTalk* (www.pinpub.com), cover Automation occasionally—the Office servers are the Automation target only for some of those articles.

For immediate help when you're stuck, your best bet can be to try the FoxPro forums and newsgroups. The FoxPro community has a well-earned reputation for its helpfulness—enough members are doing Automation work that simple questions are answered quickly. More difficult ones sometimes go unanswered. There are on-line communities for the Office applications, as well. We have less experience with them, but we have found those we've dealt with to be friendly and knowledgeable. See Appendix A, "On-line User Communities," for a list of on-line user communities for Visual FoxPro and the Office applications.

Taking up a collection

The object models of the Office applications (along with most COM servers) contain lots of collections, the OOP world's version of arrays. A collection contains references to a number of objects, generally of the same type, and provides access to those objects. Generally, a collection has a plural name, such as Slides, and contains objects that are referred to in the singular: the Slides collection contains a series of Slide objects. Just to be sure that you're good and confused while looking in the Help file, most of the time, you access the collection by a property of the same name: the Presentation object has a Slides property, which references the Slides collection. The Slides collection references a series of Slide objects. Just remember that the collection is plural (as is usually the property to access it), and the object is singular, and you shouldn't have much trouble.

Most collections, including those in Office, have a few standard methods and properties. The Count property tells you how many items are in the collection. Item, which is a method in some collections and a property in others (it's a method in the Office apps), provides access to the individual members of the collection.

Item typically takes a single parameter or index (number) and returns a reference to that member of the collection. In many cases, you can specify the item you want by name rather than number. For example, consider Visual FoxPro's Projects collection (which is a COM collection, rather than native to VFP). If the TasTrade project is open and is the first open project, you can access it as _VFP.Projects.Item[1] or _VFP.Projects.Item["TasTrade.PJX"].

In addition, most collections let you omit the Item keyword and simply attach the parameter/index to the collection name. So you can write _VFP.Projects["TasTrade.PJX"] or _VFP.Projects[1] and still get a reference to the project.

As with Visual FoxPro's arrays, you can use either square brackets or parentheses to access the elements of a collection. In this book, we use square brackets for both arrays and collections and leave parentheses to indicate functions and methods.

Changing the collection

Once you get past Count and Item, there's more diversity. Most, but not all, collections have an Add method, which allows you to add a new item of the appropriate type to the collection. For example, you use the Add method of Word's Documents collection to create a new, empty document, and the Add method of Excel's Workbooks collection to create a new, empty workbook. In fact, you also use the Add method of Excel's Worksheets collection to add a new worksheet to an existing Workbook.

There's no common technique for removing items from collections. That's because some types of items remove themselves when they no longer belong in the collection. For example, when you close a Workbook in Excel, it removes itself from the Workbooks collection.

The methods that do remove objects from collections tend to belong to the object itself, not to the collections. Although adding and removing may seem like complementary operations to us, from an object point of view, they really aren't. When you're adding, you have only the collection to work with; you don't yet have the thing you're adding. When you're ready to remove it, you have it in hand and can ask it to remove itself. So Add methods belong to collections, while Remove methods (or the methods that cause members to be removed) belong to members of a collection.

Some collections have a fixed number of entries. For example, the Borders collection in Excel represents the four borders of a range. This collection always has four items; there's no way to add items to it or remove items from it. (Word and PowerPoint also have similar Borders collections, with a fixed number of entries.)

Other collections are modified by other actions in the system. For example, Word's Revisions collection contains the changes that have been made to a document. You can't add or remove items directly because they're handled through a different mechanism.

Self-referential object models

When you start digging around the Office object models, it can be a little confusing (okay, very confusing!). You find that one object has a property that's a reference to a collection of another sort of object, or maybe it's a reference to another object. The property frequently (but not always) has the same name as the collection or other object. When you're digging in Help, it sometimes takes two or three jumps to get to something useful.

Here's an example. Say you start on Word's object model diagram and click on the Documents collection. That takes you to the Help page for the Documents collection (shown in Figure 2—look behind the dialog). What you're probably interested in, though, is the Document object, not the collection, so on the Documents page, you click on Document. That brings you to the Help page for Document. From there, you may decide to find out about the Paragraphs property, so you click Properties. **Figure 10** shows the Document page and the resulting dialog.

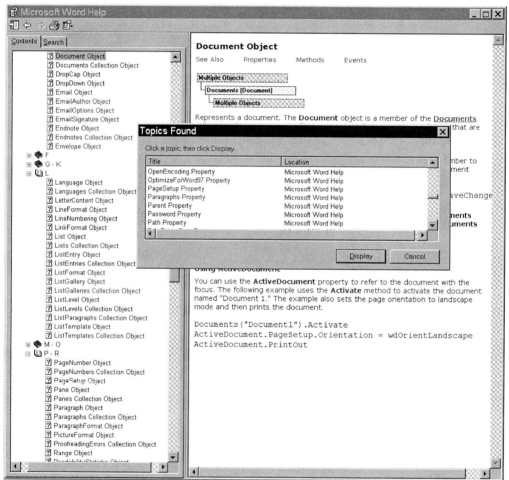

Figure 10. *From Document to Paragraphs. Many objects have properties that reference collections, using the same name as the collection. While this makes sense, it can make getting help a little long-winded, especially since often, we're ultimately headed for the individual property, not the collection.*

Choosing the Paragraphs property from the dialog brings up Help for that property, as shown in **Figure 11**. To get to Help for the Paragraphs collection requires a click on Paragraphs; to get to the actual Paragraph object—usually our actual destination—requires yet another click once we get to Paragraphs. (The See Also for the Paragraphs property does actually offer a direct jump to Paragraph, but to find that out, you'd have to click on See Also.) This is one of our least favorite things about the VBA Help system. We wish it were smart enough to offer some kind of consolidated help for the property and collection.

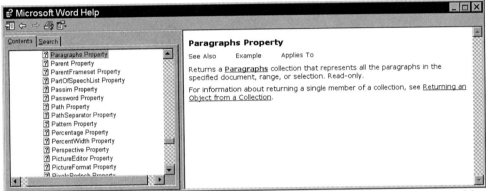

Figure 11. *Not so helpful. This Help entry and others like it, while accurate, add an extra step when you're navigating from one object to another in the Help system.*

There's a flip side to the issue of same-named properties and collections/objects. In some situations, the properties that access the collections or other objects don't have the same names as their targets. For example, a number of objects reference Word's ParagraphFormat object through a property named Format. Since the reference properties almost always use the object names, watch out for the special cases.

Moving on

One of the biggest lessons we've learned in writing Automation code is that you can't automate what you don't understand. In this chapter, we've explored different ways to become familiar with the Automation servers in Microsoft Office, but there's one more that we haven't mentioned.

Use the products. We use Office. Word, in particular, is part of our normal working environment, and much of what we know about automating it comes from hard-won expertise in using it. (On the other hand, we'd be lying if we didn't admit that we've become more powerful Word users through things we learned from Automation programming.)

When you're stuck on a hairy Automation problem, go do it interactively a few times until you really understand both the process and the result. You wouldn't expect to be able to write good programs in a language in whose environment you weren't comfortable working. Why would you expect to do it with Automation?

Add that kind of practice to the exploration tools described in this chapter, and you'll be comfortable in the Office Automation environment before you know it. Now, on to Visual FoxPro's role as Automation client.

Chapter 3
Visual FoxPro as an
Automation Client

Some aspects of Visual FoxPro are relevant, whatever product you're automating.

No matter what you're automating, much of what you do in Visual FoxPro is the same. This chapter takes a look at the things that stay the same across all servers and across the Office servers.

Managing servers

The first step with any server is getting a reference. There are two possibilities for an Automation server: you can create a new instance, or you can get a reference to an existing server, if one exists. There are also two VFP functions that you can use, CreateObject() and GetObject(), but they don't map exactly to the two techniques.

CreateObject() always creates a new instance of the server and returns a reference to it. Here's the syntax for creating Automation objects:

```
oServer = CreateObject( cServerClass )
```

cServerClass is the appropriate name for the main class of the Automation server. For the Office applications, it's "<appname>.Application" where <appname> is "Word" or "Excel" or whatever. For example, to open PowerPoint, issue this command:

```
oPowerPoint = CreateObject( "PowerPoint.Application" )
```

Note that the syntax for creating Automation objects is almost identical to that for creating native objects. The only difference is the class of the object created. This is polymorphism (one of the pillars of OOP) at work.

If the server is already open and you'd like to use the existing instance, you can use the GetObject() function instead. GetObject() takes two parameters. For this use, omit the first parameter and pass the server class as the second. Here's the syntax:

```
oServer = GetObject( , cServerClass )
```

If the server is already open, GetObject() finds it and returns a reference to that instance. However, if the server is not open, this version of the function generates an error.

For example, to attach to an open instance of Excel, use this command:

```
oExcel = GetObject( , "Excel.Application")
```

There's another way to start a server—by passing GetObject() the name of a file and letting it figure out which server to use:

```
oDocument = GetObject( cFileName )
```

VFP looks up the file's extension in the registry to figure out what application it belongs to, opens that application, then opens the file; it works pretty much as if you'd double-clicked the file in Windows Explorer, except that you get an object reference to the file as a "document," so that you can manipulate it as an object. This example opens the file "C:\Documents\MyFile.DOC" in Word and returns a reference to it:

```
oDocument = GetObject( "C:\Documents\MyFile.DOC" )
```

In some situations, the filename may not be sufficient to determine what application to open or what to make of the file. In that case, you can also pass the name of the class within the server. For example, if the file has a TXT extension, but you want Word to open it as a document, pass "Word.Document" as the second parameter, like this:

```
oDocument = GetObject( "Example.TXT", "Word.Document" )
```

However, you can't just pass the file type automatically. Most of the time, either VFP or the server application chokes when it receives the second parameter unnecessarily.

We should point out that there's a third VFP function in this family, CreateObjectEX(). It's used for creating objects on a different machine and is part of DCOM. Since this book doesn't cover DCOM, we don't discuss it here.

Displaying the Office servers

When you instantiate an Automation server, by default it's invisible. It doesn't show up on the taskbar. In Windows NT, it's shown on the Processes page of Task Manager, but not on the Applications page. It does show in Windows 95/98's Close Program dialog. It's generally a good thing that it keeps itself somewhat hidden. Often, you're doing something behind the scenes and there's no reason for a user to see it happening. However, while debugging and in some other circumstances, you may want to make the Automation process visible.

Why not just make the server application visible all the time? Speed. Not surprisingly, manipulating documents is faster when you can't see them. It's also tidier—although watching a spreadsheet or presentation being built is pretty cool the first few times, after a while, users are likely to get tired of watching.

This is one area where Outlook is the odd man out. These commands apply to Word, Excel, and PowerPoint (and, for that matter, to Visual FoxPro when it's used as a server), but not to Outlook. To make the Automation server visible, set its Visible property to .T.; set Visible to .F. to turn it off. (Actually, in PowerPoint, you can set Visible to .T., but setting it to .F. generates an error message. Word and Excel give you complete control over their visibility.) Outlook doesn't have an analogous property.

The WindowState property of the Application object determines whether the application is minimized, maximized, or "normal," meaning some user-determined size. Manipulating WindowState when the application is invisible generally makes it visible (at least to the extent of showing on the taskbar). Each of the applications has a set of constants for the three possible values of WindowState. For example, for Excel, you can make these definitions:

```
#DEFINE xlMaximized     -4137
#DEFINE xlMinimized     -4140
#DEFINE xlNormal        -4143
```

Word needs the following:

```
#DEFINE wdWindowStateNormal    0
#DEFINE wdWindowStateMaximize  1
#DEFINE wdWindowStateMinimize  2
```

The Application object of all three applications has Left and Top properties that determine where it's located on the screen, as well as Height and Width properties. You can manipulate these, unless the application is maximized. The following code (SetSize.PRG in the Developer Download files available at www.hentzenwerke.com) opens Word, sets the application window to normal, positions it a little below the upper-left corner of the screen, and then makes it visible.

```
#DEFINE wdWindowStateNormal         0

LOCAL nScreenHeight, nScreenWidth
LOCAL nWindowHeight, nWindowWidth

* Compute sizes
nScreenHeight = SYSMETRIC(2)
nScreenWidth = SYSMETRIC(1)

* Make it two-thirds the size of the screen in each dimension.
nWindowHeight = INT(.67 * nScreenHeight)
nWindowWidth = INT(.67 * nScreenWidth)

RELEASE ALL LIKE o*
PUBLIC oWord
oWord = CreateObject( "Word.Application" )

WITH oWord
  .WindowState = wdWindowStateNormal

  .Height = .PixelsToPoints( nWindowHeight, .T. )
  .Width = .PixelsToPoints( nWindowWidth, .F. )
  .Top = 10
  .Left = 10

  .Visible = .T.
ENDWITH

RETURN
```

As the example indicates, Height, Width, Top, and Left are measured in points. Word provides a number of methods for converting other measurements into points (including, in Word 2000, the PixelsToPoints method used in the example). The other applications offer fewer such methods; in fact, neither Excel nor PowerPoint includes PixelsToPoints. The conversion factor between pixels and points is about 0.75.

Unless you're doing very precise work, you can probably live with that conversion factor, so in Excel and PowerPoint, just define your own conversion, like this:

```
#DEFINE autoPixelsToPoints .75
```

You can handle converting between inches and points in the same way. There are 72 points to an inch. Define your own constant for that task, like this:

```
#DEFINE autoInToPts 72
```

Even when you're automating Word, there's some argument that you're better off doing your own conversions in VFP than using Word's built-in methods. Each call to Word is expensive. In our tests, arithmetic in VFP was about 100 times faster than calling Word's conversion methods.

Are we there yet?

All three applications start with no document open and no document window when you call CreateObject(), but they behave differently when GetObject() is used to open a specific file.

In Word, once GetObject() is through, there's a document window containing the specified document. Just set Visible to .T. for the Application object, and the document window shows:

```
oDocument.Application.Visible = .T.  && this is needed for any of the apps
                                     && but change the variable appropriately
```

PowerPoint and Excel are different. Setting Visible to .T. isn't enough. In PowerPoint, you need to call the NewWindow method to provide a document window for the specified presentation:

```
oPresentation.NewWindow()
```

Excel uses yet another approach to the same problem. There is a document window; you just can't see it. Call the Activate method for the first window in the Windows collection:

```
oWorkbook.Windows[1].Activate()
```

Working with servers

A few Visual FoxPro language features and interface components make it easier to write and maintain Automation code. Here's a look at some things to remember as you work in the wild world of Automation.

SET OLEOBJECT

This VFP command determines whether VFP searches the registry when using CreateObject() or GetObject(). When it's set to ON, VFP searches the registry; when it's set to OFF, that search is skipped. Why does this command exist? The last place VFP looks to find an object is in the registry. Before searching the registry, it loads OLE support, which takes up memory. If your application doesn't require OLE support, setting OLEOBJECT to OFF provides a bit of a performance enhancement. However, if you're using Automation, you need OLE support, as well as the ability to find the server in the registry. If you attempt to instantiate an Automation server while SET OLEOBJECT is set to OFF, an error like "Class definition WORD.APPLICATION is not found" is generated.

Use WITH...ENDWITH

Much of the code you write to automate any server involves setting properties or calling methods. It's common to have long stretches of code that consists of not much more than references to properties and methods, with perhaps a little bit of arithmetic or logic thrown in. You can make that code far more readable (and thus easier to debug and maintain) by using VFP's WITH...ENDWITH command.

A series of commands that all begin with something like oWord.ActiveDocument.Tables [3].Rows[7] just isn't going to lend itself to readability. Instead, surround the group like this:

```
WITH oWord.ActiveDocument.Tables[ 3 ].Rows[ 7 ]
  * put the commands here with a dot in front of each
ENDWITH
```

In fact, you can nest WITH commands. As you walk down the object hierarchy, doing a few things at each level, set up a WITH statement for each level—something like this:

```
#DEFINE wdAlignRowCenter    1
#DEFINE wdRowHeightExactly   2

WITH oWord.ActiveDocument
  * Do some things to the document as a whole, like
  .Save    && save using current filename

  * Then move on to the table.
  WITH .Tables[ 3 ]
    * Now issue commands aimed at the table as a whole
    .AllowPageBreaks = .T.   && allow table to break across pages

    * Then, when you're ready to talk to the single row.
    WITH .Rows[ 7 ]
      * Now issue the commands for the one row
      .Alignment = wdAlignRowCenter
      .HeightRule = wdRowHeightExactly
      .Height = .5
    ENDWITH
  ENDWITH
ENDWITH
```

The nesting makes it clear to the reader which WITH each property belongs to. VFP, of course, has no difficulty figuring it out. There's an added bonus besides readability. Code like this runs faster—FoxPro doesn't have to sort through multiple levels of hierarchy to find out what object a given property or method belongs to. In our tests, a fairly simple example that queried about a dozen properties at four levels below the Application object ran roughly twice as fast using nested WITHs as it did addressing each property directly.

Also, note that there's no rule that says the property or method has to be the first thing on the code line. It often works out that way, but it's perfectly fine to use them elsewhere. For example, the following code is acceptable:

```
WITH oExcel
  nHeight = .Height
  nWidth = .Width
ENDWITH
```

In fact, as shown by the example in the "Displaying the Office servers" section earlier in this chapter, you can call methods, perform calculations, and generally do anything you normally would inside a WITH…ENDWITH pair, as long as you make sure to include the dot before the property or method name.

Use variables for object references

Another way to make your code more readable and speed it up is to assign complex object references to local variables. Even if a WITH…ENDWITH pair isn't called for, you may be better off assigning something like oPowerPoint.ActivePresentation to a VFP variable with a name like oPres (or oPresentation, if you prefer). The variable name is easier to type and easier to read. As with the WITH statement, it gives VFP a direct route to the object you're interested in, rather than asking it to climb down the object hierarchy.

We tested the same example as for WITH (querying properties at various levels) and found that setting a local variable was as fast as—or even a little faster than—using WITH. We suspect the exact trade-off point varies, depending on factors like available memory, the number of references inside the WITH/to the local variable, and so forth. There's no question, however, that either approach is significantly faster than writing out a long reference to an Automation object. The more deeply nested the reference and the more times you need it, the more time you save.

When you use local variables, you may need to clean up afterwards. In some situations, these references can prevent the server from closing when you call the Quit method.

Loop with FOR EACH

In Chapter 2, "The Office Servers," we discussed the prevalence of collections in the Office object models (and in COM object models more generally). When you need to process all the members of a collection, VFP's FOR EACH loop is your best bet. FOR EACH lets you go through a collection (or array) without using a counter or worrying about how many members there are. Here's the syntax of FOR EACH:

```
FOR EACH oMember IN oCollection
  * issue commands for oMember
ENDFOR
```

For example, to display the name of every open document in Word, you can use this code:

```
FOR EACH oDocument IN oWord.Documents
  ? oDocument.Name
ENDFOR
```

Note, by the way, that using FOR EACH implies the use of a local variable as described in the previous section—the object reference used as the loop variable.

Debugging

Debugging Automation code is something of a challenge. As we noted in Chapter 2, the VFP Debugger isn't much help. The Watch and Locals windows only show a property of an Automation object once that property has been accessed from VFP. So you can't drill into those objects to see what's going on and really examine them the way you can with native objects. We've also sometimes found that putting COM objects (whether Automation objects or other COM objects) into the Watch window can be a good way to crash the Debugger.

So how do you debug Automation code? Carefully, and with a lot of advance planning.

Work in the Command Window

We do a lot of our testing and development in the Command Window. It's a lot easier to understand what's going on when we issue commands one at a time and examine the results. Once we're sure we know which methods to call and which properties to set to generate the desired documents, then we put them into code. We find this approach to be far more necessary (we daresay mandatory) with Automation code than with pure VFP code.

Collections and objects

Watch out for collections vs. individual objects. Since so much Automation code involves collections, it's really easy to call a method of a collection when you mean to call it for the object, or vice versa. For example, when you see something like the following, keep in mind that the object it references is an object, *not* a collection:

```
oPowerPoint.Presentations[1]
```

(This is actually another argument for using local variables. Setting oPresentation to refer to that presentation helps to avoid confusion.) A handy hint: generally, the collection object is plural (like Presentations), and the object itself is singular (like Presentation). It's pretty easy to get confused in the Help file looking for Presentation methods vs. Presentations methods, but knowing to look for the "s" (or not to) was a big breakthrough for us.

It works, but it doesn't

If your code runs, but the results are wrong, make sure you're manipulating the right objects. Recheck the appropriate sections in this book and in Help. Make sure you can perform the task (or at least a prototype of the task) interactively. We'll say it again—you can't automate what you don't understand. Try recording a macro that performs what you're trying to automate, and then examine the resulting VBA code to see whether it sheds some light on the situation.

Parameter problems

If you're having problems with type mismatch errors in method calls, try changing the order of the parameters. Sometimes (though much less often than in older versions of Office), they're wrong in the docs. Use the Object Browser to be sure of the proper order. (See Chapter 2, "The Office Servers," for more on this.)

Similarly, if you're having trouble with an invalid number of parameters, you may need to add commas to allow for omitted defaults. Again, check in the Object Browser to see the correct list of parameters for a method.

Unhelpful error messages

When an error occurs on an Automation command, it falls into one of three broad categories: you asked VFP to do something it can't do, you asked the server to do something it can't do, or something went wrong in the communication between them.

In the first case (a VFP problem), you get a normal VFP error message and can handle it as you would any other. Things to check in that situation are matching parentheses, mismatched data types, and so forth.

In the second case, you see one of just a few error messages you get when an OLE error occurs. It's almost always either 1426 or 1429. Along with it, you get an error message of varying information content. Sometimes, it's truly informative. For example, if you ask for oWord.ActiveDocument.Name when there is no active document, the error message includes "This command is not available because no document is open." That's pretty good.

But other times, the messages are pretty sparse. For example, querying a non-existent property or misspelling a method yields simply "Unknown name." We think "No such member" would be a whole lot more helpful. Really helpful would be something like "This object does not have a member called 'Mane.'" Then we'd quickly notice that we'd mistyped "Name" as "Mane" (again). But that seems to be asking for too much.

The real issue is that Visual FoxPro can't give you more information about the error than the application it's talking to gives it. That's because Visual FoxPro only knows what the server tells it. When one of these errors occurs, you need to look hard at the syntax of your command, compare it to the expected syntax, and try to figure out where you've gone wrong.

The third group of errors reflects the difficulties of communicating between two applications. These may occur if the server is shut down unexpectedly (say, if the user closes the server from outside your application) or if there's a problem opening the server. See Chapter 14, "Handling Automation Errors," for ideas on how to handle these problems gracefully.

Use the Knowledge Base

While finding things in the Microsoft Knowledge Base can be difficult, there is a tremendous accumulation of information there. When you're stuck on a tricky problem, it's worth digging in and trying a number of search combinations. If you're having a particular problem, chances are someone else has had it before you.

Try combinations like "Automation" plus "FoxPro" plus the name of the application you're having trouble with. If that doesn't work, try taking FoxPro out of the mix—maybe this is a problem in VBA, too. Search for the particular error code (not the VFP error number, but the OLE error code returned by the server), or use a phrase from the error description that comes back from the server.

Ask around

Still stuck? There are plenty of places to get on-line help with both VFP and the Office applications. Check out the list in Appendix A, "On-line User Communities." Be sure to provide enough information in your message to effectively describe your problem, but not so much detail as to make your message overwhelming. Often, the very process of trying to verify that your error occurs with the least number of simple steps will lead you to a solution, when in fact the error does not occur in the simplest case. Add complexity back in, one command at a time, and you can often isolate the source of your problem.

Time for code

At this point, it's time to dig in and start actually looking at the Office products. The next four sections of the book look at each of the Office products covered, beginning with Word. Each section starts out with a "Basics" chapter then takes off from there in a different direction, driven by the product itself.

Section II
Automating Word

Chapter 4
Word Basics

Visual FoxPro's Report Designer can't do what you need? Turn to Word instead. Its document orientation provides formatting from fonts to outlining.

Microsoft Word is an incredibly powerful word processor. It lets users create documents ranging from simple memos to complex multi-part corporate reports. It also provides tools for processing and managing those documents in a number of ways, such as checking spelling and grammar, merging with a variety of data sources, tracking changes, and much more.

Even for simple documents, Word provides myriad tools that allow users to produce attractive output. Users can work with multiple documents simultaneously, move and copy text within and between documents, and mark and name portions of a document. Formatting in Word is also quite powerful, with provision for local, page-level, and document-level control.

Word's object model

The key object in Word is Document, which represents a single, open document. The Word server has a Documents collection, which contains references to all open documents. The server also has an ActiveDocument property that points to the currently active document.

The Document object has lots of properties and methods. Many of its properties are references to collections such as Paragraphs, Tables, and Sections. Each of those collections contains references to objects of the indicated type. Each object contains information about the appropriate piece of the document. For example, the Paragraph object has properties like KeepWithNext and Style, as well as methods like Indent and Outdent.

The Word server object, called Application, has its own set of properties and methods, including a number of other collections. In addition to ActiveDocument, the Application object's properties include Visible, StartupPath, Version, and WindowState. The Application object also has methods. The simplest to understand is Quit, which shuts down the server. It has several optional parameters—the first indicates what to do if any open documents have been changed but not saved. Other methods of the Application object convert measurements from one set of units to another, check grammar and spelling, and much more.

Word Visual Basic Help contains a diagram of Word's object model. The figure is "live"—when you click on an object, you're taken to the Help topic for that object. **Figure 1** shows the portion of the object model diagram that describes the Document object.

Getting to Word

Before you can work with Word, you need an object reference to the Word Automation server or to a specific object in Word. Two VFP functions let you access Word. CreateObject() opens a new instance of Word and returns a reference to it, like this:

```
oWord = CreateObject("Word.Application")
```

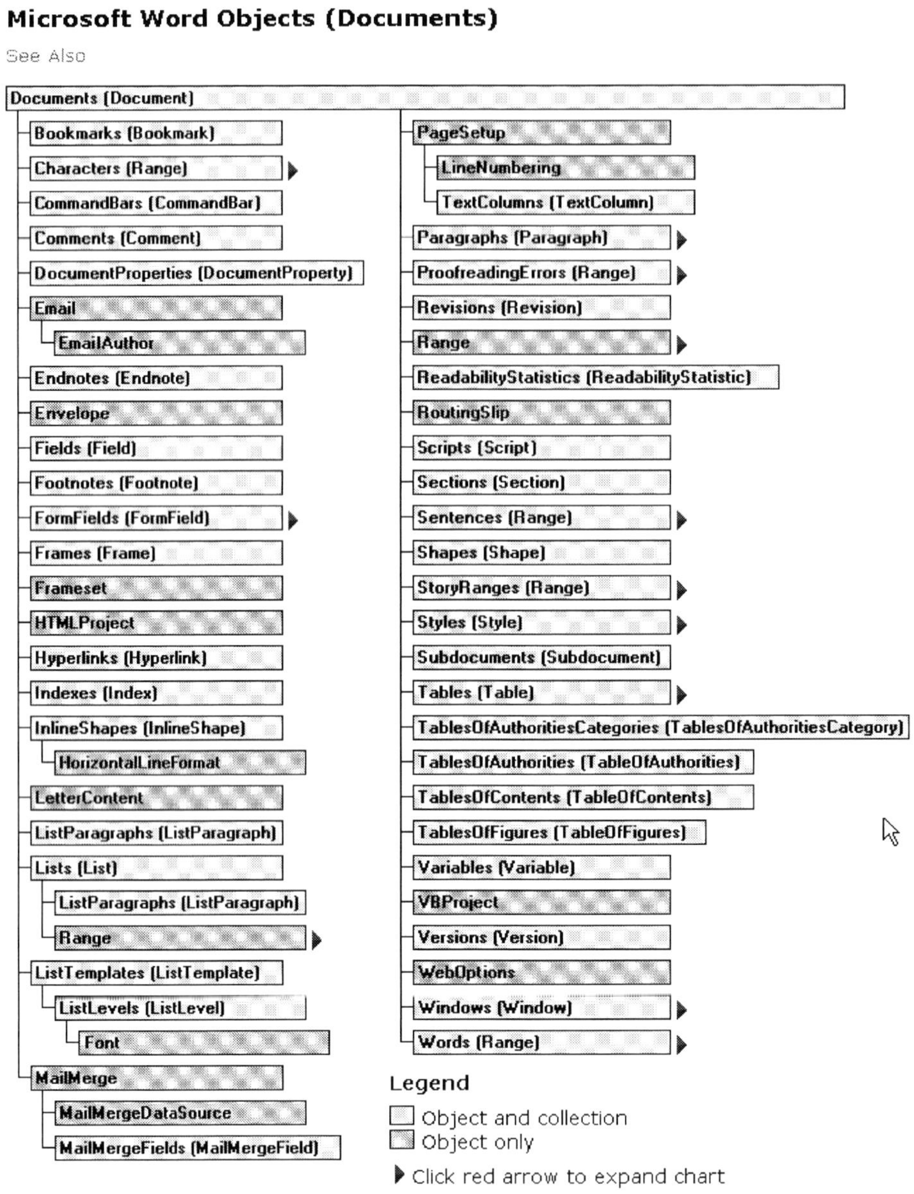

Microsoft Word Objects (Documents)

See Also

Figure 1. *The Word object model. The Help file offers a global view of Word's structure.*

GetObject() is a little more complex. It takes either of two parameters, which reflect two approaches to providing a reference to Word. If you pass it the name of an existing document, it checks whether or not Word is already open. If not, it opens Word. Either way, it opens the specified document and returns a reference to the document:

```
oDocument = GetObject("d:\writing\books\automation\chapter4.doc")
```

If you omit the first parameter to GetObject() and specify the Word Automation server as the second, it looks for an open instance of Word and returns a reference to that instance:

```
oWord = GetObject(, "Word.Application")
```

If Word isn't open, an error message is generated.

See Chapter 3, "Visual FoxPro as an Automation Client," for more general information on CreateObject() and GetObject() and their use with the Office applications.

Managing documents

The methods for creating, opening, saving, and closing documents are fairly straightforward. The only complication is in what object provides which method. The methods for creating and opening a document belong to the Documents collection. The methods for saving and closing a document belong to the Document object. Although it seems confusing at first glance, this actually makes sense because you don't have a Document object to work with at the time you create or open a document. But when it comes time to save or close it, a document reference is available.

To open an existing document, use the Open method of the Documents collection. Open has many parameters, but most of the time, the only one that matters is the first: the name and path of the file to open. The Word server doesn't recognize VFP's search path, so you usually need to provide the full path to the document, like this:

```
oDocument = oWord.Documents.Open("d:\writing\books\automation\chapter4.doc")
```

If it's successful, Open returns an object reference to the newly opened document. If the specified document doesn't exist, an error is generated, and nothing is returned. (This example, like the others in this chapter and the next two, assumes that you have an instance of Word running, with oWord holding a reference to it.)

To create a new document, use the Add method, which has only two, optional, parameters. The important one is the first, which indicates the path to the template on which the new document should be based. If it's omitted, the new document is based on the Normal template. (Templates are discussed in more detail in Chapter 5, "Intermediate Word.")

Like Open, Add returns a reference to the newly created document. This line creates a new document based on a template called "OfficeFax":

```
oDocument = oWord.Documents.Add( ;
   "C:\WINNT\Profiles\Tamar\Application Data\Microsoft\OfficeFax.DOT")
```

As with the filename in Open, the full path to the template is needed. See the section "Document templates" in Chapter 5 for information on where Word installs and keeps templates.

When you're finished working with a document, two methods are available to save it. Both methods belong to the Document object. The Save method saves the document back to its current file; if it's never been saved, a Save As dialog box appears. The SaveAs method lets you specify the filename (and a lot of other stuff) without seeing a dialog, which is usually what you want in Automation code.

If the currently active document has already been saved, this line resaves the document without user intervention:

```
oWord.ActiveDocument.Save()
```

To save the document to a different file, or to save a document for the first time without the user specifying a filename, call SaveAs and pass the filename, like this:

```
oWord.ActiveDocument.SaveAs("D:\Documents\ThisIsNew.DOC")
```

Be careful. When you pass a filename to SaveAs, it overwrites any existing file without prompting. (Of course, SaveAs, like Word's other methods, doesn't respect VFP's SET SAFETY setting, since it's not running inside VFP.)

You can check whether the document has been saved by testing its Saved property. If Saved is .T., the document is unchanged. This can be the case either because you've already saved the document and haven't changed it since, or because it's a new document and hasn't yet been modified.

In addition, the Name and FullName properties give you an alternative way to check whether a document has ever been saved. When you create a new document, Word assigns a name in the form "Document*n*," where *n* is a number. When you save the document, you can give it a more meaningful name, as well as specify the file path. The Name property of the Document contains just the file stem with no path or extension. The FullName property contains the complete filename, including the path and extension. However, before the file is saved for the first time, both Name and FullName contain the same string—the initial document name assigned by Word. You can write code like this to figure out whether to use Save or SaveAs:

```
WITH oWord.ActiveDocument
  IF .Name = .FullName
    * Prompt user to get a name,
    * then:
    .SaveAs( cFileName )
  ELSE
    .Save
  ENDIF
ENDWITH
```

Accessing parts of a document

Most of what you want to do with Word involves adding to, modifying, or reading a document, whether it's a new document you're building or an existing document you're modifying. (There's actually a third possibility. You may be working on a new document that's based on a template that contains boilerplate text that you're customizing.) There are a variety of ways to do these things, but the key to just about all of them is the Range object and, to a lesser extent, the Selection object.

The Selection object represents the currently highlighted (that is, selected) portion in a document. If nothing is highlighted, Selection refers to the insertion point. There's only one Selection object, accessed directly from the Word Application object. For example, to find out how many paragraphs are in the current selection, you can use this code:

```
nParagraphs = oWord.Selection.Paragraphs.Count
```

A Range object can represent any portion of a document. Ranges are not the same as the Selection area. You can define or modify Ranges without affecting the current Selection. You can even define multiple ranges for a document, whereas only one Selection object is available for each document. Ranges are very useful for repeatedly referencing specific portions of a document.

Ranges can be obtained in many ways. Many Word objects, like Paragraph and Table, have a Range property that contains an object reference to a Range object for the original object. For example, to create a Range from the third paragraph of the active document, you can use the following:

```
oRange = oWord.ActiveDocument.Paragraphs[3].Range
```

The Document object has a Range method that lets you specify a range by character position. For example, to get a reference to a Range containing the 100th to 250th characters in the active document (probably not a particularly useful range), use:

```
oRange = oWord.ActiveDocument.Range(100,250)
```

The Document object's Content property contains a reference to a Range that consists of the entire main document (the body of the document without headers, footers, footnotes, and so on). So the next two commands are equivalent:

```
oRange = oWord.ActiveDocument.Range()
oRange = oWord.ActiveDocument.Content
```

Beware: for a large document, creating such a variable can take a significant amount of time.

It's easy to convert Range objects to a Selection, and vice versa. Like many other objects, Selection has a Range property, which provides a Range object from the Selection. Similarly, the Range object has a Select method that highlights the range's contents, turning it into the Selection. For example, to highlight the range from the previous example, use:

```
oRange.Select()
```

Selection and Range seem quite similar, and they are in many ways, but there are differences. The biggest, of course, is that you can have multiple Ranges but only one Selection. In addition, working with a Range is usually faster than working with a Selection. On the whole, Word VBA experts recommend using Range rather than Selection wherever possible. The main reason is that using Selection is essentially duplicating screen actions with code; Range lets you operate more directly. Word's macro recorder tends to use the Selection object; this is one thing to be aware of when converting Word macros to VFP code.

Manipulating text

The Text property of Range and Selection contains whatever text is in the specified area. To bring document contents into FoxPro, create an appropriate Range and read its Text property, like this:

```
oRange = oWord.ActiveDocument.Paragraphs[7].Range
cParagraph7 = oRange.Text
```

The Text property also lets you add or change the document contents. You can add text by assigning it to the Text property.

```
oRange.Text = "This is a new sentence."
```

You can also add text to whatever's already there. Simple text manipulation does the trick.

```
oRange.Text = oRange.Text + "Add text at the end."
```

Or you can do this:

```
oRange.Text = "Add text at the beginning " + oRange.Text
```

Another possibility is to read text into VFP, manipulate it in some way, and write it back:

```
cMakeUpper = oRange.Text
cMakeUpper = UPPER(cMakeUpper)
oRange.Text = cMakeUpper
```

That example can be shortened to a single line, like this:

```
oRange.Text = UPPER(oRange.Text)
```

Using this approach, we can send the data from a record to a new, blank document:

```
USE _SAMPLES + "TasTrade\Data\Customer"

LOCAL oDocument, oRange
oDocument = oWord.Documents.Add()   && Use the Normal template
oRange = oDocument.Range()

oRange.Text = Customer_ID + ": " + Company_Name
oRange.Text = oRange.Text + "Attn: " + TRIM(Contact_Name) + ;
              " - " + Contact_Title
oRange.Text = oRange.Text + Address
oRange.Text = oRange.Text + TRIM(City) + " " + TRIM(Region) + Postal_Code
oRange.Text = oRange.Text + UPPER(Country)
```

Because Word always keeps a paragraph marker (CHR(13)) at the end of the document, it adds a paragraph marker after each addition to oRange.Text when executing this code. In other situations (including the examples that follow), you need to add the paragraph marker explicitly. The new document looks like **Figure 2**.

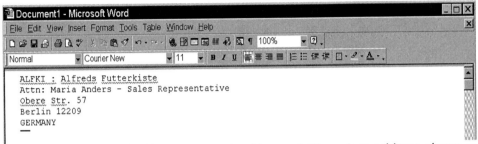

Figure 2. There's more than one way to skin a cat. The return address shown can be sent to Word in many different ways. In this case, with no special formatting involved, the fastest approach is to build the whole string in VFP, then send it to Word.

Of course, building a document by composing a single string doesn't take advantage of the special capabilities of Word. Range's InsertAfter and InsertBefore methods let you add text at the end or beginning, respectively, and expand the range to include the new text.

Here's an alternative, faster approach to creating the document shown in Figure 2:

```
#DEFINE CR CHR(13)

USE _SAMPLES + "TasTrade\Data\Customer"

LOCAL oDocument, oRange
oDocument = oWord.Documents.Add()    && Use the Normal template
oRange = oDocument.Range()

oRange.InsertAfter(Customer_ID + ": " + Company_Name + CR)
oRange.InsertAfter("Attn: " + TRIM(Contact_Name) + " - " + Contact_Title + CR)
oRange.InsertAfter(Address + CR)
oRange.InsertAfter(TRIM(City) + " " + TRIM(Region) + Postal_Code + CR)
oRange.InsertAfter(UPPER(Country))
```

In our tests, the InsertAfter version was one-and-a-half times to twice as fast as the concatenation method.

Moving in a range or selection

Besides changing the content of a range or selection, you may need to modify its extent. A number of methods change the area covered by a range or selection. One of the simplest is the Move method, which changes the boundaries of the range or selection.

Move accepts two parameters. The first indicates the unit of movement—you can move by characters, words, paragraphs, rows in a table, or the whole document. The second parameter tells how many of the specified units to move—a positive number indicates forward movement (toward the end of the document), while a negative number means backward movement (toward the beginning of the document).

In all cases, the range or selection is reduced (or "collapsed," in Word VBA terms) to a single point before being moved. Although collapsing a range or selection sounds dire, it's not. The text contained in the range/selection remains in the document—only the extent of the range or selection is changed. When moving forward, the range or selection is reduced to its end point, then moved; when moving backward, it's reduced to its beginning point before moving. You don't need to do anything special afterward. For the Automation programmer, the key issue is to understand where in the range movement begins.

Constants from the wdUnits group are used for the units of movement. **Table 1** shows the values for this group that can be passed to the Move method.

Table 1. *Word units. The constants in the wdUnits group represent portions of a document.*

Constant	Value	Description
wdCharacter	1	One character.
wdWord	2	One word.
wdSentence	3	One sentence.
wdParagraph	4	One paragraph.
wdSection	8	One section of a document. (Word allows you to divide documents into multiple sections with different formatting.)
wdStory	6	The entire length of whichever part of the document you're in. Word considers the main body of the document to be one "story," the header to be another "story," the footnotes to be a third, and so forth.
wdCell	12	One cell of a table.
wdColumn	9	One column of a table.
wdRow	10	One row of a table.
wdTable	15	The entire space of a table.

To create a range at the end of the document, you can use the following:

```
oRange  = oWord.ActiveDocument.Range()
oRange.Move( wdStory, 1)
```

Here's another way to create the document shown in Figure 2. It uses the Move method to move the Range object.

```
#DEFINE CR CHR(13)
#DEFINE wdStory 6

USE _SAMPLES + "TasTrade\Data\Customer"

LOCAL oDocument, oRange
oDocument = oWord.Documents.Add()   && Use the Normal template

oRange = oDocument.Range()
```

```
oRange.Text = Customer_ID + ": " + Company_Name + CR
oRange.Move(wdStory)
oRange.Text = "Attn: " + TRIM(Contact_Name) + " - " + Contact_Title + CR
oRange.Move(wdStory)
oRange.Text = Address + CR
oRange.Move(wdStory)
oRange.Text = TRIM(City) + " " + TRIM(Region) + Postal_Code + CR
oRange.Move(wdStory)
oRange.Text = UPPER(Country)
```

Speedwise, this version ranks between the concatenation and insert versions.

The Collapse method lets you explicitly reduce a range or selection to a single point. It takes one parameter, indicating the direction of the collapse. Passing the constant wdCollapseEnd (with a value of 0) collapses the range or selection to its end point (the point closest to the end of the document). Passing wdCollapseStart (whose value is 1) reduces the range or selection to its starting point. (That is, Collapse moves either the starting point of the range to the endpoint or the endpoint to the starting point. The range then consists of just a single point at what was previously either the end or the beginning of the range.)

The example can be rewritten yet again to use Collapse to control the range:

```
#DEFINE CR CHR(13)
#DEFINE wdCollapseEnd 0

USE _SAMPLES + "TasTrade\Data\Customer"

LOCAL oDocument, oRange
oDocument = oWord.Documents.Add()    && Use the Normal template
oRange = oDocument.Range()

oRange.Text = Customer_ID + ": " + Company_Name + CR
oRange.Collapse(wdCollapseEnd)
oRange.Text = "Attn: " + TRIM(Contact_Name) + " - " + Contact_Title + CR
oRange.Collapse(wdCollapseEnd)
oRange.Text = Address + CR
oRange.Collapse(wdCollapseEnd)
oRange.Text = TRIM(City) + " " + TRIM(Region) + Postal_Code + CR
oRange.Collapse(wdCollapseEnd)
oRange.Text = UPPER(Country)
```

In terms of timing, this version performs about the same as the Move version.

A number of other methods allow fine-tuning of movement. They include MoveEnd, MoveStart, MoveLeft, MoveRight, EndOf, and StartOf. Some methods apply only to the selection, not to ranges.

Finally, it's worth commenting that, for this particular task, the fastest approach of all is to concatenate all the strings in VFP, and then send one string to the document:

```
USE _SAMPLES + "TasTrade\Data\Customer"

LOCAL oDocument, oRange
oDocument = oWord.Documents.Add()    && Use the Normal template
```

```
oRange = oDocument.Range()
LOCAL cText
cText = ""

cText = Customer_ID + ": " + Company_Name + CR
cText = cText + "Attn: " + TRIM(Contact_Name) + " - " + Contact_Title + CR
cText = cText + Address + CR
cText = cText + TRIM(City) + " " + TRIM(Region) + Postal_Code + CR
cText = cText + UPPER(Country) + CR

oRange.Text = ""
oRange.InsertAfter(cText)
```

With VFP's speed at constructing strings, this version takes only one-third to one-quarter as long as the other approaches. Although Collapse and Move aren't the best approach in this simple case, they are essential methods for working with Word.

Bookmarks

A bookmark is a way of naming a range or location. Word maintains a collection of bookmarks, naturally called Bookmarks. To create a Bookmark, call the Bookmarks collection's Add method, passing the name for the new bookmark and the range to which it refers. For example, this code creates a bookmark called Title for the first paragraph of the document:

```
oDocument.Bookmarks.Add("Title", oDocument.Paragraphs[1].Range )
```

Why use bookmarks? Because Word does the work of maintaining them. Rather than keeping track of a variable in VFP, we can simply ask Word to hang onto a range for us. More importantly, Word can remember the range between sessions, so that when we return to a document, the bookmark is still available, still pointing to the same location.

Formatting

If all we could do was send text to Word and read the text that's already there, Automation would be useful, but not worth too much trouble. However, there's much more to automating Word than just sending and receiving text. One of the big benefits of using Word rather than VFP is the ability to apply complex formatting to documents.

Word allows documents to be formatted in a number of ways, and the objects available for formatting reflect the way Word structures its commands. For example, the Font object contains properties for the settings found in Word's Font dialog (Format|Font on the menu). The ParagraphFormat object controls the settings found in the Paragraph dialog, such as indentation, spacing, and alignment. Similarly, the settings from the Page Setup dialog are controlled by the PageSetup object. Style objects represent the preformatted and user-defined styles available in the document. These four objects manage most of the frequently used settings. Other objects control other aspects of formatting.

Setting up pages

The Page Setup dialog on Word's File menu tells Word what kind of paper to expect, where to get it, and how to lay the document out on that paper once it finds it. The dialog's controls specify the paper source (default paper tray, alternate tray, manual feed, and so forth), paper type (letter, legal, A4, and so on), and orientation of the page (portrait or landscape). The dialog is also used to determine the size of the margins, headers, and footers, to specify whether the first page of the document has a different header and footer than the rest and whether odd and even pages have different headers and footers. There are actually a lot more options there, too. Repeating our theme, Word is amazingly powerful. **Figure 3** shows the Margins page of the Page Setup dialog.

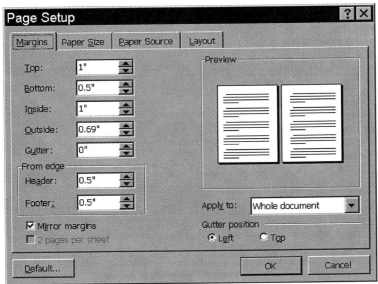

Figure 3. *The Page Setup dialog. This dialog lets you specify margins, paper size and orientation, whether headers and footers are the same or different on the first page and on odd and even pages, and much more.*

The PageSetup object is the Automation object that parallels the dialog. It has an assortment of properties that handle the various options available. Unlike many of Word's objects, most of PageSetup's properties do not refer to other objects. They're simply values, making it a little easier to work with than many of the others. (A note of caution: although the other Office applications have objects named PageSetup, each Office application's object is distinct; they can't be used interchangeably.)

Table 2 shows the most common properties of the PageSetup object, along with constant values for commonly used settings.

Table 2*. PageSetup properties. The PageSetup object mimics the Page Setup dialog on Word's File menu.*

Property	Type	Description
PaperSize	Numeric	The type of paper to use for the document, such as legal, letter, A4, and so on. wdPaperLetter 2 wdPaperLegal 4 wdPaperA4 7 wdPaper11x17 1
FirstPageTray	Numeric	The source for the first sheet of paper for the document. The first sheet is handled separately to allow, for example, letterhead for page one of a letter followed by plain paper for the rest. wdPrinterDefaultBin 0 wdPrinterUpperBin 1 wdPrinterLowerBin 2 wdPrinterManualFeed 4 wdPrinterEnvelopeFeed 5 wdPrinterAutomaticSheetFeed 7
OtherPagesTray	Numeric	The source for sheets of paper other than the first. Uses the same constants as FirstPageTray.
Orientation	Numeric	The orientation of the paper. wdOrientPortrait 0 wdOrientLandscape 1
TopMargin, BottomMargin	Numeric	The vertical margins of the page, in points.
LeftMargin, RightMargin	Numeric	The horizontal margins of the page, in points.
VerticalAlignment	Numeric	The vertical position of the text on the page. wdAlignVerticalTop 0 wdAlignVerticalCenter 1 wdAlignVerticalJustify 2 wdAlignVerticalBottom 3
DifferentFirstPageHeaderFooter	Logical or Numeric	Indicates whether the first page of the document has different headers and footers than the rest of the document. (Numeric only if undefined.)
OddAndEvenPagesHeaderFooter	Logical or Numeric	Indicates whether odd pages and even pages have different headers and footers. (Numeric only if undefined.)

Like many other measurement-related properties, the margin settings expect points rather than what's shown in the Page Setup dialog. To make specifying measurements easier, the Word Application object has a number of conversion methods, including InchesToPoints, CentimetersToPoints, PointsToInches, PointsToCentimeters, and quite a few more.

The following example creates a document, centers it vertically on the page, gives it different odd and even page headers and footers, and sets the margins to one inch everywhere but at the bottom, where 0.75" is used.

```
* Set up a document with custom margins, different odd and
* even headers and footers, and center alignment

#DEFINE wdAlignVerticalCenter 1
```

```
oDocument = oWord.Documents.Add()

WITH oDocument.PageSetup
   .VerticalAlignment = wdAlignVerticalCenter
   .OddAndEvenPagesHeaderFooter = .T.

   * Set up .75 bottom margin and 1-inch
   * top, left and right margins.
   LOCAL nThreeQuartersInPoints, nInchInPoints
   nThreeQuartersInPoints = oWord.InchesToPoints( .75 )
   nInchInPoints = oWord.InchesToPoints( 1 )

   .BottomMargin = nThreeQuartersInPoints
   .TopMargin = nInchInPoints
   .LeftMargin = nInchInPoints
   .RightMargin = nInchInPoints
ENDWITH
```

Since the number of points to the inch (or to the centimeter) never changes, you may prefer to perform these conversions yourself. You can define your own constants and perform the arithmetic in native VFP code rather than calling Automation methods to do it. Here's alternative code for the margin setting portion of the preceding example:

```
* ALTERNATE METHOD: replaces the seven lines of code, above:
   #DEFINE autoInchesToPoints 72

   .BottomMargin = 0.75 * autoInchesToPoints
   .TopMargin    = 1.00 * autoInchesToPoints
   .LeftMargin   = 1.00 * autoInchesToPoints
   .RightMargin  = 1.00 * autoInchesToPoints
```

Our tests show a speed improvement of about two orders of magnitude (that's about 100 times faster) doing the conversions ourselves. For an occasional computation, it doesn't really matter, but if you need to convert between points and other units hundreds or thousands of times, it's definitely worth using native VFP code and remembering to include the right constants everywhere.

The PageSetup object has a number of other, more obscure properties, not shown in Table 2. Though the descriptions for several properties shown in Table 2 refer to the document as a whole, each Section of a document can have its own PageSetup object whose properties apply only within that section.

PageSetup has only two methods. TogglePortrait switches Orientation between portrait and landscape. It's equivalent to setting the Orientation property directly to the opposite of its current setting. SetAsDefaultTemplate makes the current PageSetup the default for this document and for all new documents based on the active template. It's like clicking the Default button in the Page Setup dialog. (Watch out! The name of that method implies that it creates a default template. It doesn't. It creates default settings for the current template.)

Setting fonts

Fonts in Word are controlled by the Font dialog on the Format menu (shown in **Figure 4**). That dialog controls the font name, size, style (such as bold, italic, underline, and so forth), color, and effects (like strikethrough, superscripts and subscripts, and much more). It also controls more esoteric options such as kerning, animation of or around text, the vertical position of text with respect to the baseline, spacing between characters, and more. The Font object, which is similar to (though not quite the same as) Font objects in the other Office servers, manages these options.

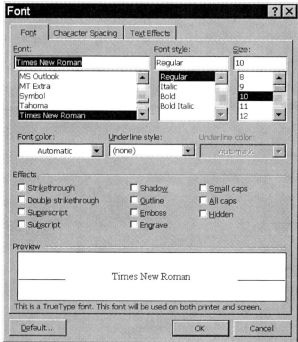

Figure 4. Specifying fonts. The Font dialog controls font, size, style, and color, as well as unusual options like kerning and spacing between characters. In Automation, the Font object manages all of these features.

Range, Selection, and Style (discussed in the section "Working with styles" later in this chapter), as well as many other objects, each have a Font property that points to a Font object. Changing the properties of the Font object modifies the font of that portion of the document. For example, to change all the customer information shown in Figure 2 to 12-point Arial, you can use this code:

```
oRange = oDocument.Range()
oRange.Font.Name = "Arial"
oRange.Font.Size = 12
```

To simplify matters, just set the desired font before sending the text to the document. Here's another version of the program to send the customer address. This one uses 12-point Arial from the start:

```
#DEFINE CR CHR(13)

USE _SAMPLES + "TasTrade\Data\Customer"

LOCAL oDocument, oRange
oDocument = oWord.Documents.Add()    && Use the Normal template
oRange = oDocument.Range()

oRange.Font.Name = "Arial"
oRange.Font.Size = 12

LOCAL cText
cText = ""

cText = Customer_ID + ": " + Company_Name + CR
cText = cText + "Attn: " + TRIM(Contact_Name) + " - " + Contact_Title + CR
cText = cText + Address + CR
cText = cText + TRIM(City) + " " + TRIM(Region) + Postal_Code + CR
cText = cText + UPPER(Country) + CR

oRange.Text = ""
oRange.InsertAfter(cText)
```

In fact, this isn't the best way to set the font for a whole document. It's better to use a template where the font of the Normal style has been set as needed. (For more information, see the section "Working with styles" later in this chapter.)

Table 3 lists Font properties you're likely to want to work with, along with Word constants for them, where appropriate.

Table 3. *Font properties. The Font object controls the appearance of the font, from the font face to its size, style, and much more. This table shows the more common properties. Check Help for more unusual settings.*

Property	Type	Description
Name	Character	The name of the font.
Size	Numeric	The size of the font, in points.
Bold	Numeric or Logical	Indicates whether the text is bold.
Italic	Numeric or Logical	Indicates whether the text is italic.
Underline	Numeric	The type of underline. wdUnderlineNone 0 wdUnderlineDouble 3 wdUnderlineSingle 1 wdUnderlineDotted 4 wdUnderlineWords 2 wdUnderlineThick 6
Superscript, Subscript	Numeric or Logical	Indicates whether the text is superscript or subscript.

It's possible for the text in a range (or whatever area the Font object covers) to have more than one font setting. When that happens, the various numeric properties get the value wdUndefined (9999999). (That's also why properties that you'd expect to be logical are listed as numeric or logical.) Font.Name is the empty string in that situation.

The next example demonstrates a related complication of working with VBA objects in Visual FoxPro. Although these logical properties (like Bold and Italic) can be set by assigning VFP's logical values .T. and .F., they can't be compared to logical values. Code like this fails with the error "Operator/operand type mismatch":

```
IF oFont.Bold
```

That's because of Bold's dual numeric/logical capabilities. When you assign logical values, Word translates them somewhere along the way, but for comparison, you have to use the numeric values. The next example (SetUserFont.PRG) defines constants TRUE and FALSE rather than using the VFP logical values. That way, the code is readable but avoids the type mismatch problem.

You can allow the user to choose the font by calling VFP's GetFont() function first. Here's a function that lets the user specify a font, prompting with the font currently in use, and changes it to the specified font. Run this code with the following syntax, making sure there's an active document with a range specified (for example, run any of the code examples in the previous sections).

```
SetUserFont(oRange.Font)
```

Listing 1 shows the code for SetUserFont (it's also included in the Developer Download files available at www.hentzenwerke.com).

Listing 1. This function lets the user choose a font, prompting with the name, size, and style of the font object it receives as a parameter.

```
* SetUserFont.PRG
* Let the user specify a font, then set
* a passed font object to use it.

#DEFINE TRUE -1
#DEFINE FALSE 0

LPARAMETERS oFont
   * oFont = Reference to a font object

LOCAL cName, nSize, cStyle
LOCAL cFontString, aFontInfo[3]

* Did we get a font object to work with?
IF VarType(oFont) <> "O"
   RETURN .F.
ENDIF

* Get current settings of font object.
WITH oFont
   cName = .Name
   nSize = .Size
   cStyle = ""
```

```
      IF .Bold = TRUE   && Can't use VFP .T. here
         cStyle = cStyle + "B"
      ENDIF
      IF .Italic = TRUE   && or here
         cStyle = cStyle + "I"
      ENDIF
ENDWITH

* Ask the user for a font
cFontString = GetFont(cName, nSize, cStyle)

IF EMPTY(cFontString)
   * User cancelled
   RETURN .F.
ELSE
   * Parse the chosen into its components
   cFontString = CHRTRAN(cFontString, ",", CHR(13))
   ALINES(aFontInfo,cFontString)

   * Apply them to the font object
   WITH oFont
      .Name = aFontInfo[1]
      .Size = VAL(aFontInfo[2])
      IF "B"$aFontInfo[3]
         .Bold = .T.   && .T. works here
      ENDIF
      IF "I"$aFontInfo[3]
         .Italic = .T.
      ENDIF
   ENDWITH
ENDIF
RETURN .T.
```

Formatting paragraphs

Paragraphs are a key concept in Word. Much of Word's formatting can be thought of as being stored "in" the marker that follows each paragraph. That's why moving text sometimes changes its formatting. If you fail to take the paragraph marker along, the moved text picks up the formatting of the new location.

At the paragraph level, you can determine alignment of text (left, right, centered, or full justification), various kinds of indentation (both amount and type), spacing of lines and paragraphs, handling of widow and orphans, and much more. Word allows regular indentation from both the left and right margins, as well as first line indents and hanging indents. Interactively, all of this is managed by the Paragraph dialog on the Format menu (shown in **Figure 5**). Behind the scenes, the ParagraphFormat object controls these settings.

Range, Selection, and Style, among others, have a ParagraphFormat object, accessed through the ParagraphFormat property. The Paragraph object has a Format property that accesses a ParagraphFormat object.

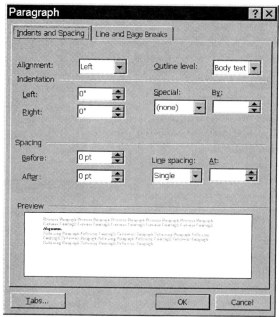

Figure 5*. The Paragraph dialog. The Indents and Spacing page shown here lets you indicate alignment, indentation, and spacing. The Line and Page Breaks page handles widow and orphan control and automatic hyphenation. The ParagraphFormat object controls these settings for Automation.*

Table 4 shows some commonly used properties of the ParagraphFormat object and the frequently used constant values for them. Like many of Word's objects, ParagraphFormat has only a few methods; none are likely to be useful in most Automation code.

This example sets the first paragraph in the current range to have a 0.5" first line indent, widow and orphan control, double spacing, and full justification:

```
#DEFINE wdAlignParagraphJustify 3
#DEFINE wdLineSpaceDouble 2

WITH oRange.Paragraphs[1].Format
  .FirstLineIndent = oWord.InchesToPoints( .5 )
  .WidowControl = .T.
  .Alignment = wdAlignParagraphJustify
  .LineSpacingRule = wdLineSpaceDouble
ENDWITH
```

This example triple spaces a range:

```
#DEFINE wdLineSpaceMultiple 5

WITH oRange.ParagraphFormat
  .LineSpacingRule = wdLineSpaceMultiple
  .LineSpacing = oWord.LinesToPoints( 3 )
ENDWITH
```

Table 4. *ParagraphFormat properties.*

Property	Type	Description
Alignment	Numeric	The alignment of text in the paragraph. wdAlignParagraphLeft 0 wdAlignParagraphRight 2 wdAlignParagraphCenter 1 wdAlignParagraphJustify 3
LeftIndent	Numeric	The indentation of the left edge of this paragraph from the left margin, in points.
RightIndent	Numeric	The indentation of the right edge of this paragraph from the right margin, in points.
FirstLineIndent	Numeric	The indentation of the first line of the paragraph. This property determines whether the paragraph has the first line indented or "outdented" (providing a hanging indent). Set a positive value to indent the first line, 0 to keep the first line flush with the rest of the paragraph, or a negative value for a hanging indent. Note that, with a hanging indent, the first line doesn't move to the left; subsequent lines move to the right.
SpaceBefore, SpaceAfter	Numeric	The amount of white space (known as *leading*) before and after the paragraph, in points.
LineSpacingRule	Numeric	The kind of line spacing in effect. This setting can entirely determine the line spacing, or it can set the stage for the LineSpacing property. wdLineSpaceSingle 0 wdLineSpaceAtLeast 3 wdLineSpaceDouble 2 wdLineSpace1pt5 1 wdLineSpaceExactly 4 wdLineSpaceMultiple 5
LineSpacing	Numeric	The actual line spacing, in points, when LineSpacingRule is wdLineSpaceAtLeast, wdLineSpaceExactly, or wdLineSpaceMultiple.
WidowControl	Numeric or Logical	Indicates whether the first and last lines of the paragraph are kept on the same page as the rest of the paragraph.
KeepTogether	Numeric or Logical	Indicates whether the entire paragraph is kept on a single page.
KeepWithNext	Numeric or Logical	Indicates whether the paragraph is kept on the same page with the paragraph that follows it.
Hyphenation	Numeric or Logical	Indicates whether the paragraph is hyphenated automatically.

Working with styles

While it's appropriate to manually adjust the formatting of a word, sentence, or paragraph here and there, the most effective way to use Word is to take advantage of styles, which are named formats that you can apply to a portion of a document. When you're working in Word, you can see the style for the insertion point in the first dropdown on the Formatting toolbar.

Word has two kinds of styles: paragraph styles and character styles. Character styles are used for fragments and control only a few settings, primarily font-related. Paragraph styles, as the name implies, apply to entire paragraphs and include a lot more options. Paragraph styles can specify font and paragraph formatting, as well as tab settings and much more. In the Style dialog available from Word's Format menu (see **Figure 6**), paragraph styles are preceded by a paragraph marker, while character styles begin with an underlined "a."

Using styles is much like using classes in an object-oriented language. They make it easy to enforce uniformity throughout and across documents, and they let you change the characteristics of sections of text with a single change. Word's styles offer some other benefits, as well. For example, each paragraph style sets the default style for the paragraph to follow. With a little more work up front, styles can be used to provide an outline for a document, as well.

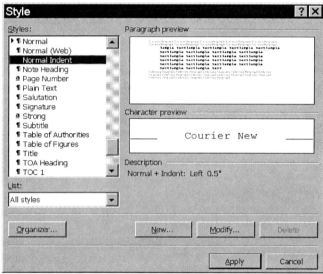

Figure 6. *Creating and choosing styles. Word's Style dialog lists the available styles. Paragraph styles are preceded by a paragraph symbol, while an underlined "a" precedes character styles. Note in the Description that the style is described in terms of another—its "base style."*

The Document object includes a Styles collection, which contains one Style object for each of the styles stored in the document. You can add your own styles using the Styles collection's Add method. Various objects' Style properties point to Style objects.

What all this fuss about styles means is that, rather than writing a lot of code to change fonts and sizes, and to set alignment and leading and other things like that, you can simply define a few custom styles or modify built-in styles, and then apply them to your documents as needed. For example, this code modifies the Normal style, which is always available, to use 16-point centered Garamond italic:

```
#DEFINE wdStyleNormal -1
#DEFINE wdAlignParagraphCenter 1

WITH oWord.ActiveDocument.Styles[ wdStyleNormal ]
  WITH .Font
    .Name = "Garamond"
    .Size = 16
    .Italic = .T.
  ENDWITH
  .ParagraphFormat.Alignment = wdAlignParagraphCenter
ENDWITH
```

To apply an existing style to a portion of a document, set the Style property of the Range or Paragraph to a built-in style using a constant, or to the name of a custom style. **Table 5** lists the constants for some of the more commonly used built-in styles. This example applies the Heading 1 style to the range referenced by oRange:

```
#DEFINE wdStyleHeading1 -2
oRange.Style = oWord.ActiveDocument.Styles[ wdStyleHeading1 ]
```

Table 5. Built-in styles. Word has more than 100 built-in styles, each referenced by a defined constant. This table shows just a few of the most common; use the Object Browser to find the rest.

Constant	Value	Constant	Value
wdStyleNormal	-1	wdStyleHeading1	-2
wdStyleBodyText	-67	wdStyleHeading2	-3
wdStyleDefaultParagraphFont	-66	wdStyleHeading3	-4

Creating custom styles

In addition to modifying the built-in styles, you can create your own custom styles. To add a new style, use the Add method of the Styles collection. Add takes two parameters: the name of the new style, and the Word constant that indicates whether it's a paragraph style (wdStyleTypeParagraph = 1) or a character style (wdStyleTypeCharacter = 2).

Every style is based on an existing style. By default, new paragraph styles are based on the Normal style, and new character styles are based on the Default Character Font style. The BaseStyle property indicates which style another style inherits from, however.

Whatever style BaseStyle points to, all other changes to the style's properties use the BaseStyle as their point of reference. If you look at the Style dialog, you see that the style's characteristics are described as "<The base style>" + "<various other characteristics>." The Description property contains the same information. So, much like classes in OOP, changes to the base style change any styles based on it.

Table 6 lists key properties of the Style object, along with significant constant values.

Table 6. Style counts. Styles are Word's version of OOP. They offer a way to provide uniform formatting within and across documents.

Property	Type	Description
BaseStyle	Character, Numeric, or Object	The name, constant value, or pointer to the style on which this style is based. See Table 5 and Help or the Object Browser for constant values for built-in styles.
Type	Numeric	The kind of style—paragraph or character. wdStyleTypeParagraph 1 wdStyleTypeCharacter 2
Builtin	Logical	Indicates whether this a built-in style.
Description	Character	The description of the style (as shown in the Style dialog).
Font	Object	Pointer to a Font object for the style.
ParagraphFormat	Object	Pointer to a ParagraphFormat object for the style.
Borders	Object	Pointer to a Borders collection for the style.
Shading	Object	Pointer to a Shading object for the style.
NextParagraphStyle	Character, Numeric, or Object	The name, constant value, or pointer to the style for the paragraph to follow this paragraph, for paragraph styles.

Listing 2 takes the simple customer address document from earlier in the chapter and begins to create a document worthy of Word. It creates several new styles to do the job. In practice, you could use the built-in Normal and Heading X (there are multiple heading levels) styles for this document, redefining them as needed. But the example shows how easy it is to create new styles. (You'll find this program as Styles.PRG in the Developer Download files available at www.hentzenwerke.com.)

Listing 2. *This program creates several custom styles, then uses them to create the document in Figure 7.*

```
* Create a formatted document by sending data from one record.
* Demonstrates Style objects, but it's more likely the needs here
* could be met by existing styles.

#DEFINE CR CHR(13)
#DEFINE wdStyleTypeParagraph 1
#DEFINE wdStyleNormal -1
#DEFINE wdAlignParagraphLeft 0
#DEFINE wdAlignParagraphCenter 1
#DEFINE wdCollapseEnd 0

USE _SAMPLES + "TasTrade\Data\Customer"

RELEASE ALL LIKE o*
PUBLIC oWord

LOCAL oWord, oDocument, oRange
LOCAL oBodyStyle, oMajorHeadingStyle, oMinorHeadingStyle

oWord = CreateObject("Word.Application")
oWord.Visible = .T.
oDocument = oWord.Documents.Add()   && Use the Normal template
oRange = oDocument.Range()

* Set up styles. Base body style on Normal.
oBodyStyle = oDocument.Styles.Add( "Body", wdStyleTypeParagraph )
WITH oBodyStyle
   * This line is overkill since it's the default
   .BaseStyle = oDocument.Styles[ wdStyleNormal ]
   WITH .Font
      .Name = "Arial"
      .Size = 12
   ENDWITH

   WITH .ParagraphFormat
      * These are fairly normal defaults, so these lines
      * may not be necessary
      .Alignment = wdAlignParagraphLeft
      .SpaceAfter = 0
   ENDWITH
ENDWITH

* Major heading is big and centered.
oMajorHeadingStyle = oDocument.Styles.Add( "MajorHeading", ;
                                    wdStyleTypeParagraph)
WITH oMajorHeadingStyle
```

```
   .BaseStyle = oBodyStyle
   .Font.Size = 20

  WITH .ParagraphFormat
     .Alignment = wdAlignParagraphCenter
     .SpaceAfter = 6  && leave a line after
     .KeepWithNext = .T.  && include at least one line of next
                          && paragraph before new page
     .KeepTogether = .T.  && keep the whole paragraph together
  ENDWITH
ENDWITH

* Minor heading is just big.
oMinorHeadingStyle = oDocument.Styles.Add("MinorHeading", ;
                                          wdStyleTypeParagraph )
WITH oMinorHeadingStyle
   .BaseStyle = oBodyStyle
   .Font.Size = 16
ENDWITH

* Now create customer report
* First, our company info centered at the top
oRange.Style = oMajorHeadingStyle
oRange.InsertAfter("Automation Sample Company" + CR)
oRange.InsertAfter("Factory Blvd." + CR)
oRange.InsertAfter("Robotville, PA 19199" + CR)

* Now leave some blank space, then put info about this customer
oRange.Collapse( wdCollapseEnd )
oRange.End = oRange.End + 1 && to allow assignment to style
oRange.Style = oBodyStyle
oRange.InsertAfter(CR + CR)

* Use minor heading for customer id and name
* Put customer id in bold
oRange.Collapse( wdCollapseEnd )
oRange.End = oRange.End + 1 && to allow assignment to style
oRange.Style = oMinorHeadingStyle
oRange.InsertAfter(Customer_ID + ": " + TRIM(Company_Name) + CR)
oRange.Words[1].Font.Bold = .t.

* Regular body style for address info
oRange.Collapse( wdCollapseEnd )
oRange.End = oRange.End + 1 && to allow assignment to style
oRange.Style = oBodyStyle
oRange.InsertAfter(TRIM(Contact_Title) + ":" + TRIM(Contact_Name) ;
                   + CR)
oRange.InsertAfter(TRIM(Address) + CR)
oRange.InsertAfter(TRIM(City) + " " + TRIM(Region) + ;
                   Postal_Code + CR)
oRange.InsertAfter(UPPER(TRIM(Country)) + CR )
* Extra line for spacing
oRange.InsertAfter( CR )

* Back to minor heading for phone number
oRange.Collapse( wdCollapseEnd )
oRange.End = oRange.End + 1 && to allow assignment to style
```

```
oRange.Style = oMinorHeadingStyle
oRange.InsertAfter( "Phone: " + TRIM(Phone) + CR)

* Fax number in regular body style
oRange.Collapse( wdCollapseEnd )
oRange.End = oRange.End + 1 && to allow assignment to style
oRange.Style = oBodyStyle
oRange.InsertAfter( "Fax:    " + TRIM(Fax) + CR )
```

Note the use of the Words collection to bold only the customer id rather than the whole line. **Figure 7** shows the resulting document in Word.

Figure 7. Using styles. Rather than formatting every item independently, styles let you define and name sets of formatting characteristics, then apply them uniformly within and across documents. Styles can be considered OOP for formatting.

In an example this small, it can be hard to see the point of creating and using styles. It's worth noting that the code in the example is divided almost exactly evenly between formatting the styles and putting the data into the document. Far more lines would have been needed to perform the same formatting without using styles. Furthermore, consider what would be needed to add more information for the same customer. Once the styles are defined, they can be used over and over. With 42 lines of code, we have three styles that can be applied wherever we need them, no matter how many more lines of code we write to send text to the document. In Chapter 5, "Intermediate Word," we'll look at creating templates, in which we can save our own styles for use in multiple documents.

Borders and shading
Word allows you to put borders around and shading behind various parts of a document to set them off from the rest of the document. You can put borders around or shade pretty much anything, from a single character to an entire page. Border styles vary from simple lines to

complex patterns and from a half-point to six points. A border can be applied on any or all sides of the text. Shading can be any color and can run the gamut from just a plain color to a patterned fill. Interactively, it's all controlled from the Borders and Shading dialog on the Format menu.

In Automation, two objects run the show. Not surprisingly, they're called Borders and Shading. Borders is a collection of Border objects.

Creating borders

Setting up borders interactively can be tricky. It's often hard to get the border where you actually want it. That's because the Borders collection can belong to different objects, and the object to which it belongs determines where the border actually appears. **Table 7** lists some of the objects that can hold a Borders collection and the interpretation of the collection in that case.

***Table 7**. Almost anything can have borders. The interpretation and size of the Borders collection depends on what object it belongs to.*

Object	Meaning of Borders
Section	Sets a Page Border for that section of the document.
Paragraphs collection	Sets borders around the group of paragraphs in the collection.
Paragraph	Sets borders for that paragraph.
Range	Sets borders for that range. When the range crosses paragraph boundaries or there's a break of some sort, such as a hard page break or a section break within the range, the range is expanded to include the complete paragraphs at each end. The border is applied to that expanded range, which is treated like a Paragraphs collection.
Table	Sets borders for the outside of the table and for the gridlines inside the table.
Rows collection	Sets borders for the rows in the collection. Applies only to the outside borders of the collection, not to the borders for each row in the collection.
Columns collection	Sets borders for the columns in the collection. Applies only to the outside borders of the collection, not to the borders for each column in the collection.
Row	Sets borders for the specified row.
Column	Sets borders for the specified column.
Cells collection	Sets borders for the cells in the specified collection. This approach works much better than using either Rows or Columns. Be sure to specify top or bottom borders when accessing Cells through a Row, and left or right borders when accessing Cells through a Column. While the others work, they're not very productive.
Cell	Sets borders for a specified cell, indicated by both row and column. This approach is also effective.
Style	Sets borders for a style.

A number of other objects reference Borders collections as well, but they're pretty esoteric.

The Borders collection contains a lot more information than most. Also, unlike most collections, you can't add members freely. The number of Border objects it contains is determined by the kind of object it belongs to. Most of the time, there are four members, accessed using these constants: wdBorderTop (-1), wdBorderLeft (-2), wdBorderBottom

(-3), and wdBorderRight (-4). For some objects, including tables, the collection has additional members. The constants are: wdBorderHorizontal (-5), wdBorderVertical (-6), wdBorderDiagonalDown (-7), and wdBorderDiagonalUp (-8).

In addition to the individual Border objects, the collection has a number of other properties. **Table 8** contains a sampling of them.

Table 8. *Borders collection properties. While most collections have few properties, Borders is particularly rich in them.*

Property	Type	Description
Count	Numeric	The number of Border objects in this collection.
InsideLineStyle	Numeric	The type of line used for the inside of a table. Can be overridden by setting borders for the individual rows, columns, or cells. Uses the constants shown for LineStyle in Table 9.
InsideLineWidth	Numeric	The size of the lines used for the inside of a table. Can be overridden by setting borders for the individual rows, columns, or cells. Uses the constants shown for LineWidth in Table 9.
OutsideLineStyle	Numeric	The type of line used for the outside border of the specified object. Uses the constants shown for LineStyle in Table 9.
OutsideLineWidth	Numeric	The size of the lines used for the outside border of the specified object. Uses the constants shown for LineWidth in Table 9.
Enable	Logical	Indicates whether or not borders should be enabled for the specified object. Setting this property to .F. turns off borders for the object.

A variety of other properties determine how far from the specified object the borders appear.

At long last, we reach the actual Border object, which describes the characteristics of a single border. **Table 9** shows its key properties.

This code creates a document and puts a page border of hot air balloons on it. **Figure 8** shows the result (substantially reduced in size).

```
#DEFINE wdArtBalloonsHotAir 12
#DEFINE wdBorderTop -1
#DEFINE wdBorderBottom -2
#DEFINE wdBorderLeft -3
#DEFINE wdBorderRight  -4

oDocument = oWord.Documents.Add()
WITH oDocument.Sections[1]
   .Borders[ wdBorderTop ].ArtStyle = wdArtBalloonsHotAir
   .Borders[ wdBorderBottom ].ArtStyle = wdArtBalloonsHotAir
   .Borders[ wdBorderLeft ].ArtStyle = wdArtBalloonsHotAir
   .Borders[ wdBorderRight ].ArtStyle = wdArtBalloonsHotAir
ENDWITH
```

Table 9. *What's in a border? These properties describe a single border.*

Property	Type	Description
LineStyle	Numeric	The type of line used for the border. For example: wdLineStyleNone 0 wdLineStyleDashDot 5 wdLineStyleSingle 1 wdLineStyleDouble 7 wdLineStyleDot 2 wdLineStyleSingleWavy 18
LineWidth	Numeric	The size of the line used for the border. You cannot set the point size for the line, but rather must use the constant value for a predefined size. Check the Object Browser for more choices. wdLineWidth025pt 2 0.25 points wdLineWidth050pt 4 0.5 points wdLineWidth075pt 6 0.75 points wdLineWidth100pt 8 1 point wdLineWidth150pt 10 1.5 points wdLineWidth225pt 18 2.25 points wdLineWidth300pt 24 3 points wdLineWidth450pt 36 4.5 points wdLineWidth600pt 48 6 points wdUndefined 9999999 Undefined
ColorIndex, Color	Numeric	The color for the line used for the border. Word offers two sets of colors. Use ColorIndex to specify a value from a short list, using the wdColorIndex constants, or use Color for a full list of RGB values, which can be passed either with VFP's RGB() function, as an actual numeric value, or by using the wdColor constants. Either property is acceptable. ColorIndex is quick and easy, but Color gives you more choices. Note that Color is new in Word 2000.
ArtStyle	Numeric	The graphic to use for a page border. More than 150 are available. Shades of PrintShop. Here's a sampling: wdArtApples 1 wdArtMusicNotes 79 wdArtBalloonsHotAir 12 wdArtPaperClips 82 wdArtBasicBlackDots 156 wdArtPencils 25
ArtWidth	Numeric	The width of the page border, in points.
Inside	Logical	Indicates whether the bordered object should have an inside border, if it supports one.

Figure 8. *Page border. The Borders collection lets you add borders to various objects. Its interpretation changes with the object.*

Shading text

After the complexities of borders, the good news is that shading is far easier. There's only one object involved, and it has only a handful of properties.

Like borders, shading can be applied at a number of levels. Many objects have a Shading property that references a Shading object. All the objects listed in Table 7 support shading except for Section, which makes sense because Section's Borders collection is really about page borders, something different than the rest.

Once you know what you want to shade, there are only three components involved in specifying shading: the background color, the foreground color, and the texture. Better yet, you can often omit the last two of these. The background color is just what it sounds like—the color to put behind the text. For most printed documents, you'll usually want some variant of gray. You can specify it with either BackgroundPatternColor or BackgroundPatternColorIndex. The difference is that BackgroundPatternColor expects an RGB value, while the longer-named property takes its value from a list of 18 predefined colors (you can look them up in the Object Browser under wdColorIndex). To specify light gray shading, try:

```
oRange.Shading.BackgroundPatternColor = RGB(230,230,230)
```

ForegroundPatternColor and ForegroundPatternColorIndex lay another color over the background color. Doing this doesn't make much sense if you don't specify a value for Texture. It's just an alternate way of specifying the shading color (or a complex way of mixing colors).

 BackgroundPatternColor and ForegroundPatternColor are new in Word 2000. In Word 97, you have to use the Index versions of the two properties and are limited to the list of predefined colors they provide.

However, Word can do much better tricks. The shading can be muted from full strength down to as low as 5 percent, with nearly 40 total steps offered. In addition, about a dozen other fill patterns are available for shading. In that case, the two colors are used as their names indicate. **Table 10** shows some of the constants available for the Texture property.

Table 10. *Textured shading. Word offers a variety of textures that allow shading to be more than just background.*

Constant	Value	Constant	Value
wdTextureNone	0	wdTextureCross	-11
wdTextureSolid	1000	wdTextureDarkCross	-5
wdTexture5Percent	50	wdTextureHorizontal	-7
wdTexture10Percent	100	wdTextureVertical	-8
wdTexture12Pt5Percent	125	wdTextureDiagonalCross	-12
wdTexture30Percent	300	wdTextureDiagonalUp	-10
wdTexture75Percent	750	wdTextureDiagonalDown	-9

This example sets up a diagonal crosshatch of orange on teal:

```
#DEFINE wdTextureDiagonalCross  -12
WITH oRange.Shading
   .Texture = wdTextureDiagonalCross
   .BackgroundPatternColor = RGB(0,192,255)
   .ForegroundPatternColor = RGB(255,128,0)
ENDWITH
```

Headers and footers

Have you ever noticed a document that included the chapter title at the top or said something like "Page 3 of 17" at the bottom of each page? Items like those are called headers and footers. Word has tremendous support for them, allowing you to put different headers on the first page of each section of a document than on the other pages, and to create separate headers and footers for odd and even pages.

Interactively, you access a document's Header and Footer through the View menu (see **Figure 9)**, which makes them available for editing and brings up a special toolbar for the purpose. The toolbar includes tools for inserting common header and footer items like page numbers, date and time, and so forth. However, headers and footers can hold any text at all, as well as graphics like company logos.

Figure 9. *Adding headers and footers. Use the View menu to make headers and footers visible interactively, so you can add to them. In the object model, they're represented by HeaderFooter objects.*

The kinds of headers and footers in a document (different first page, different on odd/even pages) are controlled through the PageSetup object and are discussed in the section "Setting up pages" earlier in this chapter. Header and footer content is stored in HeaderFooter objects, which are part of a HeaderFooters collection, accessed through the Headers and Footers properties of the Section object. Any section can have up to three of each, accessed via the constants wdHeaderFooterPrimary (1), wdHeaderFooterFirstPage (2), and wdHeaderFooterEvenPages (3).

Each HeaderFooter object represents a single header or footer. The key properties are shown in **Table 11**.

Table 11. *The HeaderFooter object. Despite its name, each instance represents a single header or footer.*

Property	Type	Description
Exists	Logical	Indicates whether the specified header or footer exists. Contradictory as this property seems, it makes sense when applied to a member of the HeadersFooters collection.
IsHeader	Logical	Indicates whether or not this is a header. If not, of course, it's a footer.
PageNumbers	Object	Pointer to a PageNumbers collection that represents page number information in this header or footer. (See the next section.)
LinkToPrevious	Logical	Indicates whether this header or footer is the same as the corresponding header or footer in the previous section of the document.

Page numbering

Page numbers can appear anywhere in a document, but are normally placed in either headers or footers. Word offers a variety of formatting options for page numbers, from normal Arabic numerals to letters, Roman numerals, and even chapter numbering (like 1–1, 1–2, and so forth). You also have a choice about the position of the number. It can go in a header or a footer, and it can be aligned left, center, or right, or at either an inside or outside margin. The last two choices apply only when the document has different odd and even page headers and footers, of course. All of those choices come just from the Insert|Page Number dialog. If you edit the header or footer manually, you can place the page number anywhere you want within it.

Word's PageNumbers collection consists of individual PageNumber objects. Each represents one occurrence of a page number in either a header or a footer. PageNumber is quite simple. Its only significant property is Alignment, which indicates the horizontal position of the page number. **Table 12** shows the possible values.

Table 12. *Aligning page numbers. These constants are the available values for the Alignment property of PageNumber.*

Constant	Value	Constant	Value
wdAlignPageNumberLeft	0	wdAlignPageNumberInside	3
wdAlignPageNumberCenter	1	wdAlignPageNumberOutside	4
wdAlignPageNumberRight	2		

The PageNumbers collection is where all the action occurs. It has a number of properties that describe page numbering within the section. **Table 13** shows the ones you're most likely to use.

To use chapter-type page numbering, the chapter numbers must be identifiable. Associating them with an outline level does that. (See the next section, "Organizing text with lists.")

Table 13. *The PageNumbers collection. Each section of a document lets you restart page numbering and change the appearance of page numbers.*

Property	Type	Description
NumberStyle	Numeric	The style to use for the page number. Check the Object Browser for additional choices. wdCaptionNumberStyleArabic — 0 wdCaptionNumberStyleUppercaseRoman — 1 wdCaptionNumberStyleLowercaseRoman — 2 wdCaptionNumberStyleUppercaseLetter — 3 wdCaptionNumberStyleLowercaseLetter — 4 wdCaptionNumberStyleHebrewLetter1 — 45
RestartNumberingAtSection	Logical	Indicates whether the page numbers start over at the beginning of this section.
StartingNumber	Numeric	The first page number for this section, if RestartNumberingAtSection is .T.
IncludeChapterNumber	Logical	Indicates whether chapter-type numbering is used. That is, should page numbers be in the format "chapter separator page"—for example, 13–4.
HeadingLevelForChapter	Numeric	The outline to be used as the chapter number in the page number
ChapterPageSeparator	Numeric	The character to use between the chapter number and the page number, for chapter-type numbering. wdSeparatorHyphen — 0 — wdSeparatorEmDash — 3 wdSeparatorPeriod — 1 — wdSeparatorEnDash — 4 wdSeparatorColon — 2
ShowFirstPageNumber	Logical	Indicates whether the page number appears on the first page of the section.

This code centers the page number in the footer, using lowercase Roman numerals.

```
#DEFINE wdCaptionNumberStyleLowercaseRoman 2
#DEFINE wdAlignPageNumberCenter 1
WITH oWord.ActiveDocument.Sections[1].Footers[1].PageNumbers
  .Add()
  .NumberStyle = wdCaptionNumberStyleLowercaseRoman
ENDWITH
oWord.ActiveDocument.Sections[1].Footers[1].PageNumbers[1].Alignment = ;
  wdAlignPageNumberCenter
```

Organizing text with lists

Word provides several alternatives for structuring text into lists. They're combined in the Bullets and Numbering dialog on the Format menu. Bullets provide a way of ticking off items that don't have a particular order, while the numbered list options are for items that need to appear in a specific order, like instructions. The third page in that dialog—the Outline Numbered tab—offers options that are even more structured and ties into Word's ability to link styles with document structure. As noted in the previous section, you need to use outline numbering in order to have pages chapter numbered.

Two sets of objects are involved in creating lists. One hierarchy (ListGalleries, ListTemplates, and ListLevels and their members) provides a set of choices for the appearance of the list, while the other (Lists and ListParagraphs and their members) contains the actual list items. This structure mirrors the way styles are applied to document contents. A variety of Style objects are available and can be applied to the contents, but any given range has only a single style. Similarly, there are a variety of list templates, but any given list has only one template applied to it.

Defining list structures

Three collections and their contents provide a wide variety of choices for formatting lists. **Figure 10** shows the hierarchy involved. The ListGalleries collection, accessed through the Application object's ListGalleries property, starts things off. Each ListGallery object represents one page in the Bullets and Numbering dialog. The constants wdBulletGallery (1), wdNumberGallery (2), and wdOutlineNumberGallery (3) are used to access them.

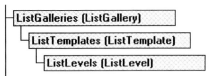

Figure 10. *Defining list structures. These three collections contain the definitions for all of the bulleted, numbered, and outline-structured lists you can create.*

Each ListTemplate object describes the way a single list is laid out. Like ListGallery, though, ListTemplate has few properties and methods itself. The only property worthy of note is OutlineNumbered, which indicates whether or not the template specifies a multi-level outline list. If not, it's restricted to a single level (which is true for all the lists shown on the first two pages of the Bullets and Numbering dialog). **Figure 11** shows the first page of the Bullets and Numbering dialog, which is not outline numbered, while **Figure 12** shows the last page, which is.

The ListLevels collection is comprised of ListLevel objects, the actual stuff of which lists are made. **Table 14** shows the interesting properties of ListLevel. If you don't like the list structures provided, this is the place to change things. For example, in the first outline numbered list (shown in the second position of the first row in Figure 12), to change the list to use square brackets rather than parentheses, you could use code like this:

```
#DEFINE wdOutlineNumberedGallery 3

LOCAL oLevel
WITH oWord.ListGalleries[ wdOutlineNumberedGallery ].ListTemplates[ 1 ]
   FOR EACH oLevel IN .ListLevels
      WITH oLevel
         * Change ")" to "]"
         .NumberFormat = STRTRAN(.NumberFormat, ")", "]")
         .NumberFormat = STRTRAN(.NumberFormat, "(", "[")
      ENDWITH
   ENDFOR
ENDWITH
```

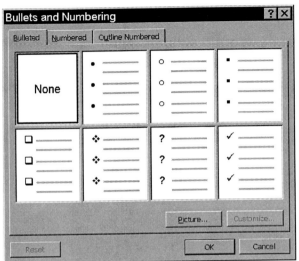

Figure 11. *List Galleries without outlines. The first two pages of the Bullets and Numbering dialog provide single-level lists. The ListGalleries collection has one member for each page of the dialog. Each choice shown (except the "None" option) is represented by one ListTemplate object.*

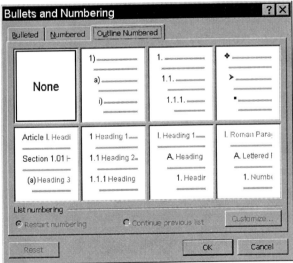

Figure 12. *Multi-level lists. The third page of the dialog offers outline numbering and provides the third member of the ListGalleries collection.*

Each level can be linked to a style using the LinkedStyle property, so that using that style automatically indicates numbering level and vice versa. Doing so provides several useful abilities. First, as noted previously, numbering within chapters is enabled. Second, Word's Outline View and Document Map become useful tools. While neither of these strictly requires numbering, both are based on the idea that a document is organized hierarchically and that the styles chosen reflect that hierarchy. (See "Organizing a document using styles" in Chapter 6 for more on this topic.) By default, the last four list templates on the Outline Numbered page are linked to the built-in Heading styles.

Table 14. *Defining list structures. ListLevel specifies how one level in a list is laid out.*

Property	Type	Description
NumberStyle	Numeric	The style for the number for this level. wdListNumberStyleBullet 23 wdListNumberStyleArabic 0 wdListNumberStyleUppercaseRoman 1 wdListNumberStyleLowercaseRoman 2 wdListNumberStyleUppercaseLetter 3 wdListNumberStyleLowercaseLetter 4
NumberFormat	Character	A string showing how to insert the level number in the proper style. Use % followed by a digit to represent the level number, except when NumberStyle is wdListNumberStyleBullet. (In that case, NumberFormat is limited to a single character.)
TrailingCharacter	Numeric	The character that follows the number. Use one of these constants: wdTrailingTab 0 wdTrailingSpace 1 wdTrailingNone 2
StartAt	Numeric	The starting number for the list.
Alignment	Numeric	The alignment of the level number or bullet. wdListLevelAlignLeft 0 wdListLevelAlignCenter 1 wdListLevelAlignRight 2
NumberPosition	Numeric	The indentation (in points) of the level number or bullet.
TabPosition	Numeric	The indentation (in points) of the tab following the level number or bullet—that is, where the text should begin on that line.
TextPosition	Numeric	The indentation (in points) of text on the second and subsequent lines of numbered or bulleted text.
Font	Object	The font to use for the level number.
LinkedStyle	Character	The name of the style linked to this level. (See the text for an explanation.)

Creating lists

The Lists collection of Document references all the lists in a document. Each List object refers to a single list. The key property of List is ListParagraphs, a collection of the paragraphs in the list. Once a list exists, you can modify its appearance by working with the properties of these objects.

The process of adding a new list to a document is roundabout, especially if you want a multi-level list. You can't just set the format you want and start adding items, as you can interactively. You need to add the text to the document, and then apply the appropriate list template. Then, for a multi-level list, you need to go back and do appropriate indenting.

Once you have the text range ready to format, use the Range's ListFormat property to access the ApplyListTemplate method. This method takes a range and turns it into a list by applying the specified ListTemplate object to it. An optional fourth parameter (not shown here) allows the list to be formatted in a way more appropriate for web pages.

```
oRange.ApplyListTemplate( oListTemplate [, lContinuePreviousList
                          [, nApplyTo  ] ] )
```

oListTemplate	Object	Reference to a ListTemplate object.
lContinuePreviousList	Logical	Indicates whether to continue numbering from the previous list or start over at 1.
nApplyTo	Numeric	The portion of the list the specified template should be applied to. Uses the following Word constants: wdListApplyToWholeList (0), wdListApplyToThisPointForward (1), wdListApplyToSelection (2). This parameter lets you change the formatting of part of a list, not necessarily the most aesthetically pleasing idea.

The other important methods are ListIndent and ListOutdent, which let you demote and promote items by one level at a time in an outline list.

Here's a brief example that creates a multi-level list:

```
#DEFINE CR CHR(13)
#DEFINE wdListApplyToWholeList 0

* Start with an empty range
oDocument = oWord.Documents.Add()
oRange = oDocument.Range()

* Now create a string containing the items to list
cItems = "First item" + CR + ;
        "Second item "+ CR + ;
        "first sub-item for item 2 " + CR + ;
        "second sub-item for item 2" + CR + ;
        "Third item" + CR
* Send the string to Word
oRange.InsertAfter(cItems)

* Apply a list template
oRange.ListFormat.ApplyListTemplate( oWord.ListGalleries[3].ListTemplates[1], ;
                        .F., wdListApplyToWholeList )

* Now handle subitems
oRange.ListParagraphs[3].Range().ListFormat.ListIndent()
oRange.ListParagraphs[4].Range().ListFormat.ListIndent()
```

Here are the results:

1) First item
2) Second item
   a) first sub-item for item 2
   b) second sub-item for item 2
3) Third item

There is an alternative to using ListIndent. Remember the ability to link styles to list levels by using LinkedStyle? Once you've done so, if you apply the specified styles to a paragraph and ApplyListTemplate, that paragraph is automatically numbered. Here's an example that shows this approach. The resulting list is shown in **Figure 13**.

```
#DEFINE CR CHR(13)
#DEFINE wdCollapseEnd 0
#DEFINE wdParagraph 4
#DEFINE wdListApplyToWholeList 0

* Start with an empty range
oDocument = oWord.Documents.Add()
oRange = oDocument.Range()

* Now create a string containing the items to list
oRange.Style = "Heading 1"
oRange.InsertAfter("First item" + CR + ;
   "Second item "+ CR )
oRange.Collapse( wdCollapseEnd )

oRange.Style = "Heading 2"
oRange.InsertAfter("first sub-item for item 2 " + CR + ;
   "second sub-item for item 2" + CR )
oRange.Collapse( wdCollapseEnd )

oRange.Style = "Heading 1"

oRange.InsertAfter("Third item")

* Now make a range of the whole thing
oRange.MoveStart( wdParagraph, -4 )

* Apply a list template that has linked styles
oRange.ListFormat.ApplyListTemplate( oWord.ListGalleries[3].ListTemplates[6], ;
                                .F., wdListApplyToWholeList )
```

I. First item

II. Second item

    A. *first sub-item for item 2*

    B. *second sub-item for item 2*

III.Third item

Figure 13. Using styles to create lists. By linking styles to list levels, you can have items indented automatically when you apply the list template.

The ListFormat object has properties to describe the appearance and structure of the level number. **Table 15** describes those you're likely to want to use. A range may contain many different lists, but it has only a single ListFormat object. The properties of ListFormat refer only to the first list in the range. To look at all the different lists in a complex range, break the range down into smaller ranges.

ListFormat is primarily concerned with the value and formatting of the paragraph number, but it also provides properties to access the list itself and the list template on which the list is based.

Table 15*. ListFormat properties. The ListFormat object, referenced through Range, controls the appearance of lists.*

Property	Type	Description
ListType	Numeric	The kind of list. wdListNoNumbering 0 wdListSimpleNumbering 3 wdListNumOnly 1 wdListOutlineNumbering 4 wdListBullet 2 wdListMixedNumbering 5
ListLevelNumber	Numeric	The indentation level for the first paragraph of this object.
ListValue	Numeric	The paragraph number without any formatting.
ListString	Character	The paragraph number with the specified formatting.
ListTemplate	Object	Reference to the ListTemplate with which the list was formatted.
List	Object	Reference to the first List contained in the ListFormat object.

Output

Producing attractive documents is a good start, but users usually want output of some sort, too. Word has a number of methods for producing output. In the interactive product, they're collected on the File menu in the Print Preview and Print menu options.

Printing

The PrintOut method of the Document object automates printing. It accepts a huge array of parameters. (This is one situation where named parameters start to look pretty good.)

Fortunately, all parameters are optional, and you won't need most of those parameters for normal processing. Unfortunately, the ones you're most likely to need are in the middle of the list rather than toward the front. The key parameters are shown here:

```
oDocument.PrintOut( lBackground, , nPrintRangeType, cFileName, cFrom, cTo, ,
              cCopies, cPageRange, , lPrintToFile)
```

lBackground	Logical	Indicates whether or not to print in the background, continuing with other code while printing.
nPrintRangeType	Numeric	Which part of the document to print. (See the text.)
cFileName	Character	If printing to file, the filename, including path, of the destination file.
cFrom, cTo	Character	If nPrintRangeType is wdPrintFromTo, the beginning and end of the print range. (See the text.)
cCopies	Character	The number of copies to print.
cPageRange	Character	If nPrintRangeType is wdPrintRangeOfPages, the print range. (See the text.)
lPrintToFile	Logical	Indicates whether to print to a file.

Incredibly, there are still eight more parameters after these. The syntax shown reflects two different approaches to specifying the pages to be printed. The nPrintRangeType parameter determines which, if either, is used. The valid constant values are wdPrintAllDocument (0), wdPrintSelection (1), wdPrintCurrentPage (2), wdPrintFromTo (3), and wdPrintRangeOfPages

(4). When wdPrintFromTo is passed, pass values for cFrom and cTo as the fifth and sixth parameters, respectively. Note that, for reasons known only to Microsoft, they're passed as characters. For example, to print three copies of pages 4–10 of a document referenced by oDocument, use:

```
oDocument.PrintOut( , , wdPrintFromTo, , "4", "10", , "3")
```

The wdPrintRangeOfPages choice lets you specify a single string and has more flexibility. In that case, pass a value for cPageRange as the eighth parameter—it can include multiple comma-separated values, and each may include a range. For example, you could pass something like "3, 4-6, 12".

To print to a file, you specify both the filename and a flag that you're printing to file, like this:

```
oDocument.PrintOut( , , , "fileoutput", , , , , , , .t.)
```

The resulting file is ready to print, complete with printer codes. Keep in mind that the file is stored in Word's current directory by default, so it's a good idea to provide the full path.

Be forewarned that printing to file sets the Print to File check box in the Print dialog and leaves it set. Omitting that parameter in a subsequent call to PrintOut defaults to .T.; you have to explicitly pass .F. to print to the printer.

Creating envelopes

Word can also automatically create and print envelopes. To do so, use the document's Envelope object. This example assumes that oRange is a range containing the customer name and address in a mailing format. It bookmarks the address (see the "Bookmarks" section earlier in this chapter for an introduction to this technique for identifying part of a document) and asks Word to create and print the envelope.

```
oDocument.Bookmarks.Add("EnvelopeAddress", oRange)
oDocument.Envelope.PrintOut(.T., , , ,.F., oWord.UserAddress)
```

First, we create a bookmark called EnvelopeAddress based on whatever is at oRange. The call to PrintOut tells Word to use whatever is at the EnvelopeAddress bookmark for the address, and to include the user's stored address (from the Tools|Options dialog's User Information page) as the return address.

The parameters for the PrintOut method of the Envelope object are different from those for the Document object. Here's a shortened version of the syntax:

```
oDocument.Envelope.PrintOut( lExtractAddress, cAddress, , lOmitReturnAddress,
                             cReturnAddress )
```

lExtractAddress	Logical	Indicates whether to extract the address from the EnvelopeAddress bookmark.
cAddress	Character	The address to use on the envelope. Ignored if lExtractAddress is .T.
lOmitReturnAddress	Logical	Indicates whether to omit the return address from the envelope.
cReturnAddress	Character	The return address to use on the envelope.

Additional parameters let you set the type and size of the envelope, as well as the printing orientation. Omitting those parameters uses the current settings.

Print preview

Perhaps all your users want is to see how the document will look when printed. That's easy. Just call the Document object's PrintPreview method. That switches Word to PrintPreview mode.

Of course, that's only useful if Word is visible. If Word is hidden, it doesn't do a bit of good. Making Word visible is as easy as setting the Application's Visible property to .T. Better yet, if you've been doing everything in the background and now you're ready to show the user what you've been up to, call PrintPreview, make Word visible, and then call Word's Activate method. That will bring Word to the front. Try it like this:

```
oDocument.PrintPreview   && Get the document ready for the user to see
oWord.Visible = .t.      && Show Word
oWord.Activate()         && Bring it to the front
```

Regardless of whether you're keeping Word hidden most of the time or showing it all along, when you're done with Print Preview, you turn it off by calling the ClosePrintPreview method of the Document object.

Putting it all together

Listing 3 shows a program (WordSample1.PRG in the Developer Download files available at www.hentzenwerke.com) that creates a document that lists all of Tasmanian Traders' customers, organized by country. It demonstrates headers, footers, page numbers, shading, and borders. **Figure 14** shows a preview of the resulting document.

Listing 3. Tasmanian Traders customer report.

```
#DEFINE wdHeaderFooterPrimary 1
#DEFINE wdGray25 16
#DEFINE wdStyleTypeParagraph 1
#DEFINE wdCaptionNumberStyleArabic 0
#DEFINE wdAlignPageNumberCenter 1
#DEFINE wdAlignParagraphCenter 1
#DEFINE wdCollapseEnd 0
#DEFINE wdLineStyleSingle 1
#DEFINE wdLineStyleNone 0
#DEFINE wdLineWidth050Point 4
#DEFINE CR CHR(13)

RELEASE ALL LIKE o*
PUBLIC oWord

LOCAL oDoc, oRange, cText, oHeaderStyle

oWord = CreateObject("Word.Application")
oWord.Visible = .T.

oDoc = oWord.Documents.Add()
* Create a style for the header text
```

```
oHeaderStyle = oDoc.Styles.Add("CenteredHeader", wdStyleTypeParagraph)
WITH oHeaderStyle
   .BaseStyle = oDoc.Styles["Heading 1"]
   .ParagraphFormat.Alignment = wdAlignParagraphCenter
ENDWITH


* Add a header
WITH oDoc.Sections[1].Headers[ wdHeaderFooterPrimary ]
   oRange = .Range()
   WITH oRange
      .Text = "Tasmanian Traders"
      .Style = oHeaderStyle
      .Shading.BackgroundPatternColorIndex = wdGray25
   ENDWITH
ENDWITH


* Add a centered page number in the footer
WITH oDoc.Sections[1].Footers[ wdHeaderFooterPrimary ].PageNumbers
   .Add()
   .NumberStyle = wdCaptionNumberStyleArabic
ENDWITH
oDoc.Sections[1].Footers[ wdHeaderFooterPrimary ].PageNumbers[1].Alignment = ;
   wdAlignPageNumberCenter


* Now create some content for the document.
* Get a list of customers organized by country.
* Sort alphabetically within countries.
SELECT Company_Name, Country ;
   FROM _SAMPLES+"\TasTrade\Data\Customer" ;
   ORDER BY Country, Company_Name ;
   INTO CURSOR CustomerByCountry


* Title for document
oRange = oDoc.Range()
oRange.InsertAfter("Customers By Country" + CR)
oRange.Style = oDoc.Styles("Heading 1")
oRange.Collapse( wdCollapseEnd )


* Loop through cursor. Put each country name bordered in heading 2 style.
* Then list each customer in that country.
LOCAL cCurrentCountry
cCurrentCountry = ""
cText = ""


SCAN
   IF NOT (Country==cCurrentCountry)
      * New country.
      oRange.InsertAfter( cText + CR )
      oRange.Style = oDoc.Styles("Normal")
      cText = ""
      oRange.Collapse( wdCollapseEnd )

      WITH oRange
         .InsertAfter( Country + CR )
         .Style = oDoc.Styles("Heading 2")
         .Borders.OutsideLineStyle = wdLineStyleSingle
         .Borders.OutsideLineWidth = wdLineWidth050Point
      ENDWITH
      oRange.Collapse( wdCollapseEnd )
      oRange.InsertAfter( CR )
```

```
        oRange.Borders.OutsideLineStyle = wdLineStyleNone
     ENDIF

     cText = cText + Company_Name + CR
     cCurrentCountry = Country
 ENDSCAN

 oRange.InsertAfter( cText )
 oRange.Style = oDoc.Styles("Normal")

 USE IN CustomerByCountry
 USE IN Customer

 oDoc.PrintPreview()
```

This chapter covered an incredible amount of material, and we're only warming up. Word has much more to offer. Stay tuned.

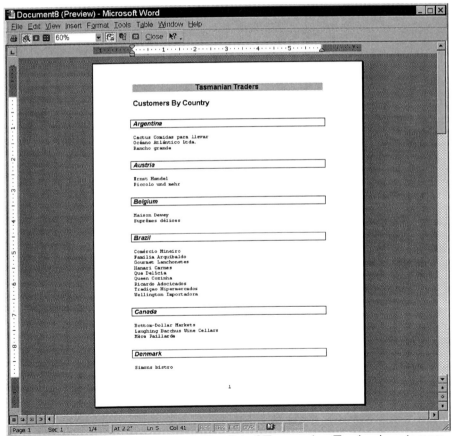

Figure 14. *The customer report. The list of Tasmanian Traders' customers demonstrates borders, shading, headers, footers, page numbers, and more.*

Chapter 5
Intermediate Word

Word offers many options for making documents more attractive and more uniform, as well as for working with existing documents.

Once you get the basics of automating Word down, there are a multitude of possibilities. This chapter looks at a variety of ways you can make Word work harder so you don't have to, including creating and using document templates, working with tables, creating multi-column documents, adding footnotes and endnotes, adding graphics to documents, automating macros, using search and replace, and auditing documents.

Document templates

Word's templates offer a way to provide standard formatting and styles for documents. Like a form class in Visual FoxPro, a template lets you specify common elements like the page setup, headers and footers, and even boilerplate text so that every new document you create contains the same things. But in other ways, templates are more like class libraries because they contain styles that can be used in the document.

Every document you create in Word is based on a template, a file with an extension of DOT. If you don't specify which template to use, the Normal template is used. By default, Normal is an empty document containing a standard set of styles. It's installed when Word is installed, along with a number of other templates. To see the available templates, choose File|New from the menu. The New dialog (shown in **Figure 1**) appears. The Normal template is shown as "Blank Document."

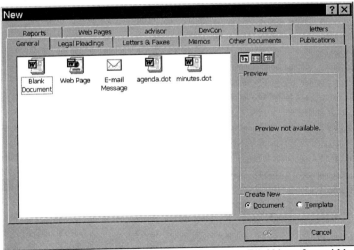

Figure 1. *Available templates. Choosing File|New from Word's menu lets you choose from among all the stored templates.*

What goes into a template?

A template can contain anything that's in a document, from the simple blank document of the Normal template to a complex legal document, complete except for the names of the parties involved. Most templates fall somewhere in between, containing some text and formatting and some custom styles.

Templates can also contain macros, including one that runs automatically when you create a document based on the template. Templates can also include bookmarks that can be filled in, either by prompting the user or by Automation. In short, templates can be as much or as little as you choose to make of them.

Finding templates

Templates are stored in several different places. The templates (and wizards) installed by Word are put into a Templates subdirectory of the Office installation. In Word 2000, they then go down one level into a subdirectory named with the numeric code for the language you're using (1033 for American English). In Word 97, there's a set of subdirectories under Templates that contains the various supplied templates and wizards. (In both cases, wizards have a WIZ extension.)

In addition, each user can set a user template directory and a workgroup template directory. The user template directory is for templates specific to the individual, while the workgroup template directory is meant for templates shared by the user's entire team. The default location for user templates varies according to the version of Word and Windows, but it isn't always in the Office directory tree. In some cases, templates are stored as part of the user's profiles in the Windows directory tree. No matter where the user template directory is, the templates in that directory appear on the General page of the New dialog. Templates in subdirectories of that directory are placed on additional pages of the dialog—the pages are labeled with the subdirectory names. Creating new subdirectories creates additional pages, as you can see in Figure 1.

The Workgroup templates setting is empty by default. When it's set, the same two-level structure applies. Templates in the directory itself appear on the General page, while subdirectories have their own pages in the New dialog.

Both can be set on the File Locations page of Word's Tools|Options dialog (see **Figure 2**).

 From the Automation point of view, you can determine (or specify) the user and workgroup template locations by checking the DefaultFilePath property of the Options object (which is a member of the Word Application object). Pass wdUserTemplatesPath (2) to find the user's own templates and wdWorkgroupTemplatesPath (3) for the workgroup's templates. (The NewDocument method of the cusWord class in the Developer Download files available at www.hentzenwerke.com accepts a template with or without a path and attempts to locate the template file before creating a new document. The cusWord class is discussed in Chapter 15, "Wrapping Up the Servers.")

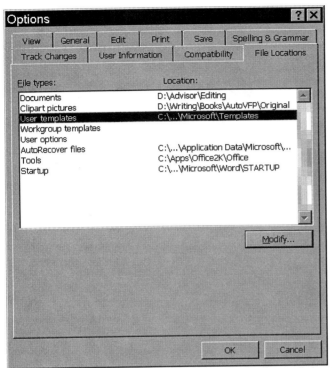

Figure 2. *Pointing to templates. Word's Options dialog lets you indicate where user and workgroup templates are stored.*

Using templates

You can use templates in several ways when automating Word. The simplest is to create new documents based on existing templates. To do so, specify a template, including the path, as the first parameter of the Documents.Add method. For example, to create a new document based on the agenda template shown in Figure 1, you would use the following code. (Unlike other examples in this book, you can't work along with this one because you don't have agenda.DOT on your machine. We'll return to this example later with one you can actually try.)

```
#DEFINE wdUserTemplatesPath 2
cTemplatePath = oWord.Options.DefaultFilePath( wdUserTemplatesPath )
* AddBS() adds a trailing backslash - before VFP 6, you need FoxTools loaded.
oDocument = oWord.Documents.Add( AddBS(cTemplatePath) + "agenda.DOT" )
```

Once you create a new document based on a template, you can treat that document just like any other new document. However, you have the advantage that it contains whatever special text, formatting, and styles were stored in the template.

Creating templates

You can also create templates with Automation. Any document can be saved as a template by passing the appropriate parameter to the SaveAs method. To create a new template, create a document, format it as desired, create any styles you want the template to have, then call SaveAs, like this:

```
#DEFINE wdFormatTemplate 1
#DEFINE wdUserTemplatesPath 2
cTemplatePath = oWord.Options.DefaultFilePath( wdUserTemplatesPath )
oDocument.SaveAs( AddBS(cTemplatePath) + "MyNewTemplate.DOT", wdFormatTemplate)
```

Now that we've created a custom template, we can create a new document based on it. Here's the example from the previous section, but using the new template rather than agenda.DOT:

```
#DEFINE wdUserTemplatesPath 2
cTemplatePath = oWord.Options.DefaultFilePath( wdUserTemplatesPath )
* AddBS() adds a trailing backslash - before VFP 6, you need FoxTools loaded.
oDocument = oWord.Documents.Add( AddBS(cTemplatePath) + "MyNewTemplate.DOT" )
```

As in interactive Word, you can store the template in a subdirectory to have it appear on a different page in the File|New dialog. Of course, if you're working with it through Automation, you don't really care where it appears. In fact, with Automation, it doesn't matter where you store templates because you can specify where Word should look for them. However, keeping them together with other templates means that interactive users can find them, as well. On the other hand, for an automated process, you may prefer to keep your templates well hidden so that users can't find them and delete them or use them in ignorance.

You can also specify that new documents you create are intended to be templates. Pass .T. as the second parameter to the Documents collection's Add method to indicate that the new document is a template rather than a regular document. Then, when you save it, it gets a DOT extension instead of DOC and the default location for it is the user templates directory. In that case, you don't need to pass the second parameter to SaveAs.

Putting templates to work

We both use templates extensively in our work to provide a uniform appearance for documents and to save time and effort. We'd no more use Word without templates than we would use VFP without classes. Especially when combined with the ability to define custom styles, templates provide a way to streamline document creation.

Tables

Word's tables seem like a natural fit for representing VFP data. A row can represent a record, with each column representing a field. What Word buys you is the ability to format the data and the table itself in sophisticated ways, well beyond the capabilities of FoxPro's Report Designer, as well as let users manipulate the results or produce output in alternative formats. A table can be formatted as a whole, but individual cells can be separately formatted, as well. Borders of tables and cells can be visible or invisible, and they can take on a range of sizes and styles. (See the section "Borders and shading" in Chapter 4 for details on formatting borders.) Both columns and rows can be individually sized.

The object hierarchy for tables is a little confusing. Each document has a Tables collection, which, in turn, contains individual Table objects. The Table object contains both Rows and Columns collections, which contain Row and Column objects, respectively. Those objects each have a Cells collection that references the individual cells in the row or column, each represented by a Cell object. While the Table object doesn't have a Cells collection, the individual Cell objects can be accessed by using the Cell method, which accepts row and column number parameters. Here are several ways to refer to the cell in the third row and fourth column of the first table in the active document:

```
oWord.ActiveDocument.Tables[1].Rows[3].Cells[4]
oWord.ActiveDocument.Tables[1].Columns[4].Cells[3]
oWord.ActiveDocument.Tables[1].Cell[3,4]
```

Interactively, you can add a table by choosing Table|Insert|Table from the menu, which brings up the dialog shown in **Figure 3**.

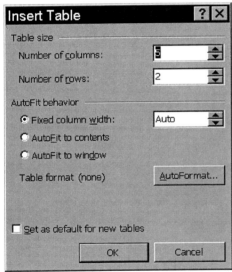

Figure 3. *Adding a table. To add a table interactively, you specify the number of columns and rows and, if you want, whether the columns should resize automatically to fit their contents. You can also specify a predefined format for the table.*

With Automation, since Tables is a collection, it's not surprising that the way to add a table to a document is to call the Add method of that collection. It takes several parameters:

```
oDocument.Tables.Add( oRange, nRows, nColumns, nTableBehavior, nAutoFit )
```

oRange	Object	Reference to a range that indicates where to insert the new table.
nRows	Numeric	The number of rows in the new table.
nColumns	Numeric	The number of columns in the new table.
nTableBehavior	Numeric	A constant that indicates whether the table automatically resizes to fit its contents.

wdWord8TableBehavior	0	Don't resize automatically.
wdWord9TableBehavior	1	Resize automatically.

nAutoFit	Numeric	If nTableBehavior is wdWord9TableBehavior, indicates which algorithm is used to resize the cells.

wdAutoFitFixed	0	Fixed column width.
wdAutoFitContent	1	Size cells to content.
wdAutoFitWindow	2	Size table to full width of window.

The last two parameters are optional. If you omit them, you get the older, Word 97 behavior of a table that doesn't resize as you fill it. However, you can change that behavior. The AllowAutoFit property and AutoFitBehavior method control this resizing capability.

Even if you're not allowing automatic resizing of columns, the AutoFit method of the Column object lets you resize individual columns based on their content. Rather than having cells change size as data is entered, you apply the changes once you've put something into the table. Column's SetWidth method lets you set a column to a specific width, in points.

Once you've added a table interactively, the Table Properties dialog on the Table menu allows you to adjust various characteristics of the table as a whole and of the individual rows, columns, and cells. **Figure 4** shows the Row page of that dialog.

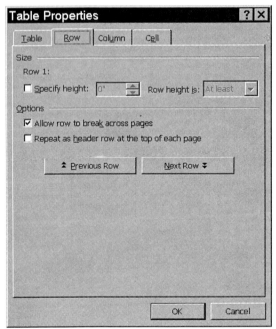

Figure 4. *Formatting a table. The Table Properties dialog lets you resize rows and columns, as well as specify other characteristics of tables and their components.*

Table 1 shows the most commonly used properties of the Table object.

Table 1. Defining tables. These properties of the Table object are the ones you're most likely to work with.

Property	Type	Description
Rows	Object	Pointer to the Rows collection for the table.
Columns	Object	Pointer to the Columns collection for the table.
Uniform	Logical	Indicates whether every row has the same number of columns. (Read-only)
Borders	Object	Pointer to the Borders collection for the table.
Shading	Object	Pointer to the Shading object for the table.
AllowAutoFit	Logical	Indicates whether columns are automatically resized as data is added to the table. Corresponds to the nTableBehavior parameter of the Tables.Add method.
AllowPageBreaks	Logical	Indicates whether the table can be split over multiple pages in the document.
AutoFormatType	Numeric	A constant indicating which, if any, of a set of predefined formats has been applied to the table. AutoFormats are applied with the AutoFormat method. Here's a sampling: wdTableFormatNone 0 wdTableFormatSimple1 1 wdTableFormatClassic1 4 wdTableFormatColorful1 8 wdTableFormatContemporary 35 wdTableFormatElegant 36 wdTableFormatGrid1 16
Spacing	Numeric	Indicates the space between cells, in points. This is the space that actually separates the cells, not the boundary between the cell border and the text.

Row and Column, not surprisingly, have a number of properties in common, including Cells to point to a Cells collection and Shading to reference a Shading object. Row also has a Borders property that references a Borders collection, though Column does not. Both objects have logical IsFirst and IsLast properties that, as their names suggest, indicate whether the particular row or column is the first or last in the collection.

At this point, the two objects part company, though there are still similarities. The size of a Row is determined by HeightRule and Height, as indicated in **Table 2**. Column width also uses two properties—PreferredWidth and PreferredWidthType, shown in **Table 3**.

Row has one other size-related property, SpaceBetweenColumns. It indicates the distance between the cell boundaries and the text. The value of the property is half what you set in Word itself because that one is measured from the text in one cell to the text in the next cell.

Row's AllowBreakAcrossRows property determines what happens when the contents of a row don't fit on the current page. If it's .T., the row can be split over two pages; if .F., a page break occurs before the row.

When a table is split over multiple pages, rows whose HeadingFormat property is set to .T. are repeated.

One big difference between Row and Column is that a Row can be a Range while a Column cannot.

Table 2. *Determining row size. Two Row properties combine to let you indicate the height of the row.*

Property	Type	Description

HeightRule	Numeric	Indicates the logic used to determine the height of this row. Use one of the following constants:
		   wdRowHeightAuto 0
		   wdRowHeightAtLeast 1
		   wdRowHeightExactly 2

Height	Numeric	The height for the row, if HeightRule is wdRowHeightExactly. The minimum height for the row, if HeightRule is wdRowHeightAtLeast. Ignored (and uninformative when queried) if HeightRule is wdRowHeightAuto; in that case, the row height is based on the row's contents.

Table 3. *Specify column width. As with rows, two properties combine to indicate the size of a column.*

Property	Type	Description
PreferredWidth	Numeric	Desired width for this column, either in points or as a percentage of the overall window width. Interpretation is determined by PreferredWidthType.

PreferredWidthType	Numeric	Indicates whether PreferredWidth is measured in points or percent, or is ignored.
		   wdPreferredWidthAuto 0 Size column by contents.
		   wdPreferredWidthPoints 1 Size column in points.
		   wdPreferredWidthPercent 2 Size column as percentage of total window.

Cell shares a number of properties with Table, Row, and Column, including Borders, Shading, HeightRule, Height, PreferredWidth, and PreferredWidthType. **Table 4** shows some other properties that are unique to Cell.

Table 4. *Cell holdings. At the bottom of the table hierarchy, cells have quite a few properties. Here are some you're likely to deal with.*

Property	Type	Description
Width	Numeric	The width of the cell, in points.
WordWrap	Logical	Indicates whether the text is wrapped into multiple lines and the cell height is increased to fit the entire contents.
FitText	Logical	Indicates whether the display size of the text (but not the actual font size) is reduced in order to make the entire contents of the cell fit onto a single line.

VerticalAlignment	Numeric	Indicates the vertical position of the text in the cell.
		   wdAlignVerticalTop 0
		   wdAlignVerticalCenter 1
		   wdAlignVerticalBottom 3

Table, Row, and Cell all have Range properties, so an entire table, row, or cell can be easily converted to a range. This means that the same techniques work for inserting text into a table as for other parts of a document. However, a Range that's created from a cell contains a

special end-of-cell marker. To access only the text in a cell, move the end of the range back one
character. Either of the following does the trick:

```
oRange.End = oRange.End - 1
oRange.MoveEnd( wdCharacter, -1 )
```

The program shown in **Listing 1** opens TasTrade's Order History view and
creates a Word table that shows the order history for the current customer. It
demonstrates a variety of features, including borders, shading, and auto-sizing of
columns. The program is OrderTblFormat.PRG in the Developer Download files available
at www.hentzenwerke.com.

*Listing 1. Creating a table. This program generates a table that contains a customer's
order history.*

```
* Create a Word table with order information for one customer
* Set up the table with two rows, formatting the second row for
* the data. Then add rows as needed for each record.


#DEFINE wdStory                    6
#DEFINE wdCollapseEnd              0
#DEFINE CR                        CHR(13)
#DEFINE wdBorderTop               -1
#DEFINE wdLineStyleDouble          7
#DEFINE wdAlignParagraphLeft       0
#DEFINE wdAlignParagraphCenter     1
#DEFINE wdAlignParagraphRight      2

RELEASE ALL LIKE o*
PUBLIC oWord

LOCAL oRange, oTable, nRecCount, nTotalOrders
LOCAL nRow

oWord = CreateObject("Word.Application")
oWord.Documents.Add()

OPEN DATABASE (_SAMPLES + "Tastrade\Data\Tastrade")
USE CUSTOMER
GO RAND()*RECCOUNT()   && pick a customer at random

* Open the Order History view, which contains
* a summary of orders for one customer.
SELECT 0
USE "Order History" ALIAS OrderHistory

* Find out how many records.
nRecCount = _TALLY

oRange = oWord.ActiveDocument.Range()

* Set up a font for the table
oRange.Font.Name = "Arial"
```

```
oRange.Font.Size = 12

* Move to the end of the document
* Leave two empty lines
oRange.MoveEnd( wdStory )
oRange.Collapse( wdCollapseEnd )
oRange.InsertAfter( CR + CR )
oRange.Collapse( wdCollapseEnd )

* Add a table with two rows
oTable = oWord.ActiveDocument.Tables.Add( oRange, 2, 4)

WITH oTable
   * Set up borders and shading.
   * First, remove all borders
   .Borders.InsideLineStyle = .F.
   .Borders.OutsideLineStyle = .F.


   * Shade first row for headings
   .Rows[1].Shading.Texture = 100

   * Put heading text in and set alignment
   .Cell[1,1].Range.ParagraphFormat.Alignment = wdAlignParagraphRight
   .Cell[1,1].Range.InsertAfter("Order Number")

   .Cell[1,2].Range.ParagraphFormat.Alignment = wdAlignParagraphLeft
   .Cell[1,2].Range.InsertAfter("Date")

   .Cell[1,3].Range.ParagraphFormat.Alignment = wdAlignParagraphRight
   .Cell[1,3].Range.InsertAfter("Total")

   .Cell[1,4].Range.ParagraphFormat.Alignment = wdAlignParagraphCenter
   .Cell[1,4].Range.InsertAfter("Paid?")

   * Format data cells
   .Cell[2,1].Range.ParagraphFormat.Alignment = wdAlignParagraphRight
   .Cell[2,3].Range.ParagraphFormat.Alignment = wdAlignParagraphRight
   .Cell[2,4].Range.ParagraphFormat.Alignment = wdAlignParagraphCenter

   * Add data and format
   * Compute total along the way
   nTotalOrders = 0
   FOR nRow = 1 TO nRecCount
      WITH .Rows[nRow + 1]
         .Cells[1].Range.InsertAfter( Order_Id )
         .Cells[2].Range.InsertAfter( TRANSFORM(Order_Date, "@D") )
         .Cells[3].Range.InsertAfter( TRANSFORM(Ord_Total, "$$$$$$$$9.99") )
         * Put an X in fourth column, if paid; blank otherwise
         IF Paid
            .Cells[4].Range.InsertAfter("X")
         ENDIF
      ENDWITH

      * Add a new row
      .Rows.Add()

      * Running Total
      nTotalOrders = nTotalOrders + Ord_Total
```

```
      SKIP
   ENDFOR

   * Add a double line before the totals
   .Rows[nRecCount + 2].Borders[ wdBorderTop ].LineStyle = wdLineStyleDouble

   * Put total row in
   WITH .Rows[ nRecCount + 2]
      .Cells[1].Range.InsertAfter("Total")
      .Cells[3].Range.InsertAfter(TRANSFORM(nTotalOrders, "$$$$$$$$$9.99"))
   ENDWITH

   * Size columns. For simplicity, let Word
   * do the work.
   .Columns.Autofit
ENDWITH
RETURN
```

The results are shown in **Figure 5**.

Order Number	Date	Total	Paid?
891	01/10/95	$806.85	X
684	08/20/94	$67.40	X
610	06/17/94	$404.65	X
312	08/14/93	$280.05	X
204	04/01/93	$884.06	X
183	03/05/93	$278.46	X
139	12/26/92	$277.05	X
101	10/24/92	$1801.16	X
Total		$4799.68	

Figure 5. *Using tables for data. A customer's order history looks good when poured into a Word table.*

The code creates a two-row table, inserts the headings, then formats the cells in the second row. The loop then inserts the data and adds a new row. Each new row picks up the formatting of the previous one, so the formats only have to be applied once.

You can combine the code (removing the part that chooses a customer record) with Styles.PRG from Chapter 4, "Word Basics" (you can see the result in Figure 7 in that chapter), and you have a reasonably attractive order history report for a customer. Wrap that in a loop with a few more commands (such as InsertBreak to add page breaks), and you can produce order histories for all customers or a selected set.

Irregular tables

Tables don't have to consist of simple grids. Not every row has to have the same number of columns. The Merge and Split methods of Cell and Cells let you combine and take apart groups of cells to create irregular tables. The Uniform property of Table indicates whether a table is regular or not; be sure to check it before using nested FOR EACH loops to try to process every row and column in a table.

The Merge method works in two ways. You can either call it for one cell and pass it another to have those two merged, or you can call it with a range of cells to have those cells merged. Here are the two syntax formats:

```
oFirstCell.Merge( oSecondCell )

oCells.Merge()
```

For example, to combine the second and third cells in row 1 of table oTable, you can use this code (all of the following assume that oTable is a reference to the table you're working with):

```
oTable.Cell(1,2).Merge( oTable.Cell(1,3) )
```

To change the fourth row of a table into a single cell, use code like this:

```
oRange = oTable.Rows[4].Range()
oRange.Cells.Merge()
```

Figure 6 shows a table (that started out with five rows and seven columns) after making those two changes.

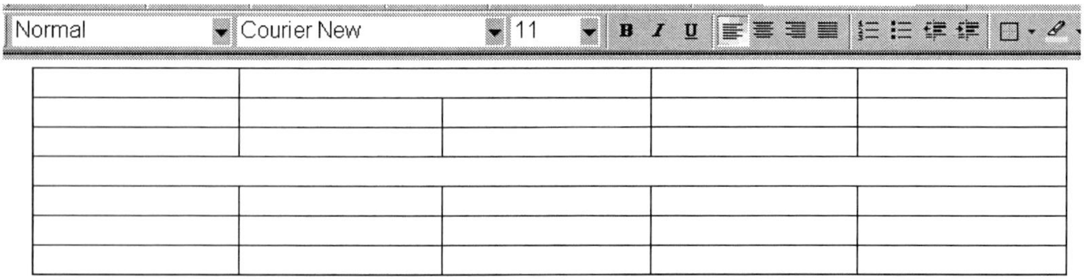

Figure 6. *Irregular table. Tables don't have to have the same number of columns in each row. The Merge and Split methods let you create irregular tables.*

Split takes a cell or collection of cells and divides it into one or more cells. It can optionally merge the cells before splitting them. Again, there are two different forms for the method, depending on whether you call it from a single cell or from a collection of cells:

```
oCell.Split( nRows, nColumns)

oCells.Split( nRows, nColumns [, lMergeFirst ] )
```

For example, to divide the first cell in row 3 into two cells in the same row, use this command:

```
oTable.Cell(3,1).Split(1,2)
```

This code takes the cells in the second row of a table, combines them, then splits them into three, resulting in just three cells in that row:

```
oTable.Rows[2].Cells.Split( 1, 3, .t.)
```

If you omit the third parameter from that call (.t.), each cell in the row would be split into three. If you pass something other than 1 as the first parameter, the single row would become multiple rows in the table.

Using Merge and Split, you can create extremely complex tables. While this provides for an attractive way to display data, keep in mind that it does make it harder to process the document. Simple FOR EACH loops through the Rows and Columns collections don't work when Uniform is .F.

Creating multi-column documents

Maybe tables are overkill for what you need. Perhaps you just need to lay out your text in multiple columns. Interactively, you do that through the Format menu by choosing Columns. That brings up the Columns dialog shown in **Figure 7**. You can specify the number of columns, the width of each, and the spacing between them.

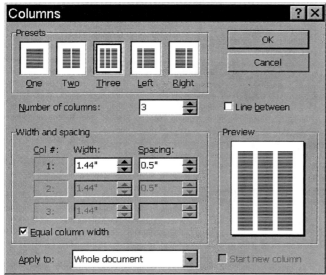

Figure 7. *Specifying columns. This Word dialog lets you indicate how many columns you want, their width, and how far apart they are.*

In Automation, columns are specified by a TextColumns collection, which is a member of a PageSetup object. (See the section "Setting up pages" in Chapter 4 for more on the PageSetup object.) In addition to the usual collection properties, TextColumns has several properties specific to its role, shown in **Table 5**.

Table 5. *Setting up columns. The TextColumns collection contains TextColumn objects, but it has several properties that apply to the collection as a whole.*

Property	Type	Description
EvenlySpaced	Logical or Numeric	Indicates whether the columns are evenly spaced.
Width	Numeric	Width of the columns in points, if they're evenly spaced.
Spacing	Numeric	Distance between columns in points, if they're evenly spaced.
LineBetween	Logical	Indicates whether a vertical line appears between columns. Not visible in the Normal view; use the Print Layout or Print Preview views to display them. Additionally, the lines are only displayed when text is contained in the columns.

As with other collections, the Add method adds new columns. But TextColumns has a special method, SetCount, which can be used to set the number of columns. Think of SetCount as a shortcut—a way to avoid having to call Add repeatedly.

The TextColumn object is a little simpler than the TextColumns collection. It has only two properties worth noting: Width and SpaceAfter. Width serves the same role here as it does for the collection, except that it affects only a single column. SpaceAfter corresponds to the collection's Spacing property. Beware: setting either Width or SpaceAfter for any column changes Width and Spacing for the collection to wdUndefined (9999999) and sets the collection's EvenlySpaced property to .F., even if the value you assign is the same as the collection-level value. To restore the collection-level values, set EvenlySpaced to .T. for the collection.

Here's the code to set up a new document with three columns—the first two equally spaced, the third wider—with a vertical line between them:

```
oDocument = oWord.Documents.Add()
WITH oDocument.PageSetup
   .TextColumns.SetCount(3)
   .TextColumns[1].Width = oWord.InchesToPoints(1.5)
   .TextColumns[1].SpaceAfter = oWord.InchesToPoints(.25)
   .TextColumns[2].Width = oWord.InchesToPoints(1.5)
   .TextColumns[2].SpaceAfter = oWord.InchesToPoints(.25)
   .TextColumns[3].Width = oWord.InchesToPoints(2.5)
   .TextColumns.LineBetween = .T.   && Put in some text to see the lines.
ENDWITH
```

When sending code to fill the columns, you move from one column to the next with the InsertBreak method. This method takes a single parameter indicating the type of break. There's a set of constants for the breaks—for a column break, it's wdColumnBreak, with a value of 8. So, to move to the next column, use this:

```
#DEFINE wdColumnBreak 8
oRange.InsertBreak( wdColumnBreak )
```

Be sure to collapse the range (see the section "Moving in a range or selection" in Chapter 4) before inserting the column break; otherwise, the column break replaces the range.

Footnotes and endnotes

Footnotes and endnotes have been the bane of students for generations, but Word makes them reasonably easy to manage. To add either a footnote or an endnote interactively, choose Insert|Footnote from the menu. The dialog shown in **Figure 8** appears. As the dialog indicates, by default, footnotes are placed at the bottom of the current page (or, if there's not enough room, at the bottom of the next page). Endnotes appear at the end of the document by default, but they can appear at the end of each section instead.

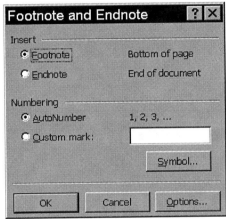

Figure 8. *Adding notes. Both footnotes and endnotes are added using this dialog. It also lets you specify numbering and placement.*

For Automation, you work with two collections, Footnotes and Endnotes, and their contained objects, Footnote and Endnote. Document and Range have Footnotes and Endnotes properties that provide access to the two collections. Although accessing the collections through a range lets you look at only the footnotes or endnotes in that range, watch out. Changing properties of the collection there affects all the footnotes or endnotes in the document, not just the ones in that range. The range just grabs a subset of the notes in the collection.

With one exception, the set of properties and methods in the Footnote and Endnote objects is identical, as is the set in the Footnotes and Endnotes collections. You can think of each case as being a subclass of the same parent class. The only difference between them is in the way that they're rendered. In fact, it's possible to convert footnotes to endnotes and endnotes to footnotes. Several methods support the switch.

The only property of Footnote and Endnote worth mentioning is Reference. It provides an object reference to a range containing the number, letter, or other symbol in the main document that points to the note. You can use it to make changes to that symbol, such as enlarging the font size or underlining. (Whether such changes are a good idea is a separate issue.)

Table 6 shows significant properties of the Footnotes and Endnotes collections, while their important methods are listed in **Table 7**.

Table 6. *Specifying footnotes and endnotes. The two collections are structurally identical—only their rendering is different.*

Property	Type	Description
Location	Numeric	Indicates where the notes appear. For footnotes, use one of these constants: wdBottomOfPage 0 wdBeneathText 1 For endnotes, use one of these constants: wdEndOfDocument 1 wdEndOfSection 0
NumberingRule	Numeric	Indicates how notes are numbered with respect to page and section breaks. wdRestartContinuous 0 Number continuously. wdRestartSection 1 Restart numbers at each section break. wdRestartPage 2 Restart numbers on each new page.
NumberStyle	Numeric	The type of numbering used for the notes. In Word 2000, about 20 styles are provided, but only a few are shown in the Footnote dialog. Others can be set through code, though not all show up properly in all versions of Word. wdNoteNumberStyleArabic 0 wdNoteNumberStyleLowercaseLetter 4 wdNoteNumberStyleUppercaseLetter 3 wdNoteNumberStyleLowercaseRoman 2 wdNoteNumberStyleUppercaseRoman 1 wdNoteNumberStyleSymbol 9 wdNoteNumberStyleHebrewLetter1 45
StartingNumber	Numeric	The number for the first note.
Separator	Object	Pointer to a range containing the separator between the main body of the document and the notes. The separator is usually a short line, but you can add text to it, remove the line, add borders, and even add graphics.
ContinuationSeparatorText	Object	Pointer to a range containing the separator between the main body of the document and the continuation of notes. Appears when notes overflow onto another page. Is usually just a short line, but as with Separator, you can remove the line, add text, add borders, and add graphics.
ContinuationNotice	Object	Pointer to a range containing a message that's displayed when notes overflow onto another page. This message is displayed at the end of the filled page. This is usually empty, but it doesn't have to be. Like the others, you can add text, borders, graphics, and so forth.

***Table 7**. Manipulating footnotes and endnotes. Collection-level methods let you manage the properties that separate notes from the main body of the document and change note types.*

Method	Description
ResetSeparator	Restores the default separator.
ResetContinuationSeparator	Restores the default continuation separator.
ResetContinuationNotice	Restores the default continuation notice.
Convert	Converts all notes in the specified range or document to the other type. That is, if the method is called from a Footnotes collection, it converts the notes to endnotes and adds them to the document's Endnotes collection; if it's called from an Endnotes collection, it converts them to footnotes and adds them to the Footnotes collection. In either case, they're correctly interspersed with existing notes of the other type.
SwapWithEndnotes	Converts all footnotes to endnotes and endnotes to footnotes. This method must be called from a Footnotes collection.

As with other collections, the key to adding new members is the Add method. For footnotes and endnotes, three parameters are required, as follows:

```
oNotes.Add( oRange [, oReferenceMark [, cText ] ] )
```

oRange	Object	A range where the note number or symbol is inserted.
oReferenceMark	Object	A range that contains a custom symbol to be used to mark the footnote or endnote. If this parameter is omitted, the note is numbered in accordance with the rule established by NumberingRule and StartingNumber.
cText	Character	The text for the footnote or endnote.

This code creates a range from the first sentence in an existing range, and adds an endnote to it.

```
#DEFINE wdCharacter 1

oNoteRange = oRange.Sentences[1]
* Back up one character to eliminate the trailing blank
oNoteRange.MoveEnd( wdCharacter, -1 )

* Allow note to be auto-numbered
oRange.Endnotes.Add( oNoteRange, , "This is the new endnote")
```

In the next example, a footnote is added, and it's given a special marker—an asterisk (*)—rather than using the default numbering. The note is attached to text that's just been inserted.

```
#DEFINE wdCollapseEnd 0
oRange.InsertAfter("Be sure to check out WhirlyGig 2000!")
oRange.Collapse( wdCollapseEnd )
oDocument.Footnotes.Add( oRange, "*", ;
    "WhirlyGig 2000 is a trademark of MonsterMega Corporation, Ltd.")
```

Adding graphics to documents

They say a picture's worth a thousand words. Certainly a document with pictures is a lot more pleasant to look at and easier to read than one without. Word provides several ways to add graphical objects to documents. All of them begin by choosing Insert|Picture from the menu. At that point, the next step depends on the type of graphical object you want to add.

Let's start with graphics that you have sitting in a file somewhere, such as a BMP or JPG or GIF. For those, you choose From File, and the Insert Picture dialog shown in **Figure 9** appears. This dialog is a specialized version of the normal Open File dialog. The Open button is labeled "Insert," and if you drop it open, there are a couple of extra choices. These options hark back to the traditional meaning of OLE—object *linking* and *embedding*. Choosing Insert makes a copy of the picture in the document with no connection back to the original file; that is, it embeds the picture in the document. Link to File creates a connection between the picture file and the document; that is, it links the picture to the document—changes to the picture are reflected in the document. Insert and Link does both—it embeds the picture in the document, but also maintains a link to the file so that the document is updated by changes to the picture file. Each of these options has its place—choose the right one for your situation, based on factors such as whether you expect the picture to change, whether you want changes in the picture to be reflected in your document, the size of the picture file, whether users can be trusted not to delete the picture, and so forth.

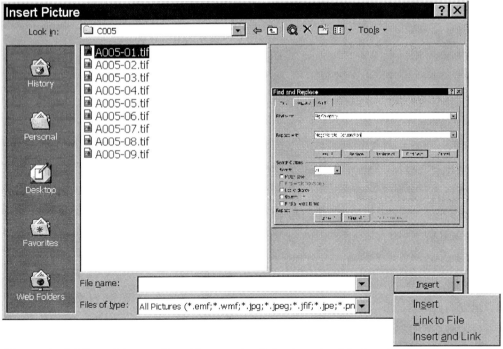

Figure 9. Adding pictures. Graphics can be linked, embedded, or both. When a picture is linked, changes to the graphic file are reflected in the document.

The list of graphical objects you can add also includes various kinds of drawings, like AutoShapes and WordArt. To add an AutoShape to your document, choose Insert|Picture|AutoShapes from the menu. This opens the AutoShapes toolbar (shown in **Figure 10**). When you click on one of the buttons, a menu of shapes of that type appears (see **Figure 11**). Choose one, and Word switches to Page Layout view if necessary and puts the chosen shape wherever you click. The AutoShapes toolbar stays open so you can add as many shapes as you want.

Figure 10. *The AutoShapes toolbar. This toolbar appears whenever you choose Insert|Picture|AutoShapes from the menu.*

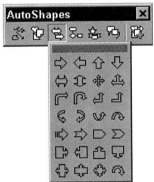

Figure 11. *Choosing an AutoShape. The items on the AutoShapes toolbar look like buttons, but each opens a menu of shape items.*

Each of the other kinds of graphic objects has its own approach. None of them are really native to Word; they all call on other applications (such as Microsoft Clip Gallery and Microsoft Graph) to supply the data to be displayed.

The two faces of graphics

Graphics in Word can be placed on two different layers of the document. Pictures that come from files normally live on the same layer as the text in the document. AutoShapes and other drawing objects are positioned as free-floating objects on a separate layer above the text. This means that they can cover the text and graphics in the main layer. Two different collections are used to manage the two types of graphic objects. Objects in the text layer are stored in the InlineShapes collection, while those that float over the text layer are controlled by the Shapes collection. Each contains a corresponding object type: InlineShape and Shape, respectively.

Working with InlineShapes

Instead of a single Add method, the InlineShapes collection has several different methods for adding different kinds of objects.

Perhaps the most important of the Add methods for the InlineShapes collection is AddPicture, which lets you add a graphic from a file. This is the programmatic equivalent of the Insert Picture dialog, shown in Figure 9. The syntax for AddPicture is as follows:

```
oDocument.InlineShapes.AddPicture( cPictureFile, lLinkToFile,
                            lSaveWithDocument, oRange )
```

cPictureFile	Character	The name, including the path, of the file that contains the graphic to be added to the document.
lLinkToFile	Logical	Indicates whether a link to the original field should be maintained—in OLE terms, whether the picture is linked.
lSaveWithDocument	Logical	Indicates whether the picture is saved in the document or only linked—in OLE terms, whether the picture is embedded.
oRange	Object	Pointer to the location where the picture should be inserted.

For example, to add the TasTrade bitmap to the beginning of a document, use code like this:

```
oRange = oDocument.Paragraphs[1].Range()
* Add picture, don't link, do embed
oDocument.InlineShapes.AddPicture( ;
   _SAMPLES + "TASTRADE\BITMAPS\TTRADESM.BMP ", ;
   .F., .T., oRange )
```

The results for a new document are shown in **Figure 12**.

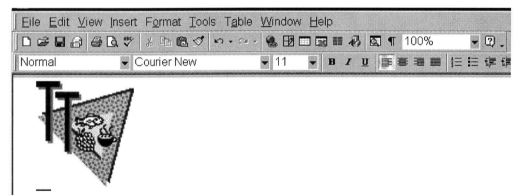

Figure 12. *Adding a graphic. To add a picture with Automation, you specify the filename, whether to link, whether to embed, and where to put it.*

The other methods add other kinds of objects to the collection, like horizontal lines, bullets made from pictures, and OLE objects. See the Help file for details.

The InlineShape object itself is a container for the picture or other object. It doesn't hold the actual graphic or OLE object, but like VFP's OLE Container control, it provides a place for it to hang its hat. InlineShape has information about the format of the object it represents, as well as what type of object it is. The information that's available varies, depending on the type of object and whether it's linked or embedded. **Table 8** lists the key properties of InlineShape and the constant values relevant for adding graphics.

Table 8. *Adding graphics and other objects on the text layer. The InlineShape object contains format and other information about objects that move with the document text.*

Property	Type	Description
Type	Numeric	The kind of graphic or other object. wdInlineShapePicture 3 Not linked wdInlineShapeLinkedPicture 4 Linked
Height, Width	Numeric	The size of the inline shape, in points. This is the actual space used for the shape in the document—it's unrelated to the size of the underlying graphic. LockAspectRatio determines whether these can be changed independently.
ScaleHeight, ScaleWidth	Numeric	Percentage of the original height and width at which the object should be displayed. When these are changed, Height and Width also change. LockAspectRatio determines whether these can change independently.
LockAspectRatio	Logical	Indicates whether Height and Width must stay in the same relative proportions. When .T., changing Height also changes Width, and changing ScaleHeight also changes ScaleWidth.
PictureFormat	Object	For picture objects, reference to a PictureFormat object, which controls those items managed interactively through the Format Picture item on Word's menu (either Format|Picture from the main menu or Format Picture from the context menu for a picture). These include cropping, brightness, and contrast. See Help for more information.
LinkFormat	Object	For linked objects, reference to a LinkFormat object, which contains information about the linked object, including the name of the file and the type of object. See Help for more information.
Borders	Object	Reference to a Borders collection for the InlineShape.

There are a number of other properties, many of them specific to particular types of objects or situations.

When processing the InlineShapes collection, be sure to check Type before assuming that properties like PictureFormat or LinkFormat are available. Different object types use different subsets of the properties, and accessing properties that aren't in use is a good way to cause an error.

Working with Shapes

Like InlineShapes, the Shapes collection doesn't have a method called simply Add. It has a number of specific methods for adding various types of objects. Shapes has its own version of AddPicture, with a somewhat different parameter list:

```
oDocument.Shapes.AddPicture( cPictureFile, lLink, lSaveWithDocument,
                             nLeft, nTop, nWidth, nHeight, oAnchor )
```

nLeft, nTop	Numeric	The position of the picture relative to the object referenced by oAnchor. Both default to 0. (Optional)
nWidth, nHeight	Numeric	The size of the picture. Defaults to the actual size of the picture. (Optional)
oAnchor	Object	A Range object that indicates where the picture is to be "anchored" in the document.

The other parameters have the same meaning here as they do for the InlineShapes collection's AddPicture method.

 The anchor parameter to Shapes.AddPicture is a position in the document from which the picture is allowed to float. This gives Word the flexibility to move the picture around and put it where there's room for it. In addition, pictures added through Shapes can have text wrapped around them, in a number of different ways. InlineShapes pictures cannot, as they always occupy the entire width of the page or column, even if that leaves considerable white space.

There are a couple of downsides to using Shapes for adding graphics. The first is minor. The graphics don't show up in Word's Normal view; you have to switch to Print Layout or Web Layout (in Word 97, use Page Layout view) to see them. That can be misleading when you're editing a document, but is less of an issue for Automation.

The other issue is more serious. Because Word can move these graphics around, it does. Controlling where a picture added through the Shapes collection appears is difficult. As the document changes, the pictures can jump around the document.

Choosing the right way to add graphics requires evaluation of the pros and cons of each approach. Different documents may call for different choices.

The AddShape method lets you add AutoShapes. Here's the syntax:

```
oDocument.Shapes.AddShape( nShape, nLeft, nTop, nWidth, nHeight, oAnchor )
```

The parameters are the same as for the Shapes collection's AddPicture method, except for the additional nShape parameter. This is a numeric value that indicates which AutoShape to add. As you'd expect, there's a set of constants available for these. Look up AutoShapeType in Help to see the list, or, for a more useful list of them, check out the msoAutoShapeType constants in the Object Browser. The list corresponds to the shapes available on the AutoShapes toolbar.

Shapes supports a number of other objects and has corresponding Add methods for those, as well. See Help for details.

The Shape object is the analogue to InlineShape and contains information about the picture or other object once you've added it to the document. Shape has some of the same properties as InlineShape, but it also has additional properties that address specific issues of floating graphics.

As elsewhere, Type identifies the kind of item the Shape contains. However, it references a different set of constants. In this case, they come from Office itself. **Table 9** lists a few of the permitted values.

Table 9. *What kind of shape am I? The Type property of Shape accepts values from Office's msoShapeType set of constants.*

Constant	Value	Constant	Value
msoPicture	13	msoAutoShape	1
msoLinkedPicture	11	msoChart	3

Height, Width, PictureFormat, and LinkFormat are the same for Shape as for InlineShape. ScaleHeight and ScaleWidth are methods rather than properties here (check Help for the parameters).

This example adds the TasTrade bitmap as a floating graphic attached to the first paragraph of the document:

```
oRange = oDocument.Paragraphs[1].Range()
* Add picture, don't link, do embed.
* By omitting the size, it defaults to the size of the graphic.
oDocument.Shapes.AddPicture( ;
   _SAMPLES + "TASTRADE\BITMAPS\TTRADESM.BMP ", ;
   .F., .T., 100, 100, , , oRange )
```

In order to see this picture, you have to be in a view other than Normal. Set the Type property of the View object of the Document's ActiveWindow to wdPrintView (3) or wdWebView (6). To return to the Normal view, set the property to wdNormalView (1).

```
#DEFINE wdPrintView 3
oDocument.ActiveWindow.View.Type = wdPrintView
```

With Shape objects, you can decide whether text is wrapped around the graphic and, if so, how wrapping works. Several properties and methods control this ability. The WrapFormat property references a WrapFormat object. That object's Type property offers the first level of settings for wrapping. Set it to wdWrapNone (3) to prevent text from wrapping around a graphic; in that case, the graphic appears in front of the text. The default is wdWrapSquare (0), which draws an imaginary square around the graphic (regardless of its actual shape) and puts text up to the edges of that square. There are several other choices, as well.

WrapFormat's Side property determines whether text appears on both sides of a graphic, if that's a possibility. The possible values are wdWrapBoth (0), wdWrapLargest (3), wdWrapLeft (1), wdWrapRight (2). The trickiest option here involves allowing text and graphics to occupy the same space, but making both of them visible. **Figure 13** shows an AutoShape with text superimposed.

Figure 13. *Combining graphics and text. By manipulating the Shape object's ZOrder method, you can put text on top.*

The secret to creating this kind of effect is to call the Shape's ZOrder method and pass msoSendBehindText (5) as a parameter. ZOrder has more options for Shape than it does in Visual FoxPro. In addition to bringing an object to front (msoBringToFront, or 0) or sending it to back (msoSendToBack, or 1), you can send it behind text as in Figure 13 or bring it in front of text (msoBringInFrontOfText, or 4), and a couple of other choices, as well.

Here's the code to create Figure 13 at the beginning of a document:

```
#DEFINE msoShape16PointStar 94
#DEFINE msoSendBehindText 5
#DEFINE wdWrapNone 3
#DEFINE wdWrapBoth 0
#DEFINE CR CHR(13)

LOCAL oDocument, oRange, oShape

oDocument = oWord.Documents.Add()
oRange = oDocument.Range()

* Add the text
oRange.Font.Name = "Calligrapher" && or choose your favorite
oRange.Font.Size = 18
oRange.InsertAfter( CR + "    Gold" + CR + "    Medal")

* Now add the shape
oShape = oDocument.Shapes.AddShape( msoShape16PointStar, 0, 0, 81, 81, oRange )
oShape.WrapFormat.Type = wdWrapNone
oShape.WrapFormat.Side - wdWrapBoth
oShape.ZOrder( msoSendBehindText )
```

Working with existing documents
Once you've created documents, there are various reasons why you might want to go through them to make changes or simply look at their contents. Word contains a number of tools that make it easy to go through a document and look inside. It's possible to examine both the contents of a document and the structure.

Search and replace
Search and replace is one of the killer features that made word processors a success when they were first introduced. The ability to go through a document and change every occurrence

of "Big Company" to "MegaMonster Corporation" with just a few keystrokes made friends of secretaries throughout the civilized world. Word takes this ability much, much further.

You can search for either text or formatting, or some combination of the two. Searching can be case-sensitive or case-insensitive. You can search just to locate the search phrase, or find it and replace it with another phrase. When you replace, you can choose to replace all occurrences or check each occurrence as it's found and replace it or not. **Figure 14** shows the Find and Replace dialog, accessed through the Edit menu in Word.

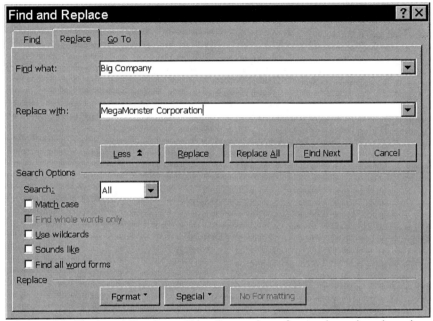

Figure 14. *Find and Replace. Word's version of search and replace is extremely powerful. You can search for text only, formatting only, or text and formatting. You can replace all instances or check them out one at a time.*

Searching is handled by the Find object, which is accessed through the Find property of a Range object. It has an assortment of properties, such as Text, MatchCase and MatchWholeWord, that determine what it's searching for. Some properties, like Font and ParagraphFormat, are references to other objects. The Format property determines whether formatting is considered in the search. Set it to .F. to search for the string specified by Text, regardless of format. **Table 10** lists some commonly used properties of Find.

The Execute method actually performs the search. In its simplest form, it uses the current settings of the Find object. It can also accept a number of parameters, most of which duplicate properties of the Find object. More about that later.

Table 10. *Setting up a search. The Find object's properties determine what to look for.*

Property	Type	Description
Text	Character	The string to search for. If it's empty and Format is .T., the search is based on formatting only.
MatchCase	Logical	Indicates whether the search is case-sensitive. Defaults to .F. (case-insensitive).
MatchWholeWord	Logical	Indicates whether the search looks only for whole word matches. Defaults to .F. (matches within words).
MatchSoundsLike	Logical	Indicates whether the search looks for matches that sound like the search string. Defaults to .F. (actual matches only).
MatchWildcards	Logical	Indicates whether the search string contains wildcards that should be matched appropriately. This is an incredibly powerful setting that is, in our opinion, vastly underused by Word users (ourselves included). Defaults to .F. (no wildcards).
MatchAllWordForms	Logical	Indicates whether other forms of the search string should be replaced with corresponding forms of the replacement string. For example, if the search and replacement strings are singular nouns, and this setting is .T., plural versions of the search string would be replaced by plural versions of the replacement string. Defaults to .F. (match the string only as provided).
Format	Logical	Indicates whether to include formatting in the search. If .F., ignore the format-related properties of this object in the search.
Font	Object	Reference to a Font object, indicating the font to match if Format is .T.
ParagraphFormat	Object	Reference to a ParagraphFormat object, indicating the paragraph formatting to match if Format is .T.
Style	Object	Reference to a Style object, indicating the style to match if Format is .T.
Forward	Logical	Indicates the direction of the search. Set to .T. to search toward the end of the document, .F. to search toward the beginning.
Wrap	Numeric	Specifies what happens when a search begins in the middle of a document and reaches the end. wdFindStop 0 Stop the search. wdFindContinue 1 Continue the search at the other end of the document. wdFindAsk 2 Ask the user what to do.
Found	Logical	Indicates the result of the last search.
Replacement	Object	Reference to a replacement object with information for replace. (See the text.)

As noted previously, Find is a member of Range (and Selection), but not of Document. The search begins at the beginning of the range, unless Forward is .F., in which case it starts at the end. The Wrap property determines what happens when it reaches the end (or beginning, when searching backward) of the range.

To search the whole document, create a range at the beginning of the document. When Execute finds a match, the range's boundaries are changed to cover only the matched item.

For example, to search for the first occurrence of the string "Visual FoxPro", regardless of case, in the current document, use the following code:

```
oRange = oWord.ActiveDocument.Range(0,0) && Start of document
WITH oRange.Find
  .Text ="Visual FoxPro"
```

```
  .MatchCase = .F.
  .Format = .F.
  lFound = .Execute()
ENDWITH
```

When this code is done, if lFound is .T., a match was found and oRange contains the matching text.

Things get a little more complex when you want to replace the found text. There are two ways to go about it. The last two parameters of Find's Execute method let you specify a replacement string and the number of replacements to perform (none, one, or all). Here's the syntax for Execute:

```
oRange.Execute( cText, lMatchCase, lMatchWholeWord, lMatchWildcards,
                lMatchSoundsLike, lMatchAllWordForms, lForward, nWrap, lFormat,
                cReplaceWith, nReplace)
```

cText	Character	Corresponds to the Text property.
lMatchCase	Logical	Corresponds to the MatchCase property.
lMatchWholeWord	Logical	Corresponds to the MatchWholeWord property.
lMatchWildcards	Logical	Corresponds to the MatchWildcards property.
lMatchSoundsLike	Logical	Corresponds to the MatchSoundsLike property.
lMatchAllWordForms	Logical	Corresponds to the MatchAllWordForms property.
lForward	Logical	Corresponds to the Forward property.
nWrap	Numeric	Corresponds to the Wrap property.
lFormat	Logical	Corresponds to the Format property.
cReplaceWith	Character	The replacement string.
nReplace	Numeric	Indicates whether to replace the search string with cReplaceWith every time it's found, just once, or not at all. Use these constants:
		wdReplaceNone 0
		wdReplaceOne 1
		wdReplaceAll 2

Technically, cReplaceWith and nReplace aren't really the last two parameters. There are several more that may be accepted, depending on what language you're using. They relate to language-specific features. Check Help if you're working in a language other than English.

Going back to the previous example, we can replace every instance of "Visual FoxPro" with "Visual FoxPro!" by changing the Execute line to:

```
#DEFINE wdReplaceAll  2
lFound = .Execute( , , , , , , , , , "Visual FoxPro!", wdReplaceAll )
```

The alternative approach uses a Replacement object referenced through the Find object's Replacement property. Replacement is like a simpler version of Find—it can format the Text property with Font, ParagraphFormat, and Style properties, among others. You can fill in Replacement's properties to specify exactly what should replace the found item, like this:

```
#DEFINE wdReplaceAll  2
WITH oRange.Find
  * what to look for
  .Text ="Visual FoxPro"
  .MatchCase = .F.
```

```
  .Format = .F.

  * what to replace it with
  .Replacement.Text = "Visual FoxPro!"
  .Replacement.Font.Bold = .T.
  .Replacement.ParagraphFormat.LeftIndent = 12

  * go!
  lFound = .Execute( , , , , , , , , , , wdReplaceAll )
ENDWITH
```

It's also possible to search for and replace only formatting. Both Find and Replacement have a method called ClearFormatting that resets all format-related properties to their defaults, so you can start from scratch.

To change every occurrence of 12-point Arial to 16-point Times New Roman, use code like this:

```
#DEFINE wdReplaceAll  2
oRange = oWord.ActiveDocument.Range(0,0)
WITH oRange.Find
  * make sure to clean up from last search
  .ClearFormatting

  * what to look for
  .Text =""
  .Format = .T.
  .Font.Name = "Arial"
  .Font.Size = 12

  * what to replace it with
  WITH .Replacement
     .ClearFormatting
     .Text = ""
     .Font.Name = "Times New Roman"
     .Font.Size = 16
  ENDWITH

  * go!
  lFound = .Execute( , , , , , , , , , , wdReplaceAll )
ENDWITH
```

Of course, with styles, you shouldn't often have to change fonts like that, but it's easy to search for and replace styles, too. Just use the Style property of the Find and Replacement objects.

With a little creativity, it's possible to find and replace pretty much anything you want in a document. You can also combine VFP's data-handling strength with VBA for power searching. Imagine putting a collection of search and replacement strings in a table, then using Automation to make all the changes without intervention.

Exploring document structure

Several properties and methods let you find out about such things as the number of words and pages in a document or range, the author of the document, its title, the template on which it's based, and so forth. You can also provide some of this information and other data about the document.

Statistics like the number of words and pages are available interactively through the Word Count item on the Tools menu. Choosing that option displays the dialog shown in **Figure 15**.

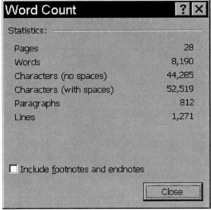

Figure 15. *It's in there. The Word Count dialog actually shows a variety of statistics about the document or range. The same information is available through the ComputeStatistics method.*

With Automation, you access the same information by using the ComputeStatistics method of the Document and Range objects. It accepts a parameter that indicates what statistic to compute and returns the appropriate value. **Table 11** shows constants for the items you're most likely to want to compute.

Table 11. *What do you want to compute today? The ComputeStatistics method takes one of these constants and tells you how many of the specified objects are in the document or range.*

Constant	Value	Constant	Value
wdStatisticWords	0	wdStatisticCharacters	3
wdStatisticLines	1	wdStatisticParagraphs	4
wdStatisticPages	2	wdStatisticCharactersWithSpaces	5

For example, to see how many words are in the current document, use:

```
#DEFINE wdStatisticWords 0
nWords = oWord.ActiveDocument.ComputeStatistics( wdStatisticWords )
```

Note that some of these values are also available by checking the Count property of the appropriate collection. For example, you can determine the number of paragraphs in a range like this:

```
nParagraphs = oRange.Paragraphs.Count
```

Be forewarned. Calling ComputeStatistics sets the document's Saved property to .F. That's right—even if you make no other changes to a document, computing the number of words or pages or whatever is enough for the document to think it's been changed.

Additional information about a document is available through the Properties dialog on the File menu. This multi-page dialog (shown in **Figure 16**) includes some of the same information as the Word Count dialog, but it also contains document properties like the author, title, subject, and many more. In addition to the properties built into the dialog, you can specify custom properties and provide values for them (using the Custom page). File properties can be displayed in the File|Open dialog and can be used to search for documents.

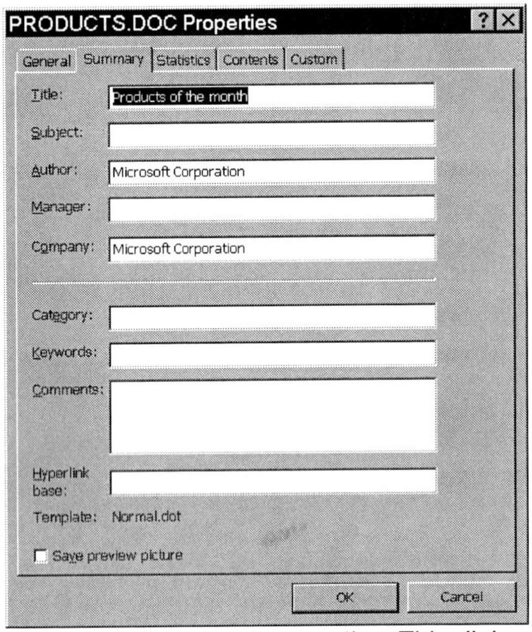

Figure 16. *Document properties. This dialog shows you the information stored with a document. In addition to the pre-defined properties, you can add your own custom properties.*

Two DocumentProperties collections contain all the properties. They're accessed through two properties of Document: BuiltinDocumentProperties and CustomDocumentProperties. DocumentProperties and DocumentProperty are Office objects, not Word-specific objects.

To check the value of a specific document property, you can look it up by name, then check its Value property. For example, to see the author of the active document:

```
? oWord.ActiveDocument.BuiltinDocumentProperties[ "Author" ].Value
```

See the DocumentProperty object in Help for a list of the built-in properties.

To add custom properties, use the Add method of the DocumentProperties collection. Here's the syntax:

```
oDocument.CustomDocumentProperties.Add( cPropertyName, lLinked, nPropertyType,
                                    uValue )
```

cPropertyName	Character	The name for the new custom property.
lLinked	Logical	Indicates whether the new custom property is linked to the contents of the document. Pass .F. to simply provide a value. If .T., must pass the optional fifth parameter (not discussed here).
nPropertyType	Numeric	The data type for the new custom property. Use one of these constants:

		msoPropertyTypeNumber	1
		msoPropertyTypeBoolean	2
		msoPropertyTypeDate	3
		msoPropertyTypeString	4
		msoPropertyTypeFloat	5

| uValue | Depends on nPropertyType | The value to assign the new custom property. |

This code adds a property called VFPVersion to the document and sets it to the version of Visual FoxPro used to create the document:

```
#DEFINE msoPropertyTypeString 4
oDocument.CustomDocumentProperties.Add( "VFPVersion", .F., ;
   msoPropertyTypeString, VERSION() )
```

Before adding a custom property, check the list of built-in properties carefully. There are quite a few of them.

Traversing a document with the collections

It's possible to "walk" through a document in a number of different ways by using the collections of the Document object along with VFP's FOR EACH loop structure. While it can be slow, for some tasks, traversing a collection is the best approach.

We don't recommend using the collections as a replacement for Find. Searching for text or formatting is much faster with Word's native search mechanism. Nor is it better to measure the size of a document by manually counting its lines, paragraphs, or words (though the Count property of the collections can be quite informative). However, looping through a collection like InlineShapes or Tables shouldn't break the efficiency bank.

 The routine in **Listing 2** example checks every graphic in a document and checks whether it's linked, but not embedded. It creates a cursor listing those that break the rule. You'll find it as FindGraphics.PRG in the Developer Download files available at www.hentzenwerke.com.

Listing 2. Finding graphics. This program traverse the InlineShapes and Shapes to find every graphic in the active document and check whether it's linked or embedded.

```
#DEFINE wdInlineShapePicture    3
#DEFINE wdInlineShapeLinkedPicture 4
#DEFINE msoPicture 13
#DEFINE msoLinkedPicture 11
```

```
* Create the log file
IF NOT USED("Graphics")
   CREATE CURSOR Graphics (cDocument C(100), cGraphic C(100), ;
                           lLinked L, lEmbedded L, tWhen T)
ENDIF

* Now find the graphics.
WITH oWord.ActiveDocument
   * Do graphics in the text layer first.
   FOR EACH oShape IN .InLineShapes
      DO CASE
      CASE oShape.Type = wdInlineShapeLinkedPicture
         * Linked, may or may not be embedded
         IF oShape.LinkFormat.SavePictureWithDocument
            * It's embedded, so log it
            INSERT INTO Graphics ;
               VALUES (.FullName, oShape.LinkFormat.SourceFullName, ;
                       .T. , .T. , DATETIME())
         ENDIF

      CASE oShape.Type = wdInlineShapePicture
         * Embedded!
         INSERT INTO Graphics VALUES (.FullName, "", .F. , .T., DATETIME())

      OTHERWISE
         && Not interested in these
      ENDCASE
   ENDFOR

   * Now free-floating graphics
   FOR EACH oShape in .Shapes

      DO CASE
      CASE oShape.Type = msoLinkedPicture
         * Linked, may or may not be embedded
         IF oShape.LinkFormat.SavePictureWithDocument
            * It's embedded, so log it
            INSERT INTO Graphics ;
               VALUES (.FullName, oShape.LinkFormat.SourceFullName, ;
                       .T. , .T., DATETIME())
         ENDIF

      CASE oShape.Type = msoPicture
         * Embedded!
         INSERT INTO Graphics VALUES (.FullName, "", .F. , .T., DATETIME())

      OTHERWISE
         && Not interested in these
      ENDCASE
   ENDFOR
ENDWITH

RETURN
```

Automating macros

Although you can perform pretty much any Word action through Automation, if you already have a Word macro to do a particular thing, it might make more sense to use the existing macro than to rewrite it in VFP. This is especially true if the macro doesn't involve transferring information between the two applications, or if it's part of a pre-packaged set of macros.

The Application object's Run method allows you to execute Word macros. You pass the name of the macro and up to 30 parameters. For example, AcceptAllRevisions is a custom macro that accepts all revisions and turns off revision tracking. This line executes it:

```
oWord.Run("AcceptAllRevisions")
```

In this case, it wouldn't be hard to create the same functionality through Automation since the macro has just two lines, but there are situations where rewriting an existing macro as Automation code would present a problem. In those cases, Run provides an easy solution.

Putting it all together

Listing 3 (WordSample2.PRG in the Developer Download files available at www.hentzenwerke.com) shows a program that creates an employee list for Tasmanian Traders. The list uses a table organized by country, with a heading for each country centered in the table. For each employee, it includes name, birth date, date of hire, and a photo. The notes stored for each employee are listed as endnotes to the document. **Figure 17** and **Figure 18** show two pages of the resulting document.

Listing 3. Building a complete document. This program creates an employee listing, using a table, endnotes, and graphics. The results are shown in Figure 17 and Figure 18.

```
* This is the "putting it all together" example for Chapter 5.
* It demonstrates the use of tables, graphics, and endnotes.
* The program creates a document that shows all the TasTrade
* employees in a table organized by country.

#DEFINE CR CHR(13)
#DEFINE wdHeaderFooterPrimary 1
#DEFINE wdGray25 16
#DEFINE wdAlignParagraphCenter 1
#DEFINE wdCollapseEnd 0
#DEFINE wdWord9TableBehavior 1
#DEFINE wdAutoFitContent 1
#DEFINE wdTableFormatList7 30
#DEFINE wdCellAlignVerticalCenter  1

RELEASE ALL LIKE o*
PUBLIC oWord

LOCAL oDocument, oRange, oTable, oRow, nRow
LOCAL nCountries, nEmployees, cCountry
```

```
oWord = CreateObject("Word.Application")
oWord.Visible = .t.

oDocument = oWord.Documents.Add()

* Set font for Normal style
WITH oDocument.Styles["Normal"].Font
   .Name = "Arial"
   .Size = 12
ENDWITH

* Add a header
WITH oDocument.Sections[1].Headers[ wdHeaderFooterPrimary ]
   oRange = .Range()
   WITH oRange
      .Text = "Tasmanian Traders"
      .Style = oDocument.Styles["Heading 1"]
      .ParagraphFormat.Alignment = wdAlignParagraphCenter
      .Shading.BackgroundPatternColorIndex  = wdGray25
   ENDWITH
ENDWITH

* Open the data
OPEN DATA _SAMPLES + "TasTrade\Data\TasTrade"

* Run a query to collect the right data in the right order
SELECT Country, Title, First_Name, Last_Name, Birth_Date, ;
      Hire_Date, Notes, Photo_File ;
   FROM Employee ;
   ORDER BY Country, Title, Last_Name, First_Name ;
   INTO CURSOR Emps
nEmployees = _TALLY

* Add a heading
oRange = oDocument.Range()
WITH oRange
   .Style = oDocument.Styles["Heading 1"]
   .ParagraphFormat.Alignment = wdAlignParagraphCenter
   .InsertAfter("Employees" + CR + CR)
   .Collapse( wdCollapseEnd )
   .Style = oDocument.Styles["Normal"]
ENDWITH

* Figure out the number of different countries
SELECT Country, COUNT( * ) ;
   FROM Emps ;
   GROUP BY Country ;
   INTO CURSOR Countries

nCountries = _TALLY

* Now add the table, with one Row for each Employee plus one for each Country
* Set up the table to resize itself based on the content of the cells.
oTable = oDocument.Tables.Add( oRange, nEmployees + nCountries + 1, 6, ;
                              wdWord9TableBehavior, wdAutoFitContent )
* Apply one of the built-in formats
oTable.AutoFormat( wdTableFormatList7,  .T., .T., .T., .T., .T., .F., ;
                  .F., .F., .F.)
```

```
* Set up table heading row
WITH oTable.Rows[1]
   .Range.Style = oDocument.Styles[ "Heading 2" ]
   .Cells[1].Range.InsertAfter("Title")
   .Cells[2].Range.InsertAfter("First Name")
   .Cells[3].Range.InsertAfter("Last Name")
   .Cells[4].Range.InsertAfter("Birthdate")
   .Cells[5].Range.InsertAfter("Hired")
   * Set up this row to be repeated on subsequent pages
   .HeadingFormat = .T.
ENDWITH

* Now loop through the employee data, sending it to the table.
* Keep track of the current country. For each new country,
* create a "header" row in the table.
cCountry = ""
nRow    = 1

SELECT Emps
SCAN
   * Grab the current row
   nRow = nRow + 1
   oRow = oTable.Rows[ nRow ].Range()

   IF NOT (Country == cCountry)
      * Change of country
      oRow.Cells.Merge()
      oRow.Style = oDocument.Styles[ "Heading 3" ]
      oRow.ParagraphFormat.Alignment = wdAlignParagraphCenter
      oRow.InsertAfter( Country )
      cCountry = Country
      nRow = nRow + 1
      oRow = oTable.Rows[ nRow ].Range()
   ENDIF

   * Now insert the data for this employee
   WITH oRow
      .Cells.VerticalAlignment  = wdCellAlignVerticalCenter
      .Cells[1].Range.InsertAfter( Title )
      .Cells[2].Range.InsertAfter( First_Name )
      .Cells[3].Range.InsertAfter( TRIM(Last_Name) )

      * Add an endnote for the memo information
      oDocument.EndNotes.Add(.Cells[3].Range(), , Notes )

      .Cells[4].Range.InsertAfter( Birth_Date )
      .Cells[5].Range.InsertAfter( Hire_Date )

      * Add the picture in the last cell
      oPicture = oDocument.InlineShapes.AddPicture ( ;
                          _SAMPLES + "TasTrade\" + Photo_File, ;
                          .t., .f., .Cells[6].Range() )
   ENDWITH

   WITH oPicture
      .ScaleHeight = 50
      .ScaleWidth = 50
   ENDWITH
```

```
ENDSCAN

oDocument.PrintPreview()

RETURN
```

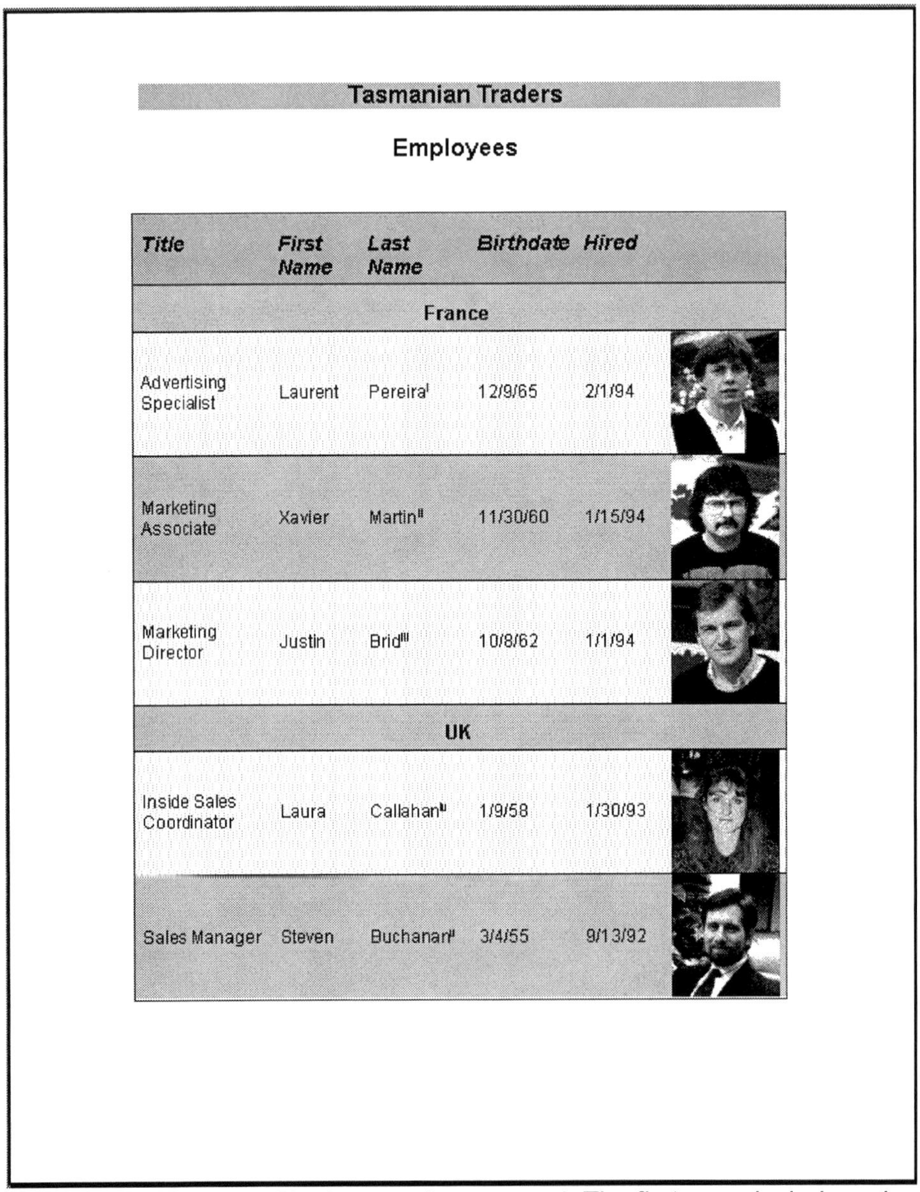

Tasmanian Traders

Employees

Title	First Name	Last Name	Birthdate	Hired	
France					
Advertising Specialist	Laurent	Pereira[i]	12/9/65	2/1/94	
Marketing Associate	Xavier	Martin[ii]	11/30/60	1/15/94	
Marketing Director	Justin	Brid[iii]	10/8/62	1/1/94	
UK					
Inside Sales Coordinator	Laura	Callahan[iv]	1/9/58	1/30/93	
Sales Manager	Steven	Buchanan[v]	3/4/55	9/13/92	

Figure 17. Tasmanian Traders employee report. The first page includes a heading then jumps right into the table. You can put graphics in a table as well as text, and not every row has to have the same number of columns.

Tasmanian Traders				
Title	**First Name**	**Last Name**	**Birthdate**	**Hired**
Entry Clerk	Andrew	Fuller[iii]	2/19/42	7/12/91
Mail Clerk	Tim	Smith[iiii]	6/6/73	1/15/93
Receptionist	Caroline	Patterson[xiii]	9/11/72	5/15/93
Sales Manager	Margaret	Peacock[iii]	9/19/37	3/30/92

[i] Laurent Pereira graduated from the Ecole Supérieure des Sciences Economiques et Commerciales in 1989. He plans to continue his studies in 1994 at the University of Bochum.
[ii] Xavier Martin is a graduate of the University of Chicago (BA) and the ESC Bordeaux (Ecole Supérieure de Commerce de Bordeaux). Mr. Martin has travelled widely in Eastern Europe, most recently in the Czech Republic, Poland, and Hungary for purposes of establishing a network of contacts for future sales activities. Mr. Martin is completely fluent in German and French (he is a native speaker of both languages); he also speaks English and understands Polish.
[iii] Justin Brid graduated from HEC Paris (Hautes Etudes Commerciales de Paris) in 1986 with high honors. Mr. Brid attended the American Graduate School of International Management (Thunderbird) in Glendale, Arizona. Prior to his employment with Tasmanian Traders, he held positions with several Import/Export companies (Culinary Specialties) in Germany, Switzerland, and Austria. Mr. Brid is equally fluent in French and German; he also speaks English and reads Spanish.
[iii] Laura received a BA in psychology from the University of Washington. She has also completed a course in business French. She reads and writes French.
[ii] Steven Buchanan graduated from St. Andrews University, Scotland, with a BSC degree in 1976. Upon joining the company as a sales representative in 1992, he spent 6 months in an orientation program at the Seattle office and then returned to his permanent post in London. He was promoted to sales manager in March 1993. Mr. Buchanan has completed courses in Successful Telemarketing and International Sales Management. He is fluent in French.

Figure 18. *Using endnotes for additional information. Although the information from the employee notes field could have been placed in the table, putting it in endnotes gives the table an uncluttered look.*

With the material in this chapter and the preceding one, you can handle most everyday word processing tasks. Now we move on to the more unusual tasks—the things you don't see every day but still might be asked to make Word do.

Chapter 6
Advanced Word

Word can produce some very complicated documents. Several features help bring order to longer documents: outlines, tables of contents, and indexes. Our look at Word finishes with the prototypical blend of word processing and databases: mail merge.

Several of Word's more complex abilities can provide the finishing touches to documents you create via Automation. This chapter looks at outlines, tables of contents, and indexes. In addition, it explores perhaps the most sought after of Word's capabilities from the database point of view: mail merge.

Organizing a document using styles

Both outlines and tables of contents are based on styles. In each case, you associate a style with each heading level, and Word does the rest. (In fact, Word can use this approach for multi-level lists, as well. See "Organizing text with lists" in Chapter 4.) The first step in creating either an outline or a table of contents is to use styles for each heading level in your document. You can use the built-in styles or create your own set of styles. As an extra benefit, this makes it easy to ensure that headings at the same level look the same throughout.

Word recognizes nine heading levels. Not coincidentally, the Normal template includes nine styles, named "Heading 1" through "Heading 9," that are linked to those nine heading levels. The easiest way to prepare for outlines and tables of contents is to use those built-in heading styles in your own documents. **Figure 1** shows them in outline view.

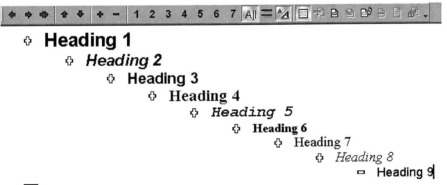

Figure 1. *Built-in heading styles. You can use these styles for your headings to simplify creation of outlines and tables of contents, or you can set up your own.*

You can use other styles, if you prefer. Set the heading level for a style through the OutlineLevel property of the Style object's ParagraphFormat object. The OutlineLevel property uses a set of constants with names like wdOutlineLevel1—the value of each is its outline level.

To demonstrate this use of styles, **Listing 1** is a program that creates a report of TasTrade sales organized by country. Within each country, customers are listed alphabetically. The report's title uses the Heading 1 style. Country names use Heading 2, and company names use Heading 3. The sales by year for each company (rounded to the nearest dollar) make up the body of the report and use the Body Text style. This program is included as MultiLevel.PRG in the Developer Download files available at www.hentzenwerke.com.

***Listing 1**. Using heading styles. This program creates a document that makes both outlining and table of contents creation simple.*

```
* Create a multi-level document using built-in
* heading styles.

#DEFINE wdCollapseEnd 0
#DEFINE CR CHR(13)

LOCAL oDocument, oRange
LOCAL cCountry, cCompany, nYear

* Create an instance of Word.
* Make it public for demonstration purposes and so
* that you can use oWord in the following examples.
RELEASE ALL LIKE o*
PUBLIC oWord
oWord = CreateObject("Word.Application")
* Make Word visible.
oWord.Visible = .T.
oDocument = oWord.Documents.Add()

OPEN DATA _SAMPLES + "TasTrade\Data\TasTrade"

* Collect customer/order information. Result contains one record per
* company per year, order by country, then company,
* then year in descending order
SELECT Company_Name, Country, YEAR(Order_Date) AS Order_Year, ;
       ROUND(SUM(Order_Line_Items.Unit_Price*Order_Line_Items.Quantity - ;
           (0.01 * Orders.Discount * Order_Line_Items.Unit_Price * ;
           Order_Line_Items.Quantity)) + Orders.Freight, 0) AS OrderTotal ;
FROM Customer ;
    JOIN Orders ;
       ON Customer.Customer_Id = Orders.Customer_Id ;
    JOIN Order_Line_Items ;
       ON Orders.Order_Id = Order_Line_Items.Order_Id ;
   GROUP BY 3, 2, 1 ;
   ORDER BY 2, 1, 3 DESC ;
   INTO CURSOR CompanyInfo

* Send data to document, as follows:
* Country is Heading 2
* Company is Heading 3
* Total with some text is Body Text

oRange = oDocument.Range()
WITH oRange
```

```
      .Style = oDocument.Styles[ "Heading 1" ]
      .InsertAfter("Tasmanian Traders Sales by Country and Company" + CR)
      .Collapse( wdCollapseEnd )
ENDWITH

cCountry = ""
cCompany = ""
nYear = 0

SCAN
   WITH oRange
      .Collapse( wdCollapseEnd )
      IF NOT (Country == cCountry)
         .Style = oDocument.Styles[ "Heading 2" ]
         .InsertAfter( Country + CR )
         .Collapse( wdCollapseEnd )
         cCountry = Country
         cCompany = ""
         nYear = 0
      ENDIF

      IF NOT (Company_Name == cCompany)
         .Style = oDocument.Styles[ "Heading 3" ]
         .InsertAfter( Company_Name + CR )
         .Collapse( wdCollapseEnd )
         cCompany = Company_Name
         nYear = 0
      ENDIF

      .Style = oDocument.Styles[ "Body Text" ]
      .InsertAfter( "Total Sales for " + TRANSFORM(Order_Year,"9999") + ;
                    " = " + TRANSFORM(OrderTotal,"@B, $$ 99,999,999") + CR)
      .Collapse( wdCollapseEnd )
   ENDWITH
ENDSCAN
```

Figure 2 shows a portion of the resulting document.

Working with outlines

Outlines in Word are more a state of mind than a separate entity. They allow you to hide the details of a document while still showing its structure. Because different portions of an outline can be expanded different amounts, Word's outlines also provide you with the effect of a drill-down report.

Once you use appropriate styles to create the headings in a document, you've outlined the document. To see the outline, all you have to do is switch to Outline View by choosing View|Outline from the menu. As Figure 1 shows, Outline View includes a special toolbar for working with outlines. It allows interactive users to expand and collapse the outline, to determine which heading levels are visible, to decide whether to show all body text or just the first line, and to manipulate items in the outline, changing their level. When a document is displayed in Outline View, printing it prints the displayed outline, not the entire document. We suppose this is what you should get from a WYSIWYG word processor, but it's something of a surprise, since other views don't affect printing.

Tasmanian Traders Sales by Country and Company

Argentina

Cactus Comidas para llevar
Total Sales for 1995 = $1,012 |
Total Sales for 1994 = $699
Total Sales for 1992 = $17,738

Océano Atlántico Ltda.
Total Sales for 1995 = $2,948
Total Sales for 1994 = $112
Total Sales for 1993 = $2,133
Total Sales for 1992 = $367

Rancho grande
Total Sales for 1995 = $697
Total Sales for 1994 = $1,986

Austria

Ernst Handel
Total Sales for 1995 = $31,221
Total Sales for 1994 = $47,050
Total Sales for 1993 = $24,476
Total Sales for 1992 = $5,372

Piccolo und mehr
Total Sales for 1995 = $3,345
Total Sales for 1994 = $8,816
Total Sales for 1993 = $12,072

Figure 2. Multi-level document. The headings in this document, created by the program in Listing 1, use the built-in heading styles.

As Views are a visual issue and Automation is usually performed behind the scenes, what does all this mean for Automation? You probably won't need to display an outline in an Automation setting, but you may need to print it, requiring a switch to Outline View. Fortunately, this switch to Outline View and subsequent outline manipulation can be done even when Word is hidden.

The key object for working with outlines is the View object, accessible through the View property of the Window object. The Window object is accessed using the ActiveWindow property of Document. So, to set the ActiveDocument to OutlineView, use code like:

```
#DEFINE wdOutlineView 2
oWord.ActiveDocument.ActiveWindow.View.Type = wdOutlineView
```

Figure 3 shows the results of issuing this code against the multi-level document from Figure 2. Other values for View's Type property include wdNormalView (1) and wdPrintPreview (4).

```
✦ ✦ ✦  ✦ ✦  ✦ −   1  2  3  4  5  6  7  All ☰ ⌦ ☐ ⌧ ⬚ ⬚ ⬚ ⬚ ⬚ ⬚ .
```

◊ **Tasmanian Traders Sales by Country and Company**
   ◊ *Argentina*
      ◊ **Cactus Comidas para llevar**
```
                  □  Total Sales for 1995 = $1,012
                  □  Total Sales for 1994 = $699
                  □  Total Sales for 1992 = $17,738
```
      ◊ **Océano Atlántico Ltda.**
```
                  □  Total Sales for 1995 = $2,948
                  □  Total Sales for 1994 = $112
                  □  Total Sales for 1993 = $2,133
                  □  Total Sales for 1992 = $367
```
      ◊ **Rancho grande**
```
                  □  Total Sales for 1995 = $697
                  □  Total Sales for 1994 = $1,986
```
   ◊ *Austria*
      ◊ **Ernst Handel**
```
                  □  Total Sales for 1995 = $31,221
                  □  Total Sales for 1994 = $47,050
                  □  Total Sales for 1993 = $24,476
                  □  Total Sales for 1992 = $5,372
```
      ◊ **Piccolo und mehr**
```
                  □  Total Sales for 1995 = $3,345
                  □  Total Sales for 1994 = $8,816
                  □  Total Sales for 1993 = $12,072
                  □  Total Sales for 1992 = $1,612
```
   ◊ *Belgium*
      ◊ **Maison Dewey**
```
                  □  Total Sales for 1995 = $4,331
                  □  Total Sales for 1994 = $5,271
                  □  Total Sales for 1993 = $1,546
```
      ◊ **Suprêmes délices**
```
                  □  Total Sales for 1995 = $5,582
                  □  Total Sales for 1994 = $10,945
                  □  Total Sales for 1993 = $8,248
                  □  Total Sales for 1992 = $5,321
```

Figure 3. *Document outline. If a document's headings use the right styles, creating an outline is as easy as switching to Outline View.*

Once you're in Outline View, you can expand and collapse the outline, either as a whole or parts of it, using View's ExpandOutline and CollapseOutline methods. Each accepts a single, optional, parameter—the range to be expanded or collapsed. If the parameter is omitted, the current selection/insertion point determines what is expanded or collapsed. For example, to collapse the detail for the vendor "Cactus Comidas para llevar" in Figure 3, issue this code:

```
oRange = oWord.ActiveDocument.Paragraphs[3].Range()
oWord.ActiveDocument.ActiveWindow.View.CollapseOutline( oRange )
```

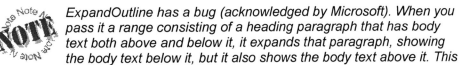

ExpandOutline has a bug (acknowledged by Microsoft). When you pass it a range consisting of a heading paragraph that has body text both above and below it, it expands that paragraph, showing the body text below it, but it also shows the body text above it. This expansion error causes problems when you attempt to collapse this part of the outline. In order to do so, you have to collapse a much larger portion of the outline than you should.

The ShowHeading method lets you determine how many levels of headings are displayed overall. You pass it a number—all headings up to and including the specified level are displayed, while all headings below that level, plus body text, are hidden. For example, to display headings up to level 3, use this code:

```
oWord.ActiveDocument.ActiveWindow.View.ShowHeading( 3 )
```

If you want to display all headings, call the ShowAllHeadings method:

```
oWord.ActiveDocument.ActiveWindow.View.ShowAllHeadings()
```

To show only the first line of body text, set the ShowFirstLineOnly property to .T.; this is a good way to get a summary of the document without showing just the headings. (In the example shown in Figure 3, changing this property doesn't make a difference because each paragraph has only a single line.) If you're showing all levels, it gives you the first line of each paragraph. Unfortunately, this property works only on screen; it doesn't affect printed output.

Notwithstanding the inability to use ShowFirstLineOnly, once you've arranged the outline the way you want it, call Document's PrintOut method (described in the "Printing" section in Chapter 4) to print your outline.

Creating a table of contents

When you have a document with headings that use heading level styles, creating a table of contents is a piece of cake. One call to the Add method of the document's TablesOfContents collection and you're done. All you need to know is where to put the table of contents (a range) and which heading levels you want to include. This code adds a table of contents right at the beginning of the document. It includes headings through level 3.

```
#DEFINE wdNormalView 1
oWord.ActiveDocument.ActiveWindow.View.Type = wdNormalView
oRange = oWord.ActiveDocument.Range(0,0)
oWord.ActiveDocument.TablesOfContents.Add( oRange, .T., 1, 3 )
```

Figure 4 shows one page of the results for the document in Figure 2.

TablesOfContents is a collection of TableOfContents objects. (Note the plural "Tables" in the collection name.) Each TableOfContents object represents one table of contents in the document. Why would you have more than one? Because you might have a separate table of contents for each chapter or each major section in a document.

QUICK-Stop.........................9
Toms Spezialitäten.........................9
Ireland.........................9
Hungry Owl All-Night Grocers.........................9
Italy.........................9
Franchi S.p.A.........................9
Magazzini Alimentari Riuniti.........................9
Reggiani Caseifici.........................9
Mexico.........................10
Ana Trujillo Emparedados y helados.........................10
Antonio Moreno Taquería.........................10
Centro comercial Moctezuma.........................10
Pericles Comidas clásicas.........................10
Tortuga Restaurante.........................10
Norway.........................10
Santé Gourmet.........................10
Poland.........................10
Wolski Zajazd.........................10
Portugal.........................11
Furia Bacalhau e Frutos do Mar.........................11
Princesa Isabel Vinhos.........................11
Spain.........................11
Bólido Comidas preparadas.........................11
FISSA Fabrica Inter. Salchichas S.A.........................11
Galería del gastrónomo.........................11
Godos Cocina Típica.........................11
Romero y tomillo.........................11
Sweden.........................12
Berglunds snabbköp.........................12
Folk och fä HB.........................12
Switzerland.........................12
Chop-suey Chinese.........................12
Richter Supermarkt.........................12
UK.........................12
Around the Horn.........................12
B's Beverages.........................12
Consolidated Holdings.........................13
Eastern Connection.........................13
Island Trading.........................13
North/South.........................13
Seven Seas Imports.........................13
USA.........................13
Great Lakes Food Market.........................13
Hungry Coyote Import Store.........................13
Lazy K Kountry Store.........................13
Let's Stop N Shop.........................13
Lonesome Pine Restaurant.........................14
Old World Delicatessen.........................14
Rattlesnake Canyon Grocery.........................14
Save-a-lot Markets.........................14
Split Rail Beer & Ale.........................14
The Big Cheese.........................14

***Figure 4**. Table of contents. Using built-in heading styles makes it a breeze to create a table of contents.*

The Add method takes quite a few parameters. Here's the syntax, listing the ones you're most likely to use:

```
oDocument.TablesOfContents.Add( oRange, lUseHeadingStyles, nFirstHeadingLevel,
                                nLastHeadingLevel, lUseFields, ,
                                lRightAlignPageNums, lIncludePageNums,
                                cAddedStyles )
```

oRange	Object	Range where the table of contents should be placed.
IUseHeadingStyles	Logical	Indicates whether the table of contents should be created based on built-in heading styles. Defaults to .T.
nFirstHeadingLevel	Numeric	The lowest numbered heading style to be included in the table of contents. Defaults to 1.
nLastHeadingLevel	Numeric	The highest numbered heading style to be included in the table of contents. Defaults to 9.
lUseFields	Logical	Indicates whether items marked as table of contents fields are included in the table of contents. See Help for more information. Defaults to .F.
lRightAlignPageNums	Logical	Indicates whether page numbers are right-aligned on the page. Defaults to .T.
lIncludePageNums	Logical	Indicates whether page numbers are included in the table of contents. Defaults to .T.
cAddedStyles	Character	A comma-separated list of styles other than the built-in heading styles that should also be used in creating the table of contents.

Once you create the table of contents, you can set the character that fills the space between the entries and the page numbers on each line by using the TabLeader property of the TableOfContents object (not the collection). **Table 1** shows constant values for TabLeader.

Table 1. *Filling the space. The TabLeader property determines how the space between the headings and the page numbers in a table of contents is filled.*

Constant	Value	Constant	Value
wdTabLeaderSpaces	0	wdTabLeaderLines	3
wdTabLeaderDots	1	wdTabLeaderHeavy	4
wdTabLeaderDashes	2	wdTabLeaderMiddleDot	5

Several other properties of TableOfContents let you change parameters set by Add, such as IncludePageNumbers, RightAlignPageNumbers, LowerHeadingLevel (corresponds to nFirstHeadingLevel) and UpperHeadingLevel (corresponds to nLastHeadingLevel).

As you may have guessed from our comments on the lUseFields parameter, there is another approach to creating a table of contents. It involves marking each item you want listed with a code. For details, see the topic "Use field codes for indexes, tables of contents, or other tables" in the regular Word Help.

Creating indexes

Long documents are far more useful when they're indexed. Unfortunately, the best way to produce a high-quality index is still the old-fashioned way—by having a person do it. That's because no automated technique can read the contents of a manuscript and decide whether a particular use of a word or phrase deserves to be mentioned in the index. In fact, this problem is the reason that so many search engines produce irrelevant results so much of the time.

Nonetheless, Word offers a couple of ways to create indexes. Only one of the techniques is really suited to Automation, however, as the other involves a great deal of human intervention.

The easily automated technique uses a concordance table listing all the words to be indexed and the index entries for them.

Deciding what to index

The concordance table is a separate document containing a standard Word table with two columns. You can create it interactively or through Automation. **Table 2** is part of a concordance table for Chapter 3 of this book, "Visual FoxPro as an Automation Client" (though not the one actually used to index the book).

Table 2. Creating an index. One way to index a document is by using a table that lists the terms to be indexed together with the index entries.

1426	error:1426
1429	error:1429
Activate	Activate
Application	Application
client	client
collection	collection
collections	collection
Command Window	Command Window
CreateObject()	CreateObject()
CreateObjectEx()	CreateObjectEx()
DCOM	DCOM
debugger	debugger
debugging	debugging

The table shows several items worth noting. First, if a word appears in several forms in the document, you need to list all those forms in the table. (Notice "collection" and "collections" in the first column, both being indexed to "collection.")

Second, you can handle multiple levels in the index within the table by separating them with a colon in the second column. Note the entries for 1426 and 1429. In the index, these will both be part of a general entry for "error," but sub-divided into "1426" and "1429."

Third, most rows in the table have the same thing in the two columns. If you're creating the table interactively, this is a great place to take advantage of a Word feature that's usually an annoyance. In Word, the Edit|Repeat Typing menu option (the shortcut is Ctrl-Y) is almost always available. When you're creating a concordance table, you can use it to cut your typing almost in half. Type the string into the first column, then hit Ctrl-Y to repeat it in the second column.

Finally, Word is unfortunately not smart enough to notice when one index phrase is contained in another. For example, Table 2 contains the word "client." If we added "client application" to the table, when the index is created, a phrase like "Using VFP as our client application" would be indexed twice—once for "client" and once for "client application." Beware of this issue as you decide what to put in the table.

Marking items for the index

Once you have the concordance table, the next step is to get the relevant items in the document marked. This is the part where the concordance table gets put to work and actually saves time. Interactively, choose Insert|Index and Tables from the menu. This displays the dialog shown in **Figure 5**. Choose AutoMark and select your concordance file.

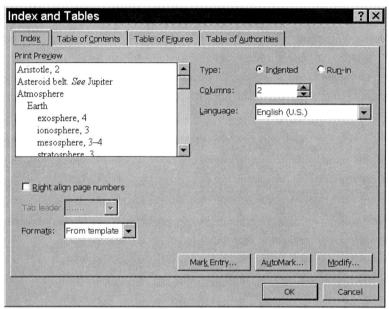

Figure 5. *Creating an index. To mark items in a document based on the concordance table, choose AutoMark from this dialog.*

Word goes through the document and adds special fields to the document everywhere it finds an item from the left column of the concordance table.

To automate this process, you use the AutoMarkEntries method of the document's Indexes collection, like this:

```
oDocument.Indexes.AutoMarkEntries( "d:\autovfp\chapter3\wordlist.DOC" )
```

Generating the index

After the items are marked, creating the index itself is simple. Interactively, you position the cursor where the index is to be placed, then bring up the Index and Tables dialog (shown in Figure 5) again, choose a format from the Formats dropdown, check Right align page numbers, if you want, and choose OK. **Figure 6** shows part of the index generated for Chapter 3, "Visual FoxPro as an Automation Client," based on the concordance in Table 2.

Activate 4
Application 1, 2, 3, 4
collection 4, 6, 7
Command Window 7
CreateObject() 1, 4, 5
DCOM 2
debugging 2
Developer Download files 3
error 1426 8
error 1429 8
object reference 2, 6, 7
Office 1, 2, 6, 8, 9
Outlook 2
parameter 1, 2, 8
PixelsToPoints 3
polymorphism 1
PowerPoint 1, 2, 4
registry 5
server 1, 2, 5, 6, 8, 9
SET OLEOBJECT 4, 5

***Figure 6**. Generated index. Applying the concordance table in Table 2 to Chapter 3 results in this index.*

To produce the index with Automation, you use the Add method of Indexes, passing it the range where the index is to be placed and several other parameters. This example creates the same index as in Figure 6, positioning it at the end of the document.

```
#DEFINE wdCollapseEnd 0
#DEFINE wdHeadingSeparatorNone 0
#DEFINE wdIndexIndent 0
#DEFINE wdTabLeaderDots 1

oRange = oDocument.Range()
oRange.Collapse( wdCollapseEnd )

oIndex = oDocument.Indexes.Add( oRange, wdHeadingSeparatorNone, .T., ;
                                wdIndexIndent, 2, .F.)

* Change leader to dots
oIndex.TabLeader = wdTabLeaderDots
oIndex.Update()
```

The Add method has a number of parameters. In the example, following the range, we specify that no punctuation is needed to separate entries for each letter of the alphabet in the index. Other choices include wdHeadingSeparatorBlankLine (1) and wdHeadingSeparatorLetter (2). The Index object's HeadingSeparator property matches up to this parameter.

The third parameter corresponds to the RightAlignPageNumbers property of the Index object and determines whether the page numbers immediately follow the entry or are right-justified.

The fourth parameter determines how the index handles sub-entries. The default value, wdIndexIndent (0), lists each sub-entry indented on a separate line beneath the main heading. The alternative option, wdIndexRunIn (1), separates the sub-entries with semi-colons on the same line with the main heading. Don't use it when you're right-aligning the page numbers—it looks terrible in that case.

The fifth parameter specifies the number of columns in the index, two in the example. It corresponds to the NumberOfColumns property of the Index object.

The final parameter shown in the example indicates that accented letters should be combined with the basic letters. Pass .T. to separate accented letters into separate index listings. This parameter corresponds to Index's AccentedLetters property.

Add has several additional parameters, but they're fairly obscure. See Help for details.

Formatting indexes

As with tables of contents, once you've added an index, you can use its properties to change its appearance. The Index object has a number of properties that affect its look—a number of them correspond to parameters of the Indexes collection's Add method, as noted previously. In addition, as with TableOfContents, the TabLeader property lets you vary the character that appears between the entry and the page number(s). The constants are the same as for TableOfContents—see Table 1.

The Update method (used in the example in the previous section), as its name suggests, updates the index. It's useful both when the marked index entries change and when you've changed formatting.

Merging documents with data

Mail merge is another of the killer functions that put word processors on everybody's desk. The ability to write a document once, then merge it with data repeatedly to produce personalized documents made sense to businesses, academics, and home users, too.

Word offers a variety of ways to merge data and documents. The best known is the most complex—using the built-in mail merge ability. However, it's also possible to merge documents by using Find and Replace and by combining the built-in mail merge capabilities with some manual labor. We'll take a look at each of these approaches here and tell you why we think the third approach is the best suited to Automation.

Word's mail merge structure

Mail merge has been included in Word for many versions. Interactively, there's a wizard called the Mail Merge Helper (see **Figure 7**) that guides users through the process. Even with this tool, though, setting up a new mail merge document, connecting it to data, and generating results is not simple. We've both spent many hours on the phone walking relatives and friends through the process.

Behind the Mail Merge Helper, there are a number of objects. Help lists no fewer than eight different objects whose names begin with "MailMerge." But it's not the complexity of the object model that leads us to recommend alternative approaches; it's the fragility of the connection between the document and the data.

When you indicate that a Word document is a mail merge document, you specify the data source for the merge. It can be another Word document, a text file, or any of a variety of database files, including FoxPro, of course. For most data sources, Word uses ODBC to read the data.

If the data file is deleted or moved or something happens to the ODBC driver, the merge stops working. Many people using FoxPro 2.x tables in mail merge got a nasty surprise when they installed Service Pack 3 for VFP 6 (or anything else that installed ODBC 4.0) because it disabled the ODBC driver for FoxPro 2.x tables and failed to automatically substitute the VFP driver for it. Mail merges that had been working for years failed.

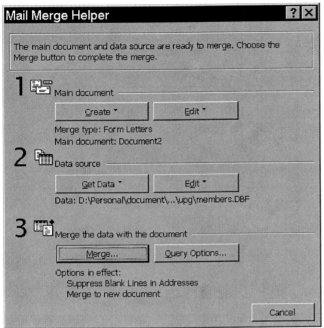

Figure 7. *Mail merge. This dialog walks interactive users through the steps needed to use Word's built-in mail merge facility.*

The need to deal with ODBC drivers and connections makes this approach harder and, especially, riskier than it needs to be. Unless you're dealing with extremely large tables, there are other, simpler ways to solve this problem. If you are dealing with large tables, plan to control the ODBC aspects yourself rather than relying on what's on the user's machine. (To learn about managing ODBC and connections, check out the book's sister volume in the Essentials series, *Client-Server Applications with Visual FoxPro 6.0 and SQL Server 7.0*.) The key thing you'll need to do is pass the connection string to the OpenDataSource method of the MailMerge object (discussed later in this chapter).

Substituting data with Find and Replace

One alternative to Word's mail merge is to use the Find and Replace objects. Since these were discussed in detail in Chapter 5 (see "Search and replace"), we'll talk here only about the specific issues involved in using them for merging documents and data.

The basic idea is to create a document that contains the desired result except for a set of strings that are to be replaced by data from your database. Alternatively, you can use a template from which you create a document, then replace the strings.

The main issue is making sure that you only replace what you mean to replace. When you're working interactively, this isn't a problem because you can see each match before you agree to replace it. With Automation, however, you need a better solution. One possibility is to enclose the strings with a special character or characters. For example, you might surround the strings to be replaced with angle brackets (like "<name>") or exclamation points ("!name!"). Then, the code to replace the string would look something like this:

```
#DEFINE wdReplaceAll 2
oRange = oDocument.Range(0,0)
WITH oRange.Find
   .Text = "!Name!"
   .Replacement.Text = TRIM(Employee.First_Name) ;
                    - " " + TRIM(Employee.Last_Name)
   .Execute( , , , , , , , , , , wdReplaceAll)
ENDWITH
```

The biggest problem with this approach is trying to find an appropriate special character to delimit your strings. You really need to be sure it's something that won't appear elsewhere in the document. While it's unlikely that a special character like an exclamation point would surround text, there's always the off chance that a user might choose to do something strange.

You can use a table to drive this approach. Consider putting the strings and formatting to be found and substituted into a table, and having a single method to perform the search and replace. Nonetheless, while searching for and replacing delimited strings is a viable solution to merging data into documents, we still think there's a better way.

Drop back 10 yards and punt

So what's a body to do? There's Word with a perfectly good mail merge engine, but the need to use ODBC to access FoxPro tables is a serious impediment. On the other hand, the rest of the mail merge facilities are really useful. The solution is to avoid the ODBC aspects while taking advantage of everything else Word has to offer.

The way to do that is to create the data source for a mail merge on the fly, sending FoxPro data to Word, and attaching it to the document just long enough to merge it. This strategy is appropriate when the amount of data to be merged is small to moderate, but it may need to be reconsidered for extremely large data sets. (However, realize that no matter what approach you use, the data has to be sent to Word somehow, so this method may be as good as any other and it does afford you more control over the process and less likelihood of trouble caused by end users than the traditional approach.)

The documents involved in mail merge

Once you take ODBC out of the picture, mail merge involves two or three documents. The first is what Word calls the *main document*. That's the document that contains the text of the letter, envelope, labels, or whatever it is you're trying to create. Most of this document looks like any other document. The exception is that, in a few places, it contains *fields*—special markers that indicate that something is to be substituted at that location. Word actually offers a wide range of fields, including such things as the date, time, and page number. For mail merge, we're specifically interested in fields of the type MergeField.

The second document in a mail merge is the *data source*. This is the document that contains the data to be substituted into the fields. It contains an ordinary Word table with one column for each MergeField. In the strategy we describe, we'll build this document on the fly.

The third document is optional. It's the *result* created by merging the main document with the data source. We prefer to merge to a new document rather than directly to the printer, but there may be situations where you choose to skip this step.

The objects involved in mail merge

The main object in mail merge is, in fact, called MailMerge—it's accessed through the MailMerge property of Document. MailMerge's Fields property references a MailMergeFields collection, made up of MailMergeField objects—these objects represent the mail merge fields in the main document. When the document is attached to a data source, the DataSource property of MailMerge accesses a MailMergeDataSource object. Its DataFields property references a collection of MailMergeDataField objects that provide information about the fields in the data source. MailMergeDataSource also has a FieldNames property that references a MailMergeFieldNames collection with information about the field names for the data.

   If this seems like a lot of objects, that's because it is, but in the strategy described here, you'll need to work directly with only the MailMerge and MailMergeFields objects.

Creating a main document

The first step is creating a main document. There are several ways to do this, not all involving Automation. Your users may simply create a main document using the Mail Merge Helper. The problem with that approach, of course, is that such documents will have data sources attached, but there are some solutions (discussed in the next section, "Attaching a data source").

   Users can also create main documents manually by inserting mail merge fields by choosing Insert|Field from the menu. The dialog shown in **Figure 8** appears. To add a mail merge field, choose Mail Merge in the left column and MergeField on the right, then type the field name in the Field codes box, as shown in the figure.

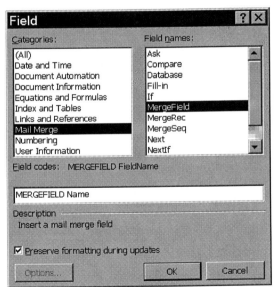

Figure 8. *Inserting mail merge fields. Users can build mail merge documents manually rather than using the Mail Merge Helper.*

   Of course, you can build main documents with Automation just like other documents. In fact, you can also use a hybrid approach, initially setting up the document with Automation, then allowing a user to edit it.

To add a mail merge field to a document, use the Add method of the MailMergeFields collection. It calls for two parameters, as follows:

```
oDocument.MailMerge.Fields.Add( oRange, cField )
```

oRange	Object	Reference to a range where the mail merge field is to be added.
cField	Character	The mail merge field to be inserted.

Attaching a data source

One of the things that makes the Mail Merge Helper so helpful is that it provides a list of the fields in the data source and lets you choose from that list as you create the main document. **Figure 9** shows part of the Mail Merge toolbar with the Insert Merge Field dropdown open, showing a list of the fields from TasTrade's Employee table.

***Figure 9**. Adding fields interactively. When a main document is attached to a data source, you can add fields by choosing them from the Mail Merge toolbar.*

Using header sources for field lists

If we want users to be able to create and edit main documents, we need a way to provide them with a list of fields, even though we don't want to create permanent connections between main documents and data sources. Several methods of the MailMerge object let us set up field lists.

In fact, there are two kinds of connections a main document can have to data. It can be connected to an actual data source that contains records available for merging. However, a main document can instead be connected to a *header source*, a document that provides only field names for the merge, but no actual merge data.

The advantage of a header source is that it's small and easy to create. We can use a header source to provide users with a list of fields while creating or editing the main document, but wait to create the complete data source until the user is ready for the actual merge. We can also create the header source and hide it from the user, when that's an appropriate strategy. (That might be appropriate where users are known to delete files when they shouldn't.)

       Listing 2 is a program that attaches a header source to a main document, based on the field list in a table or view. (It's CreateHeaderSource.PRG in the Developer Download files available at www.hentzenwerke.com.) The key to the whole process is the call to the CreateHeaderSource method of MailMerge—the rest is just typical FoxPro string manipulation. You might call this routine like this:

```
DO CreateHeaderSource WITH oDocument, _SAMPLES+"TasTrade\Data\Employee", ;
                 "C:\Temp\EmployeeHeader.DOC"
```

***Listing 2**. Creating a header source. This program generates a header source on the fly from any table or view and attaches it to a document.*

```
* CreateHeaderSource.PRG
* Create a header source for the current document
* based on a table or view
* Assumes:
*      Word is open.

LPARAMETERS oDocument, cCursor, cDocument
    * oDocument = the document for which a header source is to be created.
    * cCursor = the filename, including path, of the table or view.
    * cDocument = the filename, including path, where the
    *             header source document is to be stored.

* Check parameters
IF PCOUNT()<3
   MESSAGEBOX("Must provide table/view name and document name")
   RETURN .F.
ENDIF

IF VarType(oDocument) <> "O"
   MESSAGEBOX("No document specified")
   RETURN .F.
ENDIF

IF VarType(cCursor) <> "C" OR EMPTY(cCursor)
   MESSAGEBOX("Table/View name must be character")
   RETURN .F.
ENDIF

IF VarType(cDocument) <> "C" OR EMPTY(cDocument)
   MESSAGEBOX("Document name must be character")
   RETURN .F.
ENDIF

LOCAL nFieldCount, cFieldList, aFieldList[1], nField

* Open the table/view
USE (cCursor) AGAIN IN 0 ALIAS MergeCursor
SELECT MergeCursor

* Get a list of fields
```

```
nFieldCount = AFIELDS( aFieldList, "MergeCursor" )
* Go through the list, creating a comma-separated string
cFieldList = ""
FOR nField = 1 TO nFieldCount
   IF aFieldList[ nField, 2] <> "G"
      * Can't use General fields
      cFieldList = cFieldList + aFieldList[ nField, 1] + ","
   ENDIF
ENDFOR
cFieldList = LEFT( cFieldList, LEN(cFieldList) - 1 )

* Attach the header to the document
oDocument.MailMerge.CreateHeaderSource( cDocument, , , cFieldList )

USE IN MergeCursor

RETURN
```

The resulting header file is simply a one-row Word table, each column containing a fieldname.

When you open a main document interactively and the header source or data source is missing, Word insists that you either find the missing source or take action. In Word 2000, when the same thing happens with Automation, Word simply opens the file and detaches the header source or data source itself.

 Unfortunately, in Word 97, when you open a main document with Automation and the data source is missing, Word insists on your finding the missing data source, though it's surprisingly inventive if you point to the wrong file.

The OpenHeaderSource method of MailMerge attaches an existing header source to a main document. OpenDataSource attaches an existing data source to a main document. Both take long lists of parameters, but in each case, only the first is required—it's the name of the header/data source file, including the path. Here's an example:

```
oDocument.MailMerge.OpenHeaderSource( "C:\Temp\EmployeeList.DOC" )
```

Using a data source at merge time

 The header source allows your users to create their own main documents using a list of merge fields. Header sources contain no data—you need the ability to create and attach a complete data source on the fly. The CreateDataSource method lets you build a new data source. As with CreateHeaderSource, you build a Word table, then attach it to the main document. Most of the work is pretty straightforward. **Listing 3**, included as CreateDataSource.PRG in the Developer Download files available at www.hentzenwerke.com, creates and attaches a data source to a document. It accepts the same three parameters as CreateHeaderSource in Listing 2. Because the slowest part of the process is sending the actual data from VFP to Word, be sure to create a cursor or view that contains only the data you need for the mail merge before you call CreateDataSource. Do your filtering of both fields and

records on the VFP side. The EditDataSource method opens the DataSource associated with a
main document. If it's already open, it activates it.

Listing 3. *Build a better data source. This program creates a data source on the fly.
Rather than dealing with ODBC, send just the records and fields you need to a Word
data source when you're actually ready to do a mail merge.*

```
* CreateDataSource.PRG
* Create a data source for the current document
* based on a table or view
* Assumes:
*       Word is open.

LPARAMETERS oDocument, cCursor, cDocument
   * oDocument = the document for which a header source is to be created.
   * cCursor = the filename, including path, of the table or view.
   *           Data should already be filtered and sorted.
   * cDocument = the filename, including path, where the
   *             data source document is to be stored.

* Check parameters
IF PCOUNT()<3
   MESSAGEBOX("Must provide table/view name and document name")
   RETURN .F.
ENDIF

IF VarType(oDocument) <> "O"
   MESSAGEBOX("No document specified")
   RETURN .F.
ENDIF

IF VarType(cCursor) <> "C" OR EMPTY(cCursor)
   MESSAGEBOX("Table/View name must be character")
   RETURN .F.
ENDIF

IF VarType(cDocument) <> "C" OR EMPTY(cDocument)
   MESSAGEBOX("Document name must be character")
   RETURN .F.
ENDIF

LOCAL nFieldCount, cFieldList, aFieldList[1], nField
LOCAL oWord, oRange, oSourceDoc, oRow, oTable

* Get a reference to Word
oWord = oDocument.Application

* Open the table/view
USE (cCursor) AGAIN IN 0 ALIAS MergeCursor
SELECT MergeCursor

* Get a list of fields
nFieldCount = AFIELDS( aFieldList, "MergeCursor" )
* Go through the list, creating a comma-separated string
cFieldList = ""
FOR nField = 1 TO nFieldCount
   IF aFieldList[ nField, 2 ] <> "G"
```

```
      * Can't use General fields
      cFieldList = cFieldList + aFieldList[ nField, 1] + ","
   ENDIF
ENDFOR
cFieldList = LEFT( cFieldList, LEN(cFieldList) - 1 )

WITH oDocument.MailMerge
   * Attach the data to the document
   .CreateDataSource( cDocument, , , cFieldList )
   .EditDataSource
   oSourceDoc = oWord.ActiveDocument
   oTable = oSourceDoc.Tables[1]
   oRow = oTable.Rows[1]

   * Now open the data source and put the data into the document
   SCAN
      WITH oRow
         FOR nField = 1 TO nFieldCount
            DO CASE
            CASE TYPE( FIELDS( nField )) = "C"
               * Get rid of trailing blanks
               .Cells[ nField ].Range.InsertAfter( ;
                  TRIM( EVAL(FIELDS( nField ))))
            CASE TYPE( FIELDS( nField )) = "G"
               * Do nothing
            OTHERWISE
               * Just send it as is
               .Cells[ nField ].Range.InsertAfter( EVAL(FIELDS( nField )))
            ENDCASE
         ENDFOR
      ENDWITH
      oRow = oTable.Rows.Add()
   ENDSCAN
   oRow.Delete()
   oSourceDoc.Save()
ENDWITH

USE IN MergeCursor

RETURN
```

Performing the mail merge

Once you've jumped through all the hoops to get the data there, actually performing the mail merge is the easy part. Just call the MailMerge object's Execute method and—poof!—the main document and the data source are merged to a new document. This is all it takes:

```
oDocument.MailMerge.Execute()
```

Of course, you probably want to exercise more control than that over the merge. Various properties of the MailMerge object let you set things up before you call Execute. The two you're most likely to deal with are Destination and SuppressBlankLines. SuppressBlankLines is a logical that indicates whether lines in the document that are totally empty should be eliminated. The default is .T.

Destination determines where the merge results are sent. The default is wdSendToNewDocument (0), our preference. Our choices are wdSendToPrinter (1), wdSendToEmail (2), and wdSendToFax (3). There are several properties, all of which begin with "Mail," dedicated to particulars of the case where results are sent to e-mail.

Determining the document type

The MailMerge object has a couple of other important properties. State lets you check, for any document, what role it plays in the mail merge process. **Table 3** shows the possible values for State.

Table 3. What kind of a document am I? MailMerge's State property tells you what kind of document you're dealing with.

Constant	Value	Constant	Value
wdNormalDocument	0	wdMainAndHeader	3
wdMainDocumentOnly	1	wdMainAndSourceAndHeader	4
wdMainAndDataSource	2	wdDataSource	5

MainDocumentType tells what kind of main document you have. **Table 4** shows the values this property can take.

Table 4. Merge document types. The MainDocumentType property classifies documents into the various kinds of merge documents you can create.

Constant	Value	Constant	Value
wdNotAMergeDocument	-1	wdEnvelopes	2
wdFormLetters	0	wdCatalog	3
wdMailingLabels	1		

Rescuing abandoned mail merge documents

You may be faced with main documents that have been detached from their data sources and for which you don't have access to the appropriate tables. It turns out that it's quite easy to go through these documents and build a header source or a data source for them, as well.

 Listing 4 shows ExtractDataSource.PRG (also included in the Developer Download files available at www.hentzenwerke.com), which traverses the MailMergeFields collection of the document to create a list of fields, then uses that list to create a data source (albeit an empty one).

Listing 4. Restoring data sources. When main documents get detached from their data sources, this program can create an empty data source that allows the document to be edited.

```
* ExtractDataSource.PRG
* Process an existing document and create a data source document
* based on the fields used on the document.

LPARAMETERS oDocument, cSourceName
```

```
* oDocument = the existing mail merge document
* cSourceName = the filename, including path, for the data source

#DEFINE wdNotAMergeDocument -1

* Should check parameters here. Omitted for space reasons

WITH oDocument
   IF .MailMerge.MainDocumentType = wdNotAMergeDocument OR ;
      INLIST(.MailMerge.State, 0, 1)
      * Need to create a data source
      * Go through fields and create a list
      LOCAL oField, cCode, cField, cFieldList, cHeaderName

      cFieldList = "'"
      FOR EACH oField IN .MailMerge.Fields
         cCode = oField.Code.Text
         * Parse out extraneous information
         cField = ALLTRIM( STRTRAN(STRTRAN(cCode, ;
                  "MERGEFIELD",""), "\* MERGEFORMAT", "") )
         IF NOT cField+"," $ cFieldList
            cFieldList = cFieldList + cField + ","
         ENDIF
      ENDFOR

      IF LEN(cFieldList) > 1
         cFieldList = LEFT(cFieldList, LEN(cFieldList)-1) + "'"
      ENDIF

      * Now create a data source document.
      .MailMerge.CreateDataSource( cSourceName, , , cFieldList )
   ENDIF
ENDWITH

RETURN
```

Putting it all together

 To demonstrate this chapter's main lesson, we have a two-part process. **Listing 5** shows a program (WordSample3Pt1.PRG in the Developer Download files available at www.hentzenwerke.com) that creates a template for product information sheets for Tasmanian Traders. The template is a mail merge main document attached to a header source only. The program runs a query that collects the data needed (in a real application, you'd probably have a view for this data), then calls on CreateHeaderSource.PRG (see Listing 2) to attach the header. It then populates and saves the template. **Figure 10** shows the completed template.

Listing 5*. Creating a mail merge template. This program generates both a header source and a main document, in this case, a template for a main document.*

```
* Create a main document for product sheets.
* The document is created as a template so that it can
* then be used with File|New.
```

```
#DEFINE CR CHR(13)
#DEFINE TAB CHR(9)
#DEFINE wdHeaderFooterPrimary 1
#DEFINE wdGray25 16
#DEFINE wdAlignParagraphCenter 1
#DEFINE wdCollapseEnd 0
#DEFINE wdParagraph 4
#DEFINE wdWord 2
#DEFINE wdLineStyleDouble 7
#DEFINE wdUserTemplatesPath 2
#DEFINE wdGoToBookmark -1

LOCAL oWord, oDocument, oRange, oBorderRange, cTemplatePath

* Open Word and create a new template document
oWord = CreateObject("Word.Application")
oWord.Visible = .T.
oDocument = oWord.Documents.Add(, .T.)

* Create a cursor of all products
OPEN DATABASE _SAMPLES + "TasTrade\Data\TasTrade"
SELECT product_name, english_name, category_name, ;
       quantity_in_unit, unit_price, ;
       company_name, contact_name, contact_title, ;
       address, city, region, postal_code, country, ;
       phone, fax ;
    FROM products ;
       JOIN supplier ;
         ON products.supplier_id = supplier.supplier_id ;
       JOIN category ;
         ON products.category_id = category.category_id ;
    ORDER BY Category_Name, Product_Name ;
    INTO CURSOR ProductList

* Attach a header source to the template document
DO CreateHeaderSource WITH oDocument, DBF("ProductList"), ;
                           AddBs(SYS(2023)) +"ProdHeader.DOC"

USE IN ProductList

* Now set up the product sheet
* First, assign a font for Normal
WITH oDocument.Styles["Normal"].Font
   .Name = "Times New Roman"
   .Size = 12
ENDWITH

* Add a header
WITH oDocument.Sections[1].Headers[ wdHeaderFooterPrimary ]
   oRange = .Range()
   WITH oRange
      .Text = "Tasmanian Traders"
      .Style = oDocument.Styles[ "Heading 1" ]
      .ParagraphFormat.Alignment = wdAlignParagraphCenter
      .Shading.BackgroundPatternColorIndex  = wdGray25
   ENDWITH
ENDWITH
```

```
* Page heading
oRange = oDocument.Range(0,0)
WITH oRange
   .Style = oDocument.Styles[ "Heading 2" ]
   .ParagraphFormat.Alignment = wdAlignParagraphCenter
   .InsertAfter( "Product Information" + CR + CR )
   .Collapse( wdCollapseEnd )

   * First, add fixed text and set up bookmarks where we want
   * the merge fields to go.
   * Add Product Category
   .Style = oDocument.Styles[ "Heading 3" ]
   .InsertAfter( "Product Category: "  )
   .Collapse( wdCollapseEnd )
   oDocument.Bookmarks.Add( "ProductCategory", oRange )
   .InsertAfter( CR )
   .Expand( wdParagraph )
   .Borders.OutsideLineStyle = wdLineStyleDouble
   .Collapse( wdCollapseEnd )
   .InsertAfter( CR )

   * Add Product Name
   .InsertAfter( "Product Name: " )
   .Collapse( wdCollapseEnd )
   oDocument.Bookmarks.Add( "ProductName", oRange )
   .Collapse( wdCollapseEnd )
   .InsertAfter( CR )
   oBorderRange = oRange.Paragraphs[1].Range()
   .InsertAfter( "English Name: " )
   .Collapse( wdCollapseEnd )
   oDocument.Bookmarks.Add( "EnglishName", oRange )
   .InsertAfter( CR )
   .Collapse( wdCollapseEnd )
   oBorderRange.MoveEnd( wdParagraph, 1 )
   oBorderRange.Borders.OutsideLineStyle = wdLineStyleDouble

   * Now units and price
   .Style = oDocument.Styles[ "Normal" ]
   .InsertAfter( CR + "Sold in units of: " )
   .Collapse( wdCollapseEnd )
   oDocument.Bookmarks.Add( "Quantity", oRange )
   .InsertAfter( " at a price of: " )
   .Collapse( wdCollapseEnd )
   oDocument.Bookmarks.Add( "UnitPrice", oRange )
   .InsertAfter( " per unit." + CR + CR )
   .Collapse( wdCollapseEnd )

   * Now supplier information
   * To make things line up, we'll need a tab, so set it up.
   WITH oDocument.Paragraphs.TabStops
      .ClearAll()
      .Add( oWord.InchesToPoints( 1 ) )
   ENDWITH

   .InsertAfter( "Supplier: " + TAB )
   .Collapse( wdCollapseEnd )
   oDocument.Bookmarks.Add( "CompanyName", oRange)
   .InsertAfter( CR + TAB)
   .Collapse( wdCollapseEnd )
```

```
oDocument.Bookmarks.Add( "Address", oRange )
.InsertAfter( CR + TAB )
.Collapse( wdCollapseEnd )
oDocument.Bookmarks.Add( "City", oRange )
.InsertAfter( CR + TAB )
.Collapse( wdCollapseEnd )
oDocument.Bookmarks.Add( "Region", oRange )
.InsertAfter( CR + TAB )
.Collapse( wdCollapseEnd )
oDocument.Bookmarks.Add( "PostalCode", oRange )
.InsertAfter( CR + TAB )
.Collapse( wdCollapseEnd )
oDocument.Bookmarks.Add( "Country", oRange )
.InsertAfter( CR )
.InsertAfter( "Contact: " + TAB )
.Collapse( wdCollapseEnd )
oDocument.Bookmarks.Add( "ContactName", oRange )
.InsertAfter( CR + TAB)
.Collapse( wdCollapseEnd )
oDocument.Bookmarks.Add( "ContactTitle", oRange )
.InsertAfter( CR )
.InsertAfter( "Phone: " + TAB )
.Collapse( wdCollapseEnd )
oDocument.Bookmarks.Add( "Phone", oRange )
.InsertAfter( CR )
.InsertAfter( "Fax: " + TAB )
.Collapse( wdCollapseEnd )
oDocument.Bookmarks.Add( "Fax", oRange )
.InsertAfter( CR )

* Now insert a mail merge field at each bookmark

oRange = oDocument.Bookmarks[ "ProductCategory" ].Range()
oDocument.MailMerge.Fields.Add( oRange, "Category_Name" )

oRange = oDocument.Bookmarks[ "ProductName" ].Range()
oDocument.MailMerge.Fields.Add( oRange, "Product_Name" )

oRange = oDocument.Bookmarks[ "EnglishName" ].Range()
oDocument.MailMerge.Fields.Add( oRange, "English_Name" )

oRange = oDocument.Bookmarks[ "Quantity" ].Range()
oDocument.MailMerge.Fields.Add( oRange, "Quantity_In_Unit" )

oRange = oDocument.Bookmarks[ "UnitPrice" ].Range()
oDocument.MailMerge.Fields.Add( oRange, "Unit_Price" )

oRange = oDocument.Bookmarks[ "CompanyName" ].Range()
oDocument.MailMerge.Fields.Add( oRange, "Company_Name" )

oRange = oDocument.Bookmarks[ "Address" ].Range()
oDocument.MailMerge.Fields.Add( oRange, "Address" )

oRange = oDocument.Bookmarks[ "City" ].Range()
oDocument.MailMerge.Fields.Add( oRange, "City" )

oRange = oDocument.Bookmarks[ "Region" ].Range()
oDocument.MailMerge.Fields.Add( oRange, "Region" )
```

```
   oRange = oDocument.Bookmarks[ "PostalCode" ].Range()
   oDocument.MailMerge.Fields.Add( oRange, "Postal_Code" )

   oRange = oDocument.Bookmarks[ "Country" ].Range()
   oDocument.MailMerge.Fields.Add( oRange, "Country" )

   oRange = oDocument.Bookmarks[ "ContactName" ].Range()
   oDocument.MailMerge.Fields.Add( oRange, "Contact_Name" )

   oRange = oDocument.Bookmarks[ "ContactTitle" ].Range()
   oDocument.MailMerge.Fields.Add( oRange, "Contact_Title" )

   oRange = oDocument.Bookmarks[ "Phone" ].Range()
   oDocument.MailMerge.Fields.Add( oRange,"Phone" )

   oRange = oDocument.Bookmarks[ "Fax" ].Range()
   oDocument.MailMerge.Fields.Add( oRange, "Fax" )

ENDWITH

cTemplatePath = oWord.Options.DefaultFilePath( wdUserTemplatesPath )
oDocument.SaveAs( AddBs(cTemplatePath) + "ProdInfo")

RETURN
```

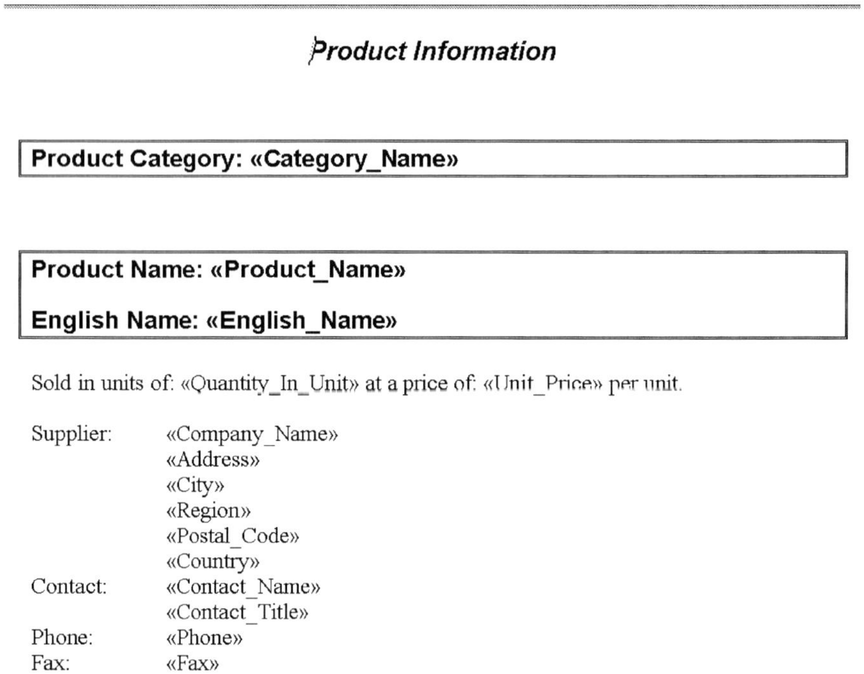

Product Information

Product Category: «Category_Name»

Product Name: «Product_Name»

English Name: «English_Name»

Sold in units of: «Quantity_In_Unit» at a price of: «Unit_Price» per unit.

Supplier:	«Company_Name»
	«Address»
	«City»
	«Region»
	«Postal_Code»
	«Country»
Contact:	«Contact_Name»
	«Contact_Title»
Phone:	«Phone»
Fax:	«Fax»

Figure 10. *Creating mail merge documents. This template was created by Listing 5. It has a header source and is based on a query from the TasTrade database.*

The second part of the process is to create an actual data source when you're ready to perform the mail merge. **Listing 6** shows the code (WordSample3Pt2.PRG in the Developer Download files available at www.hentzenwerke.com) that creates the new document from the template, calls on CreateDataSource.PRG (see Listing 3), then performs the merge and shows the result. **Figure 11** shows part of the result.

***Listing 6**. Performing a merge. This code uses the template created by Listing 5 to generate a new document, creates a data source, and executes the merge.*

```
* Create the Product Information sheets based on the
* template, using mail merge
#DEFINE wdUserTemplatesPath 2
#DEFINE wdWindowStateMaximize 1

LOCAL cTemplatePath, oDocument, oMergedDocument

* Create an instance of Word.
* Make it public for demonstration purposes.
RELEASE ALL LIKE o*
PUBLIC oWord
oWord = CreateObject("Word.Application")

* Make Word visible.
oWord.Visible = .t.

* Create a new document based on the template
cTemplatePath = oWord.Options.DefaultFilePath( wdUserTemplatesPath )
oDocument = oWord.Documents.Add( AddBs(cTemplatePath) + "ProdInfo" )

* Run the query to create a cursor of all products
* Create a cursor of all products
OPEN DATABASE _SAMPLES + "TasTrade\Data\TasTrade"
SELECT product_name, english_name, category_name, ;
          quantity_in_unit, TRANSFORM(unit_price, "@$") AS unit_price, ;
          company_name, contact_name, contact_title, ;
          address, city, region, postal_code, country, ;
          phone, fax ;
   FROM products ;
      JOIN supplier ;
         ON products.supplier_id = supplier.supplier_id ;
      JOIN category ;
         ON products.category_id = category.category_id ;
   ORDER BY Category_Name, Product_Name ;
   INTO CURSOR ProductList

* Now create and attach a data source
DO CreateDataSource WITH oDocument, DBF("ProductList"), ;
                        AddBs(SYS(2023)) + "ProdData"

USE IN ProductList

* Perform the mail merge
oDocument.MailMerge.Execute()
oMergedDocument = oWord.ActiveDocument

WITH oMergedDocument
```

```
   IF .ActiveWindow.WindowState <> wdWindowStateMaximize
      * Move it to make it visible - for some reason, it comes up
      * way off screen
      .ActiveWindow.Left = 0
      .ActiveWindow.Top = 0
   ENDIF

   * Preview it
   .PrintPreview()
ENDWITH

RETURN
```

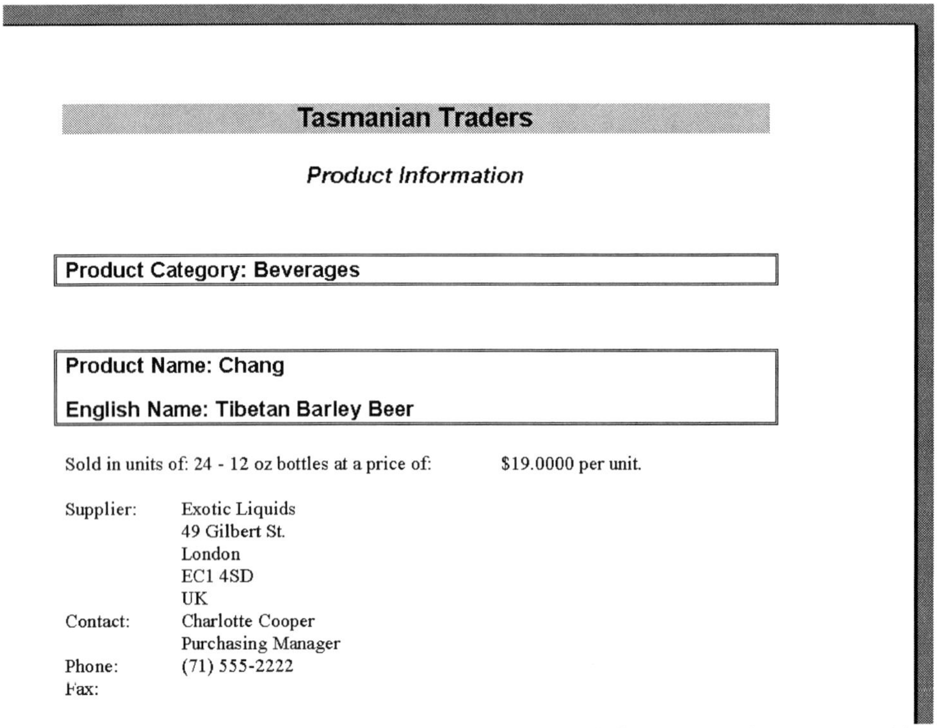

Tasmanian Traders

Product Information

Product Category: Beverages

Product Name: Chang

English Name: Tibetan Barley Beer

Sold in units of: 24 - 12 oz bottles at a price of: $19.0000 per unit.

Supplier: Exotic Liquids
49 Gilbert St.
London
EC1 4SD
UK
Contact: Charlotte Cooper
Purchasing Manager
Phone: (71) 555-2222
Fax:

***Figure 11**. Mail merge results. This is the product information sheet created by the programs in Listings 5 and 6. There's one sheet for each product.*

We'd like to say, "That's all, folks!" But the truth is that, even with three full chapters devoted to it, there's far more to Word than we've been able to cover here. So, if there's something you want to do in a document and we haven't shown you the way, just dig in and try it. Remember the keys to figuring it out. First, try to do it interactively. Try recording a macro. Use the Word VBA Help file and the Object Browser to find out what objects, methods, and properties are involved. Word's object model is extremely rich. If you can imagine it, it can probably be done.

Section III
Automating Excel

Chapter 7
Excel Basics

Excel has some capabilities that aren't found in FoxPro. Want a tabular report that the average end user can manipulate? Try Excel. Need some mathematical calculations that FoxPro doesn't provide? Excel can do it. Want some graphs? Excel has an excellent graphing engine.

Working with Excel through Automation has a lot in common with automating Word—chalk one up for polymorphism. Unfortunately, there are more differences than similarities, since the two servers have different abilities and purposes.

The object model

Like Word, Excel's top-level object is the Application object, which has properties and methods that relate to Excel as whole. A number, like StartupPath, Version, and WindowState, are the same, while others, like Calculation, which determines when calculations occur, are specific to Excel. The Application object also provides access to all other objects in Excel.

The fundamental object in Excel is a Workbook. This corresponds to an XLS file. The Excel Application object keeps track of all its open workbooks in a Workbooks collection, and uses the ActiveWorkbook property to return a reference to the active Workbook object.

Each Workbook has two main collections, Worksheets and Charts, which represent the pages of the workbook and the graphs it contains, respectively. Workbook has ActiveSheet and ActiveChart properties containing references to the current Worksheet and Chart objects. Excel also provides a shortcut by offering ActiveSheet, ActiveChart, and ActiveCell properties at the Application level.

As with Word, the Excel Visual Basic Help file contains a live diagram of the object model. **Figure 1** shows the portion of the object model diagram that describes the Worksheet object.

Déjà vu

If you're reading this book from start to finish, as you read this chapter, you'll say to yourself, "Gosh, I've read this before!" Office 2000 is object-oriented, and it's polymorphic. Polymorphism literally means "many forms," and when applied to OOP, it means that different objects have properties and methods that behave consistently. To write a file to disk, you use the Save method, whether you are in Word, Excel, PowerPoint, or Outlook. This does not mean that the Save commands do exactly the same thing—there are different things that need to happen when a Word document is saved than when an Excel spreadsheet is saved. There may even be different parameters for each. However, you can be sure that the Save command will save your work to disk.

Microsoft Excel Objects (Worksheet)

See Also

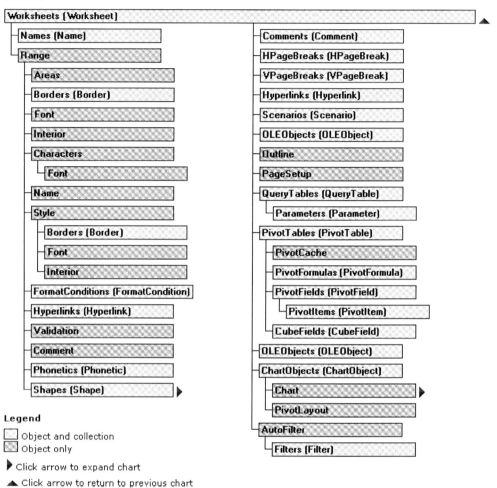

Figure 1. The Excel object model. This diagram is available in the Help file and shows the hierarchy of available objects.

The benefit of polymorphism is that once you know how to do something in one tool, you know how to do it in the rest. In Office, this is usually true. However, polymorphism does include the ability for methods to accept different parameters, because different objects are exactly that—different. So you need to be aware that syntax can (and does) change between Office applications.

There are so many similarities between the Office applications that we could have written this chapter to say things like, "Just use the CreateObject() function as explained in the Word chapter, but use "Excel.Application" instead." We felt that it would be better to have a complete explanation for each application to keep you from having to flip back and forth in the book. It also makes it easier to explain the subtle syntax differences that exist between applications. After we get past the basics of opening and saving files, we get into enough application-specific features that it will seem less repetitive.

The benefit of polymorphism is that once you know how to do something in one object, you know how to do it in all of them. However, explaining similar concepts for each object makes for redundant text. Just think of this redundant text as a "feature."

Getting a handle on the application

To open Excel with Automation, use the following command (type along in the Command Window, if you want to):

```
oExcel = CreateObject("Excel.Application")
```

Nothing happens! Check the task manager; Excel is up and running, but it's just not visible. Like the other Office applications, Excel is hidden when it's instantiated through Automation, and it's up to you to tell it when to become visible. This is a powerful feature—automating Excel without having to update the screen can shave 10 percent to 30 percent off your run time! When you're ready to show Excel to your users, set the Application's Visible property:

```
oExcel.Visible = .T.
```

If you're following along in FoxPro's Command Window, you'll see that Excel is visible, but there's no spreadsheet; just a gray screen. When the user starts Excel interactively, it's assumed that the user wants to jump right into a blank worksheet and begin typing. Automation does not assume anything! You have total control.

 All of the Excel examples assume that you've already created an Excel server object, accessed by a variable called oExcel.

Managing workbooks and worksheets

Time for some clarification that seems to get new Automation programmers: a collection object is indicated by a plural noun, and an object in the collection is the same noun in singular form. Workbooks (with an "s") is a collection of all the open Workbook (no "s") objects. A Workbook (no "s") object corresponds to an XLS file. Each Workbook has a collection called Worksheets (with an "s"). Each Worksheet (no "s") is displayed as a tab, with the tab headings near the bottom of the window.

Opening a new workbook

Since Excel opens without an available workbook, you need to add a new one or open an existing one. To create a new Workbook object, use the Add method of the Workbooks collection. The number of Worksheets a Workbook contains when added is controlled by the Application object's SheetsInNewWorkbook property (set manually in Excel by selecting

Tools|Options from the menu, choosing the General tab, and using the Sheets in New Workbook spinner). Setting this property affects all new workbooks added after the change (it does not affect those already open). Issuing the following command before opening a new workbook gives it four worksheets:

```
oExcel.SheetsInNewWorkbook = 4
```

Since users control this property, prepare your code to handle differences in this setting. Don't assume that the user hasn't played with the defaults; use the SheetsInNewWorkbook property to ensure you have enough worksheets.

Open a new worksheet using the Add method. It takes one optional parameter, which specifies a template file.

```
oWorkbook = oExcel.Workbooks.Add()
```

The variable oWorkbook points to your new workbook. There are several other ways to reference this Workbook object. One is to use the Application's ActiveWorkbook property: oExcel.ActiveWorkbook. Any time you add a new Workbook, it automatically becomes the active workbook. Another way to access this Workbook is through its index in the Workbooks collection. It is the first workbook opened, so it can be accessed as oExcel.Workbooks[1]. The Workbooks collection provides an alternate reference, which is the workbook name (appropriately stored in the Name property of a Workbook object).

The default name of a workbook is "Book" concatenated with the number corresponding to the order in which it was opened. "Book1" is the first Workbook object's Name property. The Name property is read-only. The only way to set it is to use the SaveAs method (see the section "Saving the workbook" later in this chapter).

Opening an existing workbook

There are two ways to open an existing workbook. The Open method assumes you already have a reference to the Excel Application object and will open an existing file. Visual FoxPro's GetObject() function gives you greater control over the visibility of the Workbook and does not require an Excel Application object reference.

The Open method of the Workbooks collection opens an existing workbook, given the filename:

```
oWorkbook = oExcel.Workbooks.Open("c:\my documents\sample.xls")
```

The filename is the only required parameter for the Open method. There are 12 other parameters (fortunately, all optional) to control whether links should be updated, provide a password, describe the layout of a text file to import, and other features. We invite you to check out the Help file for more information on these features.

An alternative way to open a workbook is to use the GetObject() function. GetObject() has two forms. In the first, you pass it the filename to open:

```
oWorkbook = GetObject("c:\my documents\sample.xls")
```

GetObject() returns a reference to the Workbook object (not the Application object, as with CreateObject()). If Excel was not running (or was running but not visible), you need to make the application visible to see it. To get to the Application object, use the Workbook's Application property, which references the Application object:

```
oWorkbook.Application.Visible = .T.
```

The new workbook is still not visible. Remember, Automation doesn't assume anything! The Workbook object is available to automate; its window is hidden. Again, there's a performance advantage to running all the Automation commands and then displaying it. To see the window, use the Window's Activate method (the example assumes that the window you're activating is the first window opened):

```
oWorkbook.Windows[1].Activate()
```

There are times when you want to hide the window while your Workbook is building. Assuming it is the active window, issue the oWorkbook.ActiveWindow.Close method.

The GetObject() function has an alternate syntax that allows you to prevent multiple occurrences of an object. If you are programming Office 97, this may be an important issue. You may want to use an already open instance of Excel to avoid using more memory to open another instance. In Office 2000, one of the new features is that there is only one instance of the application; the Office application itself provides better memory management. However, the GetObject() syntax still works for Excel 2000 (and opens it if it is not already open). Issuing the following opens Excel and returns a reference to the Application:

```
oExcel = GetObject("", 'Excel.Application')
```

Note that the syntax to open a filename returns a reference to the Workbook.

 If there are no instances of Excel 97 running, issuing GetObject(, 'Excel.Application') produces the following error: "OLE error code 0x800401e3: Operation unavailable." See the "Print Preview" section later in this chapter for an example of detecting if Excel is already running.

Saving the workbook

As you look through the list of methods for the Workbook object, you find references to Save and SaveAs. You would think that the Save method would be used to save any old workbook, and SaveAs would save it in a different format. However, in Excel (and PowerPoint, but not Word), the Save method takes no parameters. It uses a default filename consisting of the following:

- **The default file location**. Users can change this from the Tools|Options menu item, using the General Tab, by specifying the Default File Location. In Automation code, you check (or set) the DefaultFilePath property of the Application object.

This setting is saved when you close Excel; be sure to restore the user's settings if you change it.

- **The Workbook's Name property**. Remember, this defaults to "BookX" and is read-only.

- **The XLS extension**.

So, by default, the Save method saves the spreadsheet as something like "C:\My Documents\Book1.XLS." To name it something meaningful, use the SaveAs method, which allows you to specify a fully qualified filename. SaveAs also sets the Name property to the name part of the filename (not the path or the extension). SaveAs takes many optional parameters for such things as passwords, adding the file to the Most Recently Used list, backups, and so on. See the Help file for those parameters.

The most important parameter is the first one, which specifies the filename. Remember to fully qualify the path; if you don't, the default file location is used.

```
oWorkbook.SaveAs('c:\ExcelData\FirstTest.XLS')
```

An optional second parameter is the file format. If it's not specified, the default is the version of Excel in use (or, if the file was saved previously, the format in which the file was saved). The Help file lists 41 types (for Office 2000), including multiple versions for Lotus, dBASE, and Excel; HTML; DIF, SYLK and CSV, and others. These files require converters installed with Office; if the user elected not to install a particular converter, your error handler should be ready to deal with the resulting error. Some file formats save only the current worksheet; others save the entire workbook. The Excel Help file has excellent information if you look up the keyword "Save_As." In particular, the topic "File format converters supplied with Microsoft Excel" has valuable information about each of the file formats. In the VBA Excel Help file, there's a particularly good topic, "Saving Documents as Web Pages."

Avoiding Excel's user dialogs
When using SaveAs, saving to a file that already exists raises a user dialog, shown in **Figure 2** (of course, if the user has the Office Assistant on, it will explain the error). If the application is not Visible, the message box will pop up. If there is a visible window, both the window title bar and the button on the taskbar will flash. When the Excel window is minimized (or obscured) and the taskbar is in AutoHide mode (where you have to run the mouse down to the bottom of the screen), it appears to the user that you have a hang. If the user does see the flashing and selects Excel, then presses either "No" or "Cancel," the following error will result: "OLE IDispatch exception code 0 from Microsoft Excel: Unable to get the SaveAs property of the Workbook class." Be prepared to handle this error (#1428). Better yet, prevent this error from happening.

Figure 2*. The dialog that's raised when overwriting a file. Note that the user has three choices, and only "Yes" lets your program proceed without errors.*

There are a couple of steps you can take to thwart this error. First, check to see whether oWorkbook.Name is different from the first name of the file (no path, no extension). Use VFP's JUSTSTEM() function to return the first name of the file. If the two differ, use the SaveAs property to set the filename (and the Name property is then set to the first name of the file). If they are the same, use the Save command, which assumes you want to overwrite the file. Second, before you use the SaveAs feature, be sure that the filename in question doesn't exist:

```
MyFile = "c:\ExcelData\MyFile.XLS"

* Use JUSTFNAME() to calculate this in VFP 6.0;
* or the FoxTools function in previous versions
MyFileJustName = JustFName(MyFile)

* Determine whether to use SaveAs or Save
IF oWorkbook.Name <> MyFileJustName

   * IF the file already exists, delete it
   IF FILE(MyFile)
     * Warning: you may be deleting a file that doesn't
     * have anything to do with the situation at hand. Be
     * sure your app is aware of this.
     ERASE (MyFile)
   ENDIF

 * Save it without fear of the user dialog box
   oWorkbook.SaveAs(MyFile)

ELSE

   * Save it, since it's already been saved with SaveAs
   oWorkbook.Save()

ENDIF
```

Working with worksheets

Each Workbook can contain many Worksheets in the Workbook's Worksheets collection. Worksheets store the data. The Worksheets collection object (it's plural, so it's a collection) stores as many Worksheet (singular) objects as Excel can handle (in Excel 2000, the number of worksheets is limited by available memory). Just as with the other objects in collections, there are a number of ways to return a reference to a worksheet (there must be at least one Worksheet in a Workbook). There's the ActiveSheet property of the Workbook: oWorkbook.ActiveSheet. There's the index in the collection: oWorkbook.Worksheets[1]. Then there's the worksheet name, which defaults to "Sheet" plus the number corresponding to its index when opened: oWorkbook.Worksheets["Sheet1"]. The Name property of the worksheet is read/write, so you can set the name to something that the users will appreciate, as the name shows on the tab at the bottom of the sheet.

You can also grab a reference as you add a worksheet. Polymorphism is hard at work here; I'm sure you've guessed that you use the Add method. The syntax is a little different:

```
oWorksheet = oWorkbook.Worksheets.Add([oBefore |, oAfter], [nCount], [nType])
```

oBefore	Object	The object reference to the worksheet before which the new sheet is added. (Optional)
oAfter	Object	The object reference to the worksheet after which the new sheet is added. (Optional)
nCount	Numeric	The number of sheets to be added. (Default = 1) (Optional)
nType	Numeric	One of the sheet type constants. Unless you're writing Excel 4 macros, the only applicable constant is xlWorksheet (-4167), which is the default. (Optional)

If no parameters are passed, the new sheet is placed just before the ActiveSheet. You cannot specify both an oBefore object and an oAfter object, so just pass a blank parameter for the one you're not using. VBA allows named parameters, which make this kind of syntax much easier to use, where the parameter looks something like this: Before:=oMySheet. This syntax makes it easy to remember to pass only one of the parameters. But VFP does not support named parameters, so we must give them in the order listed. The following code sample shows how to add one worksheet before sheet one, then another after sheet one:

```
* Get a reference to the first worksheet
* oWorkbook is assumed to point to a workbook
oWorksheet1 = oWorkbook.Worksheets[1]

* Add a sheet before sheet one.
oWorksheet2 = oWorkbook.Worksheets.Add(oWorksheet1)

* Add a sheet after sheet one. Note the use of an empty
* first parameter.
oWorksheet3 = oWorkbook.Worksheets.Add(,oWorksheet1)
```

Adding a third parameter tells how many sheets you want added. If you want three sheets added before sheet one, then give the following command:

```
oWorkbook.Worksheets.Add(oWorksheet1, , 3)
```

Note that the second parameter is empty. The fourth parameter, nType, is really for backward compatibility. Leave out the fourth parameter, for simplicity.

Rows, columns, cells, and ranges

A worksheet is composed of cells, which have addresses in the form X9, where X is one or two letters indicating the column, and 9 is one or more digits indicating the row. The top left cell in a worksheet is A1. The 29th cell in the 32nd column is AF29.

A group of cells is called a *range*. Generally, a range is a rectangular group of contiguous cells, such as from D2 to F8. A range can also be a single cell. Using the Union method, you can concatenate ranges. A range is actually an object, and is accessed through the worksheet's Range property.

To specify a range, you use the Range property to specify the addresses for the range boundaries. For example, to access the data in cell C5, use:

```
? oExcel.ActiveSheet.Range("C5").Value
```

To create a range containing a rectangular range of cells from D12 to F19, use:

```
oRange = oExcel.ActiveSheet.Range("D12:F19")
```

Another way to access cells is by using the Rows, Columns, and Cells properties of Worksheet and Range. These properties takes appropriate index values and return a range containing the specified cells. To check the value of all cells in the third row of a range, you can write:

```
FOR nColumn = 1 TO oRange.Columns.Count
   ? oRange.Cells[3, nColumn].Value
ENDFOR
```

To see the contents of all cells in a range, use:

```
FOR nRow = 1 TO oRange.Rows.Count
   FOR nColumn = 1 TO oRange.Columns.Count
      ? oRange.Cells[nRow, nColumn].Value
   ENDFOR
ENDFOR
```

Note that the indexes for Cells list the row, then the column (just as arrays in VFP do), but the addresses of cells list the column first.

Relatively speaking

So far, we've used *absolute* addresses, meaning that the cell's address is relative to the first cell on the spreadsheet. We can also use *relative* addressing, which is based on a distance from the specified starting point. To create a range relative to another range, use the Offset property. This example creates a range 20 rows down and 30 rows to the left of oRange. The new range has the same size and shape:

```
oRange2 = oRange.Offset(20, 30)
```

Lots of ranges

Ranges don't have to consist of a single rectangle, either. Multiple groups can be listed when creating a range:

```
oRangeMixed = oExcel.ActiveSheet.Range("F21:F30, H21:H30")
```

The Union method combines several ranges into one. Here, the two ranges oRange and oRange2 are consolidated into a single range referenced by oBigRange:

```
oBigRange = oExcel.Union(oRange, oRange2)
```

Traversing a range with a loop like the preceding one doesn't work for a range composed of non-contiguous cells. The Areas collection has an entry for each rectangular portion (called an *area*) of the range, so to traverse all of the cells in a range, whether or not it's rectangular, you can use code like this:

```
FOR nArea = 1 TO oRange.Areas.Count
    FOR nRow = 1 TO oRange.Areas[nArea].Rows.Count
        FOR nColumn = 1 TO oRange.Areas[nArea].Columns.Count
            ? oRange.Areas[nArea].Cells[nRow, nColumn].Value
        ENDFOR
    ENDFOR
ENDFOR
```

Handling values and formulas

As the previous examples indicate, you can access the contents of a cell through its Value property. But, when working with spreadsheets, it's not always the value of a cell we're interested in. To access the formula contained in a cell, use the Formula property:

```
? oExcel.ActiveSheet.Range("C22").Formula
```

If a cell contains only a value, Formula returns the value as a string, while Value returns numbers as numbers. If there's a real formula in the cell, it's returned in the format you'd use to enter it in Excel, beginning with "–".

You can set values and formulas by assigning them to the appropriate cells:

```
oExcel.ActiveSheet.Range("C13").Value = 100
oExcel.ActiveSheet.Range("C22").Formula = "=SUM(C5:C20)"
```

Adding, copying, and moving data (including formulas)

While it's possible to copy VFP tables and views to XLS format using the COPY TO or EXPORT command, Automation provides more flexibility in the process, including the ability to put data from more than one table into a worksheet.

Populating the worksheet cell by cell

Automation allows data values to be input cell by cell. The usual method is to set up a SCAN loop, and set the values for each cell that correspond to the data in each record. Set a Range object to just the cells to be populated for the first record, and use the Columns collection to set the values of the cells. Just before the SCAN loops, use the Offset method to move the range down one row. The Offset method lets you move the Range for each iteration, without having to keep track of the row, like this:

```
SCAN
  * Do your processing and formatting here…

  * Move range down one row
  oRange = oRange.Offset(1,0)
ENDSCAN
```

Plugging in data using this method is extremely flexible, since you can populate the spreadsheet without having to create a master cursor or table, as you would to COPY TO or EXPORT. You have complete control of the cells and can conditionally decide on the cell values based upon the data. This is an excellent replacement for that report you need that requires four different conditional detail bands (when the report writer supports only one), or multiple columns that list the child records from different child tables (since we can't SET SKIP TO several tables at once).

When you have Excel pull in an XLS generated from a table or view, the column headers are automatically set to the field names. The users might appreciate "Order Num," "Date," and "Amount," instead of "cOrd_ID," "dOrd_Date," and "nOrd_Total." Explicitly setting the column headers (using the Value property of each cell) is necessary whether you pull in an XLS or add the data cell by cell.

Formulas are easy to program, as long as you are familiar with Excel's formulas. Whatever you type into the cell is what you generate in a character string. For example, to sum cells C6 to C11, set the value of a cell to "=SUM(C6:C11)". Just like using Excel interactively, if you forget the equal sign, the formula becomes a character string.

 The example shown in **Listing 1** demonstrates creating a spreadsheet by entering the data cell by cell. It uses the TasTrade Order History view and adds data for one customer's orders. This example is available as XLAddData.PRG in the Developer Download files available at www.hentzenwerke.com.

***Listing 1**. Adding data to a spreadsheet. This sample uses TasTrade's Order History view to create a simple spreadsheet for one customer's orders.*

```
* Put order information for one customer into an Excel worksheet

* Clean out any existing references to servers.
* This prevents memory loss to leftover instances.
RELEASE ALL LIKE o*

* For demonstration purposes, make oExcel available after
* this program executes.
PUBLIC oExcel
```

```
LOCAL oBook, oRange

* Open the Order History view, which contains
* a summary of orders for one customer.
OPEN DATABASE _SAMPLES + "\TASTRADE\DATA\Tastrade"
USE CUSTOMER IN 0
SELECT 0
USE "Order History" ALIAS OrderHistory

* Add a workbook, using default settings
oExcel = CREATEOBJECT("Excel.Application")
oExcel.Visible = .T.
oBook  = oExcel.Workbooks.Add()

WITH oExcel.ActiveSheet
   * Put customer name at top
   .Range("B2").Value = Customer.Company_Name

   * Put column headings in Row 5
   .Range("A5").Value = "Order Number"
   .Range("B5").Value = "Date"
   .Range("C5").Value = "Amount"

   oRange = .Range("A6:C6")
ENDWITH

* Loop through orders and send data
SCAN
   WITH oRange
      .Columns[1].Value = Order_Id
      .Columns[2].Value = Order_Date
      .Columns[3].Value = Ord_Total
   ENDWITH

   * Move range down one row
   oRange = oRange.Offset(1,0)
ENDSCAN

* Now add total row
nLastRow = oRange.Row && Row property always give first row of range
                     && This range has only one row
nTotalRow = nLastRow + 2

WITH oExcel.ActiveSheet
   .Cells( nTotalRow, 1 ) = "Total"

   * Need to convert nLastRow to char to use in formula for sum
   oExcel.ActiveSheet.Cells( nTotalRow, 3 ).Formula = ;
      "=SUM( C6:C" + LTRIM(STR(nLastRow)) + " )"
ENDWITH

USE IN OrderHistory
USE IN Customer
```

Figure 3 shows the results. The spreadsheet is successfully populated. However, some formatting is called for.

	A	B	C
1			
2		Alfreds Futterkiste	
3			
4			
5	Order Num	Date	Amount
6	953	2/7/95	$507.06
7	836	12/9/94	$835.43
8	703	9/6/94	$337.44
9	693	8/27/94	$851.22
10	644	7/19/94	########
11	63	8/21/92	$857.58
12			
13			
14	Total		########

Figure 3. *Results of the code shown in Listing 1. Literal headings, data from tables, and formulas are all successfully imported. A little formatting, discussed in subsequent sections, takes care of the display issues.*

Pulling in a generated XLS

This method of populating the data cell by cell performs well on small data sets. Once the data gets lengthy (say, more than 300 records), you are better off using EXPORT or COPY TO ... TYPE XL5, and pulling the data in. The code to do this is straightforward:

```
m.DataFile = "C:\My Documents\MyWorksheet"
SELECT DataTable
COPY TO (m.DataFile) TYPE XL5

* Open the data worksheet created by COPY TO...
oDataBook = oExcel.Workbooks.Open(m.DataFile + ".XLS")
```

Moving worksheets

When you use the COPY TO command, you create a workbook with a single worksheet. If you run into a need to combine several of these XLS files into a multi-sheet workbook, use the following trick: use the Worksheet object's Move method to move the sheet between workbooks. The following example assumes you want to move the first (only) worksheet from the oDataBook object (the one created from the XLS file) into the oOtherWorkBook object:

```
oDataBook.Worksheets(1).Move(oOtherWorkBook.ActiveSheet)
RELEASE oDataBook
```

This little trick moves the only worksheet from oDataBook to oOtherWorkBook. Since that leaves oDataBook with no worksheets, Excel automatically closes the workbook. All you need to do is delete the XLS file, and release the oDataBook variable to ensure that the reference to the object is released so the Application object closes gracefully.

Fill 'er up

There are times when you want to take a number or formula and replicate that formula a specific number of times. For example, you may want to copy a formula from the first cell to all of the cells in a column. The FillDown, FillUp, FillLeft, and FillRight methods of the Range object automatically copy the cell contents. For example, the FillDown method takes the cell at the top of the range and copies its contents down. The following code sets the first cell to a value of 1, then uses the FillDown method to copy the top cell of the range to every other cell in the range:

```
oExcel.ActiveSheet.Range("A1").Value = 1
oSheet.Range("A1:A10").FillDown
```

After running this code, the first 10 rows in column A are filled with the number 1. "Not so impressive, just copying a number," you say? Well, imagine if that cell were a complex formula, and you had to replicate that formula down a column. The FillDown command begins to look pretty good.

Excel has a feature that allows you to fill up ranges with automatically generated data. For example, you can number a list (say, from 1 to 50), or make a column of dates that represent Fridays for the next 12 weeks. The Range object's DataSeries method calculates the values of cells, according to the parameters of the series. The syntax is as follows:

```
oExcel.ActiveSheet.Range("A1").DataSeries(nRowCol, nType, nDate, nStep,
                                          xStop, xTrend)
```

nRowCol	Numeric	A value indicating whether the data series is entered in Rows or Columns. If omitted, it uses the shape of the specified range. (Optional)
		xlRows 1 xlColumns 2
nType	Numeric	A value indicating the type of series. (Optional)
		xlDataSeriesLinear -4132 xlGrowth 2
		xlChronological 3 xlAutoFill 4
nDate	Numeric	Used only if nType is xlChronological (3). A value indicating the kind of chronological series. (Optional)
		xlDay (default) 1 xlWeekDay 2
		xlMonth 3 xlYear 4
nStep	Numeric	A value representing the increment between each value in the series. The default is 1. (Optional)
xStop	Numeric or date	A value representing the value at which to stop. The type can be numeric or a date (or whatever type of series you are building). The default is the end of the range. (Optional)
xTrend	Logical or Numeric	True (or -1) to set a linear trend line (regression analysis) to forecast future trends, False (or 0) to create a standard series. The default is False (or 0). (Optional)

The following code creates a simple series, numbering the rows from 1 to 50. Note that if you don't fill in a value in the first cell of the series, there is nothing with which to start the series, and the command will appear to execute without error, but the resulting range is blank.

```
#DEFINE xlColumns            2
#DEFINE xlDataSeriesLinear  -4132
#DEFINE xlDay                1
oExcel.ActiveSheet.Range("A1").Value = 1
```

```
oExcel.ActiveSheet.Range("A1:A100").DataSeries(xlColumns, ;
    xlDataSeriesLinear, xlDay, 1, 50, .F.)
```

This next code example shows how to format a series of dates. This example shows a greater step value, calculating dates that are a week apart (actually, it's a list of Fridays between the starting date, a Friday, and the end of the year).

```
#DEFINE xlColumns         2
#DEFINE xlChronological   3
#DEFINE xlDay             1

oExcel.ActiveSheet.Range("B1").Value = "10/22/1999"
oExcel.ActiveSheet.Range("B1:B100").DataSeries(xlColumns, ;
    xlChronological, xlDay, 7, "12/31/99", .F.)
```

 Excel interprets the "12/31/99" string as a date data type. You could also use hyphens, too. Excel does some conversion on dates, as they are stored as a numeric value, called a "serial value." This value represents the number of days since December 31, 1899. Therefore, a value of 1 is January 1, 1900.

Excel uses formatting to display the cell as a date value, or you can select a numeric format to see the serial value. Additionally, time values are stored as a fraction of a day; a value of 1.5 is 12 PM on 1/1/1900. Again, you'd use Excel's formatting features to display the date, time, or both. See the section "Formatting values" later in this chapter for the details on formatting dates and times.

Note that this method calculates the dates and enters them as a value, not as a formula. If you change one date, don't expect the others to change.

Formatting

Getting FoxPro data into Excel is pretty cool. But it's even cooler to make it look good. Excel has a rich range of formatting options for a cell, including changing font attributes, formatting the way a value looks (such as percentages or negative numbers), and setting borders and shading.

Column widths and alignment

 Let's revisit the spreadsheet we created in Figure 3, using the XLAddData.PRG in the Developer Download files available at www.hentzenwerke.com. The formatting issue that first jumps out at us is the series of cells filled with pound signs, indicating that the column width is too small.

One really cool method is AutoFit, which works on the columns within a given range. In Figure 3, we can AutoFit the column widths for the first three columns. If, however, we ask for the whole range, the title in cell B2, "Alfreds Futterkiste" causes column B to be much wider than necessary, making it hard to read across each row. While the AutoFit method affects all columns in the range, it only calculates the maximum width for those cells actually contained in the calling range. By specifying A5:C14, it calculates the maximum width for columns A, B, and C, but only using those cells in rows 5 through 14. The AutoFit method takes no parameters. Here's an example of using AutoFit:

```
oSheet.Range("A5:C14").Columns.AutoFit()
```

As **Figure 4** shows, it looks a bit better. While AutoFit generates a column width to fit the longest cell, it's just barely wide enough for the longest cell. You may want to explicitly set a column or two.

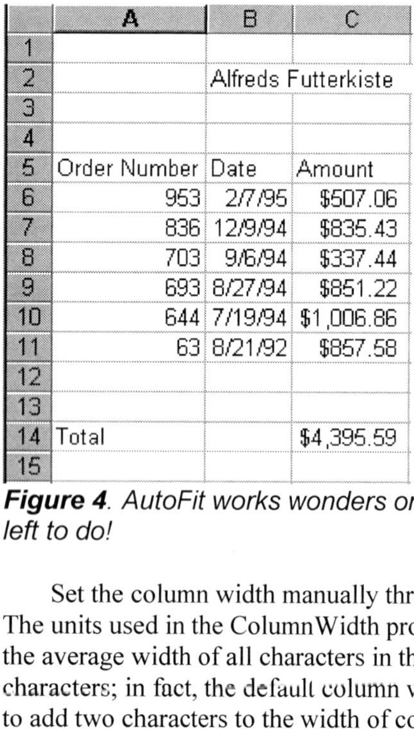

	A	B	C
1			
2		Alfreds Futterkiste	
3			
4			
5	Order Number	Date	Amount
6	953	2/7/95	$507.06
7	836	12/9/94	$835.43
8	703	9/6/94	$337.44
9	693	8/27/94	$851.22
10	644	7/19/94	$1,006.86
11	63	8/21/92	$857.58
12			
13			
14	Total		$4,395.59
15			

Figure 4. AutoFit works wonders on columns. But there's still a lot of formatting left to do!

Set the column width manually through the Columns collection's ColumnWidth property. The units used in the ColumnWidth property are in characters, where one character is equal to the average width of all characters in the default font. The property can be set to fractional characters; in fact, the default column width is 8.43 characters. The following code shows how to add two characters to the width of column B.

```
WITH oExcel.ActiveSheet.Columns[2]
   .ColumnWidth =.ColumnWidth + 2
ENDWITH
```

Alignment

By default, character data is left-aligned, while numeric and date/time data is right-aligned, and all are aligned at the bottom of the cell. Range's HorizontalAlignment and VerticalAlignment properties store the values for the alignment settings. As with most Office properties, there are a series of constants. **Figure 5** shows the constant names, values, and an example cell formatted with the alignment. Both HorizontalAlignment and VerticalAlignment act on the same cell, which allows a large number of possibilities for aligning the text in cells.

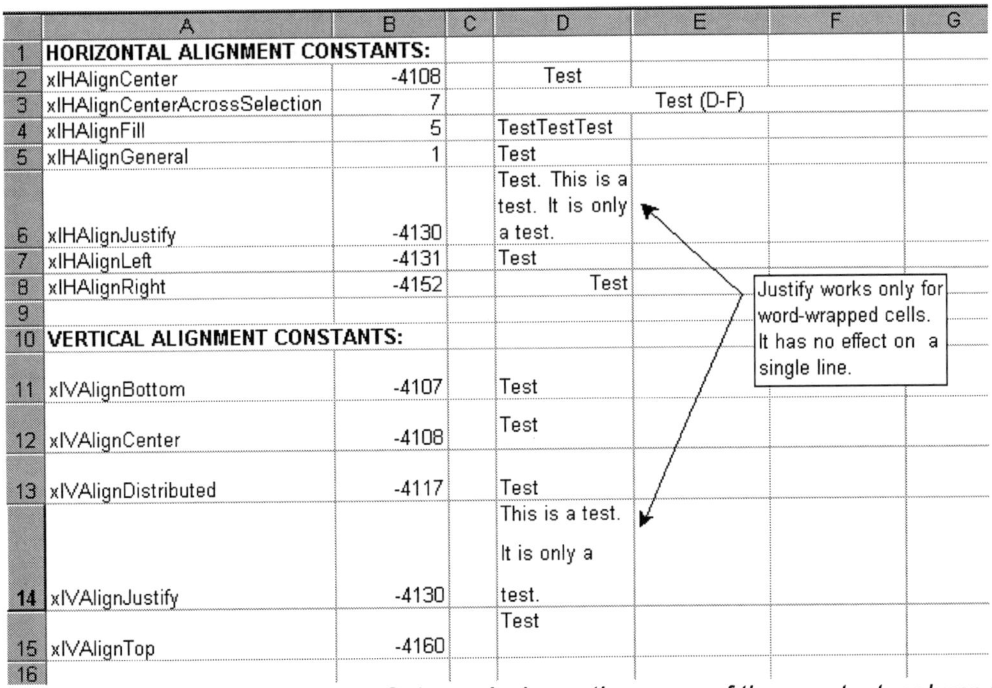

	A	B	C	D	E	F	G
1	HORIZONTAL ALIGNMENT CONSTANTS:						
2	xlHAlignCenter	-4108		Test			
3	xlHAlignCenterAcrossSelection	7			Test (D-F)		
4	xlHAlignFill	5		TestTestTest			
5	xlHAlignGeneral	1		Test			
6	xlHAlignJustify	-4130		Test. This is a test. It is only a test.			
7	xlHAlignLeft	-4131		Test			
8	xlHAlignRight	-4152		Test			
9							
10	VERTICAL ALIGNMENT CONSTANTS:						
11	xlVAlignBottom	-4107		Test			
12	xlVAlignCenter	-4108		Test			
13	xlVAlignDistributed	-4117		Test			
14	xlVAlignJustify	-4130		This is a test. It is only a test.			
15	xlVAlignTop	-4160		Test			
16							

Callout: Justify works only for word-wrapped cells. It has no effect on a single line.

Figure 5. Alignment constants. Column A shows the name of the constant, column B shows the value, and column D shows a formatted cell containing the word "Test" (except for the Justify constants, which require a word-wrapped cell to show an effect). Note that the Center Across Selection alignment is centered over three columns.

You'll see that xlHAlignGeneral and xlHAlignLeft look similar; that's because the cell contains text. The General format is the default format, which left-aligns text but right-aligns numbers and dates. xlHAlignLeft and xlHAlignRight force the alignment to the left or right, regardless of the datatype contained in the cell.

Looking again at the TasTrade example, we can center the client name over the first three columns, and then format the column headings using the following code:

```
#DEFINE xlHAlignCenterAcrossSelection    7
#DEFINE xlHAlignCenter                -4108

* Center the client name across the first three columns.
oSheet.Range("A2:C2").HorizontalAlignment = xlHAlignCenterAcrossSelection

* Center each of the column titles.
oSheet.Range("A5:C5").HorizontalAlignment = xlHAlignCenter
```

If you want to explore using the Justify alignment, the text must wrap within the cell (otherwise, it will simply left-justify the text). Use the WrapText property to set the cell to wrap words:

```
oSheet.Range("A5").WrapText = .T.
```

Fonts

Excel's Font object is much like Word's, with properties for Name, Size, Bold, Italic, and so forth. In Excel, fonts are controlled through the Font tab on the Format Cells dialog (see **Figure 6**). If we compare this dialog to Word's dialog box, we find that Excel has a subset of the Font properties that Word has. Fortunately, most of the properties that Excel's Font object has are found in Word, and are named similarly.

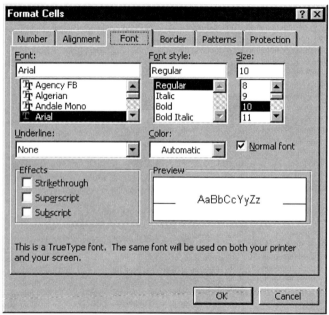

Figure 6*. The Excel Font tab on the Format Cells dialog. Excel provides a wide variety of font formatting features.*

To access the Font object, use the Range object's Font property (quite a few other objects, such as the various text objects on a chart, use the Font property, too). To set a range (in this example, the range is cell B2) to 14-point bold Times New Roman, use the following:

```
WITH oSheet.Range("B2").Font
    .Name = "Times New Roman"
    .Size = 14
    .Bold = .T.
ENDWITH
```

Table 1 shows the font properties most commonly used in Excel. There are a few others available, though not nearly as many as there are in Word's Font object. Look in the Help file under "Font Object" for more properties.

Table 1. Font properties. The Font object controls the appearance of the font from the font face to its size, style, and much more. This table shows the more common properties. Check Help for additional settings.

Property	Type	Description
Name	Character	The name of the font.
Size	Numeric	The size of the font in points.
Color	RGB Color	The color of the font.
Bold	Numeric or Logical	Indicates whether the text is bold.
Italic	Numeric or Logical	Indicates whether the text is italic.
Underline	Numeric	The type of underline. xlUnderlineStyleDouble -4119 xlUnderlineStyleDoubleAccounting 5 xlUnderlineStyleNone -4142 xlUnderlineStyleSingle 2 xlUnderlineStyleSingleAccounting 4
Superscript, Subscript	Numeric or Logical	Indicates whether the text is superscript or subscript, respectively.

Excel has some properties that we list as "Numeric or Logical." These properties can be set with VFP's logical values of .T. and .F., or -1 (for true) and 0 (for false). However, when you query these properties, Excel returns a numeric value. So while you can turn on italics with oRange.Font.Italic = .T. or oRange.Font.Italic = -1, you must remember that it returns a numeric, as in IF oRange.Font.Italic = -1...ENDIF.

Formatting values

Excel offers a feature to format numbers that acts like FoxPro's InputMask property on steroids. It's found on the Format Cells dialog, pictured in **Figure 7**. There are 12 categories, with each category having as many as 31 predefined codes. Plus, if you can't find one that meets your needs, you can define your own.

You're probably expecting to see a long list of properties with a long list of constants representing each number format. Nope, not this time. There's only one property, and that's the Range's NumberFormat property. It gets set to a string representing the format, much like the way VFP's InputMask property works. You can see some sample strings if you select the Custom category on the Number tab in the Format Cells dialog box (see Figure 7).

The most commonly used codes for format strings are shown in **Table 2**. As in VFP's InputMask codes, the pound sign (#) displays a number, and a comma puts in a thousands separator. Many symbols, such as %, $, and € (the Euro symbol), are literals; you still need to put in placeholders to display the numbers. Codes that pertain to the same data type can be mixed and matched to precisely set the formatting of a cell.

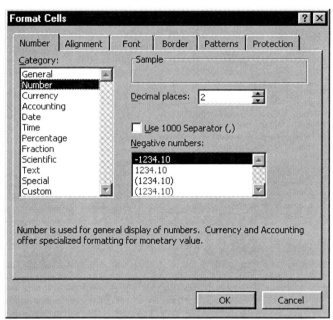

Figure 7*. The Number tab on the Format Cells dialog in Excel. Like FoxPro's InputMask property on steroids, Excel offers seemingly unlimited ways to format the way the data looks.*

Table 2*. Commonly used codes for formatting numbers. There are many more available; see the Help topic "About number formats" in the regular Excel Help file.*

Code	Description	Example value	Example string	Example output
"General"	Resets to the default format.	1234.5	"General"	1234.5
#	Displays a number (blank if a leading or trailing 0).	1234.5	"#####.#"	1234.5
0	Displays a number, including leading or trailing 0's.	1234.5	"00000.00"	01234.50
,	Adds a Thousands separator.	1234.5	"##,###.##"	1,234.5
%	Displays numbers as a percentage.	.08	"##%"	8%
$	Inserts the dollar sign.	1.25	"$##.00"	$1.25
€	Inserts the Euro symbol.	3.00	CHR(128) + "##.00"	€3.00
M	Displays the month as a number from 1–12.	10/22/99	"M"	10
Mmm	Displays the month as a three-character abbreviation.	10/22/99	"Mmm"	Oct
D	Displays the day as a number from 1–31.	10/22/99	"D"	22
Ddd	Displays the day as a three-character day of week.	10/22/99	"Ddd"	Fri
Yy	Displays a two-digit year.	10/22/99	"Yy"	99

Let's look at some numeric examples. These examples assume you have a blank sheet, referenced by oSheet. The results of all the numeric code examples are shown in **Figure 8**, at the end of the numeric examples. For our first example, let's format 1234.5 to appear as 1,234.50:

```
oSheet.Range("A1").Value = "Format a Cell"
oSheet.Columns[1].ColumnWidth = 15
oSheet.Range("A2").Value = 1234.5
oSheet.Range("A2").NumberFormat = "##,###.#0"
```

If it should be currency, with a thousands separator—like $1,234.50—try the following NumberFormat:

```
oSheet.Range("A3").Value = 1234.5
oSheet.Range("A3").NumberFormat = "$##,###.#0"
```

For those of you who use different currencies, use the ASCII code representing your currency symbol: € is CHR(128), £ is CHR(163), and ¥ is CHR(162).

Excel allows four sections of codes, sort of like an inline case statement, which are: positive numbers, negative numbers, zero values, and text. Specify a string for each section, separated by a semi-colon. Here's an example of how to format negative numbers with parentheses in lieu of a minus sign, using column B:

```
oSheet.Range("B1").Value = "Format +/-"
oSheet.Columns[2].ColumnWidth = 15
oSheet.Range("B2").Value = 1234.5
oSheet.Range("B3").Value = 0
oSheet.Range("B4").Value = -1234.5
oSheet.Range("B2:B4").NumberFormat = "##,###.#0;(##,###.#0)"
```

Cell B2 displays 1,234.50, and B4 displays (1,234.50). One of the issues we've encountered a lot is how to handle zeroes—in this case, the zero displays as ".0," but in many cases, we want the cell left blank. Using the same sequence of numbers, this time in column C, try this:

```
oSheet.Range("C1").Value = "Format +/-/0"
oSheet.Columns[3].ColumnWidth = 15
oSheet.Range("C2").Value = 1234.5
oSheet.Range("C3").Value = 0
oSheet.Range("C4").Value = -1234.5
oSheet.Range("C2:C4").NumberFormat = "##,###.#0;(##,###.#0);;"
```

If you look at Figure 8, you'll see the results of leaving the third section of the NumberFormat string blank: nothing displays for zeroes. What if you want to set a zero-value cell to show "N/A"? Not hard at all. Change the format string to this:

```
[##,###.#0;(##,###.#0); "N/A";]
```

Beware: Excel needs literal strings delimited in double quotes only, so be sure to delimit the whole FoxPro string with square brackets or single quotes. Should you forget, you'll get an error indicating that Excel is "unable to set the NumberFormat property."

The fourth section of NumberFormat allows you to format text cells. Text formats a bit differently; the entire value of the cell's text string is denoted by the @ sign, and you can place literal text (delimited by double quotes only) on either side of the @ sign. Why would you want to add to text? Perhaps your data holds only the client name, and it should say "Client Totals." Here's an example that includes formatting the text (see Figure 8 for the results):

```
* Enter some data
oSheet.Range("A6").Value = "January"
oSheet.Range("A7").Value = 102
oSheet.Range("B7").Value = "Widget"
oSheet.Range("A8").Value = -24
oSheet.Range("B8").Value = "Whatzit"
oSheet.Range("A9").Value = 0
oSheet.Range("B9").Value = "Whatnot"
oSheet.Range("A10").Value = "February"
oSheet.Range("A11").Value = 123
oSheet.Range("B11").Value = "Widget"
oSheet.Range("A12").Value = 0
oSheet.Range("B12").Value = "Whatzit"
oSheet.Range("A13").Value = 332
oSheet.Range("B13").Value = "Whatnot"

* Format the first column, using all four sections.
oSheet.Range("A6:A13").NumberFormat = [$###;($###);"No"; @" Totals"]

* Format the second column for text only. Literal
* strings are placed on both sides of the cell's actual value.
oSheet.Range("B6:B13").NumberFormat = ["Total "@" Sales"]
```

	A	B	C
1	Format a Cell	Format +/-	Format +/-/0
2	1,234.50	1,234.50	1,234.50
3	$1,234.50	.0	
4		(1,234.50)	(1,234.50)
5			
6	January Totals		
7	$102	Total Widget Sales	
8	($24)	Total Whatzit Sales	
9	No	Total Whatnot Sales	
10	February Totals		
11	$123	Total Widget Sales	
12	No	Total Whatzit Sales	
13	$332	Total Whatnot Sales	
14			
15			

Figure 8. *The combined results of the numeric formatting examples. Cell A2 shows basic formatting; A3 shows currency; B2:B4 format positive and negative numbers differently; and C2:C4 differentiate positive, zero, and negative values. A6:B13 show the use of all four formatting sections in column A, and column B's text is formatted, too.*

Dates also have a number of formats. By using "D" for day, "M" for month, and "Yy" for year, along with any literals, you can conjure up nearly any format. When D and M are used, the day and month are displayed as a number, without a leading zero. Use Dd or Mm to provide a leading zero. Three characters, as in Ddd or Mmm, provide a three-character abbreviation, as in "Fri" or "Jan." Four characters, as in Dddd or Mmmm, display the full name, as in "Friday" or "January." A string of Yyyy gives a Y2K-compliant, four-digit year. If you want a military format date, try the following:

```
oSheet.Range("A1").Value = "01/01/2000"
oSheet.Range("A1").NumberFormat = "Dd-Mmm-Yyyy"
```

The cell displays "01-Jan-2000." What if you wanted it to read, "Saturday, January 1, 2000"? Change the format string to "Dddd, Mmmm D, Yyyy" to display the desired format.

There are many combinations and permutations for formatting cells. Rather than boring you for the next several pages by attempting to explain every detail, we'll just point you to the Excel Help file (the regular Excel Help, not the VBA Help), which covers this in detail. Search for the topic "About number formats," which will explain everything you've ever wanted to know about NumberFormat strings.

Borders

The Borders collection contains Border objects, with each object representing the eight borders of the cell. This collection wouldn't be complete without a series of constants describing the eight different borders: xlDiagonalDown (5), xlDiagonalUp (6), xlEdgeBottom (9), xlEdgeLeft (7), xlEdgeRight (10), xlEdgeTop (8), xlInsideHorizontal (12), and xlInsideVertical (11). The xlEdge borders represent the outer perimeter of a range of cells. The xlInside borders are those that are on the interior of a multi-cell range. If the range is a single cell, the xlInside borders are ignored.

Table 3 shows the properties for each border. The LineStyle and Weight properties are set through constant values.

Table 3. Border properties. Borders can be placed around any range, and their appearance can be altered with these properties.

Property	Type	Description			
Color	RGB Color	The color of the border.			
LineStyle	Numeric	The numeric value corresponding to a preset line style.			
		xlContinuous	1	xlDot	-4118
		xlDash	-4115	xlDouble	-4119
		xlDashDot	4	xlLineStyleNone	-4142
		xlDashDotDot	5	xlSlantDashDot	13
Weight	Numeric	The width of the line. This uses constants, not points.			
		xlHairline	1	xlMedium	-4138
		xlThin	2	xlThick	4

If you want to put a dotted border on the bottom of a range of cells, use this code:

```
#DEFINE xlEdgeBottom     9
#DEFINE xlDot           -4118

oSheet.Range("A2:C2").Borders(xlEdgeBottom).LineStyle = xlDot
```

There are a few situations we've found with this process. For the most part, you can set any LineStyle you want. When you set the width, the results become unpredictable, usually resulting in a continuous line, and occasionally in a random color. For example, the following code produces a thick solid line, rather than a thick dash-dot line:

```
#DEFINE xlEdgeBottom     9
#DEFINE xlDashDot        4
#DEFINE xlThick          4

oSheet.Range("A2:C2").Borders(xlEdgeBottom).LineStyle = xlDashDot
oSheet.Range("A2:C2").Borders(xlEdgeBottom).Weight = xlThick
```

What seems to work is any Weight with a continuous line, or any LineStyle without setting the Weight property. In VFP, setting the BorderWidth property to anything greater than 1 implies a single-line border. What we've found with Excel's borders may parallel VFP's design. We've not found any documentation one way or the other on Excel's design.

Shading

Shading a range of cells is accomplished with the Interior object. Note that in Word, a Shading object is used, and in PowerPoint, a Fill object is used.

Table 4 shows the properties of the Interior object. Basically, you select a pattern, then apply a PatternColor to the pattern, and the Color property becomes the background color. However, it's tricky to predict the outcome. Just because the Color property is the background color does not mean that it is the less predominant color. **Figure 9** illustrates this situation. White (actually, the automatic color) is the Color setting, and the PatternColor setting is black. Looking at the samples of the available patterns, you can see that some are predominantly white, and some are predominantly black.

It's obvious that Excel gives us lots of control over the patterning a cell. Here's a design caution: if you attempt to pattern a cell with anything other than a solid color, any text that's under about 36 points and appears on that pattern is difficult to read. We haven't found a terrific business need for patterns other than solid.

Actually, to shade a cell, you don't need to do anything other than change the Interior.Color property. Since it functions as a background color, and there's no pattern to display, the cell is shaded, and it only takes one line of code (rather than setting the Pattern to xlPatternSolid, and then setting the PatternColor). Shading is accomplished like this:

```
oSheet.Range("A14:C14").Interior.Color = RGB(192,192,192) && Light Gray
```

Table 4. *Interior decorating. The Interior object has several properties to change the display of the cell.*

Property	Type	Description
Color	RGB Color	The background color that shows through the pattern. If the pattern is a fine pattern (like the xlPatternLight patterns), this color becomes the predominant color, as the pattern itself does not dominate the cell.
InvertIfNegative	Logical or Numeric	Whether the pattern is inverted if the value of the shaded cell is negative. True (.T. or 1) to invert if negative, False (.F. or 0) to remain the same when negative.
Pattern	Numeric	Patterns the range with one of 20 predefined patterns. xlPatternAutomatic -4105 xlPatternHorizontal -4128 xlPatternChecker 9 xlPatternLightDown 13 xlPatternCrissCross 16 xlPatternLightHorizontal 11 xlPatternDown -4121 xlPatternLightUp 14 xlPatternGray8 18 xlPatternLightVertical 12 xlPatternGray16 17 xlPatternNone -4142 xlPatternGray25 -4124 xlPatternSemiGray75 10 xlPatternGray50 -4125 xlPatternSolid 1 xlPatternGray75 -4126 xlPatternUp -4162 xlPatternGrid 15 xlPatternVertical -4166
PatternColor	RGB Color	The foreground color of the pattern. The Color property provides the background color.

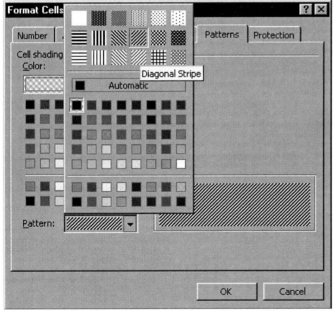

Figure 9. *The Format Cells dialog, with the Diagonal Stripe pattern selected. Note that the PatternColor is black, and the Color is Automatic, or white (it's obscured by the pattern window). Looking at all the pattern samples, it's easy to see the effect of the Color and PatternColor properties.*

Styles

Like Word, Excel has the ability to work with styles. Styles are quite useful to standardize the look of your spreadsheet. By assigning all the formatting properties—including fonts, alignment, numeric formatting, color, borders, and shading—to a single Style, you don't have to spend time cutting and pasting code over and over again (and hoping that you cut and pasted the right formatting code).

The Workbook object has a Styles property, which returns a Styles collection object. The Styles collection starts out with a few default styles, called Normal, Comma, Comma[0], Currency, Currency[0], and Percent. The styles with the "[0]" suffix omit the two decimal places after the number. You can also define your own styles. The Normal style is the default style. Use this to return to the default. Use the others to quickly set the most common numeric formatting.

While the default styles are helpful, they're rather plain. Our clients demand pizzazz, so we want something a little more sophisticated than just commas in our numbers. Since Office is polymorphic, and the Style object belongs to the Styles collection, we know to look for an Add method. Once the Style is added, we can change its attributes. All of the formatting discussed in this chapter has been illustrated with the Range object, but it also works on the Style object.

The following code creates a Style suitable for a title. The style uses 14-point Times New Roman, makes it bold, centers it, and shades it in light gray.

```
#DEFINE xlHAlignCenter  -4108
#DEFINE xlVAlignCenter  -4108
#DEFINE xlEdgeBottom        9
#DEFINE xlEdgeTop          10
#DEFINE xlEdgeRight         8
#DEFINE xlEdgeLeft          7
#DEFINE xlDouble        -4119
#DEFINE xlMedium        -4138


* Add the new style
oSheet.Parent.Styles.Add("Title")

* Change the attribute of the style
WITH oSheet.Parent.Styles("Title")

  * Font
  .Font.Name = "Times New Roman"
  .Font.Size = 14
  .Font.Bold = .T.

  * Alignment
  .HorizontalAlignment = xlHAlignCenter
  .VerticalAlignment   = xlVAlignCenter

  * Shading
  .Interior.Color = RGB(220, 220, 220)   &&  Light Gray

ENDWITH

* Set cell A1 to have a value, then apply the style.
oSheet.Range("A1").Value = "Testing"
oSheet.Range("A1").Style = "Title"
```

The only aspect that seems radically different between Styles and Ranges is the Border object. The whole series of constants changes, and it's not documented in the Help file. The only way to find out about it is to run the macro recorder and verify that the constants it's recording for Styles are very different from those used for Ranges. The constants needed for the Border object are: xlLeft (-4131), xlTop (-4160), xlBottom (-4107), xlRight (-4152), xlDiagonalUp (6), and xlDiagonalDown (5). Note that the inside borders are missing; we're not sure where they've gone.

If it's any consolation, there is a bit of consistency with borders. The same bug that affects the Weight property also happens with Styles, too.

Output

Once you have a good-looking spreadsheet, inevitably, your users will want it printed.

Page Setup

Excel has a robust set of features used to print out a page, as evidenced by **Figure 10**, the Page Setup dialog. Excel's Page Setup dialog corresponds to its PageSetup object. Each worksheet (and each chart) has its own PageSetup object.

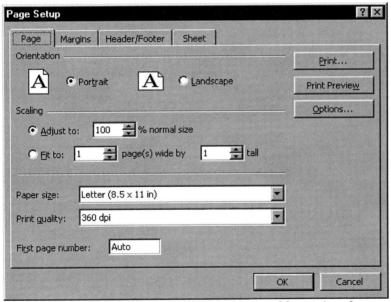

Figure 10. *Setting up the pages. This is one of four tabs of properties used when printing.*

The PageSetup has 35 properties and one method…that's robust! Quite a number of them are useful for everyday tasks. **Table 5** shows most of the properties—they are grouped by the tab on which they're found on the Page Setup dialog (a helpful order if you're using the macro recorder to help you).

Table 5. *The PageSetup object's properties. Reminder: the properties listed as Logical or Numeric can be set with either logical or numeric values, but they should be tested against numeric values only.*

Property	Type	Description
Orientation	Numeric	The orientation of printing on the paper. xlPortrait 1 xlLandscape 2
Zoom	Numeric or Logical	If numeric, applies the percentage (between 10 and 400) to scale the worksheet. If set to False (.F. or 0), FitToPagesTall and/or FitToPagesWide are used to scale the worksheet.
FitToPagesTall	Numeric or Logical	Scales the vertical print area to fit this many pages. If False (.F. or 0), no vertical scaling occurs. Ignored if the Zoom property is numeric and not zero.
FitToPagesWide	Numeric or Logical	Scales the horizontal print area to fit this many pages. If False (.F. or 0), no horizontal scaling occurs. Ignored if the Zoom property is numeric and not zero.
PaperSize	Numeric	One of about 45 preset paper sizes. Some of the most common are: xlPaperLetter 1 xlPaperLegal 5 xlPaperA4 9 xlEnvelope9 19
FirstPageNumber	Numeric	The page number used to start numbering pages. The default is 1.
TopMargin	Numeric	The distance from the top of the page to the top of the first line of text, in points.
HeaderMargin	Numeric	The distance from the top of the page to the top of the first line of text in the header, in points.
LeftMargin	Numeric	The distance from the left edge of the page to the left edge of the text, in points.
RightMargin	Numeric	The distance from the right edge of the page to the right edge of the text, in points.
BottomMargin	Numeric	The distance from the bottom edge of the page to the bottom line of text, in points.
FooterMargin	Numeric	The distance from the bottom edge of the page to the bottom line of the footer text, in points.
CenterHorizontally	Logical or Numeric	True (.T. or -1) to center the text horizontally on the page; False (.F. or 0) to start printing at the left margin.
CenterVertically	Logical or Numeric	True (.T. or -1) to center the text vertically on the page; False (.F. or 0) to start printing at the top margin.
LeftHeader	Character	These properties set the left, center, or right portions of the header or footer, as indicated. They can be set to a character string or codes, or a combination of the two. A complete set of codes is in the Excel VBA Help file under the topic "Formatting Codes for Headers and Footers."
CenterHeader	Character	
RightHeader	Character	
LeftFooter	Character	Prints the current date &D Prints the name of the file &F Prints the name of the active worksheet &A
CenterFooter	Character	Prints the current page number &P Prints the ampersand character &&
RightFooter	Character	Prints the total number of pages in the document &N
PrintArea	Character	The range of cells to print—for example, "A1:Z40". If blank, it will print them all.
PrintGridlines	Logical or Numeric	True (.T. or -1) to print the cells' gridlines, False (.F. or 0) to omit them.

Table 5, *continued*

Property	Type	Description
BlackAndWhite	Logical or Numeric	True (.T. or -1) to print colors in high-contrast shades of gray for the best possible printing on a black and white printer; False (.F. or 0) to print in color, or to let the colors print in whatever shades of gray the printer is programmed for.
Draft	Logical or Numeric	True (.T. or -1) to print the data without graphics; False (.F. or 0) prints everything.
Order	Numeric	The order in which pages are printed and numbered when a worksheet is too big to fit on one page. xlDownThenOver 1 xlOverThenDown 2

These properties are pretty straightforward. Here's some sample code that ensures that the spreadsheet will print on one sheet, with half-inch margins, in landscape orientation, with page numbers in the upper-left header.

```
#DEFINE xlLandscape   2
#DEFINE autoIn2Pts   72

oSheet.PageSetup.Orientation = xlLandscape
oSheet.PageSetup.FitToPagesTall = 1
oSheet.PageSetup.FitToPagesWide = 1
oSheet.PageSetup.TopMargin    = .5 * autoIn2Pts
oSheet.PageSetup.BottomMargin = .5 * autoIn2Pts
oSheet.PageSetup.LeftMargin   = .5 * autoIn2Pts
oSheet.PageSetup.RightMargin  = .5 * autoIn2Pts
oSheet.PageSetup.LeftHeader = "Page &P"
```

Print Preview

In some of our Automation applications, we display the final document in Print Preview mode. This lets the user analyze the data, then decide whether it's important enough to print, or if the data needs more review. Excel's printing is based on the worksheets, not the workbooks. You'll invoke the PrintPreview method from the Sheet object. This also means that you will see one sheet in the PrintPreview; you cannot scroll between sheets in a workbook (while Excel users are quite used to this, it comes as a shock to VFP developers, who can scroll through the whole report, and Word users, who can scroll through the whole document).

To invoke the Print Preview mode, use the sheet's PrintPreview method:

```
oSheet.PrintPreview()
```

However, this puts FoxPro in a wait state; the user needs to click on either the flashing window title or the flashing button on the menu bar. Once the user has done so, the PrintPreview window is displayed. But FoxPro cannot continue until the PrintPreview window is closed. Be sure that the Excel Application object's window is in a Normal state before issuing the PrintPreview command, and even then, the user may not see any of the flashing items and assume that the app has hung.

An alternative syntax, using the PrintOut method and the PrintPreview parameter, still suffers from the same problem.

```
oSheet.PrintOut(,,,.T.)
```

There is a way to display the PrintPreview screen, but it requires the user to close the PrintPreview window before your FoxPro app can continue. It uses some API calls to manipulate the windows. The FindWindowA function obtains a window handle to the application based on its class and its window name. **Table 6** shows the classes of the Office applications (valid for 97 and 2000), as well as the various versions of FoxPro. The SetWindowPos function sets the window to be the topmost window (or not) based on the window handle. You must remember to set the window back to NoTopMost, to ensure that other apps can be brought forward.

Table 6. *Class names used in FindWindowA. Passed to the API along with the window caption, it returns a valid window handle, which you can use to manipulate the window with other APIs.*

Application	Class
Excel 97 and 2000	XLMAIN
Outlook 97 and 2000	rctrl_renwnd32
PowerPoint 97	PP97FrameClass
PowerPoint 2000	PP9FrameClass
Word 97 and 2000	OpusApp
VFP 3.0 and 5.0	Fox4000001
VFP 6.0	VFP66400000

```
#DEFINE swp_nosize       1
#DEFINE swp_nomove       2
#DEFINE hwnd_topmost    -1
#DEFINE hwnd_notopmost  -2

* FindWindowA returns the window handle from the window's caption
DECLARE LONG FindWindowA IN WIN32API STRING class, STRING title
* SetWindowPos moves the window to the top, using the window handle
DECLARE SetWindowPos IN WIN32API LONG HWND, LONG hwndafter, ;
        LONG x, LONG Y, LONG cx, LONG cy, LONG flags

* Capture the window handles for both Excel and VFP.
hWndXL  = FindWindowA("XLMAIN", oExcel.Caption)
hWndVFP = FindWindowA("VFP66400000", _VFP.Caption)

* Bring VFP to the top, and instruct the user to
* close PrintPreview
= SetWindowPos(hWndVFP, hwnd_topmost, 0,0,0,0, swp_nosize + swp_nomove)
= MessageBox("Close this MessageBox, and then Excel will come forward." + ;
             CHR(13) + "Close Print Preview when ready to return to FoxPro.")

* Now bring the Excel window to the top
= SetWindowPos(hWndVFP, hwnd_notopmost, 0,0,0,0, swp_nosize + swp_nomove)
```

```
= SetWindowPos(hWndXL, hwnd_topmost, 0,0,0,0, swp_nosize + swp_nomove)

* Issue the PrintPreview method. Make sure your code
* can tolerate a wait state, and that the user knows
* to close the PrintPreview window to continue
oSheet.PrintPreview()

* Now put the Excel window to NoTopMost, so VFP can come forward
= SetWindowPos(hWndXL, hwnd_notopmost, 0,0,0,0, swp_nosize + swp_nomove)

* Bring the VFP window forward, then set it NoTopMost so other
* applications can be brought forward.
= SetWindowPos(hWndVFP, hwnd_topmost, 0,0,0,0, swp_nosize + swp_nomove)
= SetWindowPos(hWndVFP, hwnd_notopmost, 0,0,0,0, swp_nosize + swp_nomove)
```

This may work for many applications, especially if you put up a message box explaining what to do just before you call this routine.

Printing

A little less problematic than PrintPreview is printing the spreadsheet. The bulk of the properties that control printing are set in the PageSetup object. Once you're ready to print, the PrintOut method is called. While it has some parameters to control the start and end page numbers, the number of copies, and the device to which the output is sent (printer name, preview, or filename), it does its job just fine without any parameters. It assumes you want it all printed to the default printer.

```
oSheet.Printout()
```

The Excel VBA Help file does a fine job of explaining the parameters; see the "PrintOut Method" topic.

Saving the data in different formats

Excel 2000 has constants defined for 41 different formats (though all might not be available, depending on several factors, like the language [such as U.S. English], or whether the user has installed them, and so on). Quite a number of these formats are variations on the spreadsheet theme, including eight versions of Excel, and seven WK* versions. Also available are formats for CSV, SYLK, DBF, DIF, text, and HTML, among others.

The SaveAs method takes many parameters, though the most useful are the first two. The first parameter is the new filename. The filename must be fully qualified; Excel has no knowledge of VFP's SET DEFAULT setting. The second parameter is a numeric value that represents the format. Of course, we need the table of constants, shown in **Table 7**. We'll show a few—you can find the rest in the Object Browser.

You'll notice the xlWorkbookNormal value. Use this to save a copy of the file in the current version's format.

Table 7*. File format constants for Excel. Excel supports saving in many different formats. Here are a few of the 41 in Excel 2000.*

Constant	Value	Constant	Value
xlCSV	6	xlSYLK	2
xlDBF3	8	xlTextWindows	20
xlDIF	9	xlWK4	38
xlExcel9795	43	xlWorkbookNormal	-4143

Putting it all together

Listing 2 shows a program (XLSample1.PRG in the Developer Download files available at www.hentzenwerke.com) that creates a workbook with worksheets for the order history of the first three clients (the first three is just a number chosen from the air; you can play around with the loop counter, if you desire). This example covers entering data, adding a totaling formula, formatting cells, setting up the sheets to print, viewing the PrintPreview, and finally saving the spreadsheet (also see **Figure 11**).

Listing 2*. Tasmanian Traders customer history workbook. This example covers many of the topics in this chapter, including adding data and formulas, formatting cells, saving the spreadsheet, previewing, and others.*

```
* Put order information for several customers into an Excel worksheet
* Change the LoopCounter constant to change the number of customers
* entered into Excel.

* Clean out any existing references to servers.
* This prevents memory loss to leftover instances.
RELEASE ALL LIKE o*

#DEFINE xlEdgeBottom                    9
#DEFINE xlEdgeTop                       8
#DEFINE xlContinuous                    1
#DEFINE xlMedium                     -4138
#DEFINE xlHAlignCenter               -4108
#DEFINE xlHAlignCenterAcrossSelection   7
#DEFINE xlVAlignBottom               -4107
#DEFINE xlAutomatic                  -4105
#DEFINE xlPortrait                      1
#DEFINE autoIn2Pts                     72

#DEFINE swp_nosize      1
#DEFINE swp_nomove      2
#DEFINE hwnd_topmost   -1
#DEFINE hwnd_notopmost -2

#DEFINE LoopCounter     3
```

```
LOCAL oBook, oRange, oSheet

* Open the Order History view, which contains
* a summary of orders for one customer.
CLOSE DATA
OPEN DATABASE _SAMPLES + "\TASTRADE\DATA\Tastrade"
USE CUSTOMER IN 0
SELECT 0
USE "Order History" ALIAS OrderHistory

* Add a workbook, using default settings
oExcel = CREATEOBJECT("Excel.Application")
oExcel.Visible = .T.
oBook  = oExcel.Workbooks.Add()
oSheet = oBook.ActiveSheet

* Add styles to the workbook
WITH oBook
  .Styles.Add("Bold")
  WITH .Styles["Bold"]
    .Font.Bold = .T.
    .Font.Size = 12
    .HorizontalAlignment = xlHAlignCenter
    .VerticalAlignment   = xlVAlignBottom
    .WrapText = .T.
  ENDWITH
ENDWITH

FOR I = 1 TO LoopCounter

  REQUERY()

  WITH oSheet
    * Name the sheet with the Customer ID
    .Name = Customer.Customer_ID
    .Select()

    * Put customer name at top
    .Range("A2").Value = Customer.Company_Name

    * Put column headings in Row 5
    .Range("A5").Value = "Order Number"
    .Range("B5").Value = "Date"
    .Range("C5").Value = "Amount"

    oRange = .Range("A6:C6")
  ENDWITH

  * Loop through orders and send data
  SCAN
    WITH oRange
      .Columns[1].Value = Order_Id
      .Columns[2].Value = Order_Date
      .Columns[3].Value = Ord_Total
    ENDWITH
```

```
  * Move range down one row
  oRange = oRange.Offset(1,0)
ENDSCAN

* Now add total row
nLastRow = oRange.Row && Row property always give first row of range
                      && This range has only one row
cLastRow = ALLTRIM(STR(nLastRow))

WITH oSheet
  .Cells[ nLastRow , 1 ] = "Total"

  * Need to convert nLastRow to char to use in formula for sum
  .Cells[ nLastRow , 3 ].Formula = ;
    "=SUM( C6:C" + LTRIM(STR(nLastRow - 1)) + " )"
ENDWITH

* Start Formatting the sheet
WITH oSheet
  * Apply the Bold Style to column headers
  WITH .Range("A5:C5")
    .Style = "Bold"
    .Borders[xlEdgeBottom].LineStyle = xlContinuous
  ENDWITH

  * Apply Bold Style to Total label
  .Range("A" + cLastRow).Style = "Bold"
  .Range("A" + cLastRow + ":C" + cLastRow).Borders[xlEdgeTop].LineStyle = ;
    xlContinuous

  * Apply Bold Style to client name, then override
  * the horizontal alignment to spread it across columns
  .Range("A2").Style = "Bold"
  .Range("A2:C2").HorizontalAlignment = xlHAlignCenterAcrossSelection

  * Change the format of the date column
  .Range("B6:B" + cLastRow).NumberFormat = "Dd-Mmm-YYY"

  * Fix the column width
  .Range("A5:C" + cLastRow).Columns.AutoFit()

  * For some reason, the first column doesn't expand enough
  * without the column header wrapping one character of the
  * last word. Add another character to the column width
  .Range("A5").Columns.ColumnWidth = .Range("A5").Columns.ColumnWidth + 1

  * AutoFit ensures that the largest value just barely fits.
  * We prefer a little more space between the last two columns, so
  * add another character to each of these columns, too
  .Range("B5").Columns.ColumnWidth = .Range("B5").Columns.ColumnWidth + 1
  .Range("C5").Columns.ColumnWidth = .Range("C5").Columns.ColumnWidth + 1

  * Now set up the page to print
  WITH .PageSetup
    * Don't assume that these are the defaults;
    * these are things users can change!
```

```
      .Orientation = xlPortrait

      .FitToPagesTall = 1
      .FitToPagesWide = 1

      .CenterHorizontally = .T.
      .CenterVertically   = .T.

      .TopMargin    = 1.0 * autoIn2Pts
      .BottomMargin = 1.0 * autoIn2Pts
      .LeftMargin   = 1.5 * autoIn2Pts
      .RightMargin  = 1.5 * autoIn2Pts
      .HeaderMargin = 0.5 * autoIn2Pts
      .FooterMargin = 0.5 * autoIn2Pts

      .LeftHeader  = "TasTrade Client ID &A"
      .RightHeader = "Page &P of &N"
      .RightFooter = "Printed On &D"
    ENDWITH

  ENDWITH


  * Add another sheet for the next client
  IF I <> LoopCounter
    oSheet = oBook.Worksheets.Add()
  ENDIF

  * Get next client
  SKIP IN Customer

ENDFOR

* PrintPreview the workbook.
* Declare the APIs…
* FindWindowA returns the window handle from the window's caption
DECLARE LONG FindWindowA IN WIN32API STRING class, STRING title
* SetWindowPos moves the window to the top, using the window handle
DECLARE SetWindowPos IN WIN32API LONG HWND, LONG hwndafter, ;
        LONG x, LONG Y, LONG cx, LONG cy, LONG flags

* Capture the window handles for both Excel and VFP.
hWndXL  = FindWindowA("XLMAIN", oExcel.Caption)
hWndVFP = FindWindowA("VFP66400000", _VFP.Caption)

* Bring VFP to the top, and instruct the user to
* close PrintPreview
= SetWindowPos(hWndVFP, hwnd_topmost, 0,0,0,0, swp_nosize + swp_nomove)
= MessageBox("Close this MessageBox, and then Excel will come forward." + ;
             CHR(13) + "Close Print Preview when ready to return to FoxPro.")

* Now bring the Excel window to the top
= SetWindowPos(hWndVFP,  hwnd_notopmost, 0,0,0,0, swp_nosize + swp_nomove)
= SetWindowPos(hWndXL, hwnd_topmost, 0,0,0,0, swp_nosize + swp_nomove)
```

```
* Issue the PrintPreview method to show the first client.
* Make sure your code can tolerate a wait state, and that the
* user knows to close the PrintPreview window to continue

oSheet.PrintPreview()

* When the user closes PrintPreview, it returns to here.
* Bring VFP to the top, then notify user.
= SetWindowPos(hWndXL,  hwnd_notopmost, 0,0,0,0, swp_nosize + swp_nomove)
= SetWindowPos(hWndVFP, hwnd_topmost, 0,0,0,0, swp_nosize + swp_nomove)
= MessageBox("Building the Excel file is complete." + CHR(13) + ;
             "Ready to save the Excel file.")

* Reset Excel and VFP to NoTopMost
= SetWindowPos(hWndXL,  hwnd_notopmost, 0,0,0,0, swp_nosize + swp_nomove)
= SetWindowPos(hWndVFP, hwnd_notopmost, 0,0,0,0, swp_nosize + swp_nomove)


* Save the file.
* Set up the file name
XLFile = FULLPATH(CURDIR()) + "XLSample1.XLS"
XLFileJustName = JUSTSTEM(XLFile)

* Determine whether to use SaveAs or Save
IF oBook.Name <> XLFileJustName

   * If the file already exists, delete it
   IF FILE(XLFile)
     ERASE (XLFile)
   ENDIF

 * Save it without fear of the user dialog box
   oBook.SaveAs(XLFile)

ELSE

   * Save it, since it's already been saved with SaveAs
   oBook.Save()

ENDIF

=MessageBox("Excel file saved as:" + CHR(13) + XLFile)

oExcel.Quit()
RELEASE oExcel

USE IN OrderHistory
USE IN Customer
```

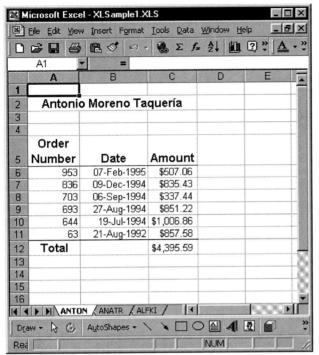

Figure 11. *The finished Tasmanian Traders customer history workbook This example covers entering data, adding a total formula, formatting cells, setting up the sheets to print, viewing the PrintPreview, and finally saving the spreadsheet.*

We've covered a lot in this chapter, yet Excel has even more to offer. We've worked on the mechanics of building a workbook with standard spreadsheet features; in the next chapter, we'll cover the more advanced Excel features that help your users analyze their data.

Chapter 8
Advanced Excel Features

Excel has many advanced features for analyzing data, standardizing worksheets, and adding pictures and shapes.

Excel's analysis features are very powerful. The PivotTable is awesome in its ability to analyze and format cross-tabbed data. What-if analysis is made easier with data tables, allowing you to see multiple results using several inputs. Goal Seek is a way to solve for one of the parameters in a function. Excel has even more analytical tools, and these will get you started.

Also included in the advanced category are using templates and automating macros. These help standardize your spreadsheets.

Finally, you can add shapes and graphics to make your worksheets really stand out.

PivotTables

PivotTables are cool. They're cross-tabs on steroids, created from a simple list of data that contains the cross-tab categories in the data within each column—the same list you'd have to SCAN and conditionally set a slew of variables, or write a complicated SQL statement to build a cross-tab. VFP does have Cross-Tab and PivotTable Wizards, but they are much more limited than Excel's engine.

On the surface, simple PivotTables can cross-tab data, such as totaling the quantity of items for each product category sold in each month. PivotTables sound even better when you find that they can summarize multiple fields for the cross-tabs—summarize the total items sold and the total sales price by each product by month sold. They'll also do pages—summarize the total items and sales price by each product by month sold, showing a "page" for each year. You can change your mind, too: instead of showing the totals for each product by month, you can change one property to show the products sold by the buyer's country. If that weren't cool enough, it's interactive for the user—you pass Excel the data and get the PivotTable set up, and your users can slice and dice the data to their hearts' content. Less code for the developer, more features for the user—it doesn't get any better than this!

PivotTables are so cool that VFP 6.0 has a PivotTable Wizard—but it requires Excel *and* Microsoft Query to be installed before it can be used. We've found Query to be temperamental in terms of programmatically ensuring that it is properly installed and configured on a user's machine; if your application can't verify that Query's going to work, your users can (and will) get nasty error messages, prompting them to make irate tech support calls. We can solve this whole problem, though, by putting the data into Excel directly from FoxPro using Automation rather than Query, then accessing Excel directly to create and manipulate a PivotTable.

Excel has several sources of data for PivotTables: a range of data in a worksheet, several ranges that the PivotTable will consolidate, another PivotTable report, or an external data source. The external data source is accessed through On-Line Analytical Processing (OLAP), ODBC, ADO, or DAO technologies, depending on the data source. Since it's so easy to COPY TO ... TYPE XL5 and automate Excel to open the file generated by FoxPro as a worksheet, the only data source for PivotTables that we'll cover is the range in a worksheet. We won't attempt to cover the complexities of automating OLAP, ODBC, ADO, or DAO through Excel. While it is technically feasible to use these approaches (we have successfully implemented some of these technologies in our own apps), detailing the intricacies of these complex technologies is really a separate subject from the focus of this book.

PivotTable data

The first step in defining a PivotTable is to set up the data in a worksheet using a row and column format that Excel calls a *list* or *database*. Have no fear; it looks just like what FoxPro developers call a database, too. There's only one difference: the first row of a list is reserved for column labels, which are used to label the PivotTable, and is used like a field name for accessing the data in the columns.

When programming a cross-tab report, a list of the unique data items in one field becomes the labels for the columns, and a list of the unique data items in another field becomes the labels for the rows. The intersection of these rows and columns reflects a summary of the numeric data, such as a total, average, count, or some other numeric function. Just like the cross-tab report, a PivotTable uses one field each for the RowFields and ColumnFields properties and summarizes the numeric data contained in the DataFields property. We'll come back to the properties later; right now, we need to set up the data. So we know we need at least three columns (and later we'll see that we can use many more).

The TasTrade database is perfect for illustrating PivotTables. We'll illustrate the PivotTable examples with a table containing a list of all the order line items. We could almost take the Order_Line_Items table as is, except that it contains a lot of codes, for which we'd like the text descriptions. **Listing 1** (XLData.PRG in the Developer Download files available at www.hentzenwerke.com) shows how to create the cursor, copy it to an XLS file, open the XLS file in Excel, then fit the columns so we can read it better. **Figure 1** shows a portion of the resulting worksheet.

Listing 1. Creating an example cursor to use for PivotTables.

```
* Clean out any existing references to servers.
* This prevents memory loss to leftover instances.
RELEASE ALL LIKE o*

* For demonstration purposes, make oExcel and oBook
* available after this program executes.
PUBLIC oExcel, oBook

OPEN DATABASE (_SAMPLES + "\TasTrade\Data\TasTrade")
```

```
SELECT Customer.Company_Name, ;
       Customer.Country, ;
       CMONTH(Orders.Order_Date) AS Order_Month, ;
       YEAR(Orders.Order_Date) AS Order_Year, ;
       Category.Category_Name, ;
       Products.Product_Name, ;
       Order_Line_Items.Quantity, ;
       Order_Line_Items.Unit_Price * Order_Line_Items.Quantity ;
         AS Total_Price;
  FROM Orders, Order_Line_Items, Customer, Products, Category ;
 WHERE Order_Line_Items.Order_ID = Orders.Order_ID ;
   AND Orders.Customer_ID = Customer.Customer_ID ;
   AND Order_Line_Items.Product_ID = Products.Product_ID ;
   AND Products.Category_ID = Category.Category_ID ;
   INTO CURSOR Pivot

LastLine = ALLTRIM(STR(_TALLY + 1 ))
COPY TO (CURDIR() + "Pivot") TYPE XL5

oBook = GETOBJECT(CURDIR() + "Pivot.XLS")

* Open the workbook, and best-fit all the columns.
WITH oBook
  oExcel = .Application
  .Application.Visible = .T.
  .Windows[1].Activate()
  .Sheets[1].Range("A1:H" + LastLine).Columns.AutoFit()
ENDWITH
```

	A	B	C	D	E	F	G	H
1	company_name	country	order_month	order_year	category_name	product_name	quantity	total_price
2	B's Beverages	UK	May	1992	Seafood	Ikura	5	155
3	Cactus Comidas para llevar	Argentina	May	1992	Seafood	Boston Crab Meat	998	18363.2
4	Cactus Comidas para llevar	Argentina	May	1992	Dairy Products	Raclette Courdavault	24	925.2
5	Cactus Comidas para llevar	Argentina	May	1992	Grains/Cereals	Wimmers gute Semmelknödel	10	332.5
6	Folk och fä HB	Sweden	May	1992	Dairy Products	Gorgonzola Telino	15	120
7	Folk och fä HB	Sweden	May	1992	Beverages	Chartreuse verte	19	239.4
8	Folk och fä HB	Sweden	May	1992	Dairy Products	Flotemysost	15	225
9	Simons bistro	Denmark	May	1992	Seafood	Carnarvon Tigers	12	524.4
10	Vaffeljernet	Denmark	May	1992	Meat/Poultry	Thüringer Rostbratwurst	35	3010
11	Vaffeljernet	Denmark	May	1992	Condiments	Vegie-spread	6	184.2
12	Wartian Herkku	Finland	May	1992	Confections	Tarte au sucre	10	340
13	Franchi S.p.A.	Italy	May	1992	Seafood	Konbu	10	42
14	Franchi S.p.A.	Italy	May	1992	Confections	Valkoinen suklaa	4	45.2
15	Morgenstern Gesundkost	Germany	May	1992	Dairy Products	Queso Manchego La Pastora	4	104
16	Morgenstern Gesundkost	Germany	May	1992	Meat/Poultry	Perth Pasties	30	687
17	Morgenstern Gesundkost	Germany	May	1992	Condiments	Vegie-spread	20	614
18	Furia Bacalhau e Frutos do Mar	Portugal	May	1992	Produce	Tofu	20	324
19	Furia Bacalhau e Frutos do Mar	Portugal	May	1992	Confections	Sir Rodney's Scones	15	105
20	Furia Bacalhau e Frutos do Mar	Portugal	May	1992	Produce	Manjimup Dried Apples	20	742
21	Seven Seas Imports	UK	May	1992	Grains/Cereals	Tunnbröd	70	420
22	Seven Seas Imports	UK	May	1992	Produce	Manjimup Dried Apples	10	370
23	Simons bistro	Denmark	May	1992	Beverages	Ipoh Coffee	10	320
24	Simons bistro	Denmark	May	1992	Dairy Products	Flotemysost	10	150
25	Wellington Importadora	Brazil	May	1992	Seafood	Carnarvon Tigers	12	524.4
26	Wellington Importadora	Brazil	May	1992	Confections	Teatime Chocolate Biscuits	15	96
27	Wellington Importadora	Brazil	May	1992	Seafood	Inlagd Sill	10	133

Figure 1. The sample worksheet for the PivotTable examples. This worksheet contains 2,822 rows. Most columns have repeating data, and when used as a row or column field, the unique values within the column become the headings.

This worksheet has 2,822 rows, and plenty of fields to use as PivotTable rows and columns. A gentle reminder here: unlike FoxPro's tables with an unlimited number of records, Excel has a limit of 65,536 rows.

Creating a PivotTable

Once you have a list in a worksheet, you can create a PivotTable. To do so, use the Worksheet's PivotTableWizard method. The PivotTableWizard method is extremely flexible (and therefore complex). However, to use data contained on a worksheet, only the first six parameters are necessary. The PivotTableWizard's pertinent syntax is as follows:

```
oSheet.PivotTableWizard( nSourceType, oSourceData, oTableDestination,
                         cTableName, lRowGrandTotals,
                         lColumnGrandTotals )
```

nSourceType	Numeric	A numeric value that represents the kind of source data. The constant we'll discuss here is xlDatabase (1). Other constants are xlConsolidation (3), xlPivotTable (-4148), and xlExternal (2).
oSourceData	Object	A Range object that contains the data for the PivotTable.
oTableDestination	Object	A Range object that contains the location of the PivotTable (you can specify just the upper-left cell; you don't have to figure out the size).
cTableName	Character	The name of the table.
lRowGrandTotals	Logical	Indicates whether grand totals for rows should be included (most useful only if multiple row fields are used).
lColumnGrandTotals	Logical	Indicates whether grand totals for columns should be included (most useful only if multiple column fields are used).

Here's the source to add a PivotTable to the preceding spreadsheet, beginning at cell J1:

```
#DEFINE xlDatabase 1

oSourceData = oBook.Sheets[1].Range("A1:H2822")
oDestination = oBook.Sheets[1].Range("J1")
oPivotTable = oBook.Sheets[1].PivotTableWizard(xlDatabase, oSourceData, ;
    oDestination, "SalesAnalysis", .T., .T.)
```

After the PivotTableWizard method is run, the range J1:K2 is highlighted by bold, blue borders. What has been accomplished is that a PivotTable object has been created. Unlike most Wizard methods that produce a finished object, the PivotTableWizard method generates a blank object, which needs more programming to finish it.

The PivotTableWizard doesn't contain parameters for populating the PivotFields collection, which is the collection of all the fields used in the PivotTable. That's okay by us, as we can't imagine how complex the syntax would be! Use the AddFields method of the PivotTable object, which has the following syntax:

```
oPivotTable.AddFields( cRowField, cColumnField, cPageField, lAddFields )
```

cRowField	Character	The name of the field used to generate the rows of the PivotTable. The field name is a character string that matches the column label in the first row of the list. (Optional)
cColumnField	Character	The name of the field used to generate the columns of the PivotTable. (Optional)
cPageField	Character	The name of the field used to generate the pages of the PivotTable. Think of pages as a filtered view rather than a tabbed page. Pages are selected from a drop-down list at the top of the PivotTable. (Optional)
lAddFields	Logical	Indicates whether to add the fields to any existing fields (.T.) or replace the fields that are contained in the PivotTable (.F.). The default is false. (Optional)

As an example, set the rows to the country field and the columns to the category name with the following code:

```
oPivotTable.AddFields("country", "category_name")
```

This command sets the RowField and ColumnField to the country and category_name fields. A data field to summarize has not been set. This is accomplished by accessing the appropriate PivotField object directly. The PivotFields collection is generated when the PivotTableWizard method is run, and it contains one object for each field. The PivotTable's AddFields method uses the listed field names, and sets certain properties of the appropriate PivotField objects to indicate that the fields are used for RowFields or ColumnFields. One of the more than 50 properties for a PivotField object is the Orientation property, which determines the location of the field within the PivotTable. Set the Orientation property to one of the following values: xlColumnField (2), xlDataField (4), xlHidden (0), xlPageField (3), or xlRowField (1). To summarize the quantity field, give the following commands:

```
#DEFINE xlDataField 4
oPivotTable.PivotFields["Quantity"].Orientation = xlDataField
```

The resulting PivotTable is shown in **Figure 2**. It only took about a second and a half to create it on Della's test machine (after the data was built). Note that the row and column field labels are dropdowns. This interactive feature lets your users select which columns or rows to display. For example, they can choose only the Beverages and Confections categories for USA, Canada, and Mexico. To do so, the user clicks on the dropdown and then checks those items in the list he'd like to see.

You can accomplish this in code, by manipulating the PivotField object's PivotItems collection. Each PivotField has a collection of PivotItems, each correlating to a row or column. The heading labels are used as the index name. One of the 19 properties of the PivotItem object is the Visible property. Setting Visible to .F. removes it from the view. The following code leaves visible only the Beverages and Confections columns for North American countries.

```
WITH oPivotTable.PivotFields("category_name")
  .PivotItems("Condiments").Visible = .F.
  .PivotItems("Dairy Products").Visible = .F.
  .PivotItems("Grains/Cereals").Visible = .F.
  .PivotItems("Meat/Poultry").Visible = .F.
```

```
  .PivotItems("Produce").Visible = .F.
  .PivotItems("Seafood").Visible = .F.
ENDWITH
WITH oPivotTable.PivotFields("country")
  .PivotItems("Argentina").Visible = .F.
  .PivotItems("Austria").Visible = .F.
  .PivotItems("Belgium").Visible = .F.
  .PivotItems("Brazil").Visible = .F.
  .PivotItems("Denmark").Visible = .F.
  .PivotItems("Finland").Visible = .F.
  .PivotItems("France").Visible = .F.
  .PivotItems("Germany").Visible = .F.
  .PivotItems("Ireland").Visible = .F.
  .PivotItems("Italy").Visible = .F.
  .PivotItems("Norway").Visible = .F.
  .PivotItems("Poland").Visible = .F.
  .PivotItems("Portugal").Visible = .F.
  .PivotItems("Spain").Visible = .F.
  .PivotItems("Sweden").Visible = .F.
  .PivotItems("Switzerland").Visible = .F.
  .PivotItems("UK").Visible = .F.
  .PivotItems("Venezuela").Visible = .F.
ENDWITH
```

	J	K	L	M	N	O	P	Q	R	S
1	Sum of quantity	category								
2	country	Beverages	Condiments	Confections	Dairy Produc	Grains/Cere	Meat/Poultry	Produce	Seafood	Grand Total
3	Argentina	118	50	57	78	64		33	1052	1452
4	Austria	1058	1010	600	807	655	362	473	876	5841
5	Belgium	423	206	358	411	178	89	204	227	2096
6	Brazil	1282	770	768	505	315	285	194	724	4843
7	Canada	364	506	580	373	311	221	154	276	2785
8	Denmark	339	261	221	99	20	250	161	294	1645
9	Finland	200	94	159	204	140	116	93	143	1149
10	France	808	374	830	453	368	312	381	696	4222
11	Germany	1832	1380	1858	1498	890	727	772	1858	10815
12	Ireland	317	216	119	459	172	316	161	757	2517
13	Italy	247	112	174	174	158	72	105	166	1208
14	Mexico	100288	83	146	297	93	101	126	158	101292
15	Norway	64	28	26	38		5	18	58	237
16	Poland	65	42	27	35		3	28	15	215
17	Portugal	140	189	112	19	104	70	73	44	759
18	Spain	226	122	166	83	157	129	50	277	1210
19	Sweden	743	274	408	288	235	304	292	611	3155
20	Switzerland	314	160	176	162	232	183	161	375	1763
21	UK	627	431	431	653	445	324	318	600	3829
22	USA	2072	1206	1837	1657	993	1453	759	1885	11862
23	Venezuela	781	271	721	495	269	302	264	961	4064
24	Grand Total	112316	7785	9774	8788	5799	5624	4820	12053	166959

Figure 2. *A simple PivotTable. In just a few lines of code, a simple cross-tab has been generated. Note the dropdowns for the Country and Category_Name—your users can have a great time customizing the data.*

As you can see, you need to address every item individually, which means you need to know your data well. But because the resulting PivotTable is completely interactive, perhaps your users may want to manipulate the fields in Excel, rather than having you write a major front end to the PivotTable.

Using a FOR EACH loop to spin through all the PivotItems can make life a bit easier. Check the value of the PivotItem's Name field to determine whether to set the Visible property. The following code produces the same results as the preceding sample code:

```
FOR EACH oItem IN oPivotTable.PivotFields("category_name").PivotItems
  IF NOT oItem.Name $ ("Beverages Confections")
    oItem.Visible = .F.
  ENDIF
ENDFOR
FOR EACH oItem IN oPivotTable.PivotFields("country").PivotItems
  IF NOT oItem.Name $ ("Canada Mexico USA")
    oItem.Visible = .F.
  ENDIF
ENDFOR
```

Let's get a little more complicated with the PivotTable. To make this PivotTable summarize the Total_Price field, use the following:

```
#DEFINE xlDataField 4
oPivotTable.PivotFields["Total_Price"].Orientation = xlDataField
```

Figure 3 shows the results (now you can see why we removed a lot of the rows and columns…so we can show a reasonably sized example!). In fact, you can have any number of DataFields. Setting the Orientation property for a PivotField does not affect any other PivotField's status.

J	K	L	M	N
		category_name ▼		
country ▼	Data ▼	Beverages	Confections	Grand Total
Canada	Sum of quantity	364	580	944
	Sum of total_price	13829.8	13316.1	27145.9
Mexico	Sum of quantity	100288	146	100434
	Sum of total_price	1907975.7	2282.95	1910258.65
USA	Sum of quantity	2072	1837	3909
	Sum of total_price	75442.15	42674.75	118116.9
Total Sum of quantity		102724	2563	105287
Total Sum of total_price		1997247.65	58273.8	2055521.45

Figure 3. *Things get a little more complex. We've turned Visible off for a number of rows and columns and added a second DataField.*

Those Total_Price values need a little formatting to look like currency. You can set the formatting for an entire PivotField using the PivotField object's NumberFormat property (this is covered in Chapter 7, "Excel Basics"—the codes you need are listed in Table 2 in that chapter). Changing the numeric format to currency works like this:

```
oPivotTable.PivotFields["Sum of Total_Price"].NumberFormat = "$###,###,###.#0"
```

Note that the field name changes for a summary value. This is because you might have two different calculations for the same field. For example, we can add an average total price field.

First we'll set the orientation of the Total_Price field again—this adds a *second* instance of a summary data field. Its default name is "Sum of Total_Price2." Changing the name also changes the display label, so that should be the next step, then actually setting the function is the last step. Set the Function property to one of the constants shown in **Table 1**.

Table 1. *Function property values. The Function property controls how the DataField is calculated.*

Constant	Value	Constant	Value
xlAverage	-4106	xlStDev	-4155
xlCount	-4112	xlStDevP	-4156
xlCountNums	-4113	xlSum	-4157
xlMax	-4136	xlVar	-4164
xlMin	-4139	xlVarP	-4165
xlProduct	-4149		

The code to add a third summary field and set it to the average of the Total_Price field is as follows:

```
#DEFINE xlDataField   4
#DEFINE xlAverage     -4106

* Add another Total_Price summary field
oPivotTable.PivotFields["Total_Price"].Orientation = xlDataField

* Change its name
oPivotTable.PivotFields["Sum of Total_Price2"].Name = "Average Total Sale"

* Set the formula to average the data, rather than sum the data
oPivotTable.PivotFields["Average Total Sale"].Function = xlAverage

* Format it so the numbers look like currency
oPivotTable.PivotFields["Average Total Sale"].NumberFormat = "$###,###,###.#0"
```

Now, to really see the power of PivotTables, you can add a second RowField. What's the purpose of a second field? To see each country's sales broken down by year. A picture's worth a thousand words here; the next line of code adds the Order_Year field as another RowField and combines with the previous examples to produce **Figure 4**.

```
#DEFINE xlRowField 1
oPivotTable.PivotFields["Order_Year"].Orientation = xlRowField
```

We've just barely scratched the surface of PivotTables here. PivotTables are so complex, even Excel's VBA Help file has this remark in the "PivotTable Object" topic: "Because PivotTable report programming can be complex, it's generally easiest to record PivotTable report actions and then revise the recorded code." We concur; this is the only way to dive further into the complexities of this extremely rich feature of Excel.

country ▾	Data ▾	order_yea ▾	category_nam ▾ Beverages	Confections	Grand Total
Canada	Sum of quantity	1992	61	85	146
		1993	219	201	420
		1994	35	171	206
		1995	49	123	172
	Sum of total_pric	1992	$562.10	$1,871.0	$2,433.10
		1993	$12,431.20	$4,683.50	$17,114.70
		1994	$210.0	$2,243.30	$2,453.30
		1995	$626.50	$4,518.30	$5,144.80
	Average Total Sa	1992	$187.37	$623.67	$405.52
		1993	$2,071.87	$390.29	$950.82
		1994	$70.0	$320.47	$245.33
		1995	$208.83	$1,506.10	$857.47
Canada Sum of quantity			364	580	944
Canada Sum of total_price			$13,829.80	$13,316.10	$27,145.90
Canada Average Total Sale			$921.99	$532.64	$678.65
Mexico	Sum of quantity	1992		27	27
		1993	66	40	106
		1994	182	72	254
		1995	40	7	47
		1996	100000		100000
	Sum of total_pric	1992		$216.0	$216.0
		1993	$796.20	$560.0	$1,356.20
		1994	$6,729.50	$1,442.55	$8,172.05
		1995	$450.0	$64.40	$514.40
		1996	$1,900,000.0		$1,900,000.0
	Average Total Sa	1992		$108.0	$108.0
		1993	$159.24	$280.0	$193.74
		1994	$672.95	$360.64	$583.72
		1995	$225.0	$64.40	$171.47
		1996	$1,900,000.0		$1,900,000.0
Mexico Sum of quantity			100288	146	100434
Mexico Sum of total_price			$1,907,975.70	$2,282.95	$1,910,258.65
Mexico Average Total Sale			$105,998.65	$253.66	$70,750.32
USA	Sum of quantity	1992	191	190	381
		1993	615	310	925
		1994	796	899	1695
		1995	470	438	908
	Sum of total_pric	1992	$7,070.0	$2,819.20	$9,889.20
		1993	$14,599.40	$8,852.60	$23,452.0
		1994	$31,604.75	$21,474.55	$53,079.30
		1995	$22,168.0	$9,528.40	$31,696.40
	Average Total Sa	1992	$1,178.33	$281.92	$618.08
		1993	$811.08	$553.29	$689.76
		1994	$929.55	$631.60	$780.58
		1995	$1,477.87	$680.60	$1,092.98
USA Sum of quantity			2072	1837	3909
USA Sum of total_price			$75,442.15	$42,674.75	$118,116.90
USA Average Total Sale			$1,033.45	$576.69	$803.52
Total Sum of quantity			102724	2563	105287
Total Sum of total_price			$1,997,247.65	$58,273.80	$2,055,521.45
Total Average Total Sale			$18,841.96	$539.57	$9,605.24

Figure 4. *A complex PivotTable, with three DataFields and two RowFields. This only scratches the surface of what PivotTables can do.*

What-if analysis using data tables

The easiest form of what-if analysis is to add some data cells to your spreadsheet along with a formula that uses those data cells, and then change the value of the data cells to see how the formula changes. This simple analysis feature keeps many Excel users happy.

The drawback to this approach is that you see only one result at a time. Sometimes it would be nice to see the results of a series of values for one of the data cells all at the same time. For example, it's easier to figure out how much to sell an item for if you can see the retail prices for a variety of markup values. You might be looking at a widget that has a cost of $5.96. You'd like to see the sale price for this item with markups of 15, 20, 25, 30, and 35 percent. Using a data table, you can develop a chart like the one shown in **Figure 5**. A data table is built from a range containing a formula and the values to plug into the formula in a column (or row).

	A	B	C
1	Widget Cost		$5.96
2			
3	0.15	$6.85	
4	0.2	$7.15	
5	0.25	$7.45	
6	0.3	$7.75	
7	0.35	$8.05	
8			

*Figure 5. A simple data table. Data tables show multiple values of one (or two) of the cells used in a formula. In this case, the formula, =C1 * (1 + A3), is stored in cell B3. Successive lines in the table replace cell A3 in the formula with the value in column A.*

Let's look at how this table is set up. First, we have the Widget Cost in cell C1. The markup values to analyze are in A3:A7. The formula to use is "=C1 * (1 + A3)", and it's in cell B3. Here's the code to get the data set up. If you're following along in FoxPro with the book, be sure to close the last spreadsheet and start a new sheet with the first three lines of the code:

```
RELEASE oPivotTable, oBook, oSourceData, oDestination
oBook = oExcel.Workbooks.Add
oSheet = oBook.Sheets[1]

* Set up and format the Widget Cost row
oSheet.Range("A1") = "Widget Cost"
oSheet.Range("C1") = 5.96
oSheet.Range("C1").NumberFormat = "$#,###.#0"

* Add the markup values to analyze
oSheet.Range("A3") = ".15"
oSheet.Range("A4") = ".20"
oSheet.Range("A5") = ".25"
oSheet.Range("A6") = ".30"
oSheet.Range("A7") = ".35"
```

```
* Put in the formula, and format the cells (including the data table
* results) to look like currency.
oSheet.Range("B3") = "=C1 * (1 + A3)"
oSheet.Range("B3:B7").NumberFormat = "$#,###.#0"
```

One way to fill in the rest of the values is to slightly modify this formula to "=C1 * (1 + A3)" and copy it down the rest of the cells. Better yet, we could use one line to set up a data table. Use the Table method of the Range object. The layout of the data has been carefully set up to ensure that the data table will work. The formula is one column to the right of and one row up from the topmost value in the column of values to substitute into the formula. The value that we're substituting, in A3, can be anywhere in the workbook. However, because it's one of the values under consideration, it makes sense to make it look like the first value in the table—this spot in the table could be blank if the value was somewhere else.

The Table method works on a range, which is the rectangular area including the formula and the values; there should be at least two rows and two columns. In the case of this example, the range is A3:B7. The method takes two parameters. Each is a range found in the formula—the first is the range to replace with the values found in the rows in the data table range, and the second is the range to replace with the values found in the columns of the data table. In this example, only columns are used. The following line produces the data table shown in Figure 5:

```
oSheet.Range("A3:B7").Table("",oSheet.Range("A3"))
```

So why set up a data table when you can copy the formula almost as easily? There are quite a number of reasons. Perhaps the nicest reason is that you can change the formula in the data table (cell B3, in our example), and the rest of the table will change. If you examine the contents of cells B4:B7, you see that they contain the value {=TABLE(,A3)}. This means that the value of each cell is calculated from the formula at the top of the table (or the leftmost value, if using rows). No need to copy the formula to the rest of the cells if you want to change the formula.

Another reason that data tables are useful is that you can include more formulae in successive columns of the table. For example, say you'd also like to compare the Wadget costs at the same markups. Add the Wadget data to the first row, and add the Wadget formula to C3, which is next to the Widget formula in B3:

```
* Set up and format the Wadget Cost row
oSheet.Range("E1") = "Wadget Cost"
oSheet.Range("G1") = 4.23
oSheet.Range("G1").NumberFormat = "$#,###.#0"

* Put in the formula, and format the cells (including the data table
* results) to look like currency.
oSheet.Range("C3") = "=G1 * (1 + A3)"
oSheet.Range("C3:C7").NumberFormat = "$#,###.#0"
```

Now you're ready to add the data table. Expand the range to include the columns for the values, the Widget formula, and the Wadget formula.

```
oSheet.Range("A3:C7").Table("",oSheet.Range("A3"))
```

Figure 6 shows the results. No extra effort is expended to copy formulae, and you can still change either (or both) formulae and affect the respective columns in the table.

	A	B	C	D	E	F	G
1	Widget Cost		$5.96		Wadget Cost		4.23
2							
3	0.15	$6.85	$4.86				
4	0.2	$7.15	$5.08				
5	0.25	$7.45	$5.29				
6	0.3	$7.75	$5.50				
7	0.35	$8.05	$5.71				

Figure 6. A data table with two calculated columns. Column B shows the Widgets and column C shows the Wadgets, with costs calculated from column A. You can have many formulae in row 3 to include in the data table—just include the columns in the Range object.

 Yet another way to construct a data table is to allow changes in two cells in the formula. In this case, the values for the first cell go in the first column of the table, and the values for the second cell go in the first row of the table (starting in column 2). The cell at the first row and column contains the formula. **Listing 2** (XLData2.PRG in the Developer Download files available at www.hentzenwerke.com) shows the code to set up the data table shown in **Figure 7**. This data table depicts the cost to purchase up to four Widgets and includes the shipping cost (which is a flat cost, regardless of the number of Widgets purchased). The Quantity variable is placed in a column, and the Shipping Costs variable is placed in a row.

Listing 2. Setting up a data table with two variables.

```
* Clean out any existing references to servers.
* This prevents memory loss to leftover instances.
RELEASE ALL LIKE o*

* For demonstration purposes, make oExcel and oBook
* and oSheet available after this program executes.
PUBLIC oExcel, oBook, oSheet

#DEFINE xlEdgeBottom   9
#DEFINE xlEdgeRight    10
#DEFINE xlContinuous   1

oExcel = CREATEOBJECT("Excel.Application")
oExcel.Visible = .T.
oBook = oExcel.Workbooks.Add()
oSheet = oBook.Sheets[1]

* Set up the variables for the formula
```

```
oSheet.Range("A1").Value = "Widget Cost"
oSheet.Range("C1").Value = 7.00
oSheet.Range("C1").NumberFormat = "$###.00"
oSheet.Range("C1").Name = "Cost"

oSheet.Range("A2").Value = "Widget Quantity"
oSheet.Range("C2").Value = 1
oSheet.Range("C2").Name = "Quantity"

oSheet.Range("A3").Value = "Shipping"
oSheet.Range("C3").Value = 2.00
oSheet.Range("C3").NumberFormat = "$###.00"
oSheet.Range("C3").Name = "Shipping"

* Set up the row headings
oSheet.Range("C5").Value = "Shipping Costs"
oSheet.Range("C6").Value = "Ground"
oSheet.Range("D6").Value = "Overnight"
oSheet.Range("E6").Value = "2-Day"

* Set up the row values
oSheet.Range("C7").Value = 2
oSheet.Range("D7").Value = 16
oSheet.Range("E7").Value = 8

* Set up the column headings
oSheet.Range("A8").Value = "Widget"
oSheet.Range("A9").Value = "Quantity"

* Set up the column values
oSheet.Range("B8").Value = 1
oSheet.Range("B9").Value = 2
oSheet.Range("B10").Value = 3
oSheet.Range("B11").Value = 4

* Add the formula
oSheet.Range("B7").Value = "=(Cost * Quantity) + Shipping"

* Create the table
oSheet.Range("B7:E11").Table(oSheet.Range("Shipping"), oSheet.Range("Cost"))

* Format the cells for currency
oSheet.Range("C7:E11").NumberFormat = "$###.00"

* Put in the cell borders for clarity
oSheet.Range("A7:E7").Borders(xlEdgeBottom).LineStyle = xlContinuous
oSheet.Range("B5:B11").Borders(xlEdgeRight).LineStyle = xlContinuous
```

Try changing the values in the formula cells—the widget cost (C1), the shipping costs (C7:E7), and the widget quantity (B8:B11). You can also change the formula in B7. Instead of a flat shipping cost, you could change it to a per-item shipping cost by changing the formula to "=(Cost * Quantity) + (Quantity * Shipping)." Watch how the appropriate parts of the table change without having to copy formulae. It's pretty cool.

	A	B	C	D	E
1	Widget Cost		$7.00		
2	Widget Quantity		1		
3	Shipping		$2.00		
4					
5			Shipping Costs		
6			Ground	Overnight	2-Day
7		9.00	$2.00	$16.00	$8.00
8	Widget	1	$9.00	$23.00	$15.00
9	Quantity	2	$16.00	$30.00	$22.00
10		3	$23.00	$37.00	$29.00
11		4	$30.00	$44.00	$36.00

Figure 7. *A two-variable data table. The formula is "=(Cost * Quantity) + Shipping" (without range names, it's "=(C1*C2) + C3)"), and it's contained in cell B7. The table range is B7:E11. The values in the column substitute for C2 in the formula, while the values in the row substitute for C3. If you change the widget cost (C1), the shipping costs (C7:E7), or the quantities (B8:B11), the entire table is recalculated to reflect the values.*

Goal Seek

Goal Seek is a feature that allows you to set up a formula and specify the result and all but one of the values in the formula, then have Excel solve for that value. While our simple example can be solved entirely with FoxPro functions, it illustrates how the Goal Seek function works. There are many kinds of problems that can use Goal Seek; the most popular example is the PMT() function, which takes three parameters (loan amount, term in months, and the interest rate) and determines the payment. Most of us, when applying for a loan, know the loan amount, the desired term, and a desired payment. Goal Seek allows us to provide the solution to the PMT function, and then find the value of one of the parameters—the interest rate—to achieve the desired payment.

We need a simple spreadsheet with three data cells, and another cell for the payment function. Let's assume our mortgage is a $150,000, 30-year loan (360 months), and we'd like a payment of $975. All we need to find is an interest rate. First, we set up the spreadsheet with the three values (use any interest rate you want) to set up the payment, like this:

```
oSheet.Range("A1").Value = "Amount"
oSheet.Range("B1").Value = 150000
oSheet.Range("B1").NumberFormat = "$###,###"

oSheet.Range("A2").Value = "Term"
oSheet.Range("B2").Value = 360
oSheet.Range("C2").Value = "months"

oSheet.Range("A3").Value = "Rate"
oSheet.Range("B3").Value = .075
oSheet.Range("B3").NumberFormat = "0.00%"

oSheet.Range("A4").Value = "Payment"
```

```
oSheet.Range("B4").Value = "=PMT(B3/12, B2, B1)"
oSheet.Range("B4").NumberFormat = "$###,###"
```

The payment shown in cell B4 is $1,048.82 (well, technically, it's -1,048.82; it's a negative number because you owe it, so be sure to set your goal to a negative number). To get it to $975, use the GoalSeek method to solve for the interest rate. GoalSeek is a method of the Range object. The specified range is the cell containing the goal that is to be sought. The method takes two parameters: the first is the goal, or the answer for the range, and the second is the range (a cell) to change in order to solve the problem. To get the interest rate, give the following:

```
oSheet.Range("B4").GoalSeek(-975, oSheet.Range("B3"))
```

And, voila, you have the result: 6.77% (see **Figure 8**). Did you notice that the numbers flashed and recalculated? That's because Excel uses an iterative process: it changes the value of the variable's cell, then checks the result. If the result is incorrect, it gets a new value for the variable and repeats the process. Generally, this runs very quickly, although complex equations or an initial value that's drastically different from the result can slow it down. Now comes the hard part—trying to find a bank that will lend you the money at 6.77% interest.

	A	B	C
1	Amount	$150,000	
2	Term	360	months
3	Rate	6.77%	
4	Payment	($975.00)	
5			

Figure 8. The results of the GoalSeek method. The desired payment is $975, and the amount and term are fixed; GoalSeek found the necessary interest rate.

Protection

When you're creating spreadsheets for other users to use, you don't want them to inadvertently delete formulae and data that you've gone to great lengths to place into the worksheet. Excel has a number of ways to protect the data:

- Require passwords to open, edit, close, and/or save a workbook;

- Recommend that the workbook be opened as "read-only";

- Hide a cell's formula, which leaves the cell visible but hides the formula on the formula bar;

- Lock a workbook, worksheet, or cells, which leaves them visible but unchangeable.

To lock or hide cells, first set the cells' Hidden and/or Locked properties as needed, and then turn on the Worksheet's protection. If you want to protect all cells on the worksheet, do not specify Hidden or Locked; just set the worksheet's protection.

Protecting a cell

All cells are locked and visible by default. However, locking a cell only matters when a worksheet is protected, and worksheets are not protected by default. Essentially, you need to unlock the cells that the user needs to change. The Range object has a Locked property that defaults to .T. To unlock a range, issue a command like this:

```
oSheet.Range("A1:F30").Locked = .F.
```

You hide a formula by using the FormulaHidden property (the formula's result is still displayed in the cell, but the formula itself is not displayed):

```
oSheet.Range("A1:F30").FormulaHidden = .T.
```

If the Worksheet is already locked, an error is generated stating that Excel is unable to set the Locked (or FormulaHidden) property. Be sure that you are protecting cells in an unlocked worksheet. The worksheet has several logical properties that you can check: ProtectContents and ProtectData are two properties that check for data; others check for protection on different kinds of objects.

Protecting a worksheet

Once you have the Locked and FormulaHidden properties set the way you want them, you can protect the worksheet with the Worksheet object's Protect method. It takes several parameters. The first is a case-sensitive character string to use as the worksheet's password. The remaining parameters are logical values pertaining to what is to be protected. In order, they are: drawing objects, contents (all the cells of a worksheet), scenarios (an analytical tool), and user interface (if true, it doesn't protect the macros).

To set the protection of just the worksheet's cells, pass .T. as the third parameter:

```
oSheet.Protect(,,.T.)
```

To protect the worksheet with a password, pass the password string as the first parameter:

```
oSheet.Protect("ThePassword", , .T.)
```

Warning: if you forget the password of a locked document, there is no way to determine the password (with Excel or Automation) to unlock the worksheet. You have to key in the exact, case-sensitive password, or you can't unlock the worksheet. Period. Use passwords at your own risk.

To unlock the worksheet, pass .F. as the third parameter. If a password was used, you must give the exact, case-sensitive string. If you do not pass a password string, Excel will prompt the user for the password; be sure your application can handle this wait state.

Protecting a workbook

Workbooks can also be protected. The structure of a workbook, meaning the position of the sheets within the workbook, can be protected, as can the windows of the workbook. In addition, the workbook can have its own password. The Workbook's Protect method takes three parameters: the first is the case-sensitive password string, the second is a logical indicator of whether to protect the structure of the workbook, and the third is a logical indicator of whether to protect the workbook's window positions. So either of these two syntaxes will work:

```
oBook.Protect("ThePassword", .T., .T.)
oBook.Protect(,.T., .T.)
```

Again, the warning: if you forget the password of a locked workbook, there is no way to determine the password (with Excel or Automation) to unlock the workbook. You have to key in the exact, case-sensitive password, or you can't unlock the workbook. Period. Use passwords at your own risk.

The procedure for unlocking a workbook is the same as that for unlocking a worksheet.

Templates

Excel's templates offer a way to provide standard formatting and styles for documents. If you've been reading this book sequentially, you've already read about Word's templates in Chapter 5, "Intermediate Word," and how they let you specify common elements like the page setup, headers and footers, and even boilerplate text so that every new document contains the same things. Excel offers the same deal.

Every spreadsheet you create in Excel is based on a template—a file with an extension of XLT. If you don't specify which template to use, the default template is used. By default, this is an empty document containing a standard set of styles. It's installed when Excel is installed, along with a number of other templates. To see the available templates, choose File|New from the menu, just as you do in Word.

What goes into a template?

A template can contain anything that's in a spreadsheet, from the simplest spreadsheet to a complex analysis report that includes many formulae, PivotTables, and charts just waiting for a few pertinent data items to be added. Templates can also contain macros, including one that runs automatically when you create a worksheet based on the template. Just like templates in Word, Excel templates can be as much or as little as you choose to make of them.

Finding templates

Templates are stored in several different places. The templates installed by Excel 2000 are put into a Templates subdirectory of the Office installation, and then they go down one level into a subdirectory named with the numeric code for the language you're using (1033 for American English). In addition, each user can set a user template directory and a workgroup template directory.

Detailed information about how Excel stores user templates is contained in the "Finding templates" section in Chapter 5. While it is a Word chapter, this is something that Office has standardized.

One thing that is slightly different is how to find the templates path. Two properties are available from the Application object: TemplatesPath and NetworkTemplatesPath. TemplatesPath is the path to your local machine's templates, and the NetworkTemplatesPath lets you point to another set of templates on the network.

Using templates

You can use templates in several ways when automating Excel. The simplest is to create new documents based on existing templates. To do so, specify a template, including the path, as the first parameter of the Workbooks.Add method. No templates are installed with the default installation of Office/Excel, so don't expect this template name to work:

```
oBook = oExcel.Workbooks.Add( oExcel.TemplatesPath + "MyTemplate.XLT" )
```

Once you create a new workbook based on a template, you can treat that workbook just like any other new workbook. However, you have the advantage that it contains whatever special text, formatting, and styles were stored in the template.

Creating templates

You can also create templates with Automation. Any workbook can be saved as a template by passing the appropriate parameter to the SaveAs method. To create a new template, create a workbook, format it as desired, create any styles, charts, PivotTables, or other features you want the template to have, and then call SaveAs like this:

```
#DEFINE xlTemplate 17
oBook.SaveAs(oExcel.TemplatesPath + "MyNewTemplate.XLT", xlTemplate)
```

As in interactive Excel, you can store the template in a subdirectory to have it appear on a different page in the File|New dialog. Of course, if you're working with it through Automation, you don't really care where it appears. In fact, with Automation, it doesn't matter where you store templates because you can specify where Excel should look for them. However, keeping them together with other templates means that interactive users can find them, as well.

Automating macros

Although you can perform pretty much any Excel action through Automation, if you already have an Excel macro to do a particular thing, it may make more sense to use the existing macro than to rewrite it in VFP. This is especially true if the macro doesn't involve transferring information between the two applications, or if it's part of a pre-packaged set of macros. A benefit to running Excel macros rather than translating them into Automation code is that macros run faster than the analogous Automation code.

The Application object's Run method allows you to execute Excel macros. You pass the name of the macro and any parameters needed to run the macro. For example, say Macro1 is the default name for a recorded macro. It may perform a variety of tasks. This line executes it:

```
oExcel.Run("Macro1")
```

In many cases, it wouldn't be hard to create the same functionality through Automation. However, there are situations where rewriting an existing macro as Automation would present a problem. In those cases, Run provides an easy solution.

Another common situation is to write a macro using Automation code. For an example, you could write a macro to save an Excel workbook. Writing an Excel macro to save the workbook allows you to take advantage of the Excel Application's DisplayAlerts property, which takes a logical value and works in a manner similar to FoxPro's SET SAFETY command. DisplayAlerts only works in the macro environment, and it's reset to true at the end of the macro. Using the following macro allows you to save a file without all of the workarounds discussed in Chapter 7, "Excel Basics."

We're assuming that you know how to write Excel macros. Determine the code you need, and put it into a file. This example uses low-level file functions to create the file, though there are many other ways to accomplish this task in FoxPro. (In VFP 6, the StrToFile() function provides a more readable way to create files.)

```
* Open the file and put in the lines of Excel Code
m.MacroFileName = "C:\Temp\SaveMacro.Txt"
m.MFHandle = FCREATE(m.MacroFileName)

* Add the body of the macro
= FPUTS(m.MFHandle, "' QuietSave Macro")
= FPUTS(m.MFHandle, "' ")
= FPUTS(m.MFHandle, "Sub QuietSave()")
= FPUTS(m.MFHandle, "' ")
= FPUTS(m.MFHandle, "  Application.DisplayAlerts = False")
= FPUTS(m.MFHandle, "  ActiveWorkbook.Save")
= FPUTS(m.MFHandle, "End Sub")

* Close the open LL file.
=FCLOSE(m.MFHandle)
```

Once you have the macro code written to a file, you're ready to bring it into Excel. Use the Modules collection object's Add method to add a blank macro module. Then use the new Module object's InsertFile method to import the macro code. Name the Macro object, and you're ready to run it:

```
* Add a new Module to the Modules collection
oMacroModule = oExcelObject.Modules.Add()

* Pull in the file containing the macro code
oMacroModule.InsertFile(m.MacroFileName)

* Name the macro
oMacroModule.Name = "MacroSave"

* Run the macro
oExcel.Application.Run("QuietSave")
```

This example is not necessarily an endorsement of using the QuietSave macro instead of the workarounds described in Chapter 7, "Excel Basics." It's an alternate method that may or may not work for your application's environment. But it does illustrate how to generate macros using Automation.

Adding shapes

Like Word and PowerPoint, Excel can add graphics to the worksheet. Excel (well, actually Office) has a robust set of Shape objects that's available to any Office application. Chapter 5, "Intermediate Word," covered how Word deals with the Shape object, and Chapter 10, "PowerPoint Basics," goes into immense detail on the Shape object for PowerPoint. We'll cover the basics of adding a Shape object here, and point you to the PowerPoint chapter for the details.

The available shapes, called AutoShapes, provide much more than just basic drawing shapes like rectangles and circles. There are many decorative shapes, such as arrows, stars, and banners. Flowchart symbols are also available, as are many kinds of callouts. Any of these shapes can be added to a worksheet using the AddShape method of the Shapes collection. AutoShapes are used to create diagrams and illustrations, or just spruce up your worksheet.

To interactively add a shape to your worksheet, select Insert|Picture|AutoShapes from the menu to activate the AutoShapes toolbar, shown in **Figure 9**. The buttons represent the main categories of shapes, and clicking on each one opens another menu of buttons that shows the available shapes for that main category of shapes.

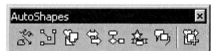

Figure 9. *The AutoShapes toolbar. This toolbar appears whenever you choose Insert|Picture|AutoShapes from the menu.*

To add a shape programmatically, use the AddShape method of the Shapes collection. This is the syntax for adding an AutoShape:

```
oShape = oSheet.Shapes.AddShape( nType, nLeft, nTop, nWidth, nHeight )
```

The first parameter is a numeric constant that indicates one of the 140 shapes available. **Table 2** lists some of the available constants. Note that their prefix is "mso," which denotes that they are available to all Office applications, not just PowerPoint. The next two parameters specify the upper-left corner of the rectangular box that contains the shape (in points, of course). The final two parameters determine the width and height of the object, in points. This rectangular box, which contains the shape, is called the *bounding box*.

The following lines of code add an arrow to the current spreadsheet. It is located half an inch from the top and left, and it's one inch long and one-half inch high. See **Figure 10** for the results.

```
#DEFINE msoShapeRightArrow 33
oSheet.Shapes.AddShape(msoShapeRightArrow, 36, 36, 72, 36)
```

Each Shape object has a number of properties, some of which contain formatting objects. **Table 3** shows the most important Shape properties.

Table 2. *A sampling of AutoShape constants and their values.*

Shape constant	Value
msoShape5PointStar	92
msoShapeArc	25
msoShapeBalloon	137
msoShapeCube	14
msoShapeDownArrow	36
msoShapeLeftArrow	34
msoShapeLineCallout1	109
msoShapeNoSymbol	19
msoShapeOval	9
msoShapeParallelogram	2
msoShapeRectangle	1
msoShapeRightArrow	33
msoShapeRoundedRectangle	5
msoShapeUpArrow	35

Table 3. *Shape properties and objects.*

Property	Type	Description
AutoShapeType	Numeric	One of the AutoShape constants, some of which are listed in Table 2.
Height	Numeric	The height of the shape, in pixels.
Width	Numeric	The width of the shape, in pixels
Left	Numeric	The position of the left side of the shape, from the left side of the worksheet, in pixels
Top	Numeric	The position of the top of the shape, from the top of the worksheet, in pixels.
TextFrame	Object	Reference to a TextFrame object. Among its properties and methods is the Character property, which points to a Character object. The Character object's Text property contains the text in the frame, and its Font property references a Font object to control the look of the text.
HorizontalFlip	Logical	True if the shape is flipped horizontally.
VerticalFlip	Logical	True if the shape is flipped vertically.
Fill	Object	Reference to a FillFormat object.
Line	Object	Reference to a LineFormat object.

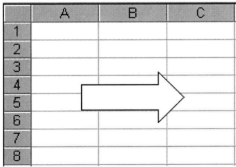

Figure 10. *Adding an AutoShape. The Shape collection's AddShape method adds one of more than 140 Office AutoShapes to your worksheet.*

The TextFrame object contains properties to format text (if any) in the shape. The most important property is the Character property, which references a Character object. The Character object's Text property contains the text, and its Font property accesses a Font object to control the look of the text. The following code adds a text string and formats the font:

```
WITH oSheet.Shapes[1].TextFrame.Characters
  .Text = "HERE"
  WITH .Font
    .Color = RGB(255, 0, 0) &&Red
    .Name = "Times New Roman"
    .Size = "12"
  ENDWITH
ENDWITH
```

Here's an interesting situation: for formatting cell borders, Chart objects, and other items in Excel, the Border object controls the border lines, and the Interior object controls the fill properties. However, Shapes are Office objects, and they use the LineFormat and FillFormat objects instead. Happily, they are similar. Sadly, they aren't the same.

Line objects store properties for color, style, transparency, pattern, weight, and arrowheads in the LineFormat object. Use the Shape object's Line property to access the LineFormat object. **Table 4** shows many of the available properties for the LineFormat object.

The colors of the line are set by using the ForeColor and BackColor properties. These properties point to a ColorFormat object. A ColorFormat object has only two properties— the one needed here is the RGB property (the other is the SchemeColor property; it's covered later). See "Formatting the Shape's border" in Chapter 10 for examples of how to use these properties.

The FillFormat object has many properties and is quite complex. To fill the shape with a color, use the FillFormat's ForeColor object. (Reminder: the FillFormat object is referenced by the Shape object's Fill property.)

```
oSheet.Shapes[1].Fill.ForeColor.RGB = RGB(192,192,192) && Light Gray
```

For more information on the FillFormat object, see the "Backgrounds" section in Chapter 11, where the FillFormat object is discussed in detail.

Table 4. *LineFormat object properties.*

Property	Type	Description
ForeColor	Object	The color of the line using a ColorFormat object.
BackColor	Object	The backcolor of a patterned line using a ColorFormat object. This is the secondary color of a patterned line, and is ignored if patterns are not used.
DashStyle	Numeric	The dash style of the line. Uses one of the following contants: msoLineDash　　　　　　4　　　msoLineDashDot　　　　　5 msoLineDashDotDot　　　6　　　msoLineLongDash　　　　7 msoLineLongDashDot　　　8　　　msoLineRoundDot　　　　3 msoLineSolid　　　　　　1　　　msoLineSquareDot　　　　2
Pattern	Numeric	The pattern applied to the line. The background of color is used as the background of the pattern. Use one of the many patterned constants, a few of which are listed here: msoPattern50Percent　　　　　　　　　7 msoPatternLargeConfetti　　　　　　　33 msoPatternLargeGrid　　　　　　　　34 msoPatternLightDownwardDiagonal　　21 msoPatternLightHorizontal　　　　　　19 msoPatternLightUpwardDiagonal　　　22 msoPatternLightVertical　　　　　　　20 msoPatternSmallGrid　　　　　　　　23 msoPatternWideDownwardDiagonal　　25 msoPatternZigZag　　　　　　　　　38
Style	Numeric	The style of the line, which can give the appearance of multiple lines. msoLineSingle　　　　1　　　msoLineThickBetweenThin　5 msoLineThickThin　　　4　　　msoLineThinThick　　　　　3 msoLineThinThin　　　2
Transparency	Numeric	The degree of transparency of the line. The value ranges between 0.0 (opaque) and 1.0 (completely clear).
Weight	Numeric	The thickness of the line, in points.
Visible	Logical	Indicates whether the line is visible.

Adding pictures

Pictures are added to the Shapes collection with the AddPicture method. The syntax is as follows:

```
oSheet.Shapes.AddPicture(cFileName, lLinkToFile, lSaveWithDocument,
                    nLeft, nTop, nWidth, nHeight)
```

cFileName	Character	The fully pathed filename of the picture.
lLinkToFile	Logical	Indicates whether to link the picture to the file from which it was created or to create a copy inside the document.
lSaveWithDocument	Logical	Indicates whether to save the linked picture with the file or to store only the link information in the document. This argument must be True if lLinkToFile is False.
nLeft, nTop	Numeric	The position (in points) of the upper-left corner of the picture, measured from the upper-left corner of the spreadsheet.
nWidth, nHeight	Numeric	The width and height of the picture, in points.

The following example adds the TasTrade logo to the worksheet. Be sure to fully qualify the path, as Excel does not know anything about VFP's defaults.

```
LogoFile = _SAMPLES + "TasTrade\Bitmaps\TTradeSm.bmp"
oSheet.Shapes.AddPicture(LogoFile, .T., .T., 32, 32, 72, 72)
```

A little playing is required when you're trying to determine the width and height of the graphic. None of the parameters are optional, so you need to know the width and height of any graphic you're adding.

Putting it all together

Listing 3 shows an example program for Tasmanian Traders' purchasing department. They would like to sell Mama's Raspberry Syrup, but Mama's Megacorp wants a $500 "marketing fee" before Tasmanian Traders can sell Mama's product. So the purchasing department has asked for an analysis of the situation. They want to know how many units of Mama's Raspberry Syrup they need to sell before they break even, and they want to see a breakdown of the sales of all condiments by year, so they can figure out whether the number required to break even is within the normal sales of all condiments. It has to look good, because Tasmanian Traders' VP of Purchasing will take this report with her when she meets with representatives of Mama's Megacorp to finalize the deal.

Here's a solution. Use a PivotTable to provide the sales breakdown, and then use the GoalSeek method to find the break-even number. Once the number is calculated, annotate it with a striking star shape to draw attention to the quantity required. Then add the TasTrade logo. **Figure 11** shows a report that will not only satisfy the requirements for the needed information, but also has visual appeal.

 Listing 3 is available as XLSample2.PRG in the Developer Download files available at www.hentzenwerke.com.

Listing 3. Tasmanian Traders' analysis worksheet for a new product. This sample demonstrates creating a PivotTable, using Goal Seek, and adding pictures and shapes. Figure 11 shows the results.

```
* Clean out any existing references to servers.
* This prevents memory loss to leftover instances.
RELEASE ALL LIKE o*

* For demonstration purposes, make certain objects
* available after this program executes.
PUBLIC oExcel, oBook, oSheet2, oPivotTable

#DEFINE xlDatabase          1
#DEFINE xlDataField         4
#DEFINE xlEdgeBottom        9
#DEFINE xlContinuous        1
#DEFINE msoShape24PointStar 95
#DEFINE autoIn2Pts          72
#DEFINE xlHAlignCenter      -4108
#DEFINE xlVAlignCenter      -4108
```

```
CLOSE DATA

OPEN DATABASE (_SAMPLES + "\TasTrade\Data\TasTrade")

SELECT Customer.Company_Name, ;
       Customer.Country, ;
       CMONTH(Orders.Order_Date) AS Order_Month, ;
       YEAR(Orders.Order_Date) AS Order_Year, ;
       Products.Product_Name, ;
       Order_Line_Items.Quantity, ;
       Order_Line_Items.Unit_Price * Order_Line_Items.Quantity ;
          AS Total_Price;
   FROM Orders, Order_Line_Items, Customer, Products ;
  WHERE Order_Line_Items.Order_ID = Orders.Order_ID ;
    AND Orders.Customer_ID = Customer.Customer_ID ;
    AND Order_Line_Items.Product_ID = Products.Product_ID ;
    AND Products.Category_ID = "    2" ;
   INTO CURSOR Pivot

COPY TO (CURDIR() + "Pivot") TYPE XL5

oBook = GETOBJECT(CURDIR() + "Pivot.XLS")

* Open the workbook, and best-fit all the columns.
* Ensure there are two sheets: Pivot for the data
* and another for the "presentation"
WITH oBook
  oExcel = .Application
  .Application.Visible = .T.
  .Windows[1].Activate()
  .Sheets[1].Range("A1:G310").Columns.AutoFit()
  oSheet2 = .Sheets.Add()
ENDWITH

* On the presentation worksheet, add the logo and title
WITH oSheet2

  * Add the TasTrade Logo
  LogoFile = _SAMPLES + "\TasTrade\Bitmaps\TTradeSm.bmp"
  .Shapes.AddPicture(LogoFile, .T., .T., ;
      0.25 * autoIn2Pts, 0.25 * autoIn2Pts, ;
      1.00 * autoIn2Pts, 1.00 * autoIn2Pts)

  * Title the worksheet
  WITH .Range["C2"]
    .Value = "Analysis for Mama's Raspberry Syrup"
    .Font.Size = 18
    .Font.Bold = .T.
  ENDWITH
ENDWITH

* Create a new PivotTable
oSourceData = oBook.Sheets[2].Range["A1:G" + ;
    ALLTRIM(STR(RECCOUNT("Pivot") + 1))]
oDestination = oSheet2.Range["C4"]
oPivotTable = oBook.Sheets[1].PivotTableWizard(xlDatabase, ;
    oSourceData, oDestination, "Analysis", .T., .T.)

WITH oPivotTable
```

```
  .AddFields("Product_Name", "Order_Year")
  .PivotFields["Quantity"].Orientation = xlDataField

  * Make the headings look nice
  .PivotFields["Product_Name"].Name = "Product Name"
  .PivotFields["Order_Year"].Name = "Year"
  .PivotFields["Sum of quantity"].Name = "Quantity Sold"

ENDWITH

WITH oSheet2

  * Format the columns a bit wider
  .Columns[4].ColumnWidth = 9
  .Columns[5].ColumnWidth = 9
  .Columns[6].ColumnWidth = 9
  .Columns[7].ColumnWidth = 9
  .Columns[8].ColumnWidth = 9

  * Find the break-even point with Goal Seek
  * Title
  .Range["C21"].Value = "Break-Even Analysis"
  .Range["C21"].Font.Bold = .T.

  * Revenue
  .Range["C22"].Value = "Price per Unit"
  .Range["D22"].Name = "UnitPrice"
  .Range["D22"].Value = 10
  .Range["D22"].NumberFormat = "$###.00"

  .Range["C23"].Value = "Units Sold"
  .Range["D23"].Name = "UnitsSold"
  .Range["D23"].Value = 100
  .Range["D23"].NumberFormat = "###.0"

  .Range("C23:D23").Borders(xlEdgeBottom).LineStyle = xlContinuous

  .Range["C24"].Value = "Total Revenue"
  .Range["D24"].Name = "TotalRevenue"
  .Range["D24"].Value = "= UnitPrice * UnitsSold"
  .Range["D24"].NumberFormat = "$##,###.00"

  * Costs
  .Range["C26"].Value = "Cost per Unit"
  .Range["D26"].Name = "UnitCost"
  .Range["D26"].Value = 7.23

  .Range["C27"].Value = "Marketing Fee"
  .Range["D27"].Name = "MarketingFee"
  .Range["D27"].Value = 500

  .Range("C27:D27").Borders(xlEdgeBottom).LineStyle = xlContinuous

  .Range["C28"].Value = "Total Costs"
  .Range["D28"].Name = "TotalCost"
  .Range["D28"].Value = "= (UnitCost * UnitsSold) + MarketingFee"
  .Range["D26:D30"].NumberFormat = "$##,###.00"

  * Profit
```

```
.Range["C30"].Value = "Profit"
.Range["D30"].Name = "Profit"
.Range["D30"].Value = "= TotalRevenue - TotalCost"

* Perform the Goal Seek
.Range["Profit"].GoalSeek(0, .Range("UnitsSold"))

* Add the shape with text indicating how many need
* to be sold to break even.
oShape = .Shapes.AddShape(msoShape24PointStar, ;
            4.8 * autoIn2Pts, 3.5 * autoIn2Pts,;
            2.0 * autoIn2Pts, 2.0 * autoIn2Pts)
cQuantity = ALLTRIM(STR(.Range["UnitsSold"].Value))

WITH oShape.TextFrame
   WITH .Characters
      .Text = "Sell " + cQuantity + " units to break even"
      .Font.Color = RGB(255, 0, 0) && Red
      .Font.Size  = 12
      .Font.Bold  = .T.
   ENDWITH
   .HorizontalAlignment = xlHAlignCenter
   .VerticalAlignment   = xlVAlignCenter
ENDWITH
ENDWITH
```

		Analysis for Mama's Raspberry Syrup					
Quantity Sold			Year				
Product Name			1992	1993	1994	1995	Grand Total
Aniseed Syrup			48	120	219	34	421
Camembert Pierrot			303	543	761	386	1993
Chef Anton's Gumbo Mix			38	169	49	120	376
Genen Shouyu			10	78	97		185
Grandma's Boysenberry Spread			23	36	156	109	324
Gula Malacca			50	260	372	51	733
Louisiana Fiery Hot Pepper Sauce			90	195	506	64	855
Louisiana Hot Spiced Okra			24	30	208	1	263
Northwoods Cranberry Sauce			92	152	134	98	476
Original Frankfurter grüne Soße			62	235	439	244	980
Sirop d'érable			55	38	410	177	680
Vegie-spread			34	229	89	147	499
Grand Total			829	2085	3440	1431	7785
Break-Even Analysis							
Price per Unit			$10.00				
Units Sold			180.5				
Total Revenue			$1,805.05				
Cost per Unit			$7.23				
Marketing Fee			$500.00				
Total Costs			$1,805.05				
Profit			$.00				

Sell 181
units to
break even

Figure 11. *TasTrade's analysis worksheet for a new product. The Goal Seek feature provides a break-even analysis, the results of which are highlighted in the shape. The number of units required can be compared to the PivotTable that contains the past sales history of all condiments. And the bitmap makes it look nice.*

This chapter covers a few of the major analysis tools available in Excel. We've touched on the more commonly used analysis tools to give you a taste of the techniques for working in Excel via Automation. There are additional tools available, which require similar techniques. The next chapter covers another kind of analysis tool: charting. Excel has a powerful charting engine to graph the results of the data analysis done in Excel.

Chapter 9
Excel's Graphing Engine

Since FoxPro lacks native graphing capabilities, Excel can step in and provide a terrific graphing engine.

Much has been written about using Microsoft Graph in VFP applications. Excel's graphing engine is based on Microsoft Graph, but it has one perk that Graph lacks: documentation. (Actually, almost any Excel graphing code also works in Graph, but this is one of those undocumented secrets you can't count on.) What you can't find out in the printed or on-line documentation and Help, you can usually find out by recording a macro.

The object model

Each Workbook has a Charts collection, which contains all of the charts in the active workbook. The Chart object contains properties that control the format and data within the chart. The SeriesCollection object stores a number of Series objects, one for each data series (a single set of data to graph) in the chart. Each Series object has a Values property, which stores the Range containing the values to plot. The Series object also has many properties to control the look of the series on the graph, such as chart type (one series can be a bar chart, while the next can be a line chart), color, borders, and so on.

The Chart object has properties to access objects that are global to the chart. For example, there are objects to format the several Axis objects, and the Floor and Walls of the PlotArea. The ChartArea (the area surrounding the chart) is formatted separately from the PlotArea (the interior of the chart, bordered on the outside by the axes). Finally, there are properties to access the Legend and ChartTitle objects.

Is it a chart or a sheet?

Excel offers two ways to place charts in a workbook. You can store the chart as an object in a worksheet, or you can store the chart as a separate worksheet (also known as a *chart sheet*). While the two kinds are each stored as Chart objects, they are stored in different collections, and each collection belongs to a different object.

Chart sheets are accessed through the Charts collection, and since they're worksheets, too, they can also be accessed through the Sheets collection (we recommend always using the Charts collection, because changing chart formatting on what appears to be a Sheet is quite confusing). The Charts collection is accessible through both the Application object and the Workbook object.

Embedded charts have their own collection, called ChartObjects. This collection belongs to the Worksheet object.

It is important to understand that chart sheets belong to the Workbook while embedded charts belong to the Worksheet. However, both kinds of charts are stored as the same Chart object and have the same properties and methods available for formatting the chart.

Regardless of whether it's an embedded chart or a chart sheet, if it's selected (either the chart sheet is the ActiveSheet or the embedded chart has "resize" handles), the Workbook object's ActiveChart property references the chart.

Setting up the data

To graph your data, the data must reside in an Excel worksheet (or series of worksheets). The section "Handling values and formulas" in Chapter 7 discusses the mechanics of adding data to worksheets. We won't cover that again here, but we will tell you how to set up the worksheet so your data easily translates into a graph.

First, we need to examine how Excel works with data. Excel charts work with sequences of data called *data series*. Each data series is a sequence of points that are plotted with the same attributes (such as color, pattern, symbol, line style, bar style—whatever is relevant to the chosen chart style). On a line chart, many lines can be plotted on a single chart; each line is a data series. On a bar chart with a three groups of color-coded bars, each color is a data series. A pie chart can graph only one data series.

Excel also uses ranges to label the category axis, and to label the data series in the legend. You can specify each data series separately, which is useful when one worksheet of data is used to create many graphs. However, Excel can accept a single rectangular range and use it to build a chart. If you're familiar with Excel's Chart Wizard, you probably already know that it defaults to using the first row and column for the headings, and then uses the remaining columns (or rows) for the data series. Understanding how Excel uses a single range for a chart makes life much easier for you; passing a single range is much easier than explicitly setting half a dozen ranges.

Setting up this single range is easy. Use column A for the category labels. The contents of each cell are the actual labels used on the X-axis, so be sure they aren't too cryptic or too long. Use subsequent columns for data series. Put the label for each series in row 1; start the data in row 2. The category headings in column A should also start in row 2. **Figure 1** shows a sample spreadsheet, ready to graph. The code to generate this spreadsheet is shown in **Listing 1** (XLGDataSetup.PRG in the Developer Download files available at www.hentzenwerke.com).

	A	B	C	D	E	F
1		1992	1993	1994	1995	1996
2	January		$1,038.10	$1,632.30	$3,530.98	
3	February		$850.40	$1,506.90	$4,723.80	
4	March		$1,383.90	$2,581.42	$5,381.84	
5	April		$1,424.70	$2,667.85		
6	May	$730.10	$929.00	$1,693.97		$19.00
7	June	$782.20	$1,361.10	$2,042.98		
8	July	$908.00	$1,485.20	$2,462.44		
9	August	$736.30	$1,254.70	$2,860.28		
10	September	$907.10	$1,633.80	$2,497.63		
11	October	$1,808.40	$2,223.60	$2,210.94		
12	November	$919.90	$1,673.20	$4,123.10		
13	December	$865.30	$1,994.80	$4,848.48		
14						

Figure 1. *A spreadsheet formatted to graph as a single range. The values in column A become the X-axis labels; the text in row 1 becomes the text to label each series in the legend for the data series stored in the column.*

Listing 1. *Code to populate the graphing data shown in Figure 1. This code uses monthly sales figures from the TasTrade sample database.*

```
* Sets up the monthly sales data by year to graph.

* Clean out any existing references to servers.
* This prevents memory loss to leftover instances.
RELEASE ALL LIKE o*

* For demonstration purposes, make oExcel and oBook
* available after this program executes.
PUBLIC oExcel, oBook

#DEFINE xlColumns 2
#DEFINE xlAutoFill 4

CLOSE ALL

* Open the Sales Summary view, which contains
* a summary of unit prices for each month and year.
OPEN DATABASE _SAMPLES + "\TASTRADE\DATA\Tastrade"
USE Customer IN 0
SELECT 0
USE "Sales Summary" ALIAS SalesSummary

* Add a workbook, using default settings
oExcel = CREATEOBJECT("Excel.Application")
oExcel.Visible = .T.
oBook  = oExcel.Workbooks.Add()

WITH oBook.Sheets[1]

   * Put the months down Column A. These are the
   * category (x) axis labels.
   .Range("A2").Value = "January"
   .Range("A2:A13").DataSeries(xlColumns, xlAutoFill, 1, 1)

   * Loop through the view. Make each year a column, and
   * ensure that there's a header.
   CurrentColumn = "A"
   CurrentYear   = "X"
   SCAN
     IF CurrentYear <> LEFT(SalesSummary.Exp_1, 4)

       * Store the Current Year
       CurrentYear = LEFT(SalesSummary.Exp_1, 4)

       * Increment the column letter (note: don't exceed
       * 25 years with this logic!)
       CurrentColumn = CHR(ASC(CurrentColumn) + 1)

       * Set the header
       .Range(CurrentColumn + "1").Value = CurrentYear
     ENDIF

     * Calculate the current row (add 1 to the value of the month);
     * make sure it's a string
```

```
      CurrentRow = ALLTRIM(STR(VAL(RIGHT(SalesSummary.Exp_1, 2)) + 1))

    * Set the value of the cell.
    .Range(CurrentColumn + CurrentRow).Value = SalesSummary.Sum_Unit_Price

  ENDSCAN

  * Widen the columns so all values are seen
  * Convert CurrentColumn from the alpha character to a numeric
  FOR I = 1 TO ASC(CurrentColumn) - 63
    .Columns[I].ColumnWidth = 12
  NEXT I
ENDWITH
```

What if you want the categories in each column, and each row is a series? You can do that. When you create the graph with the ChartWizard method (see the section "Creating a graph" later in this chapter), there's a parameter to denote whether the series are in rows or in columns.

Range names are your friend

It won't take long until your client requests a series of graphs built from the same data. Using the example data shown in Figure 1, the client may want a graph for each year, then one comparing all years on one graph. While you can build a separate worksheet with only the necessary data for the graph (which leads to redundant data), the easiest way is to put all the data on one worksheet, and then use range names for each series and for the category axis labels. Why range names? It's easier to read and debug "CategoryNames" and "Year1994" than "Sheet1!A2:A13" and "Sheet1!D2:D13."

Names are stored in the Names collection, which is accessible from the Application, Workbook, and Worksheet objects. Use the Range object's Name property to name a range. Using the data shown in Figure 1, the following code shows sample names along with their ranges. Like VFP's field names, range names must start with a letter; hence the name "Year1992" rather than "1992."

```
WITH oExcel.Sheets[1]
   .Range("A1:A13").Name = "CategoryNames"
   .Range("B1:B13").Name = "Year1992"
   .Range("C1:C13").Name = "Year1993"
   .Range("D1:D13").Name = "Year1994"
   .Range("E1:E13").Name = "Year1995"
   .Range("F1:F13").Name = "Year1996"
ENDWITH
```

Creating a graph

Polymorphism is hard at work here: use the Add method to add a chart. This time, there is a bit of a twist—you must decide which collection's Add method to use.

If you want to add an embedded chart, use the Add method of the ChartObjects collection. It takes four parameters, which are the left, top, height, and width (in points) of the chart. Issuing the following inserts a chart object below the sample data:

```
oChart = oExcel.Sheets[1].ChartObjects.Add(45.7, 173.2, 319.5, 190.5)
```

Figure 2 shows the placement of the empty ChartObject container. Don't worry—it's really a chart. The ChartWizard method can easily set the most common properties in one method call, or you can manually set them yourself. We suppose you can consider this blank graph a "feature," as it made no decisions for you about the kind of graph—so there's nothing to undo.

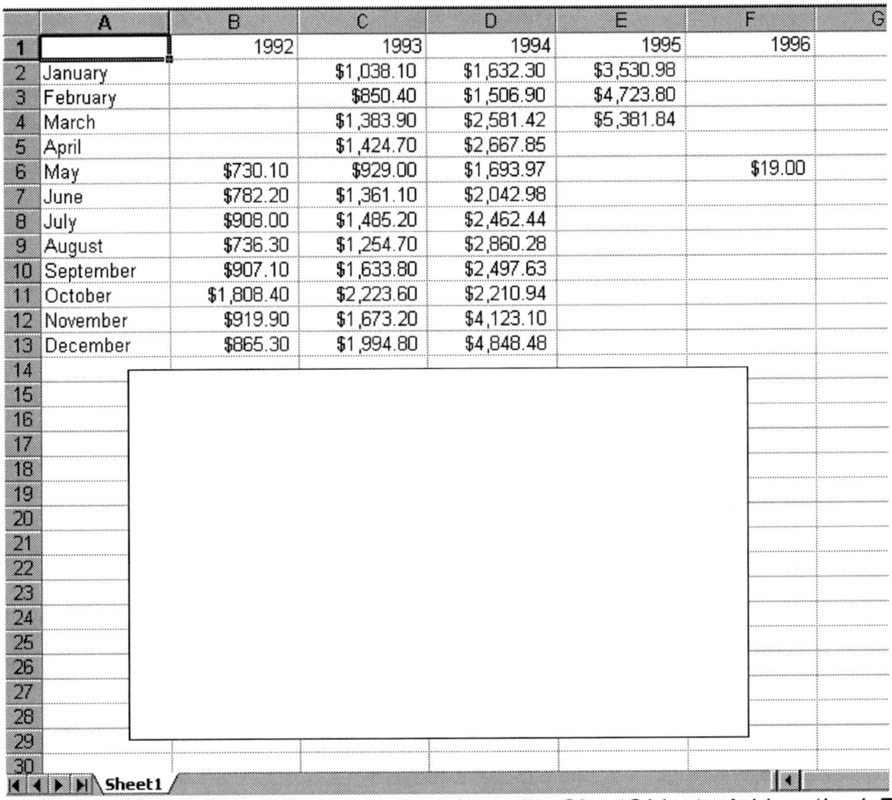

	A	B	C	D	E	F	G
1		1992	1993	1994	1995	1996	
2	January		$1,038.10	$1,632.30	$3,530.98		
3	February		$850.40	$1,506.90	$4,723.80		
4	March		$1,383.90	$2,581.42	$5,381.84		
5	April		$1,424.70	$2,667.85			
6	May	$730.10	$929.00	$1,693.97		$19.00	
7	June	$782.20	$1,361.10	$2,042.98			
8	July	$908.00	$1,485.20	$2,462.44			
9	August	$736.30	$1,254.70	$2,860.28			
10	September	$907.10	$1,633.80	$2,497.63			
11	October	$1,808.40	$2,223.60	$2,210.94			
12	November	$919.90	$1,673.20	$4,123.10			
13	December	$865.30	$1,994.80	$4,848.48			
14							
15							
16							
17							
18							
19							
20							
21							
22							
23							
24							
25							
26							
27							
28							
29							
30							

Sheet1

Figure 2. Adding an embedded chart from the ChartObjects.Add method. The new chart is blank; Excel made no assumptions about it. Use the ChartWizard method to fill it in easily, or set all of the properties manually.

How did we settle on the values to pass? With a bit of brute force in the Command Window. We created a public variable, oExcel, then ran the XLGDataSetup program. Next, we activated Excel (using Alt-Tab) and added a chart using the Chart Wizard button, and then positioned the resulting graph where we wanted it. Then we went back to VFP and queried the Left, Top, Height, and Width properties of the ChartObject object. The following commands give you the numbers you need.

```
? oExcel.Sheets[1].ChartObjects[1].Left
? oExcel.Sheets[1].ChartObjects[1].Top
? oExcel.Sheets[1].ChartObjects[1].Height
? oExcel.Sheets[1].ChartObjects[1].Width
```

If you want to add a chart sheet, use the Add method of the Charts collection. This one needs no parameters. It places the new chart sheet before the currently active worksheet. The chart sheet is named Chart*n*, where *n* is the next available chart number.

```
oChart = oBook.Charts.Add()
```

Add can also take parameters to specifically place the new chart sheet. Pass a Worksheet object as the first parameter to place the chart before the worksheet, or pass a Worksheet object as the second parameter to place it after the specified worksheet. A note of caution: passing worksheet *names* as the first or second parameter nets this error: "OLE IDispatch exception code 0 from Microsoft Excel: Unable to get the Add property of the Sheets class." Be sure to pass the Worksheet *object*.

The ActiveChart property

When the Add method is used to add an embedded chart, the resulting chart is not selected. To make it available through the Workbook's ActiveChart property, you need to use the chart's Activate method:

```
oChart.Activate()
```

Now the chart is active and available from the Workbook's ActiveChart property.

We've sometimes found that Chart object methods, particularly those for embedded charts, fail with an "Unknown name" error if called by the full ChartObject name (for example, Excel.Workbooks[1].Sheets["Sheet1"].ChartObjects[1], or any variable set to the full reference), but they appear to work just fine when called from the ActiveChart property when the same chart is definitely active (for instance, oExcel.ActiveWorkbook.ActiveChart). We're not quite sure why this is, but we're glad to find a workaround when some methods just don't want to work.

Off to see the wizard

There is a single method called ChartWizard that allows you to quickly format a chart. If you're familiar with Excel's interactive method of building a chart, the parameters will be familiar, too, because they closely parallel the tabs on the Chart Wizard's dialog box.

```
oChart.ChartWizard( [oSourceRange], [nChartType], [nChartFormat],
                     [nPlotBy], [nCategoryLabels], [nSeriesLabels],
                     [lHasLegend], [cTitle], [cCategoryTitle],
                     [cValueTitle], [cExtraTitle] )
```

oSourceRange	Object	The Range object that contains the source data for the chart.
nChartType	Numeric	The chart type. Use one of the following constants:
nChartFormat	Numeric	The variation of the chart type to use (for example, if nChartType is xlBar, then you could choose stacked bar vs. clustered bar). Use a number from 1 to however many formats are available. See the text for more information.
nPlotBy	Numeric	Indicates whether data series are stored in rows or columns. Use one of these two constants:
nCategoryLabels	Numeric	Indicates how many rows (if plotting by rows) or columns (if plotting by columns) to use as the labels on the category (X) axis.
nSeriesLabels	Numeric	Indicates how many columns (if plotting by rows) or rows (if plotting by columns) to use to label the series. Generally, the labels appear in the legend.
lHasLegend	Logical	Indicates whether the chart has a legend (.T.) or not (.F.).
cTitle	Character	A character string used to title the chart. By default, it is centered just above the plot area.
cCategoryTitle	Character	A character string used to title the category (X) axis.
cValueTitle	Character	A character string used to title the value (Y) axis.
cExtraTitle	Character	A character string used for a second value axis title in 2D charts (if two separate value axes are used), or as the series (Z) axis title in 3D charts.

For nChartType constants:

xlArea	1		xl3DArea	-4098
xlBar	2		xl3DBar	-4099
xlColumn	3		xl3DColumn	-4100
xlLine	4		xl3DLine	-4101
xlPie	5		xl3DPie	-4102
xlRadar	-4151		xl3DSurface	-4103
xlXYScatter	-4169		xlDoughnut	-4120
xlCombination	-4111			

See the text for more information.

For nPlotBy constants:

xlRows	1	xlColumns	2

The default is based on the shape of the range. If there are more rows than columns, the default is xlRows. If there are more columns than rows, the default is xlColumns. If there are an equal number of rows and columns, xlRows is used.

All this power in a single method comes with a price—it takes quite a few pages to explain all the parameters. As we explain each of the parameters, we'll also tell you which Chart object properties are set by the ChartWizard method, and whether any alternative methods are available to set these parameters. These properties and methods are discussed in the remaining sections of this chapter, so we'll note the section to reference for a complete discussion of those properties.

The source range

This is the Range object where the data resides. For embedded charts, it can be—but doesn't have to be—on the same worksheet. For chart sheets, the data is obviously not on the same worksheet. To pass the range used to populate the embedded chart shown in Figure 2, pass the following object as the oSourceRange parameter:

```
oBook.Sheets["Sheet1"].Range("A1:F13")
```

Notice that in this range, we've included the cells that contain the category and value labels. If no other parameters are passed to the ChartWizard, it assumes that no rows or columns are used as labels, so 13 categories are graphed, instead of 12 months, and six series are plotted instead of five years. If you choose to include the category and value labels, be sure to include the nCategoryLabels and nSeriesLabels parameters.

Non-contiguous ranges

It would be nice if all graphs could be graphed from contiguous ranges of data. However, you'll find that there are times when you'd like to use one worksheet to develop multiple graphs, or put data from multiple worksheets into a single graph. Either way, the series data is not contiguous.

Fortunately, Excel provides a way to use non-contiguous data. All that's necessary is to list the ranges separated by commas. Be sure to include the category label row first. For our example, let's build a graph with the months as category names, and show the years 1993 and 1994 as data series. There are two ways to do this. Using cell addresses, the code looks like this:

```
oBook.Sheets["Sheet1"].Range("A1:A13, C1:C13, D1:D13")
```

Using range names (see the section "Range names are your friend" earlier in this chapter), you get this more readable code:

```
oBook.Sheets["Sheet1"].Range("CategoryNames, Year1993, Year1994")
```

 Be sure to name the ranges using the Range object's Name property, instead of using the Names collection's Add method. We're not sure why, but a range that's added with Names.Add doesn't seem to be recognized by the ChartWizard method. You get an OLE error: 0x800a03ec, Unknown COM status code. To be fair, this isn't the only way to get that error. You can trigger this error by passing a misspelled or non-existent range name, too.

Note that for each of the ranges (including the CategoryNames range), the range includes a row for the series labels. When passing a range that includes headings, be sure that the nCategoryLabels and nSeriesLabels parameters (the fifth and sixth parameters) have a value of 1 (or more, if more rows/columns are used).

Other source properties and methods

Data series are stored in the SeriesCollection collection object, which stores a Series object for each data series. The SeriesCollection's Add method takes five parameters. They are the source range (just like the ChartWizard), a PlotBy numeric value (just like the ChartWizard's nPlotBy parameter), a logical value that's true if the first row or column contains series labels, another logical value that's true if the first column or row contains category labels, and finally, a logical value that determines whether the category labels are replaced or not. Issuing the following is similar to adding the source range through the ChartWizard (using the oSourceRange, nPlotBy, nSeriesLabels, and nCategoryLabels parameters):

```
#DEFINE xlColumns   2
oExcel.ActiveChart.SeriesCollection.Add("Sheet1!A1:F13", xlColumns, .T., .T.)
```

The Series objects store a lot of formatting information. This is covered in more detail in the "Formatting the components" section later in this chapter.

Another alternative that's new to Excel 2000 is the Chart object's SetDataSource method. This method takes two parameters: the source range and the numeric PlotBy value. The following is equivalent to the SeriesCollection.Add method and the ChartWizard method:

```
#DEFINE xlColumns   2
oExcel.ActiveChart.SetSourceData(oExcel.Sheets[1].Range("Sheet1!A1:F13"),;
      xlColumns)
```

Chart Types and Formats

The ChartWizard's second and third parameters work together. The first of these is nChartType, a numeric value that corresponds to the type of chart, such as area chart, pie chart, line chart, or bar chart. The second of these parameters, nChartFormat, is a sub-type, or a fine-tuning on the basic chart type. For example, a bar chart can be a clustered bar or a stacked bar chart. **Figure 3** shows how these two parameters work in the interactive Chart Wizard. The list to the left shows the chart type (with a thumbnail to help you out), and the chart sub-type is shown on the right, with larger icons to help you select precisely which chart to use.

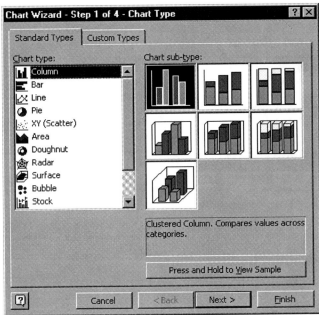

Figure 3. Chart types and sub-types, as seen from Excel's Chart Wizard. This illustrates how the nChartType (corresponds to the chart type list) and nChartFormat (corresponds to the sub-type buttons on the right) parameters work together.

There's only one problem with using Figure 3 as a reference: this is one of the few dialog boxes that does not put the options in as they're used in the corresponding method! We've shown Figure 3 to illustrate the concept of Chart Type and Chart Format, but don't rely on the dialog box to give you hints about the values to use.

The nChartType parameter uses a series of values, each with its own VBA constant name. Unfortunately, there are no constants available for the nChartFormat parameter. In fact, they don't even really correspond to the chart sub-types shown in Figure 3, because the ChartWizard method separates 3D from 2D graphs, and it mixes and matches types. Appendix B shows a complete list of the available values; **Table 1** shows the most common values.

Table 1. *Sample nChartType parameters.The Chart Format value is the column to use in the ChartWizard; the Chart Type value is the resulting value in the Chart object's ChartType property. Appendix B has the complete listing.*

Chart Format description	Chart Format value	Chart Type value
For Chart Type: xlArea	**1**	
Stacked Area	1	76
Stacked Area with black grid lines	4	76
For Chart Type: xlBar	**2**	
Clustered Bar	1	57
Stacked Bar	3	58
Clustered Bar with 0 overlap and 0 gap width	8	57
For Chart Type: xlColumn	**3**	
Clustered Column with gap width set to 150	1	51
Clustered Column, 0 overlap and 0 gap width	8	51
100% Stacked Column with series lines	10	53
For Chart Type: xlLine	**4**	
Line with markers	1	65
Line with no data markers	2	4
Data markers only (no connecting lines)	3	65
Smoothed line with no markers	10	4
For Chart Type: xlPie	**5**	
Pie with no labels	1	5
Pie with labels, highlighting first wedge	2	5
Exploded pie	4	69
For Chart Type: xl3DArea	**-4098**	
Stacked 3D area	1	78
Stacked 3D area with series labels	2	78
Area 3D elevated, vertical grid lines	7	-4098
For Chart Type: xl3DBar	**-4099**	
Clustered 3D	1	60
Stacked 3D	2	61
For Chart Type: xl3DColumn	**-4100**	
Clustered 3D	1	54
Stacked 3D	2	55
100% Stacked 3D	3	56
For Chart Type: xl3DPie	**-4102**	
3D Pie with no labels	1	-4102
3D Exploded pie	4	70

Other chart type properties

The nChartType and nChartFormat parameters set the Chart object's ChartType property. Just to be sure that life isn't too simple, Excel has 73 numeric values that don't relate well (mathematically, anyway) to the combinations of nChartType and nChartFormat parameters. You can see the resulting values enumerated in the Chart Format Value column of Table 1. We'll discuss them some more in the "Chart types" section later in this chapter.

Not only do these two parameters set the ChartType property, they also set many properties of the various Axis objects, including ScaleType, HasMajorGridlines, and HasRadarAxisLabels (if a Radar chart). Series properties are set, too, including AxisGroup, ChartType, Explosion, HasDataLabels, HasErrorBars, and various Marker properties.

For more information on these and other related properties, see the appropriate sections under "Formatting the components" later in this chapter.

PlotBy—selecting rows or columns

The nPlotBy parameter determines whether rows or columns are used as data series. Two values are available: xlRows (1) and xlColumns (2). The default depends upon the shape of the range: if there are more columns than rows, columns are the default; otherwise, the default is rows. Because of this "moving target" nature of the default value, we choose to always provide this parameter, rather than assume anything.

Other PlotBy properties

This is a well-behaved parameter, as it sets only one property without any guesswork, and it even has the same name! The Chart object's PlotBy property uses the same two values, xlRows (1) and xlColumns (2).

The category and series labels

The nCategoryLabels and nSeriesLabels parameters control how many rows or columns are used within the source range to label the categories and series. The nPlotBy parameter determines whether the category labels are rows or columns. If nPlotBy is xlRows, then the category labels are in the first n rows, and the series labels are in the first n columns. Conversely, if nPlotBy is xlColumns, then the category labels are in the first n columns, and the series labels are in the first n rows.

Generally, the value of nCategoryLabels and nSeriesLabels is 0 or 1. You can, however, use two or more columns/rows. You should experiment with the visual results; having two lines for each category may be too busy if many categories are used. Depending on space, Excel may omit the second line, anyway.

Other label properties

Category labels are stored as a range in the Series object's XValues property. Series labels are stored in the Series object's Name property. More on those in the "Data series" topic later in this chapter.

Does it have a legend?

The lHasLegend parameter determines whether the resulting chart has a legend (also known as a "key"). All it does is make the legend visible (or not). Pass a logical value indicating whether the chart should have a legend.

Other legend properties and objects

This parameter sets the Chart object's HasLegend property, which is a logical value. You can query this one and get a Boolean value (unlike many seemingly Boolean values). If the value is true, legend values are set through the Chart object's Legend object, which is discussed in detail in the "Legends" topic later in this chapter.

Title parameters

The final four parameters—cTitle, cCategoryTitle, cValueTitle, and cExtraTitle—are simply character strings that are placed in the chart as titles. The cTitle parameter is used as a chart title and is centered at the top of the chart. The cCategoryTitle and cValueTitle parameters are axis titles and are centered on the respective axis. The cExtraTitle is used only in two cases: if there is a second axis on a 2D chart, or if the chart is a 3D chart, and a third axis needs a title. See the ChartWizard example in the next section for an example showing where the titles are placed.

Other title properties

The cTitle parameter sets the Chart's HasTitle property to true and makes the ChartTitle object available (through the ChartTitle property). The remaining title parameters are axis titles, which set the corresponding Axis object's HasTitle property to True, and makes the AxisTitle object available (through the AxisTitle property). These are discussed in detail in the "Titles" topic later in this chapter.

Finally, an example of wizardry

After all the explanation of the various parameters, it's now time to see how this thing really works. For the example, we'll build a clustered column chart from the whole range of example data, plotting series by columns and using one column and row for labels. The legend is calculated, and we'll use example titles to show where the various titles go. Ready? Here goes:

```
#DEFINE xlColumn            3
#DEFINE xlColumns           2
#DEFINE autoColumnFormat    4
#DEFINE autoOneSeriesLabel  1
#DEFINE autoOneCategoryLabel 1
#DEFINE autoHasLegend       .T.

oSourceRange = oExcel.Sheets[1].Range("A1:F13")
oExcel.ActiveChart.ChartWizard(oSourceRange, xlColumn, autoColumnFormat, ;
     xlColumns, autoOneCategoryLabel, autoOneSeriesLabel, autoHasLegend, ;
     "Chart Title", "Category Title", "Value Title", "Extra Title")
```

Figure 4 shows the results of the ChartWizard method. As you can see, there's a lot of power packed into this method. As you examine the resulting graph, you see a lot of the features of the ChartWizard method. There are titles, axis labels, and a legend on a nicely formatted chart. If there's something you want to enhance, you can certainly do so. There are many properties and methods to help you refine the format—see the section "Formatting the components" later in this chapter.

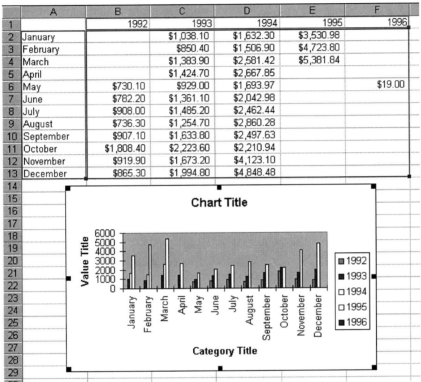

	A	B	C	D	E	F
1		1992	1993	1994	1995	1996
2	January		$1,038.10	$1,632.30	$3,530.98	
3	February		$850.40	$1,506.90	$4,723.80	
4	March		$1,383.90	$2,581.42	$5,381.84	
5	April		$1,424.70	$2,667.85		
6	May	$730.10	$929.00	$1,693.97		$19.00
7	June	$782.20	$1,361.10	$2,042.98		
8	July	$908.00	$1,485.20	$2,462.44		
9	August	$736.30	$1,254.70	$2,860.28		
10	September	$907.10	$1,633.80	$2,497.63		
11	October	$1,808.40	$2,223.60	$2,210.94		
12	November	$919.90	$1,673.20	$4,123.10		
13	December	$865.30	$1,994.80	$4,848.48		

Figure 4*. The results of the ChartWizard method. Although its parameter list is long, the ChartWizard method has a lot of power to format a chart.*

There is an alternative to using the ChartWizard. You can control each of the objects separately. It takes more code, but you gain more control. We've found that a hybrid approach works best: use the ChartWizard to get you close to what you want, and then refine the formatting from there. In the following sections, we'll discuss the various objects contained in a chart, and how to refine them. Then we'll look at the code to manually create that chart without the ChartWizard.

The anatomy of a chart

Now that we have a chart to look at, we can talk about the pieces of the chart. So many objects make up a chart that the terminology quickly gets confusing.

The *chart area* is the whole area of the chart. For embedded charts, it's the area enclosed by the border. When selected, it has eight resize handles, as shown in Figure 4. For chart sheets, the chart area is the whole sheet. The major difference between chart sheets and embedded charts is that the chart area on an embedded chart can be moved and resized (via the Top, Left,

Height, and Width properties), while the size and position of a chart sheet is fixed to the bounds of a sheet. The chart area is the only object affected by whether the chart is a chart sheet or an embedded chart. The Chart object stores the ChartArea object in the ChartArea property.

The *plot area* is the area bounded by the axes. It's the gray area shown in Figure 4. The PlotArea object is accessed from the Chart object's PlotArea property.

There are several kinds of axes available in the charts. Figure 4 shows the two most common: the *category axis*, also known as the X or horizontal axis, and the *primary value axis*, known as the Y or vertical axis. Excel provides for two value axes; if the *secondary value axis* were used, it would be shown on the right side of the graph. For some 3D charts, there is a *series axis*, also known as a Z-axis. The Axes collection is accessed through the Chart object's Axes method.

The *legend* is the box to the right of the plot area. It shows a sample of the formatting for each series along with the series labels. The Legend object is accessed via the Chart object's Legend property.

Data *series* are data points plotted with the same format. Each series is stored in an object in the SeriesCollection object. The Series object stores the data ranges for the data to graph, the category labels, and the series labels. It also stores all the formatting options, such as color options and formatting specific to the chart type (high-low bars, data markers, bar types, and so on). Each series can have its own chart type; for example, you can have one series as a line, the next as an area chart, and the third as a column chart. As long as all series use the same kind of axes, you can mix and match chart types. (In other words, a single chart can contain several different graph types, but don't plan on putting pie charts in the same chart as lines and columns.)

Within each series is a collection of data *points*. Each point can be labeled and/or formatted separately. Formatting a point calls attention to that data item—for example, it could be used to identify the high (or low) for a series. Warning: highlighting too many data points causes charts to become very confusing to the viewer. If you're highlighting more than a couple of points in a chart, be sure the points really need to be highlighted. Access the Points collection from the Series object's Points method.

Formatting the components

The GraphWizard method goes only so far in setting up a graph. Many clients are familiar with the graphs that Excel can produce and ask for many of those features. They'll ask you to move the legend to the other side, make the font bigger on the axis labels, add grid lines, change the colors (of everything—clients *love* to insist on color changes), and so on.

The following topics generally are organized to correspond to objects and collections that are part of the chart. Some objects, such as the SeriesCollection, are always available. Others, such as Title objects, are only available if a particular property, such as HasTitle, is set to true.

Whether you are building the chart from scratch or are modifying one built by the ChartWizard, you'll find what you need in the following topics. We've organized the rest of this chapter to start with a discussion of the Chart object's properties and methods, and then we'll work through the Chart object's subordinate objects.

The Chart object

We've covered many of the basics of the Chart object: how to add one, and how to use the ChartWizard method. Now we can look at the object in more detail. Many of the Chart object's properties and methods reference other objects and collections. The ChartArea and PlotArea properties reference the ChartArea and PlotArea objects, and are always available.

Some objects are not always available. Chart titles, legends, and axes are optional components. The Chart object has properties to determine whether these objects are available. The three main properties that allow access to the optional components are:

- **HasAxis**. If true, the Axes method is available to access the Axes collection.

- **HasLegend**. If true, the Legend property is available to access the Legend object.

- **HasTitle**. If true, the ChartTitle property is available to access the ChartTitle object.

There are a few properties that don't access objects. These global properties, shown in **Table 2,** affect the whole chart.

Table 2. Chart object properties. These properties do not reference other objects; they affect the look of the chart.

Property	Type	Description
ChartType	Numeric	See the next section, "Chart types," for more information.

BarShape	Numeric	Determines the shape of the bars or columns in a 3D bar or 3D column chart.
		    xlBox 0 xlCylinder 3
		    xlConeToMax 5 xlPyramidToMax 2
		    xlConeToPoint 4 xlPyramidToPoint 1
		See the next section, "Chart types," for more information.

DisplayBlanksAs	Numeric	Determines the way that blank cells plot on a chart. Uses the following values:
		    xlNotPlotted 1 Do not plot data points (for example, a line series shows a gap for blank data).
		    xlInterpolated 3 Figure out the data point from the two data points on either side (for example, a line series is drawn from the point before the blank value to the point after).
		    xlZero 2 Plot the data points as zero (for example, a line series drops to zero for the blank data).

Name	Character	Provides the name of the chart. For chart sheets, this name is used to label the sheet's tab. For both chart sheets and embedded charts, the name is used to access the Chart or ChartObject objects. The default for chart sheets is "Chart$n$," where n is the next available chart number. The default for embedded sheets is "<SheetName> Chart n" (note the spaces), where <SheetName> is the name of the current worksheet (and is inherited—if the sheet name changes, so does this part of the chart name) and n is the next available Chart object number.
PlotVisibleOnly	Logical	Indicates whether visible and hidden cells are plotted. True to plot only visible cells, false to plot both visible and hidden cells. This is only effective if the worksheet has protection features turned on.
Visible	Logical	Indicates whether the chart is visible.

Several methods take care of some cool features; these are discussed in the appropriate sections toward the end of this chapter. These are GetChartElement, PrintOut, PrintPreview, SaveAs, and Export. The SetBackgroundPicture method is discussed with the ChartArea object, as it affects the formatting of the chart area.

Chart types

We've touched on chart types a bit in the ChartWizard section. The ChartWizard method uses two parameters, a Chart Type and a Chart Format, which combine to determine how the chart looks. The results of this combination are stored as a single number in the Chart object's ChartType property (certain formats also may set some properties of the Axis and Series objects, too).

Unfortunately, we know of no algorithm to convert from the ChartWizard parameters to the ChartType values, which is why we've enumerated the values in Table 1 and Appendix B.

For each of the values, Excel has a defined constant. To conserve space in Table 1, we listed only the value. Check out the Object Browser for more information. Some of the constants are: xl3DColumn (-4100), xl3DColumnClustered (54), xlBarClustered (57), xlConeBarClustered (102), xlCylinderColClustered (92), and xlLineMarkers (65).

What are those cone and cylinder constants? Actually, you can add pyramid constants, too. These charts are not readily available to the ChartWizard. Here's a case where you need to manually set the graph type, to show the bars (or columns) as cones, cylinders, or pyramids, examples of which are shown in **Figure 5**. So, to set a graph to a columned cluster of cylinders, issue the following:

```
#DEFINE xlCylinderColClustered  92
oExcel.ActiveChart.ChartType = xlCylinderColClustered
```

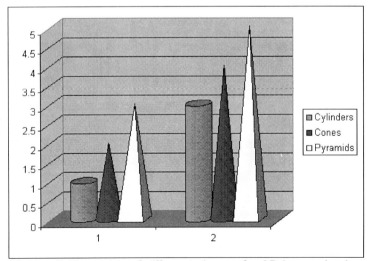

Figure 5. *Examples of different shapes for 3D bar and column charts. Cylinders, cones, and pyramids are available to add interest to your presentations.*

Actually, if you examine Appendix B, you'll find that only 33 of the 73 ChartType values are represented. The ChartWizard is excellent for setting up the most common kinds of charts, but you need to manually set the ChartType for some of the uncommon graphs.

Another way to get the cylinder, cone, and pyramid shapes in bar and column charts is to set the ChartType as a 3D bar or column chart, and then set the BarShape property. When the BarShape property is set, it updates the ChartType property to reflect the new ChartType value.

Chart object properties available only to 3D charts

Some objects and properties are available only if the chart has 3D properties. The Floor and Walls properties reference Floor and Walls objects, respectively. The walls are the sides of the 3D chart, and the floor is the bottom. These objects are similar and contain two main properties to format the objects. The Border property and the Interior property—explained later in this chapter in "The Border object" and "The Interior object" sections, respectively—control all of the formatting. Generally, you will want to set these using the same properties as for PlotArea.

The DepthPercent property stores the depth of the chart (along the Z-axis) as a percentage of the chart width. Valid values range from 20 to 2000. The HeightPercent property stores the height of the chart as a percentage of the chart width. Valid values are between 5 and 500 percent.

Two properties set the angle at which you view the chart. The Elevation is the height at which you view the chart, in degrees. **Figure 6** shows two graphs—one with the elevation set to 10, and the other with it set to the maximum value of 90. The default is 15 degrees for most chart types. The valid range for the Elevation property is -90 to 90, except for bar charts, which can range from 0 to 44.

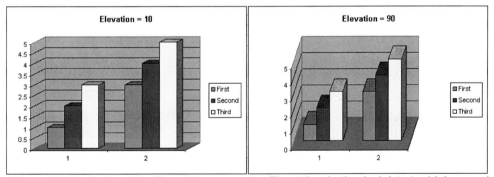

Figure 6. *Illustrating the Elevation property. Elevation is the height at which you view the chart. The chart on the left has the Elevation property set to 10, which is near eye-level. The chart on the right shows the maximum elevation, or 90, which is looking down onto the chart. The minimum value is -90, or looking from below the chart.*

The Rotation property determines how far the chart is rotated left or right (around the Y-axis), in degrees. Valid values range from 0 to 360, except for bar charts, which again can range from 0 to 44. The default is 20 for all charts. **Figure 7** shows two charts with different rotations.

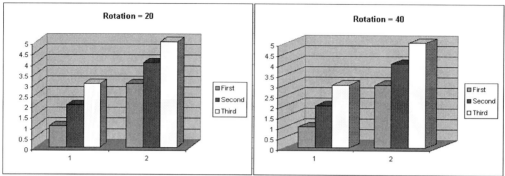

Figure 7. *Rotating the chart. The chart on the left shows the default rotation of 20 degrees, while the chart on the right shows a rotation of 40 degrees.*

The charts shown in Figure 7 are drawn in a style called isometric projection. This 3D drawing style is used for construction drawings, because accurate measurements can be made from anywhere on the chart. This is controlled by the RightAngleAxes logical property; when true, isometric projection is used—it's characterized by putting the axes at right angles to each other. When it's false, you can set the Perspective property, which takes a value between 0 and 100. Perspective is another 3D drawing style where lines that are parallel in reality, like the horizontal grid lines, are not drawn parallel and meet at a point called the vanishing point. This drawing method is used for illustration, and measurements aren't accurate because items in the foreground are necessarily larger than those in the background. Perspective is the technique that makes 3D illustrations look more realistic. When you set the value to 0, the vanishing point is far in the distance, making the lines look parallel. When set to the maximum value of 100, the vanishing point is close to the graph, which greatly distorts the graph and over-emphasizes the large end of the graph. The default value is 30. **Figure 8** shows two graphs—one has its Perspective property set to 25, and the other has it set to 100. Compare these graphs to the graphs shown in Figure 7, which have the RightAngleAxes property set to true and use the isometric projection.

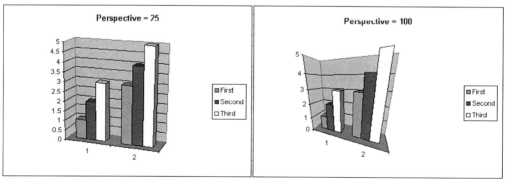

Figure 8. *A difference in perspective. Using perspective enhances the 3D illusion, as in the chart on the left (compare to the boxy look in Figure 7). The chart on the right shows the maximum perspective, which gives a very different effect.*

ChartArea

The ChartArea is the area containing the entire chart. As mentioned previously, if the chart is an embedded chart, you have access to the Top, Left, Height, and Width properties to set the size and location of the embedded chart. These properties are not available in chart sheets, because the chart is sized to take up the whole sheet; these properties are meaningless in that situation.

There is one property that does not reference an object. This is the AutoScaleFont property. Set this to false if you do not want the text to change size as the chart changes size. The default is true.

Three properties affect objects that format the entire chart area. These are the Border property (references the Border object), the Interior property (references an Interior object), and the Font property (references a Font object). These three objects are commonly used to format many chart objects (like PlotArea), and the Font and Border objects are even used in other areas in Microsoft Office.

The Border object

In Chapter 7, "Excel Basics," we looked at the Borders collection, which is used to format individual sides of each cell in a Range. Ranges work with a collection of Borders objects, one for each of the eight different borders. All other objects work with a single border, which affects all sides of the object equally. ChartArea, PlotArea, and others typically have rectangular borders, with all four sides formatted identically.

All Border objects have the same properties; these are listed in **Table 3**.

Table 3. Border properties. Borders can be placed around many objects, and their appearance can be altered with these properties.

Property	Type	Description
Color	RGB Color	The color of the border.
LineStyle	Numeric	The numeric value corresponding to a preset line style. xlContinuous 1 xlDot -4118 xlDash -4115 xlDouble -4119 xlDashDot 4 xlLineStyleNone -4142 xlDashDotDot 5 xlSlantDashDot 13
Weight	Numeric	The width of the line. This uses constants, not points. xlHairline 1 xlMedium -4138 xlThin 2 xlThick 4

To remove the border around the chart, use the following code:

```
#DEFINE xlNone -4142
oChart.ChartArea.Borders.LineStyle = xlNone
```

Remember that you can choose a fancy line style, or you can choose a continuous line style and set the weight. You cannot combine both.

The Interior object

The Interior object controls what the interior of the object looks like. To change the color, set the Color property of the Interior object to the desired RGB color. In this example, a pastel blue is chosen:

```
oExcel.ActiveChart.ChartArea.Interior.Color = RGB(192,192,255)
```

 While you can specify an RGB value, Excel will select the closest color in its palette (view this on the Format Data Series dialog, available by right-clicking any data series and selecting Format Data Series… from the pop-up menu). Excel supports only 56 colors at once; you can manipulate the palette by using the Workbook's Colors collection and changing one of the 56 colors to your RGB value. Only then can you set an object to the exact RGB value.

The Interior object also has a Pattern property. Yes, you *can* pattern the chart area, the plot area, the columns and bars, and so on, but please use this feature sparingly! Patterns can be visually overwhelming, especially if each column uses a different pattern *and* color. If the chart is in color, there should be plenty of colors to choose from. Okay, you *could* use a color and a pattern in the same color to indicate pairs of series—for example, actual vs. forecast, where the actuals are solid colors and the forecast bars are a pattern in the same color. Where patterns really excel is when you need to print in black and white, and you just can't rely on how a printer maps the colors to shades of gray.

However, we really advise against patterning the plot area, and especially the chart area. The patterns are just too small for large areas, and they tend to look ugly.

With those caveats in mind, if you want to pattern an object, here's how. Set the Color property to the "background" color of the pattern. Set the PatternColor property to the color of the pattern. Some patterns, like Checker and Gray50, use equal amounts of Color and PatternColor, so it doesn't matter which one you select. However, CrissCross is made up of thin lines, so setting PatternColor to red and Color to white gives red lines on a white background. Reversing the colors gives the illusion of red diamonds (white lines on a red background). After you've set the Color and PatternColor properties, you can set the Pattern property to the desired pattern. **Table 4** lists the pattern constants.

The following code sample sets the PlotArea to a red grid on a white background:

```
#DEFINE xlPatternGrid 15

oExcel.ActiveChart.PlotArea.Interior.Color = RGB(255,255,255) && White
oExcel.ActiveChart.PlotArea.Interior.PatternColor = RGB(255,0,0) && Red
oExcel.ActiveChart.PlotArea.Interior.Pattern = xlPatternGrid
```

This probably won't win any visual awards, but it effectively illustrates patterning the Interior object.

Table 4*. Excel Pattern constants. These can be used to pattern many objects. Be careful, though, and keep the patterning to a minimum to prevent a visual "ransom note" effect.*

Pattern constant	Value	Pattern constant	Value
xlPatternAutomatic	-4105	xlPatternHorizontal	-4128
xlPatternChecker	9	xlPatternLightDown	13
xlPatternCrissCross	16	xlPatternLightHorizontal	11
xlPatternDown	-4121	xlPatternLightUp	14
xlPatternGray16	17	xlPatternLightVertical	12
xlPatternGray25	-4124	xlPatternNone	-4142
xlPatternGray50	-4125	xlPatternSemiGray75	10
xlPatternGray75	-4126	xlPatternSolid	1
xlPatternGray8	18	xlPatternUp	-4162
xlPatternGrid	15	xlPatternVertical	-4166

The Font object

If you've been reading this book sequentially, by now you're already quite familiar with the Font object. It's discussed in the "Word Basics" chapter (Chapter 4), and again in the "Excel Basics" chapter (Chapter 7). We'll hit the highlights here and send you to the "Fonts" topic in Chapter 7 for details (Table 1 in Chapter 7 lists the commonly used Font properties in Excel).

When an object contains a Font object, the font properties are inherited by all child objects. For example, when you set the ChartArea's Font object properties, then all objects contained in the ChartArea inherit the font, unless you explicitly set the child object's font properties. Set the font properties just like you set them anywhere else:

```
oExcel.ActiveChart.ChartArea.Font.Name = "Times New Roman"
oExcel.ActiveChart.ChartArea.Font.Bold = .T.
oExcel.ActiveChart.Legend.Font.Name = "Arial"
oExcel.ActiveChart.Legend.Font.Bold = .F.
```

This example sets all text on the chart to bold Times New Roman, except text within the legend, which is set to unbolded Arial.

The PlotArea object

The PlotArea object is a child of the Chart object, and it represents the area bounded by the axes. You can resize this area, making it (and the axes that bound it) larger or smaller. The PlotArea is automatically optimized for that chart, and it usually doesn't need to be changed. But if you are trying to make the plot areas of two or more charts match in size, you need to play with the PlotArea size.

The PlotArea object has the standard Top, Left, Width, and Height properties. It also has properties for the InsideTop, InsideLeft, InsideWidth, and InsideHeight. The PlotArea object actually has two rectangular areas. The inside area is the area that defaults to gray, and it's bounded on the bottom by the category axis, on the sides by the value axes, and at the top by the maximum value. The whole plot area is the area bounded by a rectangle from the leftmost and topmost point of the primary value axis text to the rightmost and bottommost point of the secondary value axis and category axis text. Okay, a picture's worth a thousand words here. If you interactively select the PlotArea then try to move it, Excel indicates both areas with dashed lines when you move it, as shown in **Figure 9**.

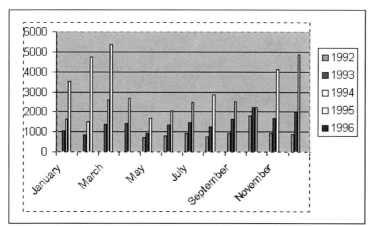

Figure 9. *Moving the PlotArea, which shows the boundaries of the outside and inside areas. The outside areas are controlled by the Top, Left, Height, and Width properties, while the inside areas are controlled by the InsideTop, InsideLeft, InsideHeight, and InsideWidth properties. The inside area properties are read-only.*

Now, the only problem is that the Inside properties are read-only. To change any of the Inside values, you need to increase or decrease the Height or Width properties, until the InsideHeight and/or InsideWidth values are appropriate.

Fortunately, the default plot area size works for most charts, and you won't have to mess with it. What you want to change are the Interior and Border properties, which work just like their ChartArea counterparts. See the "The Interior object" and "The Border object" sections earlier in this chapter.

Data series

Data series objects store the references to the data to graph, as well as the numerous properties for each series. Each Series object is stored in the SeriesCollection collection object. Before we can get to the cool part (playing with the colors and other formatting features), we need to understand how the Series object stores and manages the data properties and objects.

How data and labels are stored

When the Series objects are set from the ChartWizard or from the SetSourceData method, each column or row (depending on the nPlotBy parameter) becomes a Series object. You can also add series (either to a new chart or to an existing chart, even if it was created with the ChartWizard) using SeriesCollection's Add method. The syntax is as follows:

```
oExcel.ActiveChart.SeriesCollection.Add( oSourceRange, [nPlotBy],
      [lSeriesLabels], [lCategoryLabels], [lReplaceCategories] )
```

oSourceRange	Object	The Range object with the new data to add. You can add many series at once if the source range contains multiple series.
nPlotBy	Numeric	Indicates whether data series are stored in rows or columns. Use one of the two constants: xlRows 1 xlColumns 2 The default is xlColumns.
lSeriesLabels	Logical	Indicates whether the first row or column contains the series labels. If this argument is omitted, Excel attempts to figure it out based on the contents of the first row or column—a label is assumed to be any non-numeric data. Personally, we prefer to pass this parameter.
lCategoryLabels	Logical	Indicates whether the first row or column contains the category labels. If this argument is omitted, Excel attempts to figure it out based on the contents of the first row or column. Character and date data become labels, while numeric data is considered data to plot.
lReplaceCategories	Logical	Indicates whether the category labels that already exist in the chart should be replaced by the category labels in the source range. The default is false.

For example, starting with the data in Figure 4, if we add a column of data representing 1997 in Column G, we can update the chart with the following:

```
#DEFINE xlColumns 2
oExcel.ActiveChart.SeriesCollection.Add(oExcel.Sheets[1].Range("G1:G13"),;
     xlColumns, .T., .F., .F.)
```

To use the Add method instead of the ChartWizard method to put data into a chart that was added with ChartsObjects.Add, use the following:

```
oExcel.ActiveChart.SeriesCollection.Add(oExcel.Sheets[1].Range("A1:F13"))
```

The data portion of each series is stored in the Values property, from which you can change the series' range. From VFP, you need to set it to a Range object; from VB, you can set it to either a Range object or an array of points. When you read this Values property from VFP, you get the contents of the first cell, not a Range object or a character string representing a Range object. In all likelihood, this is due to the incompatibility of arrays between VFP and VB.

The SeriesCollection's XValues property stores the range used for the X-axis (category) values. These aren't stored in a normalized fashion, however. *Each* Series object in the collection stores an XValues value. But only the value of the first object in the collection (oChart.SeriesCollection[1]) appears to be used. Like the Values property, XValues is set to a Range (from VFP; VB also allows an array of points), but it returns only the first cell.

SeriesCollection's Name property stores the value of the series label. You set this to a range (generally representing a single cell) or a character string. This is a very handy command, because you can format your chart to readable names, while your data in the spreadsheet is abbreviated to fit in columns.

Formatting the Series

Now we're getting to the fun part. The intricacies of data storage pale in comparison to manipulating how the data looks (at least, in our opinion).

Two properties are already familiar: ChartType and BarShape. The Chart object's ChartType and BarShape properties set the formatting for the whole chart, and the Series object's properties change the format for just that particular series. The next example shows how to change the properties for each series. We'll set up some different series, so we can work on some of the other properties that affect certain types of charts.

```
#DEFINE xlArea          1
#DEFINE xlLineMarkers 65

oExcel.ActiveChart.SeriesCollection[1].ChartType = xlArea
oExcel.ActiveChart.SeriesCollection[4].ChartType = xlLineMarkers
oExcel.ActiveChart.SeriesCollection[5].ChartType = xlLineMarkers
```

Figure 10 shows the results of the code. Normally, you would not format this chart with different chart types, because each of the series represents the same kind of data. You might use different chart types if you were showing the profit, sales figures, and forecast goals. But we'll work on manipulating this data to illustrate the series concepts.

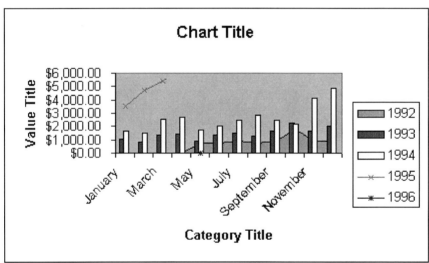

Figure 10. Each series can be a different chart type. It doesn't make sense to format this particular data set like this, but we can use the data to illustrate concepts.

There are two more objects that, by now, should be familiar. The Border and Interior objects format every series. The linear objects, like the line, use the Border properties to format the line itself; the Interior object is unavailable for lines. The other objects use the Border properties and the Interior properties to set the border (by default, it's black) and the color and patterns of the bar. See the sections "The Border object" and "The Interior object" earlier in this chapter for details.

Data labels

Data labels are text objects that label every point in the series. These properties and methods are available to the Chart, Series, and Point objects. Turn them on with the HasDataLabels property:

```
oExcel.ActiveChart.SeriesCollection[3].HasDataLabels = .T.
```

When HasDataLabels is .T., Excel labels each point with the value of the data point. Excel does a great job of centering the data label above the point, and setting the font size to something readable. However, it does not attempt to do anything about overlapping labels (if it did, then the labels wouldn't be centered at a calculated distance above the point). Turning on the labels gives us a very cluttered appearance, as shown in **Figure 11**. There are several ways to get around this problem, though none are foolproof in an automated environment, as it is difficult to query the data labels to determine whether they are overlapping.

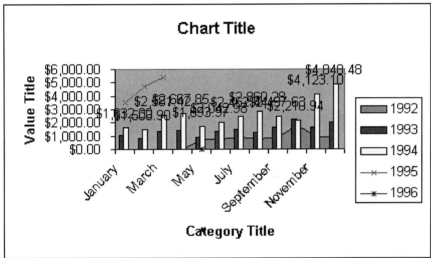

Figure 11. *Turning on data labels can give a very cluttered appearance. There are several workarounds: make the label font smaller, or turn them on for only selected points.*

One way is to change the font size. Smaller fonts won't overlap as much. The problem here is that you can get just so tiny before the font size becomes unreadable. The DataLabels property allows you to address the entire collection of data labels, or you can select individual labels to format. Here's an example of changing font properties for the entire series of data labels:

```
WITH oExcel.ActiveChart.SeriesCollection[3].DataLabels.Font
  .Name = "Times New Roman"
  .Size = 6
ENDWITH
```

Selecting a single label from the collection is as easy as addressing it by its index. For example, this sets the third data label to a font size of six:

```
oExcel.ActiveChart.SeriesCollection[3].DataLabels[3].Font.Size = 6
```

There are more options to labeling than just the point value. You can use the ApplyDataLabels method of the SeriesCollection object. It has four parameters, but the most important is the first one. You can pass one of the values given in **Table 5** to set the text of the label.

Table 5*. Values for the ApplyDataLabels method. Note that some labels are available only for certain types of charts.*

Constant	Value	Notes
xlDataLabelsShowNone	-4142	No data labels.
xlDataLabelsShowValue	2	Shows the value.
xlDataLabelsShowPercent	3	Only for pie and doughnut charts.
xlDataLabelsShowLabel	4	Shows the category label.
xlDataLabelsShowLabelAndPercent	5	Only for pie and doughnut charts.
xlDataLabelsShowBubbleSizes	6	Only for bubble charts.

Just in case these options are not enough, you can set the text of individual labels by setting the DataLabel object's Text property to anything you desire:

```
oExcel.ActiveChart.SeriesCollection[3].DataLabels[1].Text = "Test"
```

The preceding code sets the label to "Test." Setting the text value to the empty string effectively removes the label.

Error bars

Error bars show potential error amounts for each value in a series. They are available for 2D area, bar, column, line, XY (scatter), and bubble charts. The Series object's ErrorBar method is used to set the values.

```
oExcel.ActiveChart.Series[n].ErrorBar( [nDirection], [nInclude],
                [nType], [nErrorAmount], [nCustomNegAmount] )
```

nDirection	Numeric	The direction is always along the Y-axis, except in scatter charts, where you can use either xlX (-4168) or xlY (1) to indicate the direction of the error bars.
nInclude	Numeric	A value that indicates which halves of the error bar to include. Choose from one of the following: xlErrorBarIncludePlusValues 2 xlErrorBarIncludeMinusValues 3 xlErrorBarIncludeNone -4142 xlErrorBarIncludeBoth 1 The default is xlErrorBarIncludeBoth.

nType	Numeric	A value that indicates how the error bar values are calculated. Choose from one of the following: xlErrorBarTypeFixedValue 1 xlErrorBarTypePercent 2 xlErrorBarTypeStDev -4155 xlErrorBarTypeStError 4 xlErrorBarTypeCustom -4114 The default is xlErrorBarTypeFixedValue.
nErrorAmount	Numeric	The amount of the error, in units expressed by nType. If the nType parameter is xlErrorBarTypeCustom, this is the value of the positive error, as a fixed value.
nCustomNegAmount	Numeric	Used only if the nType parameter is xlErrorBarTypeCustom. This is the value of the negative error, as a fixed value.

The ErrorBars property (note that the method is singular, and the property is plural) references the ErrorBar object, with properties for additional formatting. The first is the Border property; yes, it references that same Border object to set the formatting of the error bar lines (see "The Border object" topic earlier in this chapter).

The second ErrorBar object property is the EndStyle property, which determines whether the error bars have a cap (perpendicular line at the end of the error bar) or not. It has two settings: xlCap (1) and xlNoCap (2).

Formatting data markers (line, radar, and scatter charts)

Line, radar, and scatter charts can use certain symbols to plot the points, known in Excel lingo as *data markers*. When you initially select a format with data markers, you get the default set of markers. The first series gets a six-pointed star (like an x with an additional vertical line), the second series gets an x, the third gets a triangle, the fourth gets a square, the fifth gets a diamond, and so on. Since the lines differ only by colors, it may look too busy for some people's taste. Personally, we think the first two symbols look a bit like barbed wire; we prefer the other symbols.

The Series object (and the Points object, too) uses the MarkerStyle property to set the shape of the marker. Shown in **Table 6** is a list of all the marker constants, along with their values and shapes.

Table 6. The available marker styles. Markers are used on 2D line charts and scatter charts.

MarkerStyle constant	Value	Picture
xlMarkerStyleNone	-4142	
xlMarkerStyleAutomatic	-4105	varies
xlMarkerStyleCircle	8	●
xlMarkerStyleDash	-4115	—
xlMarkerStyleDiamond	2	◆
xlMarkerStyleDot	-4118	▪
xlMarkerStylePlus	9	+
xlMarkerStyleSquare	1	■
xlMarkerStyleStar	5	✳
xlMarkerStyleTriangle	3	▲
xlMarkerStyleX	-4168	×

You can change the size of the marker with the MarkerSize property. We like the fact that this property sets the size in points, rather than relying on a series of constants!

You can change the marker color, too. You can separately set the foreground and background colors, allowing you to come up with quite a number of effects. The MarkerForegroundColor controls the border color, and the MarkerBackgroundColor controls the fill color. Set each to an RGB color value. Setting these values does not change the color of the lines connecting the markers (if any). For an example, let's change the marker of the 1995 data to an open dark blue diamond, and the lone marker of the 1996 data to a red square.

```
#DEFINE xlMarkerStyleDiamond 2
#DEFINE xlMarkerStyleSquare    1
#DEFINE ColorRed      RGB(255,  0,  0)
#DEFINE ColorWhite    RGB(255,255,255)
#DEFINE ColorDkBlue   RGB(  0, 0,128)

* Format the 1995 data to an open dark blue diamond:
WITH oExcel.ActiveChart.SeriesCollection[4]
   .MarkerStyle = xlMarkerStyleDiamond
   .MarkerForegroundColor = ColorDkBlue
   .MarkerBackgroundColor = ColorWhite
ENDWITH

* Format the 1996 data to red square on white background:
WITH oExcel.ActiveChart.SeriesCollection[5]
   .MarkerStyle = xlMarkerStyleSquare
   .MarkerForegroundColor = ColorRed
ENDWITH
```

Figure 12 shows the results of formatting the markers. Though black and white in the book, you can make out that the borders of the diamonds are darker than the line, and that the filled square is visible and is a different color than the line.

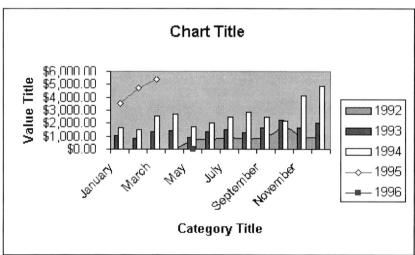

Figure 12. *The results of changing the data markers. Note that markers can be colored separately from the line.*

Smoothing lines on charts

By default, the lines on a chart are straight lines connecting each point. You can use the Series object's Smooth property to apply curve smoothing. Set this property to true to smooth the line, or false to keep the lines straight. This property applies only to line charts and scatter charts.

Formatting pie charts

Pie charts have features unique to themselves. In this example, we create a pie chart right next to the chart created for the previous examples, using the ChartWizard method.

```
#DEFINE xlPie                    5
#DEFINE autoPieNoLabels          1
#DEFINE xlColumns                2
#DEFINE autoOneSeriesLabel       1
#DEFINE autoOneCategoryLabel     1

oRange = oExcel.Sheets[1].Range("CategoryNames, Year1994")

oChart = oExcel.Sheets[1].ChartObjects.Add(372.7, 173.2, 319.5, 190.5)
oChart.Activate()
oExcel.ActiveChart.ChartWizard(oRange, xlPie, autoPieNoLabels, ;
        xlColumns, autoOneSeriesLabel, autoOneCategoryLabel)
```

The resulting graph is shown in **Figure 13**. It's a little plain-looking. The legend is bothersome too, as it's cut off part of the last entry. Fortunately, Excel gives us a range of formatting capabilities.

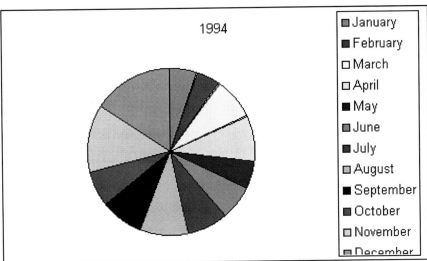

Figure 13. The default pie chart, as generated by the ChartWizard. Excel has a few formatting options to spruce this chart up.

We've already covered adding data labels by using the Series object's ApplyDataLabels method (see the topic "Data labels" earlier in this chapter). Let's look at the values that are only available to pie charts (and doughnuts): xlDataLabelsShowPercent (3) and xlDataLabelsShowLabelAndPercent (5). Displaying both the label and the percent may cause the labels to overlap, as there are so many slices to the pie in this case, so displaying only the percentage makes a good choice.

```
#DEFINE xlDataLabelsShowPercent 3
oExcel.ActiveChart.SeriesCollection[1].ApplyDataLabels( ;
       xlDataLabelsShowPercent)
```

Another possibility is the explosion effect, where one (or all) slices of the pie move out from the center of the pie. The Explosion property applies to the Series object (where all slices are exploded) and the Points object (where only that slice is exploded). The Explosion property value is a number representing the distance the slice moves from the center. Experiment a little to figure out the best value, as the value is a relative amount. One is just a tiny bit, something in the range of 5–20 looks good, and 50 separates the slices perhaps a bit too much (on this particular chart; your mileage may vary).

```
oExcel.ActiveChart.SeriesCollection[1].Explosion = 15
```

The results of formatting the labels and the explosion are shown in **Figure 14**.

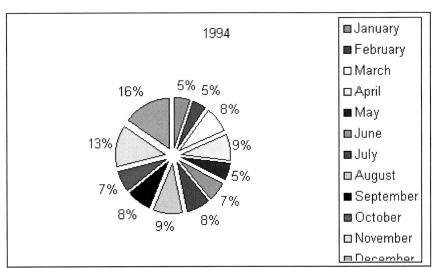

Figure 14. The pie chart with some formatting added. Percentage labels are shown, and you could add the category label, too (though it would overlap). Exploding all of the slices gives another look to the pie chart.

Formatting individual points

In the previous sections, you've seen reference to the ability to format individual points. Nearly all of the formatting features available to a Series object are available for a single point. Access the point through the Series object's Points method. You might use this feature to change the color and/or style of a marker, bar, column, or slice, to call attention to that data point. You can also add data labels to a point or two, again to draw attention to that point. You can manually set the values of the data labels, which works especially well if you want to add labels that are not part of your data in the spreadsheet.

On the example pie chart, perhaps the client wants to highlight December's slice with the category label, and to explode it (but not the rest). The following example first removes the explosion from the series, then sets up the formatting for December's slice:

```
#DEFINE xlDataLabelsShowLabelAndPercent 5

* Reset the Series explosion to 0
oExcel.ActiveChart.SeriesCollection[1].Explosion = 0

* Format the single point
WITH oExcel.ActiveChart.SeriesCollection[1].Points[12]
  .ApplyDataLabels(xlDataLabelsShowLabelAndPercent)
  .Explosion = 15
ENDWITH
```

Figure 15 shows the results of formatting a single point.

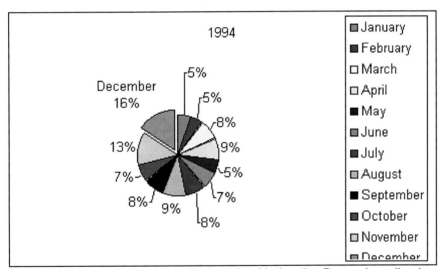

Figure 15. You can format a single point. Notice the December slice is exploded and has a different data label style.

The Legend object

The pie chart's legend has been bothering us since the first example. Access the Legend object through the Chart object's Legend property. The ChartObject also has a HasLegend property; if it's set to false, the Legend property (and therefore the Legend object) is unavailable. To quickly turn off the legend, simply set HasLegend to false:

```
oExcel.ActiveChart.HasLegend = .F.
```

This works, but it has the nasty habit of not recalculating the PlotArea to take advantage of the space previously consumed by the legend. You can also use the ChartWizard method to turn off the legend by restating the ChartFormat parameter (the second one) and the HasLegend parameter (the seventh), as in the following:

```
#DEFINE xlPie 5
oExcel.ActiveChart.ChartWizard(,xlPie,,,,,.F.)
```

This generally forces a recalculation of the plot area. However, now there's no legend, and the user is left to figure out what all of those slices mean. Perhaps we should put the legend back and figure out how to make it look better. Setting HasLegend to true recalculates the plot area, so we don't have to worry about remembering ChartWizard parameters.

```
oExcel.ActiveChart.HasLegend = .T.
```

You can change the font properties from the Legend's Font property, which accesses the Font object (explained in a previous topic in this chapter, "The Font object"). You can reduce the font a smidgen, and then you can make them fit.

```
oExcel.ActiveChart.Legend.Font.Size = ;
     oExcel.ActiveChart.Legend.Font.Size - 2
```

Figure 16 shows that changing the font size worked. You can also control the font name, bold and italic attributes, and so on. It's the same Font object used throughout the Excel model.

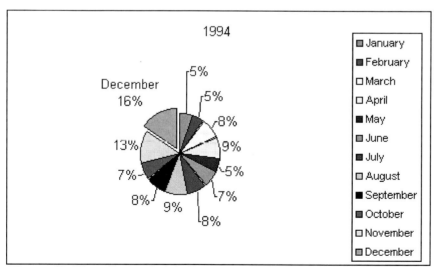

Figure 16. *The effects of globally changing the font size of the legend. By reducing the size, we've made it fit. The Legend object is as robust as the other chart objects and has many properties available to alter its format.*

What else can you do to the Legend? You can set its Border and Interior properties (see the topics "The Border object" and "The Interior object" earlier in this chapter). You can manipulate the Top and Left properties to move it around (Height and Width are calculated for you and are therefore read-only). An easier way to move it around is to use the Position property, which takes one of the following values: xlLegendPositionBottom (-4107), xlLegendPositionCorner (2), xlLegendPositionLeft (-4131), xlLegendPositionRight (-4152), or xlLegendPositionTop (-4160). This also recalculates the Height and Width, allowing the legend to stretch along the bottom.

You can also format the font properties of each legend entry separately by accessing the LegendEntries property, which references the LegendEntries collection of LegendEntry objects. You cannot change the text (you do that through the Series object or the cell with the label), but you can access the font object, as in the following, which formats December's legend entry to bold:

```
oExcel.ActiveChart.Legend.LegendEntries[12].Font.Bold = .T.
```

Each LegendEntry object has a LegendKey object, which is that little sample that identifies the series. It has a Border object and an Interior object, as well as the other formatting properties used by the Series object. We recommend setting the formatting in the Series object; however, there is one exception. We ran into a problem formatting a Series object with an entirely blank data range. This can happen if you generate data for a standard chart and no data comes up for a series—for example, if you graph monthly sales by customer for each category of products, and a customer orders no items in, say, the Beverage or Confections categories. Accessing the Series object gives an error, as the data range is empty. You can safely format the LegendKey object to customize the look of the legend key so the legend looks the same as other graphs.

Axes

The Chart object's Axes method returns an Axis object from the Axes collection. Each Axis object in the chart is contained in the Axes collection. The Axes method takes two parameters: the axis type and the axis group. The axis type is one of the following values: xlCategory (1), xlSeriesAxis (3), or xlValue (2). The axis group can be either xlPrimary (1) or xlSecondary (2). Secondary axes are available only on 2D charts, and only when a Series object's AxisGroup property is set to 2. The secondary axis allows two separate ranges of data to be graphed together. For example, the primary axis might be the value of the sales, with the secondary axis showing the percent of the total. **Table 7** shows the properties available for each Axis object.

The TickLabels object

The TickLabels object controls the format of the labels on the axis. It gives you nearly complete control over the labels. **Table 8** summarizes the important properties for the TickLabels object.

Table 7. *Properties of an Axis object. These properties give a lot of flexibility for formatting axes.*

Property	Type	Description
AxisBetweenCategories	Logical	Applies only to the category axis. True if the value axis crosses the category axis between categories (best for column charts); False if it crosses at the category (good for lines).
Crosses	Numeric	Determines the point where other axes cross this axis. Can be at the first value using xlMinimum (4) or at the last value using xlMaximum (2).
CrossesAt	Numeric	Applies only to the value axis. An integer that represents the relative value on the value axis where the category axis crosses.
Border	Object	References a Border object that takes care of the formatting of the axis line. See "The Border object" earlier in this chapter.
ScaleType	Numeric	Applies only to the value axis. The values are either xlLinear (-4132) or xlLogarithmic (-4133).
HasMajorGridlines, HasMinorGridlines	Logical	True if the axis has major or minor gridlines, respectively. Only primary axes can have gridlines.
MajorGridlines, MinorGridlines	Object	If the corresponding HasMajorGridlines or HasMinorGridlines property is true, this property references a Gridlines object. See the section "Gridlines" later in this chapter.
MaximumScaleIsAuto, MinimumScaleIsAuto	Logical	Applies only to the value axis. A logical property that indicates whether the number of minimum and maximum values is calculated by Excel. If false, set the MaximumScale or MinimumScale properties.
MaximumScale, MinimumScale	Numeric	Applies only to the value axis. If MaximumScaleIsAuto or MinimumScaleIsAuto is false, these properties contain the value of the largest/smallest values on the axis.
MajorUnitIsAuto, MinorUnitIsAuto	Logical	Applies only to the value axis. Indicates whether the number of units between tick marks is calculated by Excel. If false, set the MajorUnit/MinorUnit properties.
MajorUnit, MinorUnit	Numeric	Applies only to the value axis. If MajorAxisIsAuto or MinorAxisIsAuto is false, these properties contain the value between major/minor tick marks; otherwise, this property contains .T.
TickmarkSpacing	Numeric	Applies only to the series and category axes. Determines how many categories or series are between tick marks. Use MajorUnit or MinorUnit properties to set the value axis.
MajorTickMark, MinorTickMark	Numeric	Indicates the location of the tick mark. Use one of the following: xlTickMarkNone -4142 xlTickMarkInside 2 xlTickMarkOutside 3 xlTickMarkCross 4
TickLabels	Object	References a TickLabels object. This object is where the text properties for the tick mark are set. See the next topic, "The TickLabels object."
TickLabelPosition	Numeric	Describes the position of the labels on the axis. Values are: xlTickLabelPositionNone -4142 Suppresses labels. xlTickLabelPositionLow -4134 Nearest the axis. xlTickLabelPositionHigh -4127 On the other side of the PlotArea. xlTickLabelPositionNextToAxis 4 Nearest the axis.
TickLabelSpacing	Numeric	Determines the number of categories or series between tick mark labels. Cannot be set on the value axis.

Table 8*. Properties for the TickLabels object. The TickLabels are the text that displays along the axis.*

Property	Type	Description
Alignment	Numeric	A value that indicates how the label lines up with the axis. Choose from xlHAlignCenter (-4108), xlHAlignLeft (-4131), or xlHAlignRight (-4152).
Font	Object	Property that accesses the Font object to format the text on the axis. See the topic "The Font object" earlier in this chapter.
NumberFormat	Character	A string of codes that's used to format the numbers, much like VFP's InputMask property. See the section "Formatting values" in Chapter 7 for more information.
Orientation	Numeric	An integer value that represents the text orientation, ranging from -90 to 90. Alternatively, a constant can be used: xlTickLabelOrientationAutomatic -4105 xlTickLabelOrientationDownward -4170 xlTickLabelOrientationHorizontal -4128 xlTickLabelOrientationUpward -4171 xlTickLabelOrientationVertical -4166

Gridlines

The Gridlines object is available only to primary axes. Its only relevant property is the Border property, accessing a Border object (see the topic "The Border object" earlier in this chapter). The Border object contains the formatting of the grid lines.

Titles

Charts have two kinds of title objects: ChartTitle objects and AxisTitle objects. Their structures are similar. The ChartTitle object is accessed through the Chart object's ChartTitle property, and it's used only if the Chart object's HasTitle property is true. The AxisTitle is accessed through the Axis object's AxisTitle property, and it's used only if the Axis object's HasTitle property is true. **Table 9** shows their properties.

Putting it all together

Listing 2 shows a program (XLSample3.PRG in the Developer Download files available at www.hentzenwerke.com) that uses many of the features covered in this chapter. The first chart is a column chart that uses the data generated in Listing 1. Because the data for 1996 is incomplete, the range omits this data. To illustrate adding a Series to a graph, an Average column is created and populated using Excel's AVERAGE function. The Average series is then formatted as a Line chart. Each of the other columns is formatted to a specific color, optimized for printing (that way, it looks good when printed in this book). The axis labels are formatted, too. This chart is shown in **Figure 17**.

The second chart is a 3D pie chart, which is a chart sheet instead of an embedded chart. It uses some 3D formatting properties, and changes the formatting of some titles and data labels, as well as the color of the pie wedges. Gray was chosen as the color so it would print well. The pie chart is shown in **Figure 18**.

***Table 9**. Properties of the ChartTitle and AxisTitle objects.*

Property	Type	Description
Border	Object	References a Border object. See "The Border object" topic earlier in this chapter. By default, Titles do not have borders.
Caption, Text	Character	These two identical properties contain the title text.
Font	Object	References a Font object. See "The Font object" topic earlier in this chapter.
HorizontalAlignment	Numeric	Determines the horizontal alignment for the title. Use one of the following: xlHAlignCenter -4108 xlHAlignLeft -4131 xlHAlignDistributed -4117 xlHAlignRight -4152 xlHAlignJustify -4130
VerticalAlignment	Numeric	Determines the vertical alignment for the title. Use one of the following: xlVAlignBottom -4107 xlVAlignJustify -4130 xlVAlignCenter -4108 xlVAlignTop -4160 xlVAlignDistributed -4117
Left, Top	Numeric	Can be set to fine-tune the title's location.
Orientation	Numeric	Determines the text orientation, ranging from -90 to 90. Or a constant can be used: xlDownward -4170 xlHorizontal -4128 xlUpward -4171 xlVertical -4166
Shadow	Logical	Indicates whether there is a drop-shadow on the title box.
Interior	Object	References an Interior object, which controls the color of the title box. See "The Interior object" topic earlier in this chapter.

***Listing 2**. Tasmanian Traders Annual Sales graphs. This code covers many of the topics covered in this chapter, such as creating graphs, working with multiple ChartTypes within a chart, adding Series, formatting individual Series, and more.*

```
* Sets up the monthly sales data by year to graph.

* Clean out any existing references to servers.
* This prevents memory loss to leftover instances.
RELEASE ALL LIKE o*

* For demonstration purposes, make certain objects
* available after this program executes.
PUBLIC oExcel, oBook, oSheet, oChart

#DEFINE xlColumn                    3
#DEFINE xl3DPie                     -4102
#DEFINE xlColumns                   2
#DEFINE xlLegendPositionBottom      -4107
#DEFINE xlLineStyleNone             -4142
#DEFINE xlCategory                  1
#DEFINE xlValue                     2
#DEFINE xlPrimary                   1
#DEFINE xlFillDefault               0
#DEFINE xlLineMarkers               65
```

```
#DEFINE xlMarkerStyleDiamond     2
#DEFINE autoColumnFormat         4
#DEFINE autoPieFormat            7
#DEFINE autoOneSeriesLabel       1
#DEFINE autoOneCategoryLabel     1
#DEFINE autoHasLegend           .T.
#DEFINE autoNotHasLegend        .F.
#DEFINE rgbWhite         RGB(255, 255, 255)
#DEFINE rgbLtGray        RGB(192, 192, 192)
#DEFINE rgbMedGray       RGB(128, 128, 128)
#DEFINE rgbDkGray        RGB( 64,  64,  64)
#DEFINE rgbBlack         RGB(  0,   0,   0)

* Create the workbook and add the data
DO XLGDataSetup   && Listing 1

* Add the range names
WITH oExcel.Sheets[1]
   .RANGE("A1:A13").NAME = "CategoryNames"
   .RANGE("B1:B13").NAME = "Year1992"
   .RANGE("C1:C13").NAME = "Year1993"
   .RANGE("D1:D13").NAME = "Year1994"
   .RANGE("E1:E13").NAME = "Year1995"
   .RANGE("F1:F13").NAME = "Year1996"
ENDWITH
```

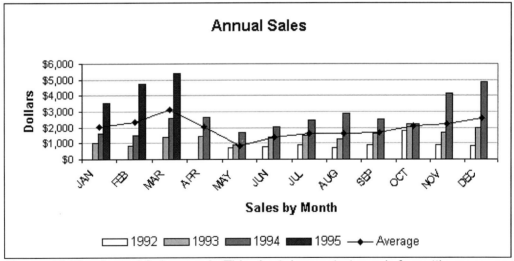

Figure 17. *The Annual Sales graph. This chart demonstrates axis formatting, using different ChartTypes by Series, moving the legend, and formatting each Series individually.*

```
* Create the first chart
oChart = oExcel.Sheets[1].ChartObjects.ADD(0, 175, 400, 200)
oChart.ACTIVATE()
```

```
* Include only the category names and years through 1995
oSourceRange = oExcel.Sheets[1].Range("A1:E13")
oExcel.ActiveChart.ChartWizard(oSourceRange, xlColumn, autoColumnFormat, ;
        xlColumns, autoOneCategoryLabel, autoOneSeriesLabel, autoHasLegend, ;
        "Annual Sales", "Sales by Month", "Dollars")

WITH oExcel.ActiveChart

  * Move the legend to the bottom, and remove the border
  .Legend.Position = xlLegendPositionBottom
  .Legend.Border.LineStyle = xlLineStyleNone

  * Format the axes.
  * On the category axis, set the size a little smaller,
  * and put the labels on a 45 degree slant.
  .Axes(xlCategory, xlPrimary).TickLabels.Orientation = 45
  .Axes(xlCategory, xlPrimary).TickLabels.Font.Size = 8

  * On the value axis, set the size a bit smaller,
  * format the values to currency, and turn on Gridlines
  .Axes(xlValue, xlPrimary).TickLabels.Font.Size = 8
  .Axes(xlValue, xlPrimary).TickLabels.NumberFormat = "$#,###;;$0"
  .Axes(xlValue, xlPrimary).HasMajorGridlines = .T.
  .Axes(xlValue, xlPrimary).MajorGridlines.Border.Color = rgbLtGray

  * Abbreviate the category labels to make more room for the chart
  FOR I = 1 TO 12
    WITH oExcel.ActiveSheet.Range("A" + ALLTRIM(STR(I + 1)))
      .Value = UPPER(LEFT(.Value, 3))
    ENDWITH
  ENDFOR

  * Center the axis within the ChartArea
  .Legend.Left = (.ChartArea.Width - .Legend.Width) / 2

ENDWITH

* Add an average column.
WITH oExcel.Sheets[1]
  * Insert the Series label
  .Range("G1").Value = "Average"

  * Insert the AVERAGE formula into each cell
  FOR I = 2 TO 13
    cI = ALLTRIM(STR(I))
    .Range("G" + cI).Value = "=AVERAGE(B" + cI + ":F" + cI + ")"
  ENDFOR

  * Name the range
  .Range("G1:G13").Name = "Average"
ENDWITH

WITH oExcel.ActiveChart

  * Add the Average series, and format it to a black line
  * with diamond markers (also black).
  .SeriesCollection.Add( oExcel.Sheets[1].Range("G1:G13"), ;
      xlColumns, .T., .F., .F.)
  WITH .SeriesCollection[5]
```

```
   .ChartType = xlLineMarkers
   .MarkerStyle = xlMarkerStyleDiamond
   .MarkerForegroundColor = rgbBlack
   .MarkerBackgroundColor = rgbBlack

   .Border.Color = rgbBlack
ENDWITH

* Change the colors of the bars to shades of gray
.SeriesCollection[1].Interior.Color = rgbWhite
.SeriesCollection[2].Interior.Color = rgbLtGray
.SeriesCollection[3].Interior.Color = rgbMedGray
.SeriesCollection[4].Interior.Color = rgbDkGray

* Format the interior color of the plot area
.PlotArea.Interior.Color = rgbWhite
ENDWITH
```

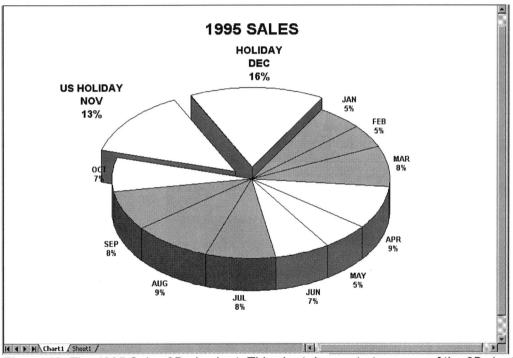

Figure 18. *The 1995 Sales 3D pie chart. This chart demonstrates some of the 3D chart features, such as Explosion, Rotation, and Elevation, as well as working with non-contiguous data ranges, and formatting titles and data labels.*

```
* Create the second chart. This time it's a chart sheet.
oChart = oExcel.Charts.Add()
oChart.ACTIVATE()
```

```
* Use only the category names and 1994 data. Note that the chart
* sheet was added before the data worksheet, which bumps the data
* worksheet to the second instance in the collection of worksheets.
oSourceRange = oExcel.Sheets[2].Range("CategoryNames, Year1994")
WITH oExcel.ActiveChart

  * Create a 3D pie chart
  .ChartWizard(oSourceRange, xl3DPie, autoPieFormat, ;
       xlColumns, autoOneCategoryLabel, autoOneSeriesLabel, ;
       autoNotHasLegend, "1995 SALES")
  * Set the elevation up a little more than the default
  .Elevation = 35

  * Rotate the chart. Rotating a pie chart changes the angle
  * of the first slice.
  .Rotation  = 30

  * Increase the title's font size
  .ChartTitle.Font.Size = 22

  WITH .SeriesCollection[1]
    * Make all DataLabels bold
    .DataLabels.Font.Bold = .T.

    * Format the November wedge by exploding it, adding
    * a custom label, and changing the label's font size
    WITH .Points[11]
      .Explosion = 15
      .DataLabel.Text = "US HOLIDAY" + CHR(13) + .DataLabel.Text
      .DataLabel.Font.Size = .DataLabel.Font.Size + 4
    ENDWITH

    * Format the December wedge by exploding it, adding
    * a custom label, and changing the label's font size
    WITH .Points[12]
      .Explosion = 15
      .DataLabel.Text = "HOLIDAY" + CHR(13) + .DataLabel.Text
      .DataLabel.Font.Size = .DataLabel.Font.Size + 4
    ENDWITH

  ENDWITH

  * Identify each quarter: Q1 and Q3 are gray, Q2 and Q4 are white
  FOR I = 1 TO 12
    IF I <= 3 OR (I >= 7 AND I <=9)
      .SeriesCollection[1].Points[I].Interior.Color = rgbLtGray
    ELSE
      .SeriesCollection[1].Points[I].Interior.Color = rgbWhite
    ENDIF
  NEXT I

ENDWITH
```

Excel's charting engine is very robust, and it offers tons of formatting options. You'll amaze your clients (and yourself) with the number of options available.

Section IV
Automating PowerPoint

Chapter 10
PowerPoint Basics

While most people view PowerPoint as a tool to create powerful presentations, a savvy developer sees lots of possibilities for visually appealing output options that aren't available with the FoxPro report writer.

PowerPoint is an excellent tool for creating visual presentations comprised of slides, where each slide contains elements of text, graphics, and even multimedia. Rich formatting features provide control over the appearance of the slide. You can change the color, font, and size of text objects, even down to changing the attributes for each character. Numerous shape elements are provided, with a myriad of formatting options, such as gradient or textured background fills, a variety of borders, and the ability to include text within the shape.

With the power and capability of computers today, and the population's desire for high-tech visual presentations, PowerPoint has the ability to add the bells and whistles that appeal to today's audiences. Objects can be set to flash, play sounds, navigate to other slides in the slide show, run macros, or even run external programs when the user moves the mouse over them, or clicks on them. In fact, you can set different actions for a mouse-over than a mouse-click. You'll feel like a Hollywood producer when you choose one of a variety of wipes, fades, and sound effects to fire for each slide as it transitions from one to the next.

PowerPoint also has tools to assist the presenter, such as storing notes for each slide. These notes can be geared for the speaker, or they can be printed to hand out to the audience. The slide show itself can be printed out in a number of formats, from one on a page to nine thumbnails on a page. With a little imagination, PowerPoint is a very valuable output alternative for FoxPro programs.

The PowerPoint object model

Like the other Office programs, PowerPoint's top-level object is the Application object, which stores the application-wide settings and options (size of main window, active printer, and so on). The Application object also provides access to all other objects in PowerPoint.

The primary object in PowerPoint is the Presentation object, which represents a single slide show presentation. A Presentation object corresponds to a PowerPoint file (PPT); PowerPoint users also refer to the PowerPoint file as a "presentation." (The term "presentation" is used in several ways in the Help files and other documentation; be sure you understand the context in which it's used, which can be difficult at 2:30 in the morning!)

The PowerPoint Application object keeps track of all open Presentation objects in the Presentations collection. Each Presentation object stores some default characteristics for the presentation. The SlideMaster object controls the default appearance of each slide object, and it manages such features as the slide background, color scheme, text styles, and headers and footers. Also available are objects that set the defaults for the print formats for notes and handouts, appropriately called NotesMaster and HandoutMaster. The SlideShowSettings object stores such information as what slide to start and end on, how to advance the slides, and whether or not to run a continuous loop. The Application's ActivePresentation property points to the active Presentation object.

Within each presentation is a Slides collection, which contains a Slide object for each slide in the presentation. Anything added to the slide—text, bitmaps, shapes, lines, and so forth—is stored in the Shapes collection. This concept is a little awkward at first, since it doesn't seem intuitive that text, lines, and bitmaps should be stored in the same collection—wouldn't the average database developer normalize these into separate tables? It helps if you define a "shape" as something with size (height, width), colors (borders, background, foreground; perhaps even a bitmap), and a text element (which isn't always used). So how do you tell all these shapes apart? The Type property contains a number describing the shape. You can also use the Name property to attach a meaningful name, much as you would name each control placed on a FoxPro form.

There are several Range objects. You can group any number of slides into a SlideRange collection object, and any number of shapes into a ShapeRange collection object. By referencing a collection of slides or objects, you can easily set the properties of all elements in the collection.

PowerPoint Visual Basic Help contains a diagram of PowerPoint's object model. (See Chapter 2, "The Office Servers," for details on how to find this Help and what to do if you can't find it.) The figure is "live"—when you click on an object, you're taken to the Help topic for that object. **Figure 1** shows the portion of the object model diagram that describes the Presentation object.

Déjà vu

If you're reading this book from start to finish, as you read this chapter, you'll say to yourself, "Gosh, I've read this before!" (especially since this is basically the same text as in Chapter 7, "Excel Basics"). Office 2000 is object-oriented, and it's polymorphic. Polymorphism literally means "many forms," and when applied to OOP, it means that different objects have properties and methods that behave consistently. To write a file to disk, you use the Save method, whether you are in Word, Excel, PowerPoint, or Outlook. This does not mean that the Save commands do exactly the same thing—there are different things that need to happen when a Word document is saved than when an PowerPoint presentation is saved. There may even be different parameters for each. However, you can be sure that the Save command will save your work to disk.

The benefit of polymorphism is that once you know how to do something in one tool, you know how to do it in the rest. In Office, this is usually true. However, polymorphism does include the ability for methods to accept different parameters, because different objects are exactly that—different. So you need to be aware that syntax can (and does) change between Office applications.

There are so many similarities between the Office applications that we could have written this chapter to say things like, "Just use the CreateObject() function as explained in the Word chapter, but use "PowerPoint.Application" instead." We felt that it would be better to have a complete explanation for each application to keep you from having to flip back and forth in the book. It also makes it easier to explain the subtle syntax differences that exist between applications. After we get past the basics of opening and saving files, we get into enough application-specific features that it will seem less repetitive.

Microsoft PowerPoint Objects

See Also

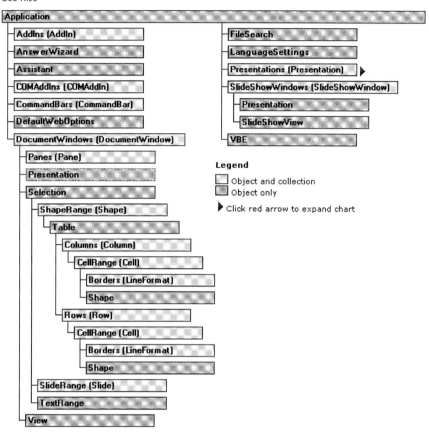

Figure 1. The PowerPoint object model. This diagram is available in the Help file and shows the hierarchy of available PowerPoint objects.

The benefit of polymorphism is that once you know how to do something in one object, you know how to do it in all of them. However, explaining similar concepts for each object makes for redundant text. Just think of this redundant text as a "feature."

Getting a handle on the application

Now that you have some background on PowerPoint's object model, type the following command into the Command Window to instantiate PowerPoint using Automation:

```
oPowerPoint = CreateObject("PowerPoint.Application")
```

It takes a second for the cursor to come back (it's going to the disk to pull up PowerPoint...give it a nanosecond!). PowerPoint is now instantiated. "Yeah, right," you say—check the Task List if you don't believe us! Remember that the Office servers instantiate as not Visible. So, type in the following command to see the instance:

```
oPowerPoint.Visible = .T.
```

You are now viewing the PowerPoint Application. The variable oPowerPoint is a handle to the PowerPoint Application object. The Application object represents the entire instance of PowerPoint. It knows what presentations are open through the Presentations collection, and it knows which one is active through the ActivePresentation property.

Controlling the size and location of the PowerPoint window is easy with the Top, Left, Height, and Width properties. These are all measured in points. The following code sets the top and left about 1" from the edge of the desktop and makes it about 4" square (remember, there are 72 points to the inch). The inches used to display the windows are virtual inches—meaning that they approximate a real inch. However, there are differences in display sizes, which makes a difference in the size of the window. On a display larger than 20", the window is about 5" square and 1.25" from the top and left. On a tiny laptop display, it may only be 3.5". The resolution of the screen is taken into account for virtual inches, so the window should be the same size on any display regardless of the resolution. In any case, the window takes up the same proportions on any screen it's displayed on. If you're following along in the Command Window, be sure your PowerPoint window is set to Normal (as opposed to minimized or maximized) before proceeding.

```
WITH oPowerPoint
   .Top = 72
   .Left = 72
   .Width = 288
   .Height = 288
ENDWITH
```

If you're following along by typing these commands in the FoxPro Command Window and the PowerPoint window was either minimized or maximized, you get the error: "OLE IDispatch error exception code 0…" PowerPoint doesn't allow you to set these properties if the application is minimized or maximized. When you write your code, you need to check the WindowState property to ensure PowerPoint's window is "normal" (neither maximized nor minimized). The WindowState property uses the following intrinsic constants (see Chapter 2, "The Office Servers," for an explanation of VBA constants): ppWindowNormal (1), ppWindowMinimized (2), and ppWindowMaximized (3). Run the following code to make the window "normal" before setting the height and width:

```
#DEFINE ppWindowNormal 1

WITH oPowerPoint
  IF .WindowState <> ppWindowNormal
    .WindowState = ppWindowNormal
  ENDIF
ENDWITH
```

A nice thing to do for your users is to change the caption on PowerPoint to let them know why the PowerPoint window suddenly appeared. Use the Caption property to change the window's title.

```
oPowerPoint.Caption = "Automated from The World's Greatest Application"
```

The Quit method closes down the PowerPoint instance. If there are any unsaved presentations open, the user is prompted to deal with them and further processing is suspended until the user answers the prompts. See the next section, "Managing presentations and slides," for information on how to save the presentations before calling the Quit method. This method accepts no parameters. It's simply:

```
oPowerPoint.Quit
```

The Quit method works differently in the various Office applications. In Word, you can pass it a parameter to automatically save changes, prompt the user for changes, or quit without saving changes. Excel behaves like PowerPoint, and prompts the user if there are unsaved changes. Outlook just shuts down without saving any changes. Be aware that, despite polymorphism, the Office object models are occasionally inconsistent!

Managing presentations and slides

When you open PowerPoint through Automation, it doesn't automatically pop open and ask the user whether he wants to open an existing presentation or create a new presentation. That's your job. PowerPoint comes up and sits there with a nice, gray screen (that is, if you've set the Visible property to true), until you tell it what to do. First, you create a Presentation object (using the Add method of the Presentations collection), and then you add Slide objects (using the Add method of the Slides collection).

Presenting: the Presentation object

The Presentations collection is an array of Presentation objects. Think of a Presentation object as a reference to a single presentation file (PPT).

When you instantiate the PowerPoint Application object with CreateObject(), it opens without any active presentations. Most often, you want to add a blank presentation. Use the Add method of the Presentations collection:

```
oPresentation = oPowerPoint.Presentations.Add()
```

oPresentation is now a reference to a Presentation object. Add takes an optional parameter that determines whether the window containing the new presentation is visible. The default is .T., so the window defaults to visible, as long as the Application object is visible. There are several ways of accessing the new Presentation object. First is the variable name that you set when you added the presentation—oPresentation. The Application object has an ActivePresentation property; use oPowerPoint.ActivePresentation to return a reference to the active presentation. Beware: if you try to access the ActivePresentation property when no presentations are open or if the Application is not visible, an error occurs. Check the value of oPowerPoint.Presentations.Count and oPowerPoint.Visible to ensure that it is greater than zero before accessing ActivePresentation.

Like other collections, Presentations offers two ways of accessing its contents. The first uses an index number corresponding to the order in which the presentations were opened—in this case, oPowerPoint.Presentations[1]. The second uses the name of the presentation (found in the Name property). For example, a presentation saved as "MyPresentation.PPT" can be referenced as oPowerPoint.Presentations("MyPresentation.PPT"). The path is not included, and presentation names are not case-sensitive.

Note that the Name property for presentations is read-only. When a presentation is added, the Name is "PresentationX," where "X" is a numeral corresponding to the number of files created during this session but not yet saved. Once the file is saved, the Name property reflects the filename and extension (but not the path) of the file saved on the disk. (The FullName property provides the name plus path of the stored file, and the Path property holds just the path.)

Opening an existing presentation

To open an existing presentation, use the Open method. The syntax of the Open method is as follows:

```
oPowerPoint.Presentations.Open( cFileName, [lReadOnly], [lUntitled],
             [lWithWindow] )
```

cFileName	Character	The filename of the presentation. Be sure to include the full path.
lReadOnly	Logical	.T. to open read-only. Default is Read/Write (.F.). (Optional)
lUntitled	Logical	.T. to open without a title. Default is .F., and the title defaults to the filename. (Optional)
lWithWindow	Logical	.T. opens a visible window, which is the default. .F. hides the opened presentation. (Optional)

So if you issue the command:

```
oWayCool = oPowerPoint.Presentations.Open("c:\My Documents\WayCool.PPT")
```

you open the WayCool.PPT presentation in a new window. The window title defaults to "WayCool.PPT," and you can reference this presentation object as oPowerPoint.Presentations("WayCool.PPT") or oPowerPoint.ActivePresentation or oWayCool.

As noted in Chapter 3, "Visual FoxPro as an Automation Client," an alternative method to open a presentation is with the GetObject() function. The following is the syntax:

```
oPresentation = GetObject("c:\My Documents\WayCool.PPT")
```

Used with only a filename as a parameter, GetObject() returns a reference to the Presentation object (not the Application object, as CreateObject() does). If PowerPoint was not running (or was running but not visible), you need to make the application visible to see it:

```
oPresentation.Application.Visible = .T.
```

The Presentation is open and available for editing. However, it does not yet have a window, and is therefore not displayed. The document opened by GetObject() respects the setting of the Application's Visible property at the time the Document object is instantiated. If the Application was not Visible (which would be the case if you use the GetObject() syntax to open a document without PowerPoint being active), you must make the document visible by giving it a window. Incidentally, this same behavior occurs when you use the Open method with the lWithWindow parameter set to False. You must use the NewWindow method to put the presentation in a window:

```
oPresentation.NewWindow()
```

Opening Presentations without making them visible can be used to your advantage. If you build the presentation when it is not visible, you see performance gains of about 30 percent. To close an open window without closing the Presentation, issue the following code:

```
oPowerPoint.ActiveWindow.Close()
```

You still have access to the Presentation, but it is not displayed in a window, so your Presentation builds significantly faster. The GetObject() function has an alternate syntax that allows you to prevent multiple occurrences of an object. If you are programming Office 97, this may be an important issue. You may want to use an open instance of PowerPoint to avoid using more memory for another instance. One of the changes in Office 2000 is that there is only one instance of the application; the Office application itself provides better memory management. However, the GetObject() syntax still works for PowerPoint 2000 (and opens the application if it is not already open). Issuing:

```
oPowerPoint = GetObject(,'PowerPoint.Application')
```

opens PowerPoint and returns a reference to the Application. Note that the syntax to open a filename returns a reference to the Presentation.

For the rest of this section, we'll assume that there is a reference to an open presentation, and that the reference is called oPresentation.

Adding slides

A PowerPoint presentation is comprised of slides. Individual slides are Slide objects belonging to a Slides collection (just like Presentation objects belonging to a Presentations collection). Add a Slide object to the presentation with the Add method:

```
oSlide = oPresentation.Slides.Add(nIndex, nLayout)
```

nIndex	Numeric	The index number of the slide.
nLayout	Numeric	One of the ppSlideLayout constants to choose one of the 29 predefined slide layout options.

Learning what options are available for the nLayout parameter is easy when you understand that the Layouts correspond to the dialog box that appears when a slide is added manually in PowerPoint, as shown in **Figure 2**. As you click on the slide layout thumbnails, the name in the lower right corner changes, and it loosely corresponds to the constant name.

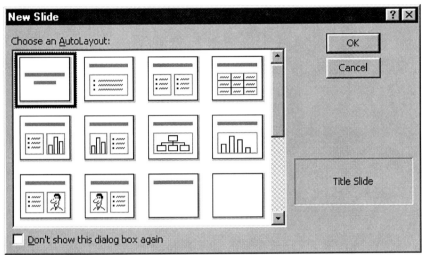

Figure 2. *The New Slide dialog box in PowerPoint. This dialog gives a visual reference to the predefined slide layouts.*

The constants for some of the most common styles are ppLayoutTitle (1), ppLayoutText (2), ppLayoutTable (4), and ppLayoutBlank (12).

The slide index represents that slide's position in the slide show. An index of 1 inserts the new slide at the beginning of the presentation. An index of 5 inserts the new slide after slide 4 and increments the indices of the following slides. Providing an index greater than one more than the total number of slides generates an error. Use oPresentation.Slides.Count to ensure that the value you pass isn't too big.

```
#DEFINE ppLayoutTitle 1

* Add a title slide to the beginning of the presentation.
oSlide = oPresentation.Slides.Add(1, ppLayoutTitle)

* Add a "blank" slide to the end of the presentation.
oSlide = oPresentation.Slides.Add(oPresentation.Slides.Count + 1,;
        ppLayoutTitle)
```

Like the Presentation object, there are several ways to access a slide. You can use the variable (oSlide, in the preceding example). You can also use the Slides property, passing either the index or the slide name, as in oPresentation.Slides[1] or oPresentation.Slides["Slide1"]. Note that there is no ActiveSlide property. You can access the active slide object with oPowerPoint.Windows[1].View.Slide, but only if the Application object is visible. There doesn't seem to be a way to determine the active slide if the Application object is invisible.

When you add a slide, its Name property defaults to the word "Slide" followed by an integer, which is the next available slide number in the slide show. If you are writing an application that goes back and edits the slides, it's prudent to set the Name property to something that is easier to remember.

There is also a SlideRange collection object, which represents a range of slides. According to the Help file, you can use the Slide collection's Range method to select a series of slides. Help says the Range method can accept an index number, a slide name, or a series of indices and slide names in a VBA array. However, arrays from FoxPro are incompatible with VBA arrays, so they will not work. You can pass a single index or a single character string representing the slide name to Range, and work on one slide. However, the syntax:

```
oPresentation.Slides["Slide3"]
```

is easier to read (and executes a little faster) than:

```
oPresentation.Slides.Range("Slide3")
```

So why did we bring it up? Because the macro recorder generates lots of statements using the Range method. There is a similar Range method for Shapes and Notes, too, and it is frequently used by the macro recorder. So if you generate code from the macro recorder, be sure to remove any references to multiple slides, and you can also remove the Range method keyword, too.

Saving the presentation

Looking quickly through the Presentation object methods, we come to Save. Instinct tells us to use just oPresentation.Save, which works, but not like you think. Remember that the Presentation's Name defaults to "PresentationX." PowerPoint saves the file in the directory from which PowerPoint was started, as "PresentationX.PPT." Perhaps not *quite* what you or your users wanted! The Save method does not accept parameters.

The not-so-intuitive solution is to use the SaveAs method. Fortunately, this tidbit of information is documented for the Save method, so when you forget it, you can find it in the Help file. The syntax of the SaveAs method is:

```
oPresentation.SaveAs(cFileName, [nFileFormat], [lEmbedFonts])
```

cFileName	Character	The fully qualified filename for the presentation.
nFileFormat	Numeric	Use one of the ppSaveAs constants to choose one of the supported formats. If not included, the presentation is saved in the format of the current presentation. (Optional)
lEmbedFonts	Logical	Use .T. if you want to embed the font information in the file. The default is .F. (Optional)

Remember to use the fully qualified filename. Just because FoxPro's default directories are set the way you want them and you're issuing commands from VFP doesn't mean that PowerPoint knows about those defaults.

Be aware that PowerPoint does not know anything about FoxPro's SET SAFETY setting. Issuing this command will overwrite an existing file without any notice.

There are ppSaveAs constants for every supported format that appears in the interactive Save As dialog box. Office 2000 supports 18 formats, including graphical formats (BMP, GIF, and JPG), previous versions of PowerPoint, data exchange formats (RTF, MetaFile), HTML, and others (Office 97 supports seven formats, which are mostly previous versions or RTF). Commonly used constants and their values are ppSaveAsPresentation (1), ppSaveAsHTML (12) (not available in Office 97), ppSaveAsShow (7), and ppSaveAsTemplate (5). So how do you know when to use SaveAs instead of Save? When you open a new document, its name is "PresentationX." Check the Name property to see if it has the name you want to use, or if it resembles the default. You may want to compare the Name property to your filename (without path) instead of the example shown:

```
#DEFINE ppSaveAsPresentation 1

IF LEFT(oPresentation.Name, 12) == "Presentation"
  oPresentation.SaveAs("C:\MyDocs\MyPresentation.PPT", ppSaveAsPresentation)
ELSE
  oPresentation.Save()
ENDIF
```

Closing presentations

You can close a presentation at any time, whether it's saved or not, by using the Close method. The Close method takes no parameters.

```
oPresentation.Close()
```

There is no warning if you close an unsaved presentation. To check whether it's saved before you close it, examine the Saved property, which contains 0 if the presentation has changed since it was created or last saved, and 1 if it's unchanged.

```
#DEFINE ppSaveAsPresentation 1

* Check to see if the presentation is saved before closing it
IF oPresentation.Saved = 0
  * Better save this presentation. Be sure it's saved with the proper name
  IF LEFT(oPresentation.Name, 12) == "Presentation"
    oPresentation.SaveAs("C:\MyDocs\MyPresentation.PPT", ppSaveAsPresentation)
  ELSE
    oPresentation.Save()
  ENDIF
ENDIF
oPresentation.Close()
```

Closing the application object

To shut down PowerPoint, call the Application object's Quit method:

```
oPowerPoint.Quit()
```

This severs the connection with the PowerPoint Application object. All presentations are closed (without saving) *unless* there are any variables pointing to object references in PowerPoint. If there is such a reference, none of the open presentations are closed, and the object references that exist are valid. When you close the last presentation (or release all object references), all remaining presentations are then closed.

 This is one instance where PowerPoint 2000 has changed the object model slightly. In PowerPoint 2000, there can be one and only one instance of a PowerPoint Application object; CreateObject() references an already running instance of PowerPoint, and creates another reference to it. In PowerPoint 97, each call to CreateObject() creates a new instance of an Application. An additional difference is that PowerPoint 97 closes without caring whether there are any open variables pointing to an instance of PowerPoint.

 To examine PowerPoint 2000's Quit behavior, run the code shown in **Listing 1**. It is saved as PPTQuit.PRG in the Developer Download files available at www.hentzenwerke.com.

Listing 1. The quirks of quitting PowerPoint 2000. As in Visual FoxPro, be sure to release all your object references to successfully close the server application.

```
* Create the Application instance
oPowerPoint = CreateObject("PowerPoint.Application")
oPowerPoint.Visible = .T.

WITH oPowerPoint
  * Create the first presentation
  oPresentation1 = .Presentations.Add()

  * Create the second presentation
  oPresentation2 = .Presentations.Add()
ENDWITH

= MESSAGEBOX("Alt-Tab to PowerPoint, and manually open a new presentation.")

* You might put in a SUSPEND here, to allow you to Alt-Tab
* to PowerPoint. Manually open a new presentation to see
* what happens to it if you don't have an object reference.

= MESSAGEBOX("Press OK to close Presentation2")
oPresentation2.Close()

= MESSAGEBOX("Press OK to close the Application Object." + CHR(13) + ;
            "Notice nothing happens.")
oPowerPoint.Quit()

= MESSAGEBOX("Press OK to close Presentation1")
oPresentation1.Close()

= MESSAGEBOX("The Application, and any presentations you manually " + ;
            "opened are still there! Press OK to release oPowerPoint.")
RELEASE oPowerPoint && Office 97 successfully terminates here.
```

```
= MESSAGEBOX("It's still there! Now press OK to release oPresentation1.")
RELEASE oPresentation1

= MESSAGEBOX("It's still there! Now press OK to release oPresentation2.")
RELEASE oPresentation2

= MESSAGEBOX("It's gone--and so are the presentations you manually " + ;
            "opened." + CHR(13) + ;
            "Remember to release ALL your variables!")
```

Just as with FoxPro forms, you need to release all the references to objects before you can destroy the instance of the main object (in PowerPoint 2000 only).

Making it look good for the users

Before moving on to adding content to the slides, let's explore some of the properties and methods that allow us to make the process of building the presentation more attractive to the user. We've already discussed Visible, Left, Top, Width, and Right. These control whether the user sees PowerPoint, and where the PowerPoint window appears on the screen. If the position and size of the window are not set in code, the PowerPoint window displays where and how the user last had it—it could be maximized, minimized, or normal anywhere on the screen.

During development, we like to have FoxPro in a normal window the full height of the screen and taking up about two-thirds of its width on one side, then forcing PowerPoint to come up two-thirds of the width on the opposite side. This way, the results of code that runs are easy to see. Users also like this arrangement for the first little while—it's quite cool to watch. They soon tire of it, though, just about the time they complain about performance (a sure sign that the novelty has worn off). Then you can add the feature to give the user the option of not seeing the final presentation until the end. It also runs approximately 30 percent faster (depending on hardware configuration and the types of slides that are built), which makes you look like a hero for being so responsive to their needs.

While PowerPoint is visible, there are reasons to bring PowerPoint in front of your application, especially if the users are attempting to watch it while it builds. This is accomplished through the Presentation's Activate method:

```
oPowerPoint.Activate()
```

This method brings the current presentation window to the top of all running Windows applications. In this situation, you'll also want to display slides as you work on them. Use Slide's Select method to bring a slide to the front:

```
oPresentation.Slides[1].Select()
```

A note to PowerPoint 97 users: the preceding line will cause an error. Use the following line, instead:

```
oPresentation.ActiveWindow.View.GoToSlide(2)
```

Just when do you show that slide? Do you issue the Select method just after you add it? If users are watching, it gives a very nice demonstration of exactly what's going on. The users can really relate to the "hard work" the computer is doing. However, after watching it a few times, users can get a little bored and wish it would run faster. To gain some performance (generally about a 15–20 percent increase), wait until the slide is completely drawn, then issue the Select method. Adding and formatting shapes on a hidden slide avoids time-consuming redraws, and your slides appear to pop up on the screen. If your users really complain, don't make the Application object visible until the end, and use a progress bar to indicate relative time remaining, instead.

Working with slide contents

Building presentations full of blank slides is straightforward. The next step is to add text and shapes to your slides. Any object on a slide, whether it is a picture, a title, text, shape, an OLE object, or something else, becomes one object in the Shapes collection. On the surface, this seems like an odd way to design a collection, as many different kinds of items obviously require different sets of properties. Looking a bit deeper, if you see each of those objects as something that takes up height and width, at a certain position, and contains a certain type of content, with text optional, then each of these strange objects starts to look as if it could belong to the same collection.

As in most COM collections, you can refer to a particular Shape object using its index in the collection (like oSlide.Shapes[7]) or its name (oSlide.Shapes["Rectangle 2"]).

The shape's name is generated when it is added to the slide. The default naming convention is the shape type keyword, followed by a number representing the number of shapes on the slide at the time the shape was added, plus one. Therefore, if a line, rectangle, text box, and AutoShape are added to a blank slide, their default names are Line 2, Rectangle 3, Text Box 4 and AutoShape 5, respectively (complete with the embedded blank). The Name property is read/write, so you have the option of changing them. If you are building an application that edits a generated presentation, it's strongly advisable to change the names into something more meaningful. However, if you are building a presentation from start to finish with no opportunity to edit it, do not take the time to change the names. There is no facility for the user to see the shape names in PowerPoint, so it seems silly to pay a minor performance penalty to change the names when the names won't be used.

Using the slide layouts

There are 29 predefined slide layouts to choose from; you must choose one when you add a slide. Each format has a predefined set of shapes, called Placeholders, ready to fill in. Depending on the format, there are between zero and five placeholders (all rectangle Shapes) already preset with default properties. This makes building slides pretty easy…just populate the properties and go!

Table 1 shows the various layouts, including the constant names and their values (so you can play with the commands interactively in the Command Window), and the number and kind of shapes on the slide. You can access the Shape objects through the Shapes collection, where they are the first several Shapes in the collection. You can also use the Placeholders collection to access them. They have the same index number as the Shapes collection, but any other shapes added to the slide do not appear in the Placeholders collection, only in the Shapes collection. The shapes are listed in their index order on the slide—for example, if you look at ppLayoutChartAndText, the title is Shapes[1] and Placeholders[1], the chart is Shapes[2] and

Placeholders[2], and the bulleted text is Shapes[3] and Placeholders[3]. The only difference between these placeholders and shapes you add yourself is that these are predefined with commonly used default settings. Unfortunately, there are no constants to denote the index of various placeholders. It's impossible to define such constants, as bulleted text could be in the second or third position depending on the slide layout used. Just be content to use this table to reference the index values you need.

Table 1. *PowerPoint slide layouts. The predefined layouts contain a variety of shapes to make it easy to build presentations without having to start from scratch.*

Constant	Value	Number of shapes	Shapes provided
ppLayoutBlank	12	0	None
ppLayoutChart	8	2	Title, chart
ppLayoutChartAndText	6	3	Title, chart, bulleted text
ppLayoutClipartAndText	10	3	Title, clip art, bulleted text
ppLayoutClipartAndVerticalText	26	3	Title, clip art, and sideways bulleted text
ppLayoutFourObjects	24	5	Title, two stacked objects next to two stacked objects
ppLayoutLargeObject	15	1	OLE object (no title)
ppLayoutMediaClipAndText	18	3	Title, media clip, bulleted text
ppLayoutMixed	-2		(Not a selectable format)
ppLayoutObject	16	2	Title, OLE object
ppLayoutObjectAndText	14	3	Title, OLE object, bulleted text
ppLayoutObjectOverText	19	3	Title, OLE object above bulleted text
ppLayoutOrgchart	7	2	Title, organization chart
ppLayoutTable	4	2	Title, table rectangle
ppLayoutText	2	2	Title, bulleted text
ppLayoutTextAndChart	5	3	Title, bulleted text, chart
ppLayoutTextAndClipart	9	3	Title, bulleted text, clip art
ppLayoutTextAndMediaClip	17	3	Title, bulleted text, media clip
ppLayoutTextAndObject	13	3	Title, bulleted text, OLE object
ppLayoutTextAndTwoObjects	21	4	Title, bulleted text next to two stacked OLE objects
ppLayoutTextOverObject	20	3	Title, bulleted text above OLE object
ppLayoutTitle	1	2	Title, subtitle
ppLayoutTitleOnly	11	1	Title (leaves room for something below it)
ppLayoutTwoColumnText	3	3	Title, two-column bulleted text
ppLayoutTwoObjectsAndText	22	4	Title, two stacked OLE objects next to bulleted text
ppLayoutTwoObjectsOverText	23	4	Title, two side-by-side OLE objects over bulleted text
ppLayoutVerticalText	25	2	Title, sideways bulleted text
ppLayoutVerticalTitleAndText	27	2	Sideways title and bulleted text (portrait layout)
ppLayoutVerticalTitleAndTextOverChart	28	3	Sideways title, sideways text, chart (portrait layout)

The wonderful thing about these default layouts is that the shapes are completely editable; PowerPoint provides you with a great default, and you can enhance it as you see fit. That means that you can move, resize, add, or delete any of these shapes.

 PowerPoint defines AutoLayouts that contain OLE objects. Adding OLE objects to the placeholders works well for interactive PowerPoint users. It was not designed to automate the placeholders to accept an OLE object (by macros or Automation). This is documented in the Microsoft Knowledge Base Article #Q160252 for PowerPoint 97, and #Q222796 for PowerPoint 2000. You can still use the Layout objects to hold pictures or text, but you can't change the placeholders into OLE objects. You must add an OLE object with the AddMediaObject method of the Shapes collection.

Shapes, shapes, and more shapes

Now comes the fun part: setting up the properties of the shapes to make this slide say something, and look great! The obvious place to start is the title slide. Not only is it the first slide in the presentation, but it also has the shapes that are the easiest to work with—both of them are text.

The following code opens a new presentation and adds a title slide. **Figure 3** shows the result. You'll reap the most benefits if you try this interactively in the Command Window, as you can play with the properties and see how they change. Just remember to replace the constants with their numeric values, because the Command Window doesn't automatically use #DEFINES. (Except, of course, if you cut and paste the code with the #DEFINES, highlight all of the commands, including the #DEFINES, and then Execute the selection. See Chapter 2, "The Office Servers," for more tips on interactive testing.)

```
#DEFINE ppLayoutTitle 1

oPowerPoint = CreateObject("PowerPoint.Application")
oPowerPoint.Visible = .T.
oPresentation = oPowerPoint.Presentations.Add()
oSlide = oPresentation.Slides.Add(1, ppLayoutTitle)
```

There are two objects on the title slide: the title and the subtitle. Table 1 tells us that the first shape is the title, and the second is the subtitle. It's easy to think that we can just set the shape's Caption property and move on, but it's not quite that simple. Remember, not every shape has text (why would you want text on a sound object?). So the Shape object model includes a TextFrame object for each Shape object. The TextFrame object only exists if the Shape object's HasTextFrame property is true. In this case, the text is visible on the slide, so it's obvious that the TextFrame object exists (with other kinds of objects, it's prudent to test HasTextFrame). The TextFrame object contains a TextRange object, which actually has the Text property, set thusly:

```
oSlide.Shapes[1].TextFrame.TextRange.Text = "PowerPoint Automation Demo"
oSlide.Shapes[2].TextFrame.TextRange.Text = "Hang on to your socks!"
```

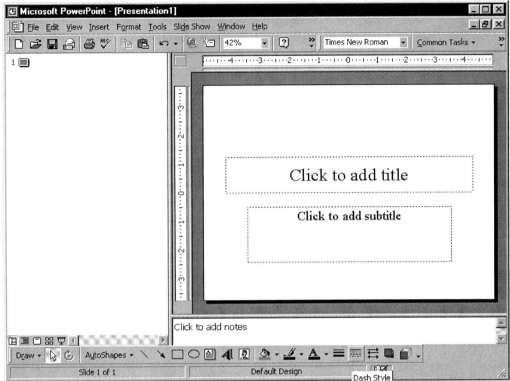

Figure 3. *Adding a title slide. Note the two shapes representing the title and subtitle.*

Voila! A complete slide, and in only six lines of code! The next step is to dress up this plain slide. For that, a better understanding of the Shape object is required.

The Shape object
The Shape object is the key object for a developer automating PowerPoint. It's more complicated than most, but also more powerful.

The Shapes collection supports a number of different types of shapes. Each type of shape is added with a different method. It's beyond the scope of this book to discuss all of them. Help does have some good information on these, but it lacks a complete list (other than the "See Also" dropdown, which only shows a few at a time). We provide the complete list in **Table 2** and discuss the ones you're most likely to use. In order to support so many kinds of objects, the Shape object uses related objects to describe the unique formatting features of some of the shapes. These are listed in the "Unique format objects" column of Table 2.

Each Slide object has several standard formatting objects, too. **Table 3** shows the formatting objects that apply to all Shapes.

Table 2. *Method names used to add shapes. Each kind of shape has its own special method. Some types use additional objects for special formatting.*

Method name	Description	Unique format objects
AddCallout	Adds a Callout shape (a text box with a leader line, usually used to point to and explain something on the slide).	CalloutFormat
AddComment	Adds a rectangle with a colored background. Like a Callout, but no leader line.	
AddConnector	Adds a line or curve that connects two other shapes.	ConnectorFormat
AddCurve	Adds a Bézier curve from a series of points.	ShapeNodes
AddLabel	Adds a text label (a rectangle with text but no border or fill).	
AddLine	Adds a line.	
AddMediaObject	Adds a multimedia object from a file.	OLEFormat, LinkFormat
AddOLEObject	Adds an OLE object from file, class name, or ProgID.	OLEFormat, LinkFormat
AddPicture	Adds a graphic from a file.	OLEFormat, PictureFormat
AddPlaceholder	Adds a Placeholder shape back if you delete one.	PlaceholderFormat
AddPolyline	Adds a series of line segments from a series of points.	ShapeNodes
AddShape	Adds one of 140 predefined AutoShapes.	
AddTable	Adds a table (PowerPoint 2000 only).	
AddTextbox	Adds a text box.	
AddTextEffect	Adds a WordArt object.	
AddTitle	Restores a title if you deleted the title Placeholder.	PlaceholderFormat

Table 3. *Formatting objects that pertain to each Shape object. The "Shape property" column is the name of the Shape object's property used to access the object. The "Object kind" column refers to the kind of object the property references; in other words, the topic to look up in the Help file.*

Shape property	Object kind	Description
ActionSettings	ActionSettings	Defines the action to occur when the mouse moves over the shape during a slide show.
AnimationSettings	AnimationSettings	Defines the special effects for the shape during a slide show.
Fill	FillFormat	Defines the shape's fill properties.
Line	LineFormat	Defines the shape's border properties (or line properties if a line).
TextFrame	TextFrame	Contains the text properties and methods, if the shape contains text.

These formatting objects have properties and methods that determine what the object looks like. These objects, along with a few other Slide properties and methods, are discussed in detail in the following sections.

Adding lines

Lines are perhaps the easiest shape to add. The parameter list is simple: the beginning and ending coordinates. Once the line is added, the LineFormat object's properties must be set to format the line to something other than the default. The LineFormat object is available to all Shapes.

The syntax for adding a Line object is:

```
oSlide.Shapes.AddLine(nBeginX, nBeginY, nEndX, nEndY)
```

The parameters represent the beginning and ending coordinates, in points. For example, to add a horizontal line four inches from the top of the slide, starting one inch from the left side and ending nine inches from the left side, use this command:

```
oLine = oSlide.Shapes.AddLine(72, 288, 648, 288)
```

Since a point is $1/72^{nd}$ of an inch, all the measurements are multiplied by 72. It's not very intuitive to look at—imagine coming back to this line of code next month! The following code is much easier to understand, and debug. You might add your own constant, perhaps called autoIn2Pts, to make the code more intuitive. (See the Note for more information.)

```
#DEFINE autoIn2Pts 72

oLine = oSlide.Shapes.AddLine(1.00 * autoIn2Pts, 4.00 * autoIn2Pts, ;
        9.00 * autoIn2Pts, 4.00 * autoIn2Pts)
```

 A point is $1/72^{nd}$ of an inch. Most of the placement of PowerPoint's objects takes place using points rather than inches or centimeters. To make your code more readable, you should probably define a constant such as autoIn2Pts to 72. If you work in the metric system, you might choose a constant such as autoCm2Pts and set it to 28.35. Then you can write code using units you are comfortable with, rather than using outrageously large numbers that don't relate to anything you understand.

Points to ponder

While we're on the subject of points, you need to know that PowerPoint stores all measurements in points. Remember that properties like Top, Left, Height, and Width don't need to be multiplied by the constants. For example, the following code draws a line the width of the title, and another one half an inch above it. The title Shape has an index of 1 (unfortunately, there are no predefined constants for the Layout objects; see Table 1 for the index values for the various shapes):

```
#DEFINE autoIn2Pts 72

WITH oSlide.Shapes[1]
   oLine = oSlide.Shapes.AddLine(.Left, .Top - (.5 * autoIn2Pts), ;
```

```
      .Left + .Width, .Top - (.5 * autoIn2Pts))
ENDWITH
```

Formatting lines

Thin, black lines can get just a bit boring. PowerPoint has so many formatting features that we need to do some exploring! Line objects store properties for color, style, transparency, pattern, weight, and arrowheads in the LineFormat object. Use the Line object's Line property to access the LineFormat object. **Table 4** shows the properties of the LineFormat object.

Table 4. LineFormat object properties.

Property	Type	Description
ForeColor	Object	The color of the line using a ColorFormat object.
BackColor	Object	The backcolor of a patterned line using a ColorFormat object. This is the secondary color of a patterned line, and it's ignored if patterns are not used.
DashStyle	Numeric	The dash style of the line. Uses one of the following contants: msoLineDash 4 msoLineDashDot 5 msoLineDashDotDot 6 msoLineLongDash 7 msoLineLongDashDot 8 msoLineRoundDot 3 msoLineSolid 1 msoLineSquareDot 2
Pattern	Numeric	The pattern applied to the line. The background of color is used as the background of the pattern. Use one of the many patterned constants. A few are listed here: msoPattern50Percent 7 msoPatternLargeConfetti 33 msoPatternLargeGrid 34 msoPatternLightDownwardDiagonal 21 msoPatternLightHorizontal 19 msoPatternLightUpwardDiagonal 22 msoPatternLightVertical 20 msoPatternPlaid 42 msoPatternSmallGrid 23 msoPatternSolidDiamond 39 msoPatternWideDownwardDiagonal 25 msoPatternWideUpwardDiagonal 26 msoPatternZigZag 38
Style	Numeric	The style of the line—which can give the appearance of multiple lines. msoLineSingle 1 msoLineThickBetweenThin 5 msoLineThickThin 4 msoLineThinThick 3
Transparency	Numeric	The degree of transparency of the line. The value ranges between 0.0 (opaque) and 1.0 (completely clear).
Weight	Numeric	The thickness of the line, in points.
Visible	Logical	A logical value determining whether the line is visible.

***Table 4**, continued*

Property	Type	Description
BeginArrowheadLength	Numeric	The length of the arrowhead at the beginning of the line. Use one of the following constants: msoArrowheadLengthMedium 2 msoArrowheadLong 3 msoArrowheadShort 1
BeginArrowheadStyle	Numeric	The shape of the arrowhead at the beginning of the line. Use one of the following constants: msoArrowheadDiamond 5 msoArrowheadNone 1 msoArrowheadOpen 3 msoArrowheadOval 6 msoArrowheadStealth 4 msoArrowheadTriangle 2
BeginArrowheadWidth	Numeric	The width of the arrowhead at the beginning of the line. Use one of the following constants: msoArrowheadNarrow 1 msoArrowheadWide 3 msoArrowheadWidthMedium 2
EndArrowheadLength	Numeric	The length of the arrowhead at the end of the line. Use one of the constants listed in BeginArrowheadLength.
EndArrowheadStyle	Numeric	The shape of the arrowhead at the end of the line. Use one of the constants listed in BeginArrowheadStyle.
EndArrowheadWidth	Numeric	The width of the arrowhead at the end of the line. Use one of the constants listed in BeginArrowheadWidth.

The colors of the line are set using the ForeColor and BackColor properties. These properties point to a ColorFormat object. A ColorFormat object has only two properties—the one needed here is the RGB property (the other is the SchemeColor property; it's covered later).

 To illustrate the use of these properties, the code in **Listing 2** generates some lines on a PowerPoint slide (the code is PPTLines.PRG in the Developer Download files available at www.hentzenwerke.com). **Figure 4** shows the results of the sample code.

Listing 2. *Example code for formatting lines. There are many ways to format a line: patterns, width, and arrowheads are shown in this example. See Figure 4 for the resulting slide.*

```
#DEFINE autoIn2Pts              72
#DEFINE ppLayoutBlank           12
#DEFINE msoLineThickThin         4
#DEFINE msoPatternSmallGrid     23
#DEFINE msoLineDash              4
#DEFINE msoArrowheadLengthMedium 2
#DEFINE msoArrowheadOval         6
#DEFINE msoArrowheadWidthMedium  2
#DEFINE msoArrowheadLong         3
#DEFINE msoArrowheadTriangle     2
#DEFINE msoArrowheadWide         3

* Clean out any existing references to servers.
* This prevents memory loss to leftover instances.
RELEASE ALL LIKE o*

* For demonstration purposes, make oPowerPoint and oSlide
```

```
* available after this program executes.
PUBLIC oPowerPoint, oSlide

* Open the server and add a presentation
oPowerPoint = CreateObject("PowerPoint.Application")
oPowerPoint.Visible = .T.
oPresentation = oPowerPoint.Presentations.Add()

* Get a new slide
oSlide = oPresentation.Slides.Add(1, ppLayoutBlank)

* Add a line, and format it to be blue, a weight of 5 points,
* and Thick Thin style
oLine = oSlide.Shapes.AddLine( ;
          1.00 * autoIn2Pts, 2.00 * autoIn2Pts, ;
          9.00 * autoIn2Pts, 2.00 * autoIn2Pts)
WITH oLine.Line   && The .Line refers to the LineFormat object
  .ForeColor.RGB = RGB(0, 0, 255)
  .Weight = 5
  .Style = msoLineThickThin
ENDWITH

* Add a line, and format it to be red on yellow,
* half an inch thick, and patterned with the small grid pattern.
oLine = oSlide.Shapes.AddLine( ;
          1.00 * autoIn2Pts, 3.00 * autoIn2Pts, ;
          9.00 * autoIn2Pts, 3.00 * autoIn2Pts)
WITH oLine.Line   && The .Line refers to the LineFormat object
  .ForeColor.RGB = RGB(255, 0, 0)
  .BackColor.RGB = RGB(255, 255, 0)
  .Weight = .5 * autoIn2Pts
  .Pattern = msoPatternSmallGrid
ENDWITH

* Add a line, and add an arrowhead to the beginning and end.
* Format the beginning arrowhead as a circle, and the ending
* arrowhead as a long, wide triangle. Make the line dashed.
oLine = oSlide.Shapes.AddLine( ;
          1.00 * autoIn2Pts, 4.00 * autoIn2Pts, ;
          9.00 * autoIn2Pts, 4.00 * autoIn2Pts)
WITH oLine.Line   && The .Line refers to the LineFormat object
  .DashStyle = msoLineDash
  .BeginArrowheadLength = msoArrowheadLengthMedium
  .BeginArrowheadStyle  = msoArrowheadOval
  .BeginArrowheadWidth  = msoArrowheadWidthMedium
  .EndArrowheadLength = msoArrowheadLong
  .EndArrowheadStyle  = msoArrowheadTriangle
  .EndArrowheadWidth  = msoArrowheadWide
ENDWITH
```

Listing 2 illustrates a few interesting nuances of formatting lines. The BackColor property is relevant only when a pattern is used, and provides the background color to fill in the line. When using arrowheads, the beginning arrowhead goes on the first X,Y coordinate passed to the AddLine method; the ending arrowhead goes on the second coordinate.

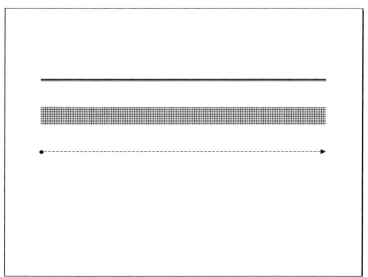

Figure 4. *Line-up time. A PowerPoint slide showing the formatted lines generated from Listing 2.*

When the Shape is something other than a line, the LineFormat object referenced by Line describes the shape's borders. In that case, the LineFormat object has all the same properties, except for the Arrowhead properties. Attempting to set the value of any arrowhead property to something other than one results in the error: "OLE IDispatch exception code 0: The specified value is out of range…"

Adding AutoShapes

Office comes with more than 140 predefined shapes for use in its applications. The available shapes provide much more than just the basic drawing shapes like rectangles and circles. There are many decorative shapes, such as arrows, stars, and banners. Flowchart symbols are also available, as are many kinds of callouts. Any of these shapes can be added to a slide using the AddShape method of the Shapes collection. AutoShapes are used to create diagrams, illustrations, or just spruce up your slides.

The syntax for adding an AutoShape is:

```
oShape = oSlide.Shapes.AddShape( nType, nLeft, nTop, nWidth, nHeight )
```

The first parameter is a numeric constant indicating one of the 140 shapes available. **Table 5** shows a sample of the available constants. Note that their prefix is "mso," which denotes that they are available to all Office applications, not just PowerPoint. The next two parameters specify the upper left corner of the rectangular box containing the shape (in points, of course). The final two parameters determine the width and height of the object, in points. This is different from a line, which requires an absolute endpoint rather than a width and height. This rectangular box, which contains the shape, is called the *bounding box*.

Table 5. *A sampling of AutoShape constants and their values.*

Shape constant	Value
msoShape5PointStar	92
msoShapeArc	25
msoShapeBalloon	137
msoShapeCube	14
msoShapeDownArrow	36
msoShapeLeftArrow	34
msoShapeLineCallout1	109
msoShapeNoSymbol	19
msoShapeOval	9
msoShapeParallelogram	2
msoShapeRectangle	1
msoShapeRightArrow	33
msoShapeRoundedRectangle	5
msoShapeUpArrow	35

The shape is placed with the current AutoShape default settings. The built-in defaults are a distinctive shade of seafoam green, with a thin black border. We'll discuss changing these lovely default colors in the section "Filling the shape" later in this chapter. So issuing the following:

```
#DEFINE msoShape5PointStar 92
#DEFINE autoIn2Pts         72

oShape = oSlide.Shapes.AddShape(msoShape5PointStar, ;
        1 * autoIn2Pts, 1 * autoIn2Pts, ;
        4 * autoIn2Pts, 4 * autoIn2Pts)
```

draws a 4" star, with the top left corner of its bounding box one inch from the top and side. See **Figure 5** for the result (on an otherwise blank slide).

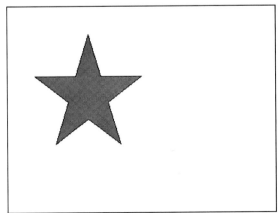

Figure 5. *Results of adding a star AutoShape. The shape is placed with the current AutoShape defaults, which include fill color, border color, and border style.*

Formatting the shape's border

Since we know how to format lines, we can figure out how to format borders. A Shape's Line property (which references a LineFormat object) controls its border. So, if you really want, you can put a 5-point-wide dashed dark blue border around the star:

```
#DEFINE msoLineDash 4

WITH oShape.Line
  .ForeColor.RGB = RGB(0, 0, 128)
  .Weight = 5
  .DashStyle = msoLineDash
ENDWITH
```

Of course, you can make the border disappear by setting its Visible property to false:

```
oShape.Line.Visible = .F.
```

Filling the shape

Now, to do something about that wonderful seafoam green color. That requires the Fill property, which references a FillFormat object. The FillFormat object's properties and methods make it extremely powerful. Not only can you change the seafoam green color to any other displayable solid color, but you can change it to a gradient fill, a texture, a pattern, a picture, or even make it semi-transparent. The FillFormat object is covered in detail in the section "Achieving consistency with Master Slides" in Chapter 11. But we do need to do something about that color...

Just like setting a line, the ForeColor property controls the color. Changing the color of the star is as easy as:

```
oShape.Fill.ForeColor.RGB = RGB(255, 255, 0)
```

Now it's yellow. If you care to pattern it, you need to set the BackColor property, then use the Patterned method to apply the patterning, using the same pattern constants as for lines. This code sets the back color to dark blue, and the pattern to msoPatternSmallGrid. The results are shown in **Figure 6**.

```
WITH oShape.Fill
  .BackColor.RGB = RGB(0, 0, 128)
  .Patterned(msoPatternSmallGrid)   && 23
ENDWITH
```

Okay, so that's not the most attractive pattern. But it gives a great example of why we might need to undo the patterning. The obvious approach is to use the Patterned method—of course, the obvious isn't always the way to go. To remove the patterning, use the Solid method to set it back:

```
oShape.Fill.Solid()
```

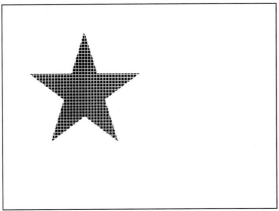

Figure 6*. The stellar results of patterning. The ForeColor is used as the color of the pattern itself, while the BackColor fills in the area behind the pattern.*

Beware! While the FillFormat and LineFormat objects have similar properties, the LineFormat object doesn't have a Solid method. To remove a pattern from a Line, set its DashStyle property to msoLineSolid (a value of 1).

Adding and formatting text

Text can be added to any shape. There are properties to set the color and font of the text. Individual characters, words, sentences, or even paragraphs can be formatted differently—for example, bolding certain words, or highlighting certain lines. You can also format the text as a bulleted list, with a wide variety of formats available for the bullets.

Adding text

Adding text to Shapes is the same as adding text to a title—especially since titles are really just Rectangle Shapes. A quick review of the process reminds us that the Shape's TextFrame property contains a TextFrame object. The TextFrame object contains properties and methods to align and anchor the text frame, and to store and format the text in the text frame.

Among the properties of the TextFrame object, the TextRange property is used to store a TextRange object. The TextRange object contains the properties that store the text and the text's formatting, along with a series of methods to manipulate the text. We'll come back to an explanation of the TextFrame properties after we look at the TextRange object—it's much easier to see how TextFrame properties affect the text when there is actually text to view!

Within the TextRange object, the text string itself is stored in the Text property. The font formatting information is stored in the TextRange's Font property, and the stored Font object is similar to the Font objects encountered in Word and Excel. The following example adds an oval and shows how to add a text string and use the basic font formatting to the shape:

```
#DEFINE msoShapeOval   9
#DEFINE autoIn2Pts    72

oShape = oSlide.Shapes.AddShape(msoShapeOval, ;
         4.0 * autoIn2Pts, 1.5 * autoIn2Pts, ;
```

```
                2.0 * autoIn2Pts, 4 * autoIn2Pts)
WITH oShape.TextFrame.TextRange
  .Text = "This is a test." + CHR(13) + "It is only a test."
  .Font.Name = "Arial"
  .Font.Size = 36
  .Font.Bold = .T.
ENDWITH
```

The Shape that is added is a tall, thin oval. **Figure 7** shows the results of the code. Note that the shape's boundaries do not affect the size and width of the text. The text is far wider than the shape. The TextFrame object has an AutoSize property that can resize the Shape to fit the text string. Setting the AutoSize property to ppAutoSizeShapeToFitText (1) automatically resizes the Shape to fit the text. **Figure 8** shows how the example shape changes when AutoSize is set to fit the text. Even if AutoSize is immediately set back to ppAutoSizeNone (0), the automatically generated size remains; it does not revert to the previous size.

Figure 7. Results of the formatted text added to an oval shape.

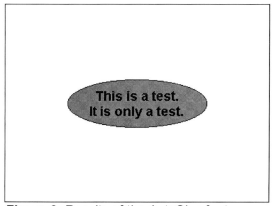

Figure 8. Results of the AutoSize feature.

Fun with text segments

The TextRange object in Office gives us a rich set of methods to work with segments of text. These chunks are commonly known as Characters, Words, Lines, Sentences, Paragraphs, and Runs. By selecting certain segments, such as a few words or a sentence, the selected text can be formatted differently than the other text. While characters, words, sentences, and paragraphs seem obvious, lines and runs need a bit more explanation. Lines correspond to the physical line in the text frame (think MLINE() here). Runs correspond to text with identical formatting attributes.

Segments of text are selected with the TextRange methods called Characters, Words, Lines, Sentences, Paragraphs, and Runs. Each method takes two optional parameters. The first is the position of the starting chunk, and the second is the number of segments you want returned (the default is 1). If you omit either parameter, you get them all. All of these methods return another TextRange object to manipulate. To see the text, you need to reference the Text property of the TextRange object. Here are a few examples, based on the text shown in Figure 8.

```
? oShape.TextFrame.TextRange.Lines[2].Text          && "It is only a test."
? oShape.TextFrame.TextRange.Words[3].Text          && "a " (note the space)
? oShape.TextFrame.TextRange.Words[5].Text          && "." (Periods are words)
? oShape.TextFrame.TextRange.Characters[4,6].Text   && "s is a"
```

Since these methods return TextRanges, you can string these methods together to get a very specific segment, such as the third word in the second sentence:

```
? oShape.TextFrame.TextRange.Sentences[2].Words[3].Text   && "only "
```

This is useful when a client has a company name displayed in a different font, or if words or sentences should be highlighted. It's useful for formatting paragraphs, too.

Formatting paragraphs

If you're saying, "There shouldn't be paragraphs on a PowerPoint slide!" give yourself a pat on the back! You understand good presentation layout! For those of you who are scratching your head wondering why, the rule of thumb is "seven lines of seven words." This is generally considered to be a maximum, too. The audience should not spend time reading lots of text on the screen, because if they are, they're not listening to the presenter. (For that matter, the presenter shouldn't read the slide to the audience, either, but we digress.)

So why would PowerPoint include a ParagraphFormat object? Polymorphism. The name is consistent with the object that performs similar functionality in other Office products, and it allows you to easily format bulleted lists. (Think of each bullet as a paragraph.) Besides, it will format the paragraph, if you (or your clients) insist on paragraphs of text.

The ParagraphFormat object has a few properties that contain the values for formatting the entire text range. The Alignment property sets the alignment of the whole text range. Alignment constants are ppAlignLeft (1), ppAlignCenter (2), ppAlignRight (3), ppAlignJustify (4), and ppAlignDistribute (5). Also available is the WordWrap property, which is a logical value.

There are properties that set the vertical spacing for each paragraph within the TextFrame. Use the SpaceBefore, SpaceAfter, and SpaceWithin numeric properties to set the spacing between lines of text. The amount of space is set by a corresponding LineRule property: LineRuleBefore, LineRuleAfter, and LineRuleWithin. The LineRule properties can be set with a logical or numeric value denoting whether the units are in number of lines (.T., or 1) or in points (.F., or 0). Either logical or numeric values may be used to set the value; however, these properties are numeric when queried. Set the LineRule properties explicitly before changing the Space properties, as changing the LineRule properties from points to lines properly converts the stored Space value, but changing from lines to points sets the corresponding Space property to zero.

Bullets

The ParagraphFormat object uses the Bullet property to store the BulletFormat object. The BulletFormat object sets all the formatting for the bullets. PowerPoint 2000 offers some nice updates to the BulletFormat object, the most notable of which is the Type property. The Type object determines what kinds of bullets are used. If no bullets should be used, set the Type property to ppBulletNone (0). To display symbols for bullets, use the ppBulletUnnumbered (1) constant. To display numbered bullets, use the ppBulletNumbered (2) constant. To display a graphic image, such as a BMP, as a bullet, use the ppBulletPicture (3) constant.

 In PowerPoint 97, the BulletFormat object does not support numbered bullets or pictures for bullets. That leaves symbol bullets, or no bullets. The 97 BulletFormat object uses a Visible object to toggle the display of bullet symbols. The Visible property is still available in PowerPoint 2000, but it is not specifically listed in the Help file under "BulletFormat Properties" or the Applies To list in the Visible property (though it is included in several examples in the Help file). This usually indicates that the property may not be available in the next version of PowerPoint. Make sure your code uses the Type property rather than the Visible property when running under PowerPoint 2000.

Controlling the size of the bullets is accomplished with the RelativeSize property. The numeric value should be between .25 and 4. This number indicates the size as a percentage of the height of the text. If you enter values larger or smaller than the expected range, no error occurs; instead, it displays the symbol as if it were set to the minimum or maximum (whichever was exceeded). This property is unchanged from PowerPoint 97.

The Character property sets the character used for the bullet. According to the Help file, this property stores the Unicode value for the symbol. Use the Unicode value only for Unicode fonts, such as Lucida Sans Unicode. If you set the Bullet object's Font property to a regular ASCII font, such as Wingdings, use the ASCII value of the character.

Numbered bullets

PowerPoint 2000 offers a series of properties to number the bullets. The Style property selects one of the approximately 28 preset styles of numbering (not all are available in every language). The numbering styles force the bulleted characters to a specific case, and with specified parentheses or periods. Of course there are the series of constants (a few samples are shown in **Table 6**)—the Help file has a complete listing (it's one of the few Help pages that shows the values of the constants, too).

Table 6*. Constants for numbering bullets. Numbered bullets is a feature new in PowerPoint 2000.*

Constant	Value	Example
ppBulletAlphaLCPeriod	0	a.
ppBulletAlphaUCPeriod	1	A.
ppBulletArabicParenRight	2	1)
ppBulletArabicPeriod	3	1.
ppBulletRomanLCParenBoth	4	(i)
ppBulletAlphaUCParenRight	11	A)
ppBulletArabicPlain	13	1
ppBulletCircleNumWDWhitePlain	19	① (Only available for 1–10)

The default value for the style is ppBulletAlphaUCPeriod (1), which is the uppercase alpha characters followed by a period.

The StartValue property contains the number of the first bullet on the slide. This is particularly useful if bulleted lists break across slides—for example, when the first three bullets are on Slide 1, and the second three are on Slide 2. You may want to break numbered bullets into two columns on the same slide, and have two text shapes numbered consecutively on the same slide. StartValue is a numeric property. If the bullet Style shows numbers, the value directly corresponds to the number displayed in the bullet. This includes Roman numerals. If the Style shows alpha characters, the value corresponds to the position in the alphabet: 1 = A, 2 = B, 26 = Z, 27 = AA, 28 = BB, and so forth. The StartValue property has a range from 1 to 32767. The default is 1.

Setting the StartValue uses the currently stored style. Since the default is uppercase alpha characters, don't be surprised to set StartValue to 3 and get "C." instead of "3." Be sure to explicitly set the Style property when you set the StartValue to avoid little surprises like that.

 Setting the values for the Style or the StartValue automatically sets the Type property to ppBulletNumbered (2). Use the Type property to test whether there are numbered bullets; do not rely on the Style or the StartValue properties alone. These properties retain their settings even if you select another type of bullet.

Picture bullets

PowerPoint 2000 includes a new feature to add a graphic file as the bullet character. This can really dress up the presentations. Adding a graphic file as a bitmap uses the lone method of the BulletFormat object—the Picture method. It accepts a single parameter, which is the fully qualified path to the file (or at least a path relative to PowerPoint's location; remember, PowerPoint does not know what FoxPro's current directories are). PowerPoint supports a wide variety of graphic formats; see the "Picture Method" topic in the Help file for a complete list.

When the Picture method runs, it sets the Type property to ppBulletPicture (3). There does not appear to be an exposed property to query what graphic file is used.

You can set the picture for each bullet individually—by using the TextRange's Paragraphs method. While the following code is technically possible, do be sure that it is visually acceptable (this particular example illustrates the technical methods, but is *not* recommended as an example of good layout!).

```
WITH oShape.TextFrame.TextRange
  * Make sure the shape has two paragraphs of text
  .Text = "Test 1" + CHR(13) + "Test 2"

  * Use some standard bitmaps that come with Windows
  .Paragraphs(1).ParagraphFormat.Bullet.Picture( ;
     GETENV("WINDIR") + "\Triangles.bmp")
  .Paragraphs(2).ParagraphFormat.Bullet.Picture( ;
     GETENV("WINDIR") + "\Circles.bmp")
ENDWITH
```

Fun with fonts

If you've been developing apps for any length of time, you can probably relate to this: you've just demonstrated your really awesome presentation that extracts the data from the tables, manipulates it a dozen ways, drops it into an incredibly well-done presentation containing 20 slides in two seconds flat—it's utterly amazing. After viewing this incredible technological feat, the client/boss pauses thoughtfully before saying, "Hmmm…can we change the font to something else?" After you pick up your bruised and battered ego off the floor (after all, you were expecting a comment something like "Wow!"), you can tell them with confidence that yes, there is a way to change the font. And the color, too (try not to appear too sarcastic when you say this through gritted teeth!).

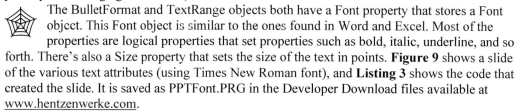 The BulletFormat and TextRange objects both have a Font property that stores a Font object. This Font object is similar to the ones found in Word and Excel. Most of the properties are logical properties that set properties such as bold, italic, underline, and so forth. There's also a Size property that sets the size of the text in points. **Figure 9** shows a slide of the various text attributes (using Times New Roman font), and **Listing 3** shows the code that created the slide. It is saved as PPTFont.PRG in the Developer Download files available at www.hentzenwerke.com.

This code shows the various properties of the Font object, as well as how to manipulate text segments and a few ParagraphFormat features.

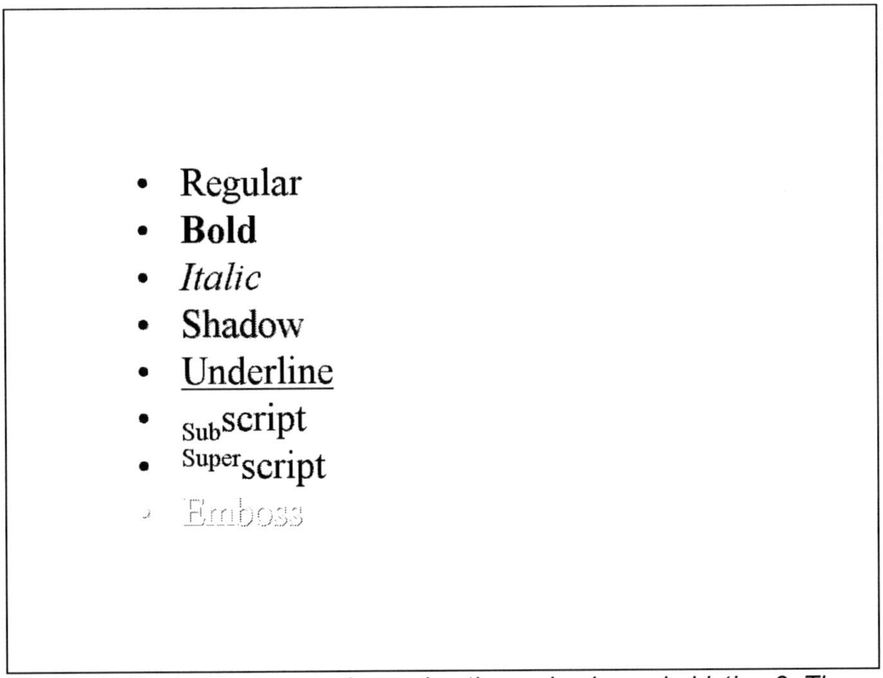

- Regular
- **Bold**
- *Italic*
- Shadow
- Underline
- Subscript
- Superscript
- Emboss

Figure 9. *Font object examples, using the code shown in Listing 3. These eight effects can also be combined, if desired.*

Listing 3. *Manipulating the Font object.*

```
#DEFINE ppLayoutBlank       12
#DEFINE msoShapeRectangle   1
#DEFINE ppAlignLeft         1
#DEFINE ppBulletUnnumbered  1

* ASSUMPTION: oPresentation is a variable pointing
*             to an open PowerPoint presentation.

* Add a new slide with a new shape
oSlide = oPresentation.Slides.Add(1, ppLayoutBlank)
oShape = oSlide.Shapes.AddShape(msoShapeRectangle, 100,100,500,350)

* Remove the shape's border and fill color.
oShape.Line.Visible = .F.
oShape.Fill.ForeColor.RGB = RGB(255,255,255)

WITH oShape.TextFrame.TextRange

  * Add the example text
  .Text = "Regular" + CHR(13) + ;
          "Bold" + CHR(13) + ;
          "Italic" + CHR(13) + ;
          "Shadow" + CHR(13) + ;
          "Underline" + CHR(13) + ;
```

```
                     "Subscript" + CHR(13) + ;
                     "Superscript" + CHR(13) + ;
                     "Emboss"

   * Make the font larger, left align the text,
   * and set the bullet format to default symbols.
   .Font.Size = 32
   .ParagraphFormat.Alignment = ppAlignLeft
   .ParagraphFormat.Bullet.Type = ppBulletUnnumbered

   * Format each of the bullets
   .Paragraphs[2].Font.Bold = .T.
   .Paragraphs[3].Font.Italic = .T.
   .Paragraphs[4].Font.Shadow = .T.
   .Paragraphs[5].Font.Underline = .T.
   .Paragraphs[6].Characters[1,3].Font.Subscript = .T.
   .Paragraphs[7].Characters[1,5].Font.Superscript = .T.
   .Paragraphs[8].Font.Emboss = .T.

ENDWITH
```

The Font object also has a property, Color, which references a ColorFormat object. The ColorFormat's RGB property sets the text color. The background color is set by the shape. The following example sets the title text to blue. If there were a bullet symbol on the title, the Font.Color property sets the color for the text and the bullet.

```
oSlide.Shapes.Title.TextFrame.TextRange.Color = RGB(0,0,128)
```

Occasionally, you may want to set the bullet color separately from the text color. To accomplish this, set the TextRange.ParagraphFormat.Bullet.Font.Color.RGB property. This sets the logical TextRange.ParagraphFormat.Bullet.UseTextColor property to .F. While you cannot explicitly set UseTextColor to .F., you can set it to .T. to return the bullet color to the text color.

The Name property sets the font. Set it to a font name, just like you set the font name properties for FoxPro objects. The font must exist on that machine, or it selects a font (generally Times New Roman). As with color, you may want to set the font of bullets separately from the text. It's done similarly, by setting the TextRange.ParagraphFormat .Bullet.Font.Name property (as opposed to TextRange.Font.Name), which then sets the TextRange.ParagraphFormat.Bullet.UseTextFont to .F. You cannot explicitly set UseTextFont to .F., but you can set it to .T. to return the bullet font to the text font.

Making it presentable

Once the slides are built, the users are going to want to do something with them. They'll probably want to run a slide show, or they're going to want to print it. Fortunately, PowerPoint exposes some methods to allow you to perform some pretty nice feats.

Running a slide show mode

Once you build a presentation, your users might like to preview it on the screen as a slide show. The Presentation's SlideShowSettings property references a SlideShowSettings object that allows you to manipulate the presentation. The only method is the Run method, which starts the slide show:

```
oPresentation.SlideShowSettings.Run()
```

This command tells PowerPoint to begin the slide show, which becomes the topmost window. Your application slips behind the slide show. When the users finish the slide show, they return to PowerPoint—*not* to your application! In addition, your application continues to run while the slide show is in progress. To handle this gracefully, be sure that the next line of your program is a wait state, so your application doesn't march along while they're watching the PowerPoint show. You probably also want code to put your application back on top after the show is over.

Printing

Presentation has a PrintOptions property that points to a PrintOptions object. The properties of PrintOptions are summarized in **Table 7**. Once the print options are set, issue the PrintOut method to print the selected items.

Table 7. *PrintOptions object properties.*

Property	Type	Description
Collate	Logical	A logical value denoting whether multiple copies should be collated.
FitToPage	Logical	True to make the slides fill the page; False to honor the values in the Page Setup dialog.
FrameSlides	Logical	True to place a thin border around slides, notes, and handouts; False to omit it.
HandoutOrder	Numeric	Sets the order of the slides on the handout: ppPrintHandoutHorizontalFirst (1)—Prints slides in rows across the page. ppPrintHandoutVerticalFirst (2)—Prints the slides in columns down the page. Default is 1; set to the number of copies needed.
OutputType	Numeric	A numeric value corresponding to what is printed (slides, handouts, or notes): ppPrintOutputSlides (1)—Default. ppPrintOutputTwoSlideHandouts (2)—Two slides per page. ppPrintOutputThreeSlideHandouts (3)—Three slides per page. ppPrintOutputFourSlideHandouts (8)—Four slides per page. ppPrintOutputSixSlideHandouts (4)—Six slides per page. ppPrintOutputNineSlideHandouts (9)—Nine slides per page. ppPrintOutputOutline (6)—Outline format. ppPrintOutputNotesPages (5)—Notes only.
PrintColorType	Numeric	A numeric value indicating how the colors should print: ppPrintColor (1)—Default. ppPrintBlackAndWhite (2)—Grayscale. ppPrintPureBlackAndWhite (3)—Strictly black and white (no fills).
PrintFontsAsGraphics	Logical	True to print the fonts as a graphical image.
PrintHiddenSlides	Logical	True to print any hidden slides.
PrintInBackground	Logical	True to print in the background (default).

Once the properties are set, invoke the PrintOut method. All parameters are optional. The syntax of the PrintOut method is as follows:

```
oPresentation.PrintOut(nFromSlide, nToSlide, cPrintToFile, nCopies, lCollate)
```

The nFromSlide and nToSlide parameters set the first and last slides to print. The cPrintToFile parameter is a fully qualified path and filename to accept the output. The remaining parameters override the settings in the PrintOptions object: nCopies overwrites NumberOfCopies, and lCollate overrides Collate.

Putting it all together

Listing 4 shows a few slides for a marketing presentation for Tasmanian Traders. The slides show what is covered in this chapter. The program creates three slides, shown in **Figures 10**, **11**, and **12**.

Listing 4. A sample presentation for Tasmanian Traders.

```
CLOSE DATA
#DEFINE ppLayoutTitle          1
#DEFINE ppLayoutText           2
#DEFINE ppBulletArabicPeriod   3
#DEFINE msoLineThickBetweenThin 5
#DEFINE autoIn2Pts             72


* Clean out any existing references to servers.
* This prevents memory loss to leftover instances.
RELEASE ALL LIKE o*

* For demonstration purposes, make oPowerPoint and oPresentation
* available after this program executes.
PUBLIC oPowerPoint, oPresentation

SET PATH TO _SAMPLES + "\TasTrade\Data\"

* Set up the data
OPEN DATABASE "TasTrade"
LogoFile = _SAMPLES + "\TasTrade\Bitmaps\TTradeSm.bmp"

USE OrdItems IN 0
USE Products IN 0

* Select the top 5 selling items of all time
SELECT TOP 5 ;
       P.English_Name, ;
       SUM(O.Unit_Price * O.Quantity) AS TotQuan ;
  FROM OrdItems O, Products P ;
 WHERE O.Product_ID = P.Product_ID ;
 GROUP BY 1 ;
 ORDER BY 2 DESC;
  INTO CURSOR TopSellers

* Select the number of products
SELECT Count(*) ;
```

```
  FROM Products ;
  INTO ARRAY aProducts

* Open PowerPoint
oPowerPoint = CreateObject("PowerPoint.Application")
oPowerPoint.Visible = .T.

* Create the presentation
oPresentation = oPowerPoint.Presentations.Add()

SlideNum = 1
```

Tasmanian Traders

Welcomes you...

Figure 10. *The Tasmanian Traders sample title slide. This slide demonstrates adding graphics and changing text attributes.*

```
* TITLE SLIDE...........
* Add the slide
oSlide = oPresentation.Slides.Add(SlideNum, ppLayoutTitle)

* Set the title text. Change it to Arial font, blue, and bold.
WITH oSlide.Shapes[1].TextFrame.TextRange
  .Text = "Tasmanian Traders"
  WITH .Font
    .Name = "Arial"
    .Bold = .T.
    .Color = RGB(0, 0, 128)
  ENDWITH
ENDWITH

* Set the subtitle text
oSlide.Shapes[2].TextFrame.TextRange.Text = "Welcomes you..."

* Add the logo.
oSlide.Shapes.AddPicture(LogoFile, .F., .T., ;
     2.0 * autoIn2Pts, 1.5 * autoIn2Pts)

* PowerPoint 97 users: the last two parameters,
* height and width, are not optional. Use this
```

```
* code instead:
*.Shapes.AddPicture(LogoFile, .F., .T., ;
*      8.5 * autoIn2Pts, 6.0 * autoIn2Pts, ;
*      1.0 * autoIn2Pts, 1.0 * autoIn2Pts)

SlideNum = SlideNum + 1
```

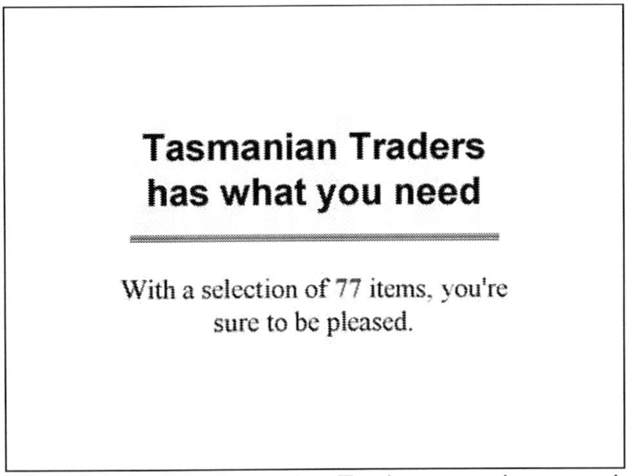

Figure 11. *The Tasmanian Traders sample second slide. This slide demonstrates adding lines and changing attributes for a segment of text.*

```
* SECOND SLIDE...........
* Add the slide
oSlide = oPresentation.Slides.Add(SlideNum, ppLayoutTitle)

* Bring the slide to the front
oSlide.Select()

* PowerPoint 97 users: oSlide.Select() will
* generate an error. Use this line instead:
* oPresentation.ActiveWindow.View.GoToSlide(2)

* Set the text of the title
WITH oSlide.Shapes[1].TextFrame.TextRange
   .Text = "Tasmanian Traders " + CHR(13) + "has what you need"
   WITH .Font
     .Name = "Arial"
     .Bold = .T.
     .Color = RGB(0,0,128)
   ENDWITH
ENDWITH

* Move the title up about half an inch
WITH oSlide.Shapes(1)
   .Top = .Top - (.5 * autoIn2Pts)
ENDWITH

* Add a line half an inch below the title that is centered and 6" long
```

```
LineTop = oSlide.Shapes[1].Top + oSlide.Shapes[1].Height + ;
    (.5 * autoIn2Pts)
LineLeft = 2 * autoIn2Pts
LineEnd = LineLeft + (6.0 * autoIn2Pts)

oLine = oSlide.Shapes.AddLine(LineLeft, LineTop, LineEnd, LineTop)

* Format the line to be red, and make it a thick line
* with two thin lines on either side
WITH oLine.Line
  .ForeColor.RGB = RGB(255,0,0)
  .Style = msoLineThickBetweenThin
  .Weight = 8
ENDWITH

* Set the text of the subtitle, and change the number to bold and red.
WITH oSlide.Shapes[2].TextFrame.TextRange
  .Text = "With a selection of " + ALLTRIM(STR(aProducts[1])) + ;
          " items, you're sure to be pleased."
  .Words[5].Font.Bold = .T.
  .Words[5].Font.Color = RGB(255, 0, 0)
ENDWITH

SlideNum = SlideNum + 1
```

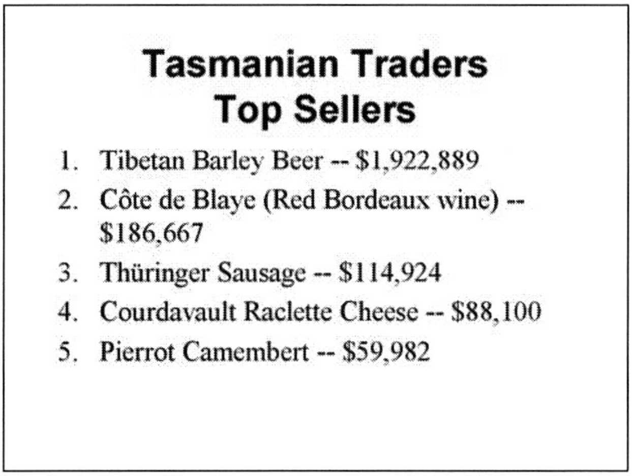

Tasmanian Traders
Top Sellers

1. Tibetan Barley Beer -- $1,922,889
2. Côte de Blaye (Red Bordeaux wine) -- $186,667
3. Thüringer Sausage -- $114,924
4. Courdavault Raclette Cheese -- $88,100
5. Pierrot Camembert -- $59,982

Figure 12. The Tasmanian Traders sample third slide. This slide demonstrates adding bulleted lists.

```
* TOP 5 SELLERS SLIDE..........
* Add the slide
oSlide = oPresentation.Slides.Add(SlideNum, ppLayoutText)

* Bring the slide to the front
oSlide.Select()

* PowerPoint 97 users: oSlide.Select() will
* generate an error. Use this line instead:
```

```
* oPresentation.ActiveWindow.View.GoToSlide(2)

* Insert the title (note the use of the Title object, instead of
* an enumerated shape object). Make the font Arial, blue, and bold.
WITH oSlide.Shapes.Title.TextFrame.TextRange
  .Text = "Tasmanian Traders" + CHR(13) +  "Top Sellers"
  WITH .Font
    .Name = "Arial"
    .Bold = .T.
    .Color = RGB(0,0,128)
  ENDWITH
ENDWITH

* Build the string to use for the top 5 sellers.
* Use a CR between each item to make each a separate bullet.
BulletString = ""
SELECT TopSellers
SCAN
  BulletString = BulletString + ;
                 TRIM(TopSellers.English_Name) + " -- $" + ;
                 ALLTRIM(TRANSFORM(TopSellers.TotQuan, "99,999,999")) + ;
                 CHR(13)
ENDSCAN

* Add the bullet string to the text frame, and make the bullets numeric.
WITH oSlide.Shapes[2].TextFrame.TextRange
  .Text = BulletString
  .ParagraphFormat.Bullet.Style = ppBulletArabicPeriod   && Available only
                                                         && in PowerPoint 2000
ENDWITH

* Run the slide show.
oPresentation.SlideShowSettings.Run()
```

Now you are capable of producing a slide show that is sure to knock the socks off your client. But wait, there's more! In addition to these basic features, PowerPoint throws in some advanced features—FREE! The next chapter explains some of the advanced features of PowerPoint.

Chapter 11
PowerPoint Advanced Features

Once you build a basic presentation, your clients will soon be begging for more. Actually, some of these advanced features (like the Master Slide feature) can be so helpful, you'll want to use them right away. Others, like animations and transitions, are fun to watch (and program). Used judiciously, these will dazzle your clients!

Now that your clients are impressed, you're ready to tackle a little more pizzazz in your presentations. Master Slides is a feature that ensures that all your slides have a consistent appearance. This chapter also covers some fancy features to animate shapes, control the transitions between slides, add multimedia, and create hot spots that run other programs. At the end are ways to add notes to be printed with your presentation.

Achieving consistency with Master Slides

The SlideMaster object sets the defaults for each slide's layout and appearance. The SlideMaster stores the defaults for colors and fonts, standard item placement, as well as objects that should appear on any slide (perhaps a company logo in the corner). The SlideMaster object is referenced by the Presentation's SlideMaster property.

Backgrounds

The plain white background on all slides is something your clients will insist that you change. You can set backgrounds individually on every slide, but that's a lot of redundant code, and it's a big performance hit. One of the first SlideMaster properties to explore is the Background property. This sets the background of all slides to be the same using a minimum of code with maximum performance.

The Background property stores a ShapeRange object. While the ShapeRange object has a number of properties, the most useful from the Background property's viewpoint is the Fill property, which references a FillFormat object, the same object used to fill shapes. You can fill the background with solid, soft yellow like this:

```
#DEFINE rgbSoftYellow  RGB(255,255,192)
oPresentation.SlideMaster.Background.Fill.ForeColor.RGB =  rgbSoftYellow
```

To provide a patterned background, set the ForeColor and BackColor properties of the FillFormat object. Then use the Patterned method, which accepts one parameter, a numeric value corresponding to the pattern (msoPattern constants). The Pattern property is set to the same value you pass to the Patterned method.

```
#DEFINE msoPatternDottedGrid  45
#DEFINE rgbDarkGray           RGB(128, 128, 128)
#DEFINE rgbMediumGray         RGB(192, 192, 192

* For a Patterned Background:
```

```
WITH oPresentation.SlideMaster.Background.Fill
  .ForeColor.RGB = rgbDarkGray
  .BackColor.RGB = rgbMediumGray
  .Patterned(msoPatternDottedGrid)
ENDWITH
```

This code produces a medium gray slide with a dotted grid (about every eight pixels) in dark gray. We're not sure this is the most aesthetically pleasing background—the pattern is too small and busy to use for projected slides. The Pattern tab on the Fill Effects dialog box in **Figure 1** shows examples of the patterns. Use of patterns may best be left to smaller shapes, which can handle smaller patterns.

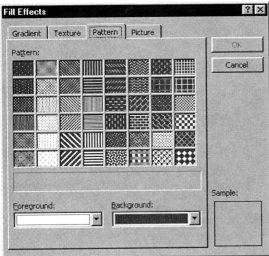

Figure 1. *The Fill Effects dialog box. This dialog shows samples of the available patterns.*

 The ForeColor represents the pattern, in this case, the dotted lines, and the BackColor shows through the pattern. Some patterns, like the dotted grid, show more background color; others show more foreground color.

Textures

If you or your client has used PowerPoint for very long, you know (or will soon be informed by your client) that there are textured backgrounds. Office provides about 25 preset textures to use. The FillFormat's PresetTextured method sets the background to the specified texture.

```
#DEFINE msoTextureSand  8
oPresentation.SlideMaster.Background.Fill.PresetTextured(msoTextureSand)
```

This line of code sets the background to a deep sand texture. If you want to find out what texture is in use, use the read-only PresetTexture property to return the numeric value.

What if your client wants a custom texture? Not to worry, PowerPoint provides a UserTextured method. This method takes one parameter, which is the fully qualified filename of a picture file to tile across the background. This filename is stored in the TextureName property (read-only). The TextureType property indicates which kind of texture is in use. The TextureType property returns msoTexturePreset (1) or msoTextureUserDefined (2).

Picture fills

You can use a bitmap as a background, too. The UserPicture method accepts a parameter consisting of a fully qualified bitmap filename. It forces the bitmap to take up the entire background—it does not tile it (use the UserTextured method to tile it). It uses some interesting smoothing techniques when you try to stretch a small bitmap across the whole slide. For an example, you might try:

```
oPresentation.SlideMaster.Background.Fill.UserPicture( ;
    GETENV("WINDIR" + "\TILES.BMP"))
```

This is a small bitmap that resembles brick; when enlarged, it has kind of a futuristic red and black look. This won't win any visual awards, but it is a striking example of how a small bitmap is smoothed over the whole screen. There isn't a documented property that corresponds to the UserPicture method to tell you what bitmap is used.

 The Background object is available for the SlideMaster as well as Shapes. These methods and properties for textures, picture fills, and gradient fills are available for shapes, too.

Gradient fills

Perhaps the most sought after background is the gradient fill—you know the kind, a nice medium blue fades from the top to a nearly black color at the bottom. **Figure 2** shows the PowerPoint dialog box that allows you to select the gradient fills interactively. This is a handy cue to remember all the various properties for setting a gradient fill.

There are three gradient color types available in PowerPoint. The GradientColorType property stores the currently selected gradient type. It is a read-only property; separate methods are used to set the gradient. This is to your benefit, as the methods used to set each type take multiple parameters, ensuring that you set all the necessary properties for the specific gradient. Here are the three gradient color types:

- Preset colors: usually employing three or more colors, there are 24 presets that have names like Daybreak, Ocean, Fog, Moss, Wheat, and Parchment (which, incidentally, are the most professional looking schemes; the rest can look very garish depending on the text colors used).

- One-color fill: the selected color graduates to shades of the same color that are lighter or darker than the selected color (as light as white or as dark as black).

- Two-color fill: the first color graduates into the second color.

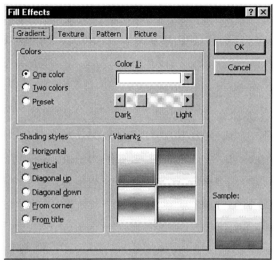

Figure 2. *PowerPoint's gradient fill option dialog box. This is a handy visual reminder of the properties that need to be set for a gradient fill.*

The preset colors are set with the PresetGradient method. This method takes three parameters:

```
oPresentation.SlideMaster.Background.Fill.PresetGradient(nStyle,
        nVariant, nType)
```

nStyle	Numeric	Indicates the shading style of the gradient:			
		msoGradientDiagonalDown	4	msoGradientDiagonalUp	3
		msoGradientFromCenter	7	msoGradientFromCorner	5
		msoGradientFromTitle	6	msoGradientHorizontal	1
		msoGradientVertical	2		
nVariant	Numeric	Indicates the choice of color order (no constants):			
		1 = Color 1 to Color 2 (top left box in the gradient dialog)			
		2 = Color 2 to Color 1 (top right box in the gradient dialog)			
		3 = Color 1 to Color 2 back to Color 1 (lower left box in the gradient dialog)			
		4 = Color 2 to Color 1 back to Color 2 (lower right box in the gradient dialog)			
nType	Numeric	Indicates the preset color scheme. Some of the 24 are:			
		msoGradientDaybreak	4	msoGradientOcean	7
		msoGradientFog	10	msoGradientParchment	14
		msoGradientMoss	11	msoGradientWheat	13

Most clients may object to the preset colors. As stated before, many are garish, and those that are professional are probably overused by their competitors. Your client may be more sophisticated than the preset colors (by the way, this is an excellent argument to dissuade a client who chooses one of the garish presets—take a look at the Rainbow type [16] to see what we mean).

The next gradient type is the one-color gradient, which uses the OneColorGradient method to set the appropriate properties. Like the PresetGradient method, it also takes three parameters;

the first two are identical to the PresetGradient method:

```
oPresentation.SlideMaster.Background.Fill.OneColorGradient(nStyle,
            nVariant, nDegree)
```

nStyle	Numeric	The shading style of the gradient. See PresetGradient for constants.
nVariant	Numeric	The choice of color order. See PresetGradient for values.
nDegree	Numeric	A value from 0 to 1, representing the darkness of the resulting color. 0 is black, and 1 is white; .25 is a dark shade of the color, and .75 is a pale shade of the color. Represents Color 2.

Notice that there is no mention of what color to use as Color 1. The ForeColor property is used for Color 1. To set the background color on the slide to go from a medium royal blue to a pale shade of the same blue, use the following code:

```
#DEFINE msoGradientHorizontal   1
#DEFINE rgbMediumBlue           RGB(0, 0, 150)

WITH oPresentation.SlideMaster.Background.Fill
  .ForeColor.RGB = rgbMediumBlue
  .OneColorGradient(msoGradientHorizontal, 1, .75)
ENDWITH
```

The final gradient type is the two-color gradient. Yep, you guessed it: use the TwoColorGradient method. This one only takes two parameters:

```
oPresentation.SlideMaster.Background.Fill.TwoColorGradient(nStyle, nVariant)
```

nStyle	Numeric	The shading style of the gradient. See PresetGradient for constants.
nVariant	Numeric	The choice of color order. See PresetGradient for values.

The two colors are set by the Foreground and Background colors. The following example sets the color to graduate from a royal blue to a pale teal:

```
#DEFINE msoGradientHorizontal   1
#DEFINE rgbMediumBlue           RGB(  0,   0, 150)
#DEFINE rgbPaleTeal             RGB(192, 255,255)

WITH oPresentation.SlideMaster.Background.Fill
  .ForeColor.RGB = rgbMediumBlue
  .BackColor.RGB = rgbPaleTeal
  .TwoColorGradient(msoGradientHorizontal, 1)
ENDWITH
```

Since you're setting a series of properties by calling methods, just what properties are you setting? **Table 1** shows the FillFormat's properties that are set through each method. These are all read-only properties that can be queried to determine what the current settings are. Be sure to check the GradientColorType property first, then query only the properties that are applicable to the gradient type. Unused properties (such as GradientDegree, if a preset or two-color gradient type) are not reset to a default value when the gradient type is changed. For example, determining that the GradientDegree is .75 does not guarantee that a one-color gradient is used—you must query GradientColorType to be sure.

Table 1. *The Gradient properties of the FillFormat object. Each type of gradient uses most of the Gradient properties—but not all. Check GradientColorType to ensure you set the appropriate properties for the gradient fill.*

Property	PresetGradient	OneColorGradient	TwoColorGradient
GradientColorType	msoGradientPresetColors (3)	msoGradientOneColor (1)	msoGradientTwoColors (2)
GradientStyle	nStyle parameter	nStyle parameter	nStyle parameter
GradientVariant	nVariant parameter	nVariant parameter	nVariant parameter
GradientDegree	NA	0 (black) – 1 (white)	NA
PresetGradientType	nType parameter	NA	NA

All the types of backgrounds (solid, patterned, picture, textured, and gradient) set properties through the FillFormat's methods. **Table 2** shows a compilation of all the properties that are set or used with each method. Remember, setting to a different background does not reset any unused properties to a default. Query the FillFormat's Type property to ensure which background format is in use.

Table 2. *The FillFormat properties set by the various FillFormat methods. Remember that the Type property is the only indicator of the background format in use—do not rely on values in the other properties solely to determine the type of background format. (Table continues on page 303.)*

Property	Solid	Patterned	Preset Texture	User Defined Texture
Read Only				
Type	msoFillSolid (1)	msoFillPatterned (2)	msoFillTextured (4)	msoFillTextured (4)
Pattern	-	msoPattern constants	-	-
TextureType	-	-	msoTexturePreset (1)	msoTextureUserDefined (3)
PresetTexture	-	-	msoTexture constants	-
TextureName	-	-	-	BMP filename
GradientColorType	-	-	-	-
GradientStyle	-	-	-	-
GradientVariant	-	-	-	-
PresetGradientType	-	-	-	-
GradientDegree	-	-	-	-
Read/Write				
ForeColor	✓	✓	-	-
BackColor	-	✓	-	-

Standardizing the appearance of text

Text is controlled by the TextStyles collection of the SlideMaster object. The collection has three objects. The first is the default style, used when a shape with text is added. The second is the title style used for all title placeholder objects. The last object is the body style, used for all of the other placeholders in an AutoLayout.

Within each TextStyle object is a collection of Level objects (Help refers to these as TextStyleLevel objects, though you access them through the Level property). Text levels are easiest to explain in terms of bullets: normally, each level is indented from the previous, and each level has a different bullet character and font characteristics—though each level does not necessarily have to be indented or bulleted. **Figure 3** shows the master slide as seen in PowerPoint, which shows the default characteristics for each level. PowerPoint supports five levels.

Each Level object contains a Font object and a ParagraphFormat object. The ParagraphFormat object contains the Bullet object. These objects are covered in Chapter 10, "PowerPoint Basics," and have the same properties and methods when used for Levels as they do for TextRanges.

You might use the TextStyles and Levels collections to change the color and font for the Title objects. Usually slide show backgrounds are a darker color, like medium to dark blue, to ensure readability. When the background is dark, the text needs to be light—perhaps a shade of yellow. Additionally, it is usual to use an eye-catching sans-serif font for a title. The following code demonstrates this. **Figure 4** shows the results.

Table 2, continued

UserPicture	Preset Gradient	One Color Gradient	Two Color Gradient
msoFillPicture (6)	msoFillGradient (3)	msoFillGradient (3)	msoFillGradient (3)
-	-	-	-
-	-	-	-
-	-	-	-
-	-	-	-
-	msoGradientPresetColors (3)	msoGradientOneColor (1)	msoGradientTwoColors (2)
-	nStyle	nStyle	nStyle
-	nVariant	nVariant	nVariant
-	nType	-	-
-	-	0.0-1.0	-
-	-	✓	✓
-	-	-	✓

```
#DEFINE ppTitleStyle  2
#DEFINE rgbYellow      RGB(255,255,0)

WITH oPresentation.SlideMaster.TextStyles[ppTitleStyle].Levels[1].Font
  .Name = "Arial"
  .Color.RGB = rgbYellow
ENDWITH
```

Figure 3. *The default SlideMaster as seen in PowerPoint. Notice the levels shown in the Object Area.*

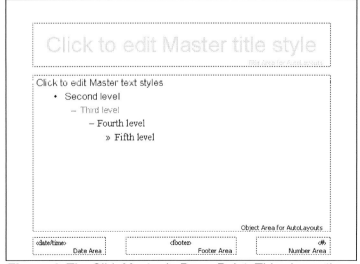

Figure 4. *The SlideMaster in PowerPoint. This shows the results of the example code that sets the Titles and Placeholder default text.*

As the example illustrates, a Title uses the Levels collection. A Title can have multiple Levels, perhaps for a title and subtitle in the same rectangle. While levels are useful for changing fonts in Titles, they really excel in placeholders, especially when bullets are used.

The next example shows how to format the first three Levels in placeholders. The ppBodyStyle constant is used to reference the third TextStyle object. The first level is formatted to dark blue. The bullet character is a dot, but we've turned it off. The character is set so it can be turned on when needed. The second level is set similarly, but the bullet is left on. The third level is slightly smaller, medium cyan, and uses an en-dash bullet character. The result is shown in Figure 4.

```
#DEFINE ppBodyStyle   3
#DEFINE rgbDarkBlue     RGB(0,   0, 128)
#DEFINE rgbMediumCyan RGB(0, 192, 192)

* Set Level One
WITH oPresentation.SlideMaster.TextStyles[ppBodyStyle].Levels[1]
  WITH .Font
    .Name      = "Arial"
    .Color.RGB = rgbDarkBlue
    .Size      = 20
  ENDWITH
  WITH .ParagraphFormat.Bullet
    * Set bullet character to a dot (use 149 if using PowerPoint 97)
    .Character = 8226
    .Visible   = .F.    && Don't show the bullet!
  ENDWITH
ENDWITH

* Set Level Two
WITH oPresentation.SlideMaster.TextStyles[ppBodyStyle].Levels[2]
  WITH .Font
    .Name      = "Arial"
    .Color.RGB = rgbDarkBlue
    .Size      = 20
  ENDWITH
  * Set bullet character to a dot (use 149 if using PowerPoint 97)
  .ParagraphFormat.Bullet.Character = 8226

ENDWITH

* Set Level Three
WITH oPresentation.SlideMaster.TextStyles[ppBodyStyle].Levels[3]
  WITH .Font
    .Name      = "Arial"
    .Color.RGB = rgbMediumCyan
    .Size      = 18
  ENDWITH
  * Set bullet character to an en-dash (use 150 if using PowerPoint 97)
  .ParagraphFormat.Bullet.Character = 8211
ENDWITH
```

Similar code can be used to set the default text for added shapes using the constant ppDefaultStyle to access the first TextStyle object.

Standardizing colors with ColorSchemes

An alternative to setting the colors on the SlideMaster is to use a ColorScheme object, which stores the colors for the eight standard elements on a slide. **Figure 5** shows the PowerPoint dialog box that allows you to customize the colors. To display it in PowerPoint, select Format|Slide Color Scheme… from the menu, then click the Custom tab. Up to 16 ColorScheme objects can exist; they're stored in the ColorSchemes collection.

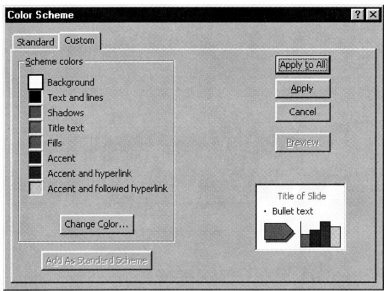

Figure 5. PowerPoint's Color Scheme dialog box. Color schemes set the eight standard colors for objects.

Although the ColorSchemes collection belongs to the Presentation object, any ColorScheme object can be referenced by the SlideMaster object, or by any slide. The Help file has quite a lengthy discussion of how to use multiple ColorSchemes within a presentation (for example, having one ColorScheme for title slides, and another for standard slides).

The most basic and practical use of a single ColorScheme is to dictate the colors of the eight elements on the SlideMaster. A ColorScheme contains a collection of eight colors, each referenced by a constant. The constants for the eight colors are: ppBackground (1), ppForeground (2), ppShadow (3), ppTitle (4), ppFill (5), ppAccent1 (6), ppAccent2 (7), and ppAccent3 (8). Beware: setting the background and fill colors in a ColorScheme overrides any of the Background or Fill object properties that are set—if you set up a gradient fill background, do not set the background color of the color scheme!

The following code changes the title colors to red and the text (ppForeground) to dark blue. Be sure to use this code instead of setting colors in the SlideMaster. Colors set explicitly through the SlideMaster's TextStyles will take precedence over the ColorSchemes (though if you look at the dialog box, the ColorSchemes color will change, but it won't change the colors on the slides).

```
#DEFINE ppTitle        4
#DEFINE ppForeground 2
#DEFINE rgbRed         RGB(255, 0,   0)
#DEFINE rgbDarkBlue    RGB(  0, 0, 128)

WITH oPresentation.SlideMaster.ColorScheme
  .Colors[ppTitle].RGB = rgbRed
  .Colors[ppForeground].RGB = rgbDarkBlue
ENDWITH
```

More on SlideMaster shapes

The five shapes on the SlideMaster are exactly that: Shape objects. You can set any of the Shape properties, not just fonts. Changing the size or borders on the SlideMaster shapes affects the placeholders on all shapes. To access the properties of the shapes, use the Shapes collection. The indices are from 1 to 5, in this order: Title Area, Object Area, Date Area, Footer Area, and Number Area. With the myriad of constants available in VBA, it is surprising there are not constants for these object. (If you expect to work with them a lot, you can certainly define your own.)

All shapes get their color from the ColorScheme object on the SlideMaster. In the example in the previous section, all the text is dark blue. Perhaps you want the footer area to be dark green instead. Override the ColorScheme setting by accessing the shape directly. The following lines of code set the text of the footer to "Tasmanian Traders" and set the color to dark green.

```
#DEFINE rgbDarkGreen   RGB(0, 128, 0)

WITH oPresentation.SlideMaster.Shapes[4].TextFrame.TextRange
  .Font.Color.RGB = rgbDarkGreen
  .Text = "Tasmanian Traders"
ENDWITH
```

The first two shapes, the Title Area and the Object Area, get their font properties from the TextStyles objects. The other three (Date Area, Footer Area, and Number Area) are not affected by TextStyles. Set font properties of these three objects separately.

Fancy features

Warning: the following features are fun to program and interesting to watch. However, the maxim "less is more" is very appropriate here. There is elegance in simplicity. Used sparingly, these features can set your presentation apart from others. Overuse them and the audience tires of all the gimmicks, leading them to ignore the slides and, quite possibly, the speaker who is presenting them. Remember, the audience sees only the presentation, not the way-cool tricks in your code.

Animations

Animations are special effects—visual and audio—that highlight important elements in a slide. Some animation effects that PowerPoint supports are objects flying in from the edge (choose your edge), text appearing letter-by-letter, and sound files playing. These animations can be timed to happen sequentially or all at once. They can happen automatically, or in response to mouse clicks. There are so many combinations and permutations of animations; we won't attempt to cover each and every one of them. The Animation dialog gives you an excellent interface in which to explore them. We'll give you an idea of what's possible to get you started.

There are 19 animation effects supported by PowerPoint 2000, many with several options, bringing the total number of effects to about 80. **Figure 6** shows PowerPoint's Custom Animation dialog, with the Effects dropdown box shown open. This dialog also gives some insight into the available collections, objects, and properties. In the upper left corner, there is a list of all the objects on the slide; each can be animated separately (or not animated at all). The Effects tab is shown, displaying the many properties involved in customizing the effect. The other tabs indicate that there are properties to set the Order and Timing of effects, to animate Charts (if any are present), and to add Multimedia effects.

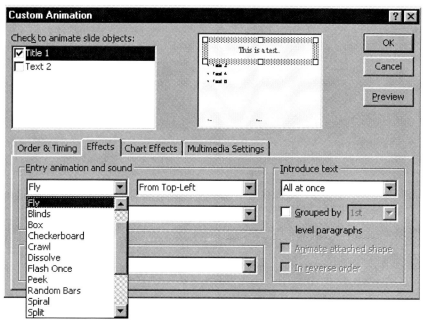

Figure 6. *PowerPoint's Custom Animation dialog. The dropdown for Effects is open, showing many of the available animation effects.*

The AnimationSettings object stores all the objects, collections, and properties that pertain to animations. The AnimationSettings object is stored in the AnimationSettings property of every Shape object. Shapes on the SlideMaster can be animated, too.

Setting the effect

The EntryEffect property sets the effect. This property is set to a numeric value, for which there are VBA constants. The constants are set up to combine the two fields in the dialog box describing what is to happen (shown in Figure 6 as "Fly") and any available options for that effect, such as where it might move from (shown in Figure 6 as "From Top-Left"). Some of the constants for the effects are: ppEffectAppear (3844), ppEffectFlashOnceFast (3841), ppEffectFlashOnceMedium (3842), ppEffectFlyFromLeft (3329), ppEffectFlyFromTopLeft (3333), ppEffectRandom (513), ppEffectZoomIn (3345), and ppEffectZoomInSlightly (3346). Use the Object Browser to look up the other 72 constants. See "Take me for a browse" in Chapter 2 for details on the Object Browser.

The following code sets the first shape on the slide to fly in from the left:

```
#DEFINE ppEffectFlyFromLeft    3329
oSlide.Shapes(1).AnimationSettings.EntryEffect = ppEffectFlyFromLeft
```

Modifying the effects

A very popular effect is to have a slide containing bulleted text, and have each of the bullets fly in from the left as the user clicks the mouse. A modification to the "fly in from left" effect is to set which levels of bullets fly in together. The TextLevelEffect tells which levels are animated. TextLevelEffect is set to a numeric value—some of the constants are ppAnimateByFirstLevel (1), ppAnimateBySecondLevel (2), ppAnimateByAllLevels (16), and ppAnimateLevelNone (0). Setting the effect to animate the first level sends each first level bullet in separately, with all its subordinates. Setting the effect to animate the second level sends each first and second level item in separately—any subordinates to the second level come in with their parent.

The following code generates an example Tasmanian Traders marketing slide, showing a bulleted list with two levels. The code sets the title and bullets to fly in from the left, one each time the mouse is clicked. The code is set to fly each of the bullets in separately (at level 2). Modify the code for a second run by changing the TextLevelEffect to ppAnimateByFirstLevel, to see that the first bullet flies in with its two subordinate bullets. **Figure 7** shows the resulting slide.

```
#DEFINE ppEffectFlyFromLeft    3329
#DEFINE ppLayoutText           2
#DEFINE ppAnimateByFirstLevel  1
#DEFINE ppAnimateBySecondLevel 2

* Add a slide--title and text objects on the layout

oSlide = oPresentation.Slides.Add(1, ppLayoutText)

* Put in the title text and set the effect
WITH oSlide.Shapes[1]
   .TextFrame.TextRange.Text = "Tasmanian Traders"
   .AnimationSettings.EntryEffect = ppEffectFlyFromLeft
ENDWITH

* Put in some bullets (at 2 levels) and set the effect
m.BulletString = "Distributor of Fine Food Products" + CHR(13) + ;
                 "Beverages" + CHR(13) + ;
```

```
                     "Desserts" + CHR(13) + ;
                 "International Shipping" + CHR(13) + ;
                 "Satisfaction Guaranteed"
WITH oSlide.Shapes[2]
  .TextFrame.TextRange.Text = m.BulletString

  * Indents "Beverages" and "Desserts"
  .TextFrame.TextRange.Sentences[2, 2].IndentLevel = 2

  .AnimationSettings.EntryEffect = ppEffectFlyFromLeft
  .AnimationSettings.TextLevelEffect = ppAnimateBySecondLevel

  * Run this again, but change the TextLevelEffect constant in the line above
  * to ppAnimateByFirstLevel to see how setting it to first level brings
  * in the two "level 2" bullets with their "level 1" parent.

ENDWITH
```

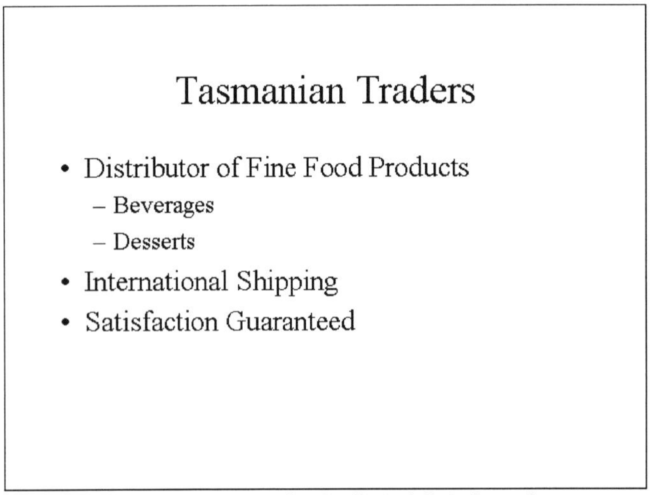

Tasmanian Traders

- Distributor of Fine Food Products
  - Beverages
  - Desserts
- International Shipping
- Satisfaction Guaranteed

Figure 7. *An example of a bulleted list. Levels are used to format the bullets and text. Level 1 has a circular bullet. Level 2 has a dash for a bullet, and has slightly smaller text.*

Automatic timing

To eliminate manual mouse clicks and let the show run automatically, use the AdvanceMode property. There are two constants: ppAdvanceOnClick (1) and ppAdvanceOnTime (2). When the AdvanceMode property is set to ppAdvanceOnTime, it checks the number of seconds stored in the AdvanceTime property. Add the following lines to the end of the previous example, and it automatically animates items one second apart.

```
#DEFINE ppAdvanceOnTime 2

* Change the Title shape's settings
WITH oSlide.Shapes[1].AnimationSettings
```

```
  .AdvanceMode = ppAdvanceOnTime
  .AdvanceTime = 1
ENDWITH

* Change the bullet text shape's settings
WITH oSlide.Shapes[2].AnimationSettings
  .AdvanceMode = ppAdvanceOnTime
  .AdvanceTime = 1
ENDWITH
```

If there are multiple shapes, the order in which the shapes are animated is set through the AnimationOrder property. By default, AnimationOrder is set to the creation order of the Shape (assuming, of course, that the Shape is to be animated at all). By setting the AnimationOrder property, you can change the order in which the objects are animated.

These are just a few of the many properties and methods available to animate shapes. See the Help file under "AnimationSettings Object" for a comprehensive list.

Transitions

Fades, dissolves, wipes; these are all various ways of transitioning between slides. Transitions can be applied to the SlideMaster, which affects all slides, or just to a single slide. The transitions are stored in the SlideShowTransition object. The SlideShowTransition object is similar to the AnimationSettings object—transitioning to another slide is similar to transitioning a single object onto the screen.

The EntryEffect property is used to store the transition effect. It uses the same set of constants as the AnimationSettings' EntryEffect property. Not all constants for EntryEffects are available for transitions, though (for example, ppFlyInFromLeft is only for animations).

Like AnimationSettings, the SlideShowTransition object has properties to advance automatically. The syntax is different than AnimationSettings, though. The SlideShowTransition object has an AdvanceOnTime logical property. The AdvanceTime property stores the number of seconds (just as in the AnimationSettings object).

The following code adds a transition to the first slide to "cover down" and automatically advance after two seconds. If this code were applied to the SlideMaster, it would affect every slide, but as written here, it only affects the first slide.

```
#DEFINE ppEffectCoverDown  1284

WITH oPresentation.Slides[1].SlideShowTransition
  .EntryEffect = ppEffectCoverDown
  .AdvanceOnTime = .T.
  .AdvanceTime   = 2
ENDWITH
```

Taking action

PowerPoint allows specific actions to be taken when the mouse is moved over or clicked on a shape. Actions include jumping to a specific slide in the slide show, running another slide show, running a separate program, playing a sound, as well as a few others. **Figure 8** shows PowerPoint's interactive Action Settings dialog, which lists the possible actions.

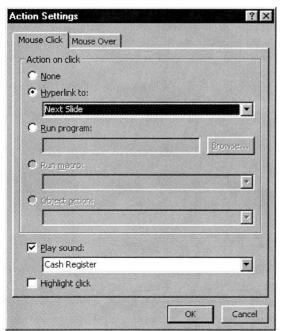

***Figure 8**. PowerPoint's Action Settings dialog. Action settings define the action taken on mouse overs and mouse clicks.*

The ActionSettings collection stores these actions. The collection contains two ActionSettings objects: one for a mouse click and one for a mouse over. The indices for the collections are ppMouseClick (1) and ppMouseOver (2).

The Action property is the property that controls the action. Set the Action property to one of the constants listed in **Table 3**.

***Table 3**. Where the action is. Set the Action property to determine the action taken when a user clicks on a shape.*

Constant	Value	Constant	Value
ppActionNone	0	ppActionHyperlink	7
ppActionNextSlide	1	ppActionRunMacro	8
ppActionPreviousSlide	2	ppActionRunProgram	9
ppActionFirstSlide	3	ppActionNamedSlideShow	10
ppActionLastSlide	4	ppActionOLEVerb	11
ppActionLastSlideViewed	5	ppActionPlay	12
ppActionEndShow	6		

The following code adds an arrow shape in the lower right corner of a slide, and sets its Action property to move to the previous slide.

```
#DEFINE msoShapeRightArrow    33
#DEFINE ppMouseClick           1
```

```
#DEFINE ppActionPreviousSlide 2

oShape = oSlide.Shapes.AddShape(msoShapeRightArrow, 600, 450, 50, 50)
oShape.ActionSettings[ppMouseClick].Action = ppActionPreviousSlide
```

PowerPoint has a feature called Action Buttons, which are a series of predefined buttons. These buttons have a consistent look, and they help the presentation designer maintain a consistent look and feel. When entered interactively in PowerPoint, the dialog box comes up with the Action defaults for the type of button selected. For example, placing the button with the End picture on it sets the Action default to jump to the end of the slide show. When these buttons are added in code (Automation or VBA macros), no default Action is specified—you must specify it explicitly using code like that shown previously.

The ActionSettings collection has additional properties to support other kinds of Actions. To enter a hyperlink, first set the Action property to ppActionHyperlink, then set the properties of the Hyperlink object. To create a hot link, set the Address property of the Hyperlink object, which stores the URL. Here's a code sample that adds a shape and attaches a hyperlink to a URL.

```
#DEFINE msoShapeRectangle 1
#DEFINE ppMouseClick       1
#DEFINE ppActionHyperlink 7

oShape = oSlide.Shapes.AddShape(msoShapeRectangle, 300, 200, 150, 100)
WITH oShape.ActionSettings[ppMouseClick]
   .Action = ppActionHyperlink
   .Hyperlink.Address = "http://www.hentzenwerke.com"
ENDWITH
```

You can even run any program, including compiled FoxPro programs, from a mouse click or mouse over. This is accomplished through the Run method. Pass it the fully qualified program name.

```
#DEFINE msoShapeRectangle 1
#DEFINE ppMouseClick       1

oShape = oSlide.Shapes.AddShape(msoShapeRectangle, 300, 200, 150, 100)
oShape.ActionSettings[ppMouseClick].Run = ;
     "C:\Program Files\Microsoft Office\Office\WINWORD.EXE"
```

Multimedia

In this world of high-tech movies and video games, multimedia in business presentations is almost expected. Multimedia has the power to enhance a presentation, making it more interesting to watch and easier for the viewer to retain what was presented. However, there's a fine line between "very interesting" and "very distracting"—again, we listen to the maxim "less is more."

While you are developing automated presentations, be sure that your program can handle scaling to the wide variety of hardware available for presentations. Even today, not all computers have good sound systems (or speakers that are decent enough to project to the whole room full of attendees), high-powered graphics cards, and lots of RAM and processor to allow the presentation to be successful. Ensure that your users have an alternative to awesome multimedia displays—if the presentation computer can't handle multimedia, the "incredibly awesome" presentation quickly is perceived as "incredibly awful."

Sounding off

Sounds are managed through the SoundEffect object. The ActionSettings, AnimationSettings, and SlideShowTransition objects (discussed earlier in this chapter) each have a SoundEffect property to access the SoundEffect object.

There are a number of sound effects available in PowerPoint without using separate sound files. These built-in sounds are accessed using the names shown in any of the PowerPoint sound effect dropdown boxes. **Figure 9** shows the Play sound dropdown on the Action Settings dialog.

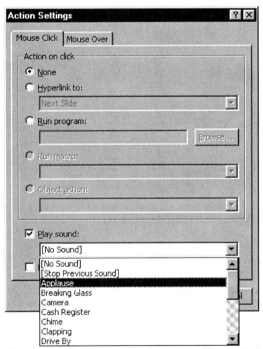

Figure 9. *PowerPoint's Action Settings dialog, showing the built-in sound effects.*

Set the Name property to the text string corresponding to the sound you wish to use. This is an exception to the long list of numeric constants usually used by VBA! The list of options are: Applause, Breaking Glass, Camera, Cash Register, Chime, Clapping, Drive By, Drum Roll, Explosion, Gun Shot, Laser, Ricochet, Screeching Brakes, Slide Projector, Typewriter, and Whoosh.

```
#DEFINE ppMouseClick  1
oShape.ActionSettings[ppMouseClick].SoundEffect.Name = "Slide Projector"
```

Setting the Name property automatically sets the Type property to ppSoundFile (2). To turn off the sound, set the Type property to ppSoundNone (0). The constant ppStopPrevious (1) stops any sound currently being played.

To specify a WAV file to play, use the ImportFromFile method to both link to the WAV file and set the object to play it. Pass the fully qualified WAV filename. Once you have imported the WAV file, it is added to the list of sounds available so it can be referenced by other objects (by its filename without the path), just like the built-in sounds. The following lines of code import the WAV file, set the shape to play it when clicked, and then use the imported file by its name to set the same sound to play on the slide show transition.

```
#DEFINE ppMouseClick  1

SoundFile = GETENV("WINDIR") + "\Media\Chord.WAV"

oShape.ActionSettings[ppMouseClick].SoundEffect.ImportFromFile(SoundFile)
oSlide.SlideShowTransition.SoundEffect.Name = "CHORD.WAV"
```

The SoundEffect object has a Play method, which plays the sound on demand. Use the Play method only when you want the sound to play while your code is running; the use of the Play method does not affect whether sounds play in the slide show. It plays the sound set for the specified object:

```
oSlide.SlideShowTransition.SoundEffect.Play()
```

This line plays whatever sound is set in the slide's SlideShowTransition object.

Motion

To add video clips, you use the Shapes collection's AddMediaObject method. As Chapter 10, "PowerPoint Basics," points out, while AutoLayouts exist with placeholders for OLE objects, they cannot be used with Automation or macros.

The AddMediaObject method takes up to five parameters. The first is the filename, and is not optional. Next are the Left and Top. These are optional; the default is zero for both. The last two, Width and Height, are also optional, and default to the width and height of the object. The following line of code shows how to add one of FoxPro's sample AVI files (it is a spinning globe, not a fox, as the name seems to indicate).

```
oShape = oSlide.Shapes.AddMediaObject( ;
     _SAMPLES + "Solution\Forms\Fox.AVI", 240, 156)
```

This adds the AVI file roughly centered in the slide.

 There wasn't any magic involved in finding the Left and Top parameters. It was done interactively. Using the FoxPro Command Window, we opened an instance of PowerPoint and added a new presentation with a blank slide. Then we issued the preceding command, leaving out the Left and Top parameters, which placed the image in the upper left corner. Activating PowerPoint, we moved the image using the

mouse to the location we wanted. Back in FoxPro's Command Window, we asked PowerPoint for the Top and Left properties, and typed the results into our code:

```
? oShape.Left
? oShape.Top
```

It's important to remember to let the tools do the work for you. FoxPro's object references persist until the variable is released, or the object in PowerPoint is unavailable (whether the presentation is closed or the object itself is deleted). Setting a reference to an object in FoxPro, switching to PowerPoint to interactively manipulate the PowerPoint objects, then querying the properties from FoxPro is a very powerful way to quickly determine the desired properties of the PowerPoint objects.

Adding the media clip with AddMediaObject sets it to play when the user clicks on it during the presentation. The AnimationSettings and ActionSettings objects change the behavior, setting it to play when the slide is selected, to continuously play while the slide is viewed, or to play when the mouse is moved over it. The ActionSettings object, which pertains to mouse clicks and movement, has no additional properties for multimedia (see the section "Taking action" earlier in this chapter). The AnimationSettings object, however, does have a number of properties relating to multimedia.

Figure 10 shows the Custom Animation dialog box, with the Multimedia Settings tab selected. This tab sets the properties of the AnimationSettings' PlaySettings object. The PlaySettings object contains a number of properties that determine how the media clip plays during a slideshow. The check box labeled "Play using animation order" corresponds to the logical PlayOnEntry property. When PlayOnEntry is true, it plays the media clip when the slide is displayed (based on the AnimationSettings object's AnimationOrder property). PlayOnEntry also respects the other AnimationSettings properties, such as AdvanceMode and AdvanceTime—if other objects that are higher in the order need mouse clicks to animate, then those lower in the order aren't animated until the mouse clicks force the preceding animations to happen. Set PlayOnEntry to false to ensure that the user must animate it manually.

The two radio buttons that set the "While playing" action correspond to the PauseAnimation property. When set to true (when the radio button reads "Pause slide show"), other automatic features of the slide show wait until the video clip has finished playing. When set to false, the other automatic features are played at the same time. This can be useful if you want several animated GIFs to play simultaneously. Set PauseAnimation to true when you only have one object to play, and do not want the slide show to advance before the object completes its play.

On the Custom Animation dialog, the Multimedia Settings tab has a "More Options" button, which corresponds to more animation properties. The check boxes correspond to the LoopUntilStopped and RewindMovie properties. To loop the animation until the user selects another action (or another action is automatically scheduled to run), set the LoopUntilStopped property to true. Setting it to false runs it once. The RewindMovie property controls whether the movie returns the view to the first frame when finished (true) or whether the movie stays on the last frame (false).

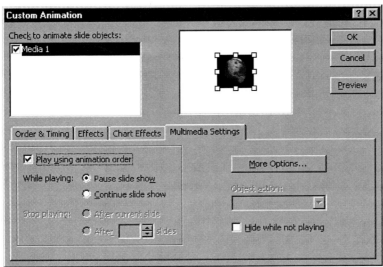

Figure 10*. Multimedia Custom Animation settings. The Multimedia Settings tab shows the properties that are available to media clips.*

A common scenario is to play the video continuously when the slide is selected. The following code adds the video clip object and sets the appropriate properties:

```
oShape = oSlide.Shapes.AddMediaObject( ;
        _SAMPLES + "\Solution\Forms\Fox.AVI", 240, 156)
WITH oShape.AnimationSettings.PlaySettings
  .PlayOnEntry = .T.
  .LoopUntilStopped = .T.
ENDWITH
```

 Many properties, such as PlayOnEntry, can be set with a logical value (.T. or .F.) or a numeric value (1 or -1). However, when you read them, they will always be numeric. This is a "feature" of how FoxPro's logical values are translated to a numeric property; the native numeric value will always be returned.

Adding notes

Notes can be entered for each slide. Notes are displayed in the bottom panel (in PowerPoint 2000), or printed with a picture of the slide on the top and the notes below, one slide per page. The notes can be used as speaker notes, or printed and passed out as handouts, with the notes annotating the slide images.

Explaining how to put notes on each slide actually is easier if we start by explaining the notes master. **Figure 11** shows the notes master view in PowerPoint. Like the Placeholders collection for slides (discussed in Chapter 10, "PowerPoint Basics"), the indices of the Placeholders collection make sense when we see them in the notes master view: 1 is the header area, 2 is the date area, 3 is the SlideMaster object, 4 is the notes body area, 5 is the footer area, and 6 is the number area (Microsoft didn't provide constants for these, but you can certainly define your own). Just as with the SlideMaster (see "Achieving consistency with Master Slides" earlier in this chapter), these Placeholders can be formatted with color, fonts, and standardized text. The NotesMaster object contains the properties that are accessed when printing the notes pages.

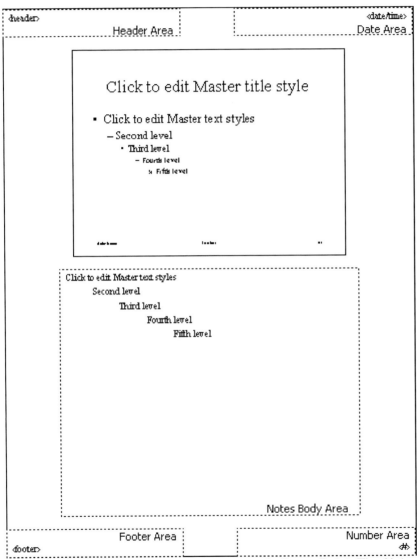

Figure 11. *The notes master page, as seen in PowerPoint. The Notes Placeholders are ordered in a left to right, top to bottom order.*

Notes can be added to each slide using the NotesPage object. The NotesPage object contains a collection of two Shape objects: one for the slide picture, and the second for the text. When viewing the notes master, these two shapes change on each page, while the others remain constant (the slide number can be set to a field that calculates the slide number). The slide image has an index of 1, while the text has an index of 2 (again, there are no Microsoft-issue constants). The following lines of code add sample speaker note text for slides 1 and 2:

```
WITH oPresentation
   .Slides[1].NotesPage.Shapes.Placeholders[2].TextFrame.TextRange.Text = ;
      "Remember to welcome the audience." + CHR(13) + "Introduce the company."
   .Slides[2].NotesPage.Shapes.Placeholders[2].TextFrame.TextRange.Text =  ;
      "Explain the marketing slogan."
ENDWITH
```

You can format notes just like any other text. See the section "Adding and formatting text" in Chapter 10, as well as "Standardizing the appearance of text" earlier in this chapter, for additional information on formatting the text.

Putting it all together

In Chapter 10, "PowerPoint Basics," we put together a little slide show demonstrating the topics we covered. In this chapter, we use the same basic slides, and add many of the additional features we covered. **Listing 1** (PPTSample2.PRG in the Developer Download files available at www.hentzenwerke.com) shows the code, while **Figure 12**, **Figure 13**, and **Figure 14** show the finished slides. Note that with the addition of color, sound, and animation, this code must be run to see the presentation. Black and white screen shots cannot show all the features.

Listing 1. A sample presentation for Tasmanian Traders.

```
CLOSE DATA
#DEFINE ppTitleStyle              2
#DEFINE ppBodyStyle               3
#DEFINE ppLayoutTitle             1
#DEFINE ppLayoutText              2
#DEFINE ppEffectCoverDown      1284
#DEFINE ppEffectDissolve       1537
#DEFINE ppEffectAppear         3844
#DEFINE ppAnimateByFirstLevel     1
#DEFINE ppAdvanceOnTime           2
#DEFINE msoGradientHorizontal     1
#DEFINE ppBulletArabicPeriod      3
#DEFINE msoLineThickBetweenThin   5
#DEFINE autoIn2Pts               72

#DEFINE rgbDarkBlue     RGB(  0,   0, 138)
#DEFINE rgbMediumBlue   RGB( 96,  96, 204)
#DEFINE rgbPaleGray     RGB(192, 192, 192)
```

```
#DEFINE rgbYellow        RGB(255, 255,   0)
#DEFINE rgbBurgundy      RGB(128,   0,   0)
#DEFINE rgbLineColor     RGB(255, 255,   0)

SET PATH TO (_SAMPLES + "\TasTrade\Data") ADDITIVE

*******************
* Set up the data
*******************
OPEN DATABASE TasTrade
LogoFile = (_SAMPLES + "\TasTrade\Bitmaps\TTradeSm.bmp")

USE OrdItems IN 0
USE Products IN 0

* Select the top 5 selling items of all time
SELECT TOP 5 ;
       P.English_Name, ;
       SUM(O.Unit_Price * O.Quantity) AS TotQuan ;
  FROM OrdItems O, Products P ;
 WHERE O.Product_ID = P.Product_ID ;
 GROUP BY 1 ;
 ORDER BY 2 DESC;
  INTO CURSOR TopSellers

* Select the number of products
SELECT Count(*) ;
  FROM Products ;
  INTO ARRAY aProducts

* Clean out any existing references to servers.
* This prevents memory loss to leftover instances.
RELEASE ALL LIKE o*

* For demonstration purposes, make oPowerPoint and oPresentation
* available after this program executes.
PUBLIC oPowerPoint, oPresentation

* Open PowerPoint
oPowerPoint = CreateObject("PowerPoint.Application")
oPowerPoint.Visible = .T.

* Create the presentation
oPresentation = oPowerPoint.Presentations.Add()

SlideNum = 1

*******************
* MASTER SLIDE
*******************
WITH oPresentation.SlideMaster

  * Set the background to a gradient fill
  WITH .Background.Fill
    .ForeColor.RGB = rgbMediumBlue
```

```
    .BackColor.RGB = rgbPaleGray
    .TwoColorGradient(msoGradientHorizontal, 1)
ENDWITH

* Set titles
WITH .TextStyles[ppTitleStyle].Levels[1].Font
  .Name = "Arial"
  .Shadow = .T.
  .Color.RGB = rgbDarkBlue
ENDWITH

* Set Body Style levels
WITH .TextStyles[ppBodyStyle]
  WITH .Levels[1]
    WITH .Font
      .Name       = "Arial"
      .Bold       = .T.
      .Color.RGB = rgbBurgundy
      .Size       = 20
    ENDWITH
    WITH .ParagraphFormat.Bullet
      * Set bullet character to a dot (use 149 if using PowerPoint 97)
      .Character = 8226
      .Visible   = .F.    && Don't show the bullet!
    ENDWITH
  ENDWITH
  WITH .Levels[2]
    WITH .Font
      .Name       = "Arial"
      .Color.RGB = rgbDarkBlue
      .Size       = 20
    ENDWITH
    * Set bullet character to a dot (use 149 if using PowerPoint 97)
    .ParagraphFormat.Bullet.Character = 8226

  ENDWITH

ENDWITH

* Add the logo.
.Shapes.AddPicture(LogoFile, .F., .T., ;
     8.5 * autoIn2Pts, 6.0 * autoIn2Pts)

* PowerPoint 97 users: the last two parameters,
* height and width, are not optional. Use this
* code instead:
*.Shapes.AddPicture(LogoFile, .F., .T., ;
*     8.5 * autoIn2Pts, 6.0 * autoIn2Pts, ;
*     1.0 * autoIn2Pts, 1.0 * autoIn2Pts)


ENDWITH
```

Figure 12. *The Tasmanian Traders sample title slide. The gradient fill background, title fonts and colors, and the logo on each slide are done through the Master Slide.*

```
********************
* TITLE SLIDE
********************
* Add the slide
oSlide = oPresentation.Slides.Add(SlideNum, ppLayoutTitle)

* Set the title text.
oSlide.Shapes[1].TextFrame.TextRange.Text = "Tasmanian Traders"

* Set the subtitle text
oSlide.Shapes[2].TextFrame.TextRange.Text = "Welcomes you..."

WITH oSlide.SlideShowTransition
   .EntryEffect = ppEffectCoverDown
   .AdvanceOnTime = .T.
   .AdvanceTime   = 2
ENDWITH

SlideNum = SlideNum + 1
```

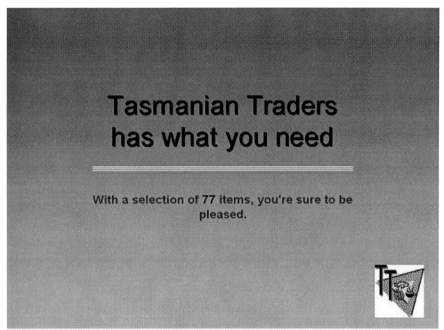

Figure 13. *The Tasmanian Traders sample second slide. As with the first slide, there is minimal formatting in the code, because the SlideMaster takes care of the majority of the formatting.*

```
*******************
* SECOND SLIDE
*******************

* Add the slide
oSlide = oPresentation.Slides.Add(SlideNum, ppLayoutTitle)

* Bring the slide to the front
oSlide.Select()

* PowerPoint 97 users: oSlide.Select() will
* generate an error. Use this line instead:
* oPresentation.ActiveWindow.View.GoToSlide(2)

* Set the text of the title
oSlide.Shapes[1].TextFrame.TextRange.Text = "Tasmanian Traders " + CHR(13) + ;
     "has what you need"

* Move the title up about half an inch
WITH oSlide.Shapes[1]
  .Top = .Top - (.5 * autoIn2Pts)
ENDWITH

* Add a line half an inch below the title that is centered and 6" long
LineTop = oSlide.Shapes[1].Top + oSlide.Shapes[1].Height + ;
     (.5 * autoIn2Pts)
LineLeft = 2 * autoIn2Pts
```

```
LineEnd = LineLeft + (6.0 * autoIn2Pts)

oLine = oSlide.Shapes.AddLine(LineLeft, LineTop, LineEnd, LineTop)

* Format the line to be a thick line
* with two thin lines on either side
WITH oLine.Line
  .ForeColor.RGB = rgbLineColor
  .Style = msoLineThickBetweenThin
  .Weight = 8
ENDWITH

* Set the text of the subtitle, and change the number to bold and blue
WITH oSlide.Shapes[2].TextFrame.TextRange
  .Text = "With a selection of " + ALLTRIM(STR(aProducts[1])) + ;
          " items, you're sure to be pleased."
  .Words[5].Font.Color = rgbDarkBlue
ENDWITH

WITH oSlide.SlideShowTransition
  .EntryEffect = ppEffectDissolve
  .AdvanceOnTime = .T.
  .AdvanceTime   = 5
ENDWITH

SlideNum = SlideNum + 1
```

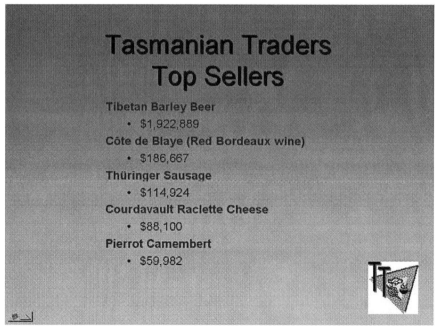

Figure 14. *The Tasmanian Traders sample third slide. Again, the bulk of the formatting is done in the SlideMaster. Fonts, colors, and backgrounds are extremely consistent, and your code is easy to maintain.*

```
*************************
* TOP SELLERS SLIDE
*************************
* Add the slide
oSlide = oPresentation.Slides.Add(SlideNum, ppLayoutText)

* Bring the slide to the front
oSlide.Select()

* PowerPoint 97 users: oSlide.Select() will
* generate an error. Use this line instead:
* oPresentation.ActiveWindow.View.GoToSlide(3)

* Insert the title (note the use of the Title object, instead of
* an enumerated shape object).
oSlide.Shapes.Title.TextFrame.TextRange.Text = "Tasmanian Traders" + ;
     CHR(13) + "Top Sellers"

* Build the string to use for the top 5 sellers.
* Use a CR between each item to make each a separate bullet.
BulletString = ""
SELECT TopSellers
SCAN
  BulletString = BulletString + ;
                 TRIM(TopSellers.English_Name) + CHR(13) + "$" + ;
                 ALLTRIM(TRANSFORM(TopSellers.TotQuan, "99,999,999")) + ;
                 CHR(13)
ENDSCAN

* Add the bullet string to the text frame.
WITH oSlide.Shapes[2]
  WITH .TextFrame.TextRange
    .Text = BulletString

    * Indent all the sales quotas
    FOR I = 1 TO 5
      .Lines[I*2, 1].IndentLevel = 2
    ENDFOR
  ENDWITH

  * Move it to the right about 1.5"
  .Left = .Left + (1.5 * autoIn2Pts)

  * Each bullet (with subordinates) appears at 1 second intervals
  WITH .AnimationSettings
    .EntryEffect = ppEffectAppear
    .TextLevelEffect = ppAnimateByFirstLevel
    .AdvanceMode = ppAdvanceOnTime
    .AdvanceTime   = 0.5
    .SoundEffect.Name = "Whoosh"
  ENDWITH
ENDWITH

oSlide.SlideShowTransition.EntryEffect = ppEffectDissolve

* Run the slideshow.
oPresentation.SlideShowSettings.Run()
```

This chapter explored the visual world of PowerPoint. We've covered many of the commonly used features of PowerPoint. There is a lot more to PowerPoint, though, so don't hesitate to use that macro recorder, the Object Browser, and the Help files to find those features that your application needs.

Section V
Automating Outlook

Chapter 12
Automating Outlook

Imagine writing applications that send you e-mail when an error occurs or put important dates (like the one your check is due) right onto the user's calendar.

Outlook often reminds us of those infomercials on late night television—it slices, it dices, it juliennes. Outlook does so many different things that it's hard to categorize. It's far more than just an e-mail client—in fact, neither of us uses it that way habitually. But it's not just a calendar/scheduler or address book, either. In many ways, Outlook is the replacement for the whole collection of items that most of us still keep on our desks—the Rolodex®, datebook, pad of paper, telephone, and collection of Post-Its™. While we're not ready to throw any of them out quite yet, we do find ourselves relying on Outlook more and more (at least while the computer is turned on).

The Outlook object model

Outlook's object model is quite different from those of the other Office applications. That's because it grew up in a different family and was adopted by Office. It's only with Office 2000 that you can use VBA to write macros for Outlook, and there's still no way to record a macro as there is in the other Office products. (This, of course, makes figuring out the syntax for automating Outlook a lot harder. You can't just record a macro and convert the code.)

Because of Outlook's varied history, the examples in this chapter have been tested only with Outlook 2000. They may well work with earlier versions, but we're making no promises on that front.

Like the other Office applications, Help has a live diagram of the object model. **Figure 1** shows the main page of the diagram.

As in the rest of Office (and many other servers), there's an Application object at the top that represents the server itself. This is the object you instantiate with CreateObject()—we'll look at that in the next section, "Getting a handle on Outlook." As you'd expect, it has a Quit method to shut the application down. However, there's no Visible property, no Top and Left properties to indicate where the application is positioned, and no StartupPath property to indicate where data is to be placed.

More striking, though, is that once you have the Application object in hand, there's no object that jumps out at you as clearly the key to the Outlook object model the way Document does in Word or Presentation does in PowerPoint. That's because there is no one dominant object—the closest is probably MAPIFolder. Each MAPIFolder represents one of Outlook's folders, so there's a MAPIFolder object for the Calendar, another for Contacts, a third for the Inbox, and so on. MAPIFolder objects are gathered into a Folders collection. To complicate (or is it confuse?) matters, MAPIFolders can be nested. In fact, the Folders collection containing the key Outlook objects is contained in another MAPIFolder object called "Personal Folders." That MAPIFolder is contained in yet another Folders collection, which is contained in a NameSpace object. (Don't worry if this seems complicated. We'll dig into it with examples later on.)

Microsoft Outlook Objects

See Also

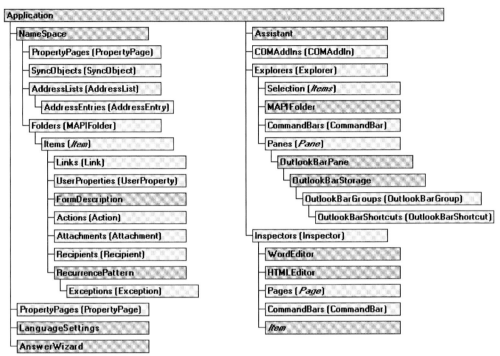

Figure 1. Outlook object model. Unlike the other Office objects, there's no obvious candidate for the key object below Application.

Getting a handle on Outlook

Although we use the same commands to start Outlook as the other Office applications, this is yet another area where things are different as much as they're the same. Again, VFP's CreateObject() function is the key to starting the Outlook Automation server. However, unlike the others, if Outlook is already open, this command:

```
oOutlook = CreateObject("Outlook.Application")
```

attaches to the running Outlook instance rather than starting a new one. It's as if you used GetObject(), not CreateObject(). In fact, you get the same result by issuing:

```
oOutlook = GetObject(,"Outlook.Application")
```

If Outlook isn't already running, then calling CreateObject() creates an instance, as you'd expect. When you open Outlook this way, you run into yet another difference. As noted previously, Outlook's Application object doesn't have a Visible property. In order to make Outlook visible, so you can see what you're doing, you have to create and display an Explorer object, Outlook's face to the world. Here's the code:

```
#DEFINE olFolderDisplayNormal 0
oNameSpace = oOutlook.GetNameSpace("MAPI")
oExplorer = oOutlook.Explorers.Add(oNameSpace.Folders[1],olFolderDisplayNormal)
oExplorer.Activate()
```

The first line (after the #DEFINE) is likely to be the first line you issue anytime you start up a new instance of Outlook. It creates a NameSpace object within Outlook. NameSpace is at the top of the object hierarchy and is needed to climb down to other objects. (Actually, you can climb down by way of an Explorer, but for Automation work, you'll typically be working behind the scenes and won't need an Explorer.)

The next line creates an Explorer, telling it to display the first folder in the NameSpace created by the previous line. Then, the last line tells Outlook to show the newly created Explorer object. That's the line that's really equivalent to a Visible = .T. line. However, there's no corresponding Deactivate method. Once you activate the Explorer, the only way to make it go away is to call its Close method, which not only hides it, but destroys it, as well.

Once you have Outlook up and running, what can you do with it? That's what we're about to find out.

Accessing Outlook's contents

Look at the example in the previous section again. The first real line of code is fairly mysterious. It calls a method of the Application object named GetNameSpace, passing it a parameter called "MAPI." What's a NameSpace, and why does it want a "MAPI"?

This is one of those questions to which the correct answer is "because." If you look up the NameSpace object in the Outlook VBA Help file, the first sentence says, "Represents an abstract root object for any data source." Not very helpful, is it? Reading on, you find out that the only data source Outlook supports is "MAPI," which is the Mail Application Programming Interface and includes all the data stored in Outlook. Bottom line—NameSpace is simply an object that provides a gateway to the rest of the Outlook data. Perhaps at some point, Outlook's designers imagined that they'd support a variety of data stores.

We're not sure why you have to actively call GetNameSpace to load the data instead of having it loaded when Outlook starts up. But you do, so just get used to doing it automatically.

Once you get past that point, things get a little more interesting. The NameSpace object provides access to the Folder objects that are the heart of Outlook. There are a couple of ways into those Folders. You can simply climb down the hierarchy. NameSpace has a Folders collection that contains one or more items, depending on your configuration. For a stand-alone user, the only item in the collection is "Personal Folders." With Exchange Server available, the collection may also contain "Public Folders" and "Mailbox" items. Those folders each have their own Folders collections that contain a folder for each of the individual applets within Outlook. There are folders for Calendar, Tasks, Inbox, Outbox, Contacts, and so forth. You can access them, like this, if you've saved the reference to the NameSpace object in oNameSpace, as shown previously:

```
oCalendar = oNameSpace.Folders[1].Folders["Calendar"]
oInbox = oNameSpace.Folders[1].Folders["Inbox"]
```

and so forth.

However, there's a simpler way to get to the individual folders. NameSpace has a method, GetDefaultFolder, to which you can pass an appropriate constant, and receive in return a reference to the specified folder. **Table 1** shows the constants for the 10 types of folders that Outlook supports.

Table 1. *Outlook folders. These constants represent the 10 primary folder types in Outlook. Pass them to GetDefaultFolder to access Outlook's data.*

Constant	Value	Constant	Value
olFolderDeletedItems	3	olFolderContacts	10
olFolderOutbox	4	olFolderJournal	11
olFolderSentMail	5	olFolderNotes	12
olFolderInbox	6	olFolderTasks	13
olFolderCalendar	9	olFolderDrafts	16

To use this approach, call the method like this:

```
#DEFINE olFolderTasks 13
#DEFINE olFolderContacts 10
oTasks = oNameSpace.GetDefaultFolder( olFolderTasks )
oContacts = oNameSpace.GetDefaultFolder( olFolderContacts )
```

Once you have the folder for one of the Outlook applets, you can explore its contents. Each folder contains a collection of items, but the details vary significantly. We'll look at the ones we think you're most likely to want to automate here, but we won't explore all 10 in depth. If you need to work with the others, the Outlook VBA Help file should tell you what you need to know. (Actually, once you get the hang of it, looking up the specific properties isn't that big a deal.)

Once you reach the folder for a given Outlook applet, you still have to climb down through an Items collection to reach the actual contents. For example, to find out how many tasks are in the Tasks folder, you'd check:

```
? oTasks.Items.Count
```

New items of each type are created using Application's CreateItem method. You pass it a constant (or the actual value) for the kind of item you want to create, and it adds a member to the appropriate folder. **Table 2** shows the constants to pass to CreateItem.

Table 2. *Creating new items. The CreateItem method adds data. Pass one of these constants to create an item of the specified type.*

Constant	Value	Constant	Value
olMailItem	0	olJournalItem	4
olAppointmentItem	1	olNoteItem	5
olContactItem	2	olPostItem	6
olTaskItem	3	olDistributionListItem	7

For example, to create a new appointment, issue this call:

```
oAppt = oOutlook.CreateItem( olAppointmentItem )
```

Then, you can modify the properties of the new appointment such as Start, End, AllDayEvent, and so forth to properly enter it into the Calendar. Other types of items are handled similarly.

Once you've filled in the properties of the item, call its Save method to save it in the appropriate collection. Anytime you change a property, you need to call Save again to have your changes saved.

You can remove an item by calling its Delete method. This method moves the item to the DeletedItems folder, from which it can be resurrected, if necessary, but will be cleaned up, in due course. (The DeletedItems folder can be set to be emptied automatically on exit or, like the Recycle Bin, can be emptied manually.)

Sending e-mail

The first thing everyone seems to want to automate with Outlook is sending e-mail messages, whether it's to send bug reports to developers, saturate potential customers with solicitations, or just communicate between different sites running an application.

The key object for sending and receiving messages is MailItem, which represents a single mail message. To create a new MailItem object, call CreateItem, passing olMailItem (0) as the parameter:

```
#DEFINE olMailItem 0
oMailItem = oOutlook.CreateItem( olMailItem )
```

Table 3 lists key properties of MailItem.

This code creates a simple message to one person:

```
#DEFINE CR CHR(13)
WITH oMailItem
    .Subject = "Meeting next week"
    .Body = "Just confirming our meeting on Tuesday at 3." + CR + ;
            "Please bring ideas, as well as your notes from last year's event."
    .Recipients.Add("Bill Gates")
ENDWITH
```

Table 3. *What's in a message? Here are the properties of MailItem you're most likely to work with.*

Property	Type	Description
Subject	Character	The description of the message. This can be used as an index into the Items collection.
Body	Character	The content of the message.
Recipients	Object	Reference to a collection of Recipient objects, with one entry for each person to receive this message. (See the next section, "Recipients and contacts.")
To	Character	A semi-colon-separated list of recipients. Although you can specify the list of recipients by filling in this property, it's not recommended. Use .Recipients.Add() instead. (See the next section, "Recipients and contacts.")
CC	Character	A semi-colon-separated list of people receiving copies of the message (the cc: list). The caution in the To property applies to CC as well.
BCC	Character	A semi-colon-separated list of people receiving blind copies of the message (the bcc: list). The caution in the To property applies to BCC as well.
Importance	Numeric	The priority of the message (corresponding to the Importance field in the Options dialog). Uses these constants: olImportanceLow 0 olImportanceNormal 1 olImportanceHigh 2
Sensitivity	Numeric	The privacy level of the message (corresponding to the Sensitivity field in the Options dialog). Uses these constants: olNormal 0 olPersonal 1 olPrivate 2 olConfidential 3
Attachments	Object	Reference to a collection of Attachment objects, with one for each attached file. (See "Attaching files" later in this chapter.)

As with other items, once you've filled in the properties, you can call the Save method to store the new message. However, the new message isn't automatically stored in the Outbox. The folder where unsent messages are stored is determined by a setting in Outlook's Options dialog. **Figure 2** shows the Advanced E-mail Options dialog, where users make this choice. This dialog is accessed by choosing Tools|Options from the menu, then choosing E-mail Options on the Preference tab, then choosing Advanced E-mail Options on the dialog that appears.

Saving a message isn't enough to have it sent to the recipients, though. You have to call the Send method, as well. (In fact, you can just call Send and skip Save altogether.) That method, as its name suggests, sends the message immediately, routing it to the Sent Messages folder.

```
oMailItem.Save()
oMailItem.Send()
```

Figure 2. *Specifying e-mail options. This dialog lets you specify where the Save method stores new mail messages. They can be placed in any of several folders, including Drafts and Outbox.*

If Outlook isn't connected to the mail server, a send error occurs (though you don't get any indication of the error in VFP), and the message lands in the Outbox, ready to be sent the next time there's a connection. (Actually, it may land in your Drafts folder—see the next paragraph for the reason why.) However, at that time, depending on Outlook's configuration, the message isn't necessarily sent automatically—the user may have to take some action to start the process of sending and receiving messages. (None of this really has much to do with Outlook itself so much as the way Outlook is configured to send and receive mail, and none of it affects the code you write in VFP to send the mail.)

If you've been following along with the examples and, for some reason, don't have Bill Gates in your Outlook address book, that Send command resulted in another error, one that was displayed in VFP: "OLE IDispatch exception code 4096 from Microsoft Outlook: Outlook does not recognize one or more names." (Of course, if you do have Bill Gates in your Outlook address book, you probably shouldn't have sent the message, unless you happen to have a meeting with him scheduled for Tuesday at 3.) The second part of the message is actually pretty clear. It means that Outlook was asked to send a message to someone, but doesn't have that person in its Contacts folder. Fortunately, there's a way to prevent this error before it occurs. The next section shows you how.

Recipients and contacts

As Table 3 indicates, a message can be sent to more than one person, and any given person can be on any of three lists: the main list, the CC ("carbon copy") list, or the BCC ("blind carbon copy") list. All of them are managed through a single collection called Recipients, however. The Type property of the Recipient object indicates, for each recipient, to which list he or she belongs. The choices are olTo (1), olCC (2), and olBCC (3).

To add a person to the list of recipients for a message, use the Add method of the Recipients collection. It expects a single parameter, the name or e-mail address of the person to be added. Outlook has a lot of smarts built in for matching this information up to the Contacts folder. Given half a chance, it'll do the job right. The Resolve and ResolveAll methods are used for this process. Resolve belongs to the Recipient object, while ResolveAll is a collection method. Both attempt to match the current name/address information with the Contacts folder and fill in the Name and Address properties, as well as create an AddressEntry object for the Recipient when a match is found. Resolve can work with as little as a partial first or last name, if it's unique.

```
#DEFINE olMailItem 0
#DEFINE CR CHR(13)
#DEFINE olCC 2

oMailItem = oOutlook.CreateItem( olMailItem )

WITH oMailItem
   .Subject = "Send ideas now!"
   .Body = "If you have any ideas on how to proceed with " + CR + ;
           "this project, please send them to the whole group now. "

   * Add recipients
   WITH .Recipients
      .Add("Fred Smith")
      .Add("Mary Louise McGillicuddy")
      .Add("Darth") && surely the only Darth, so no last name needed
      .Add("Basil Rathbone")

      * Copy the boss
      oRecip = .Add("Ruth Less")
      oRecip.Type = olCC

      * Get Outlook to add all the e-mail addresses
      lResolved = .ResolveAll()
   ENDWITH

   * Save and send
   .Save()
   .Send()
ENDWITH
```

Of course, you can't run this example as is. You'll need to substitute people who are actually in your Outlook address book (to avoid the error message described previously). Even so, you may not want to run the whole example, since they'll wonder why you're sending them such a strange message. Fortunately, you can stop short of sending the message (that is, don't execute the Send method) and just examine it in the Drafts folder or Outbox (or whichever folder you have Outlook saving unsent messages in), then delete it before you send it.

> *We ran into a problem with the ResolveAll method in situations where not every recipient was found. What should happen is that the e-mail address gets filled for those Recipients with matching records in Contacts, and their Resolved property is set to .T. We found that, in some cases, Resolved is not set to .T., yet calling the Resolve method for the individual Recipient record does return .T. Therefore, we recommend using Resolve rather than ResolveAll if there's any chance some Recipients may not be able to be resolved. See the example in "Putting it all together" at the end of this chapter.*

Attaching files

In addition to text, you may want to send files along with a message. The Attachments collection lets you do this. Use the Add method to attach each file—doing so creates a new Attachment object in the collection. Pass the name of the file, including the path where it can be found, to Add.

```
oMailItem.Attachments.Add( "C:\My Documents\QuarterlyReport.DOC" )
```

If you're adding attachments to a message you've already saved (but not sent), remember to save the message again. If you attempt to add an attachment to an existing message and the file doesn't exist, a member is added to the Attachments collection anyway. (If you check .Attachments.Count, you'll see that it's gone up.) Be sure to use the Delete or Remove method to get rid of the spurious attachment before you go on.

Manipulating the Contacts folder

Outlook has a built-in address book, the folder called Contacts. It's like a super-Rolodex, capable of keeping track of multiple addresses, phone numbers, and e-mail addresses for each person, represented by a ContactItem object.

Surprisingly, Outlook doesn't use collections to manage the various addresses, phone numbers, and e-mail addresses. Separate properties are used for each, and the number of each type is limited (three addresses, 19 phone numbers, three e-mail addresses). **Table 4** lists some of the properties of ContactItem—see Help for more, but the pattern should be obvious from the table.

The program in **Listing 1** reads the Contacts folder and creates a cursor with an entry for each person, containing the name, selected mailing address, and primary telephone number. You'll find it as MakeContactList.PRG in the Developer Download files available at www.hentzenwerke.com.

Table 4. *I'm in the book. The ContactItem object represents a person in Outlook's address book.*

Property	Type	Description
FullName	Character	The person's full name, unparsed. The name is also available in a variety of configurations, like LastNameAndFirstName, LastFirstAndSuffix, and so forth. See Help for a complete list.
FirstName	Character	The person's first name.
LastName	Character	The person's last name.
HomeAddress	Character	The person's home address, unparsed. As with name, the components are available individually. Outlook is also capable of doing sophisticated parsing of an address it's given to break it into components.
HomeAddressStreet	Character	The street portion (first line) of the home address.
HomeAddressCity	Character	The city portion of the home address.
HomeAddressState	Character	The state portion of the home address.
HomeAddressCountry	Character	The country of the home address.
HomeAddressPostalCode	Character	The postal/ZIP code of the home address.
BusinessAddress	Character	The person's business address, unparsed. The same individual components are available as for home address.
SelectedMailingAddress	Numeric	Indicates which address is the primary address for this person. Uses these constants: olNone 0 olBusiness 2 olHome 1 olOther 3
HomeTelephoneNumber	Character	The person's home telephone number.
BusinessTelephoneNumber	Character	The person's business telephone number.
HomeFaxNumber	Character	The person's home fax number.
BusinessFaxNumber	Character	The person's business fax number.
PagerNumber	Character	The person's pager number.
CarTelephoneNumber	Character	The person's car phone number.
PrimaryTelephoneNumber	Character	The primary phone number to use for this person.
Email1Address	Character	The first e-mail address for this person.
Birthday	Datetime	The person's birthday.

Listing 1. *Collecting contact information. This program reads the Contacts from Outlook and puts them into a VFP cursor.*

```
* Read Outlook contact information into a cursor
#DEFINE olContacts 10
#DEFINE olNone 0
#DEFINE olHome 1
#DEFINE olBusiness 2
#DEFINE olOther 3

LOCAL oNameSpace, oContacts, oContact
LOCAL cFirst, cLast, cAddr, cPhone
```

```
IF VarType(oOutlook) <> "O"
     * Start or connect to Outlook
     * Make it public for demonstration purposes.
     RELEASE oOutlook
     PUBLIC oOutlook
     oOutlook = CreateObject("Outlook.Application")
ENDIF
oNameSpace = oOutlook.GetNameSpace("MAPI")

* Get Contacts folder
oContacts = oNameSpace.GetDefaultFolder( olContacts )

* Create a cursor to hold contact information
CREATE CURSOR ContactInfo ;
   (cFirstName C(15), cLastName C(20), mAddress M, cPhoneNum C(30))

* Go through contacts
FOR EACH oContact IN oContacts.Items
   WITH oContact
      cFirst = .FirstName
      cLast = .LastName
      cPhone = .PrimaryTelephoneNumber

      * Choose the right address. If the primary phone number is empty,
      * pick up the phone number associated with this address.
      DO CASE
      CASE .SelectedMailingAddress = olHome
         cAddr = .HomeAddress
         IF EMPTY(cPhone)
            cPhone = .HomeTelephoneNumber
         ENDIF
      CASE .SelectedMailingAddress = olBusiness
         cAddr = .BusinessAddress
         IF EMPTY(cPhone)
            cPhone = .BusinessTelephoneNumber
         ENDIF
      CASE .SelectedMailingAddress = olOther
         cAddr = .OtherAddress
         IF EMPTY(cPhone)
            cPhone = .OtherTelephoneNumber
         ENDIF
      CASE .SelectedMailingAddress = olNone
         cAddr = ""
      ENDCASE

      INSERT INTO ContactInfo VALUES (cFirst, cLast, cAddr, cPhone)
   ENDWITH
ENDFOR

* Show the results
BROWSE

RETURN
```

Chances are that you'll need to go the other direction, too, and create an Outlook contact from FoxPro data. While this book focuses on FoxPro solutions, be aware that Outlook supports the import of files in many formats directly, and has a pretty snappy and flexible interface to its Import Wizard. Consider exporting contact information from VFP into one of the common formats (like CSV) and then importing it into Outlook from there. Contacts are created like other Outlook items, by using the CreateItem method. The example shown in **Listing 2** (MakeContact.PRG in the Developer Download files available at www.hentzenwerke.com) adds a record from the TasTrade Supplier table to Outlook's contacts.

Listing 2. *Create an Outlook contact. This program sends data from VFP to Outlook to create a new contact.*

```
* Add supplier information

#DEFINE olContactItem 2
#DEFINE olBusiness 2

LOCAL oNameSpace, oContact

IF VarType(oOutlook) <> "O"
      * Start or connect to Outlook
      * Make it public for demonstration purposes.
      RELEASE oOutlook
      PUBLIC oOutlook
      oOutlook = CreateObject("Outlook.Application")
ENDIF
oNameSpace = oOutlook.GetNameSpace("MAPI")

* Open Supplier
OPEN DATA _SAMPLES + "TasTrade\Data\TasTrade"
USE Supplier

* Pick a random record for demonstration purposes
GO RAND() * RECCOUNT()

* Create a new contact record
oContact = oOutlook.CreateItem( olContactItem )

WITH oContact
   .FullName = Contact_Name
   .CompanyName = Company_Name
   .BusinessAddressStreet = Address
   .BusinessAddressCity = City
   .BusinessAddressState = Region
   .BusinessAddressPostalCode = Postal_Code
   .BusinessAddressCountry = Country
   .SelectedMailingAddress = olBusiness
   .BusinessTelephoneNumber = Phone
   .PrimaryTelephoneNumber = Phone
   .BusinessFaxNumber = Fax
   .Save()
```

```
ENDWITH

USE

RETURN
```

Adding appointments and tasks

Other than communicating to the outside world, you might use Outlook to keep users up to date. While you can build a calendar into your application, why duplicate effort? Why not just use the one that's already on the user's machine? It's easy to both create new appointments in Outlook and read the ones that are already there. Along the same lines, don't build a "to do" list into your application. Let your applications talk to Outlook's Task list.

As with other Outlook items, adding appointments and tasks is as simple as calling CreateItem and filling in the blanks, then calling the Save method for the new object. **Table 5** shows key properties of the AppointmentItem method. **Table 6** looks at TaskItem properties.

The MarkComplete method of TaskItem indicates that the task has been completed on the current date. It sets PercentComplete to 100 and Complete to .T. as well. We're not sure why you can't pass it a parameter to indicate when the task was done.

The code in **Listing 3** adds the birthdays of all the TasTrade employees to the Calendar as all-day events for the next two years, and creates a task of sending each of them a birthday card. The due date for the task varies depending on the country to allow sufficient time for mailing. You'll find it as MakeBdays.PRG in the Developer Download files available at www.hentzenwerke.com.

Table 5. Making appointments. These are the properties you're most likely to set for an AppointmentItem object.

Property	Type	Description
Start, End	DateTime	The start and end time, respectively, of the appointment.
Duration	Numeric	The length of the appointment, in minutes. Interacts with Start and End, of course. You can't set all three.
AllDayEvent	Logical	Indicates whether the item is an "all-day event," that is, something that lasts all day rather than occurring at a specific time.
Subject	Character	The description of the item. The subject can be used as an index into the Items collection.
Location	Character	The location of the appointment. In the Calendar, the location appears next to the subject in parentheses.
Body	Character	The notes for the appointment. These don't appear at all in the Calendar, only in the Appointment dialog itself.
ReminderSet	Logical	Indicates whether Outlook should provide a reminder for this appointment.
ReminderMinutesBeforeStart	Numeric	The number of minutes before the Start time when Outlook should provide the reminder for the appointment.

Table 6*. Describing tasks. These properties are the keys to putting a TaskItem on the Task list.*

Property	Type	Description
Subject	Character	The description of the task, it shows in the Subject column in the Task list. This property can be used as an index into the Items collection.
DueDate	DateTime	The date by which the task is supposed to be completed.
Complete	Logical	Indicates whether the task has been completed. Although this property isn't ReadOnly, it's better to use the MarkComplete method to set this property.
DateCompleted	DateTime	The date on which the task was completed. Note that this is a datetime item, but only the date portion is significant. Like the Complete property, it's better to use the MarkComplete method to set this property.
StartDate	DateTime	The date the task was started.
Status	Numeric	The current status of the task. Use one of these constants: olTaskNotStarted 0 olTaskWaiting 3 olTaskInProgress 1 olTaskDeferred 4 olTaskComplete 2
PercentComplete	Numeric	Indicates how far along the task is.
Importance	Numeric	The priority of the task (corresponding to the Priority field in the Task dialog). Uses these constants: olImportanceLow 0 olImportanceNormal 1 olImportanceHigh 2
Categories	Character	A comma-separated or semi-colon-separated list of categories in which the task should be placed.
Body	Character	Notes for the task. Displayed only in the Task dialog and in memo-style output.
ReminderSet	Logical	Indicates whether Outlook should provide a reminder for this task.
ReminderTime	DateTime	The date and time when Outlook should provide a reminder for this task.

Listing 3*. Adding appointments and tasks. This routine adds the birthdays for all the TasTrade employees to Outlook's Calendar for the next two years, as well as creating a task of sending each a birthday card each time.*

```
* Add TasTrade employee birthdays to the Calendar and
* create a task for each to send a birthday card
#DEFINE olAppointmentItem 1
#DEFINE olTaskItem 3
#DEFINE CR CHR(13)

LOCAL oNameSpace, oAppt1, oAppt2, oTask1, oTask2
LOCAL dNextBirthday

IF VarType(oOutlook) <> "O"
     * Start or connect to Outlook
     * Make it public for demonstration purposes.
     RELEASE oOutlook
     PUBLIC oOutlook
     oOutlook = CreateObject("Outlook.Application")
```

```
ENDIF
oNameSpace = oOutlook.GetNameSpace("MAPI")

* Open the Employee table
OPEN DATABASE _SAMPLES+"\TasTrade\Data\TasTrade"
USE Employee

SCAN
    * Create one appointment and one task for each employee
    * for each of two years
    oAppt1 = oOutlook.CreateItem( olAppointmentItem )
    WITH oAppt1
        * Figure out when the employee's next birthday will occur
        dNextBirthday = GOMONTH( Birth_Date, ;
                                 (YEAR(DATE()) - YEAR(Birth_Date)) * 12)
        IF dNextBirthday <= DATE()
           dNextBirthday = GOMONTH( dNextBirthday, 12)
        ENDIF

        * Set the date and make it an all-day event
        .Start = DTOT( dNextBirthday )
        .AllDayEvent = .T.

        * Use the employee's name in the subject
        .Subject = First_Name - (" " + Last_Name ) - "'s Birthday"

        * Turn off reminders for this
        .ReminderSet = .F.

        .Save()
    ENDWITH

    oTask1 = oOutlook.CreateItem( olTaskItem )
    WITH oTask1
        * Set the task name using the employee name
        .Subject = "Send a birthday card to " + First_Name - (" " + Last_Name)

        * Figure out the due date based on the country it's going to
        DO CASE
        CASE INLIST(Country , "USA", "Canada")
           .DueDate = dNextBirthday - 3
        CASE INLIST(Country, "UK", "France")
           .DueDate = dNextBirthday - 7
        OTHERWISE
           * Figure this'll take a long time
           .DueDate = dNextBirthday - 10
        ENDCASE

        * Put the mailing address in the body for convenience
        cAddress = Address + CR + ;
                   City + CR + ;
                   Region + CR + ;
                   Postal_Code + CR + ;
                   Country
        .Body = "Mailing Address (unformatted): " + CR + cAddress

        * Set a reminder one day ahead
        .ReminderTime = .DueDate - 1440*60
```

```
      .ReminderSet = .T.

      * Set the category
      .Categories = "Gifts"
      .Save()
   ENDWITH

   * Now do second year
   oAppt2 = oAppt1.Copy()
   WITH oAppt2
      * Move the date forward one year
      .Start = GOMONTH( .Start, 12 )
      .Save()
   ENDWITH

   oTask2 = oTask1.Copy()
   WITH oTask2
      * Move the date forward one year
      .DueDate = GOMONTH( .DueDate, 12 )
      .Save()
   ENDWITH

ENDSCAN

USE IN Employee
CLOSE DATA

RETURN
```

In case, like us, you don't really want to leave these items scattered throughout your copy of Outlook, **Listing 4** is an antidote program. It's included as CleanBdays.PRG in the Developer Download files available at www.hentzenwerke.com. It uses the Find method of the Items collection. Find takes a single parameter, a filter string, and returns the first item that matches that filter. The required format for the filter makes us really glad that FoxPro has three sets of character delimiters—properties of the item must be surrounded with square brackets. If no matching item is found, Find returns .null.

It's worth noting that there's also a FindNext method. In this program, it's not needed because each time we find a matching item, we delete it immediately. So, the next search is again looking for the first item that matches the filter string. (For another approach to this problem, check out the Restrict method in the Help file. It's like setting a filter on the list of items.)

Listing 4. *Finding and removing items. This program cleans up after the one in Listing 3.*

```
* Clean up birthday entries added to Outlook
#DEFINE olFolderCalendar 9
#DEFINE olFolderTasks 13

LOCAL oNameSpace, oAppt, oTask
LOCAL oAppts, oTasks, cFilter

IF VarType(oOutlook) <> "O"
      * Start or connect to Outlook
```

```
      * Make it public for demonstration purposes.
      RELEASE oOutlook
      PUBLIC oOutlook
      oOutlook = CreateObject("Outlook.Application")
ENDIF
oNameSpace = oOutlook.GetNameSpace("MAPI")

oAppts = oNameSpace.GetDefaultFolder( olFolderCalendar )
oTasks = oNameSpace.GetDefaultFolder( olFolderTasks )

* Open the Employee table
OPEN DATABASE _SAMPLES+"\TasTrade\Data\TasTrade"
USE Employee

SCAN
   * Create a filter string
   cFilter = '[Subject] = "' + First_Name - ;
           (" " + Last_Name ) - "'s Birthday" + '"'

   * Loop until there are no more matches
   oAppt = oAppts.Items.Find( cFilter )
   DO WHILE NOT IsNull( oAppt )
      oAppt.Delete()
      oAppt = oAppts.Items.Find( cFilter )
   ENDDO

   * Now do the same thing for the Tasks
   cFilter = '[Subject] = "Send a birthday card to ' + ;
           First_Name - (" " + Last_Name) +'"'
   * Loop until there are no more matches
   oTask = oTasks.Items.Find( cFilter )
   DO WHILE NOT IsNull( oTask )
      oTask.Delete()
      oTask = oTasks.Items.Find( cFilter )
   ENDDO

ENDSCAN

RETURN
```

Putting it all together

Listing 5 shows a program that adds an appointment to the calendar, adds several related tasks, then sends an e-mail to the other participants in the meeting, in this case, all the TasTrade employees. The program expects them to be in the Outlook address book—however, it produces a message box showing the list of everyone to whom it was unable to send a message. (Like the other e-mail example in this chapter, you need to substitute people who are actually in your Outlook address book for this example to run correctly.) **Figure 3** shows the appointment the program sets up, while **Figure 4** shows one of the resulting tasks. You'll find Listing 5 as OutlookSample.PRG in the Developer Download files available at www.hentzenwerke.com.

Listing 5. *Plan a meeting. This program sets up a meeting by adding it to the calendar, adding several tasks, and sending an e-mail to all employees.*

```
#DEFINE olMailItem 0
#DEFINE olAppointmentItem 1
#DEFINE olTaskItem 3
#DEFINE CR CHR(13)
#DEFINE olImportanceHigh 2
#DEFINE MB_ICONINFORMATION    64       && Information message
#DEFINE MB_OK    0       && OK button only
#DEFINE OneDayInSeconds 86400

LOCAL oNameSpace, oMessage, oAppt, oTask

IF VarType(oOutlook) <> "O"
    * Start or connect to Outlook
    * Make it public for demonstration purposes.
    RELEASE oOutlook
    PUBLIC oOutlook
    oOutlook = CreateObject("Outlook.Application")
ENDIF

oNameSpace = oOutlook.GetNameSpace("MAPI")

* First, set up the appointment
oAppt = oOutlook.CreateItem( olAppointmentItem )
WITH oAppt
    .Subject = "Monthly Staff Meeting"
    .Location = "Conference Room A"
    .Start = {^ 2000/02/01 9:00}
    .Duration = 90
    .ReminderSet = .T.
    .ReminderMinutesBeforeStart = 15
    .Save()
ENDWITH

* Now, set up some associated tasks
* First, the agenda
oTask = oOutlook.CreateItem( olTaskItem )
WITH oTask
    .Subject = "Staff Meeting Agenda"
    .DueDate = {^ 2000/01/31 12:00}
    .Categories = "Staff Meeting"
    * get a reminder one day before it's due
    .ReminderSet = .T.
    .ReminderTime = .DueDate - OneDayInSeconds
    .Save()
ENDWITH

* Next, the snacks
oTask = oOutlook.CreateItem( olTaskItem )
WITH oTask
    .Subject = "Order refreshments"
    .DueDate = {^ 2000/01/30 17:00}
    .Categories = "Staff Meeting"
    * get a reminder half an hour ahead
    .ReminderSet = .T.
    .ReminderTime = .DueDate - 30*60
```

```
    * Put the information about what and where to order in the task
    .Body = "Get bagels and danish from the kosher bakery"
    .Save()
ENDWITH

* Finally, send a notice out to all employees
OPEN DATA _SAMPLES + "TasTrade\Data\TasTrade"
USE Employee

* Create a cursor to keep track of the employees we were unable to mail to
CREATE CURSOR EmailProbs (cFullName C(40))

oMessage = oOutlook.CreateItem( olMailItem )
WITH oMessage
    .Subject = "Monthly Staff Meeting"
    .Body = "The monthly staff meeting will be held on " + ;
                "Tuesday, February 1 at 9:00 A.M. " + ;
                "in Conference Room A. Everyone is expected to attend." + ;
                + CR + CR + ;
                "Please bring your sales reports for December and " + ;
                "preliminary figures for January." + ;
                + CR + CR + ;
                "Refreshments will be served, as usual."

    .Importance = olImportanceHigh

    * Now loop through Employee, adding recipients
    SELECT Employee
    SCAN
        oRecipient = .Recipients.Add( First_Name - (" " + Last_Name ) )
        IF NOT oRecipient.Resolve()
            * Either this name is ambiguous or there's no
            * e-mail address for this person on file.
            * Log the omission
            INSERT INTO EmailProbs VALUES (oRecipient.Name)

            * Remove this person
            oRecipient.Delete()
        ENDIF

    ENDSCAN

    IF .Recipients.Count > 0
        * Send it
        .Send()
    ELSE
        * No recipients, so get rid of the message
        .Delete()
    ENDIF
ENDWITH

* Report the failed e-mails
SELECT EmailProbs
IF RECCOUNT() = 0
    MESSAGEBOX( "All e-mails sent", ;
                MB_ICONINFORMATION+MB_OK, ;
                "Outlook Automation Sample")
ELSE
    * Build a string containing the list of failures
```

```
      cFailString = ""
      SCAN
         cFailString = cFailString + cFullName + CR
      ENDSCAN
      MESSAGEBOX("E-mail was not sent to the following employees: " + ;
                CR + cFailString, ;
                MB_ICONINFORMATION+MB_OK, ;
                "Outlook Automation Sample")
ENDIF

USE IN EmailProbs
USE IN Employee

RETURN
```

Outlook is a rich program for managing personal data, such as schedules, "to do" lists, address books, and e-mail. While its object model is not polymorphic with the rest of Office, it provides plenty of opportunities for Automation.

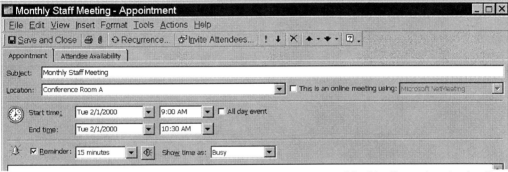

Figure 3. *Automated scheduling. This appointment was added to the calendar by the program in Listing 5.*

Figure 4. *Tell me what to do. This is one of two tasks created by Listing 5.*

Section VI
Advanced Topics

Chapter 13
Inter-Office Communication

Once you've figured out the servers as individual applications, the next natural step is to get them talking to each other, or talking back to your FoxPro application.

It doesn't take long before you, your clients, or your boss comes up with the idea that you ought to be able to cut and paste between the cool applications you've developed. After all, an interactive user can press Ctrl-C and Ctrl-V to copy and paste between various Office applications. How hard can it be to automate it? Fortunately, it's not hard at all. We'll cover several ways to get data from one server to appear in another server.

The next idea that seems obvious to the developer is that the Office servers are wonderfully object-oriented, complete with their polymorphic properties, methods, and events. Events—VFP allows you to run code on certain events; it might be feasible to do the same in the Office servers. Wouldn't it be nice to get the Office server to tell your VFP application when the user tries to save, print, or exit the document that your application so carefully opened? It's quite possible with VFP's VFPCOM.DLL utility, which binds the server's events to VFP procedures.

Communicating between Office applications

There are two basic methods to automate sharing data between two Office applications: one is to cut the selection to the clipboard, and paste it in the other application. This is a nice, simple method. The second method is to add it as an OLE object, which then gives the user a lot of control over the end product, as OLE's in-place editing features can then be used to tweak the appearance, if necessary. Several methods are available to add an OLE object.

Copying and pasting between applications

The interactive method of copying between applications goes something like this: open the application with the source data, select the source data, and use Cut or Copy to paste it to the clipboard. Then open the target application, locate the position to paste the data, and paste the contents of the clipboard. The same process applies to automated copying and pasting.

To illustrate automating a copy and paste procedure, we'll build a small spreadsheet, and place it into a Word document.

Setting up the source data

 For this example, the source is a small spreadsheet. Chapters 7, 8, and 9 ("Excel Basics," "Advanced Excel Features," and "Excel's Graphing Engine," respectively) explain the details of setting up a spreadsheet, so we won't go into that here. **Listing 1** shows the code to build a sample spreadsheet, which is shown in **Figure 1**. Listing 1 is available as SourceSetup.PRG in the Developer Download files available at www.hentzenwerke.com.

Listing 1. *A sample Excel spreadsheet, which we'll use in our copying examples. See Figure 1 for the results.*

```
* Clean out any existing references to servers.
* This prevents memory loss to leftover instances.
RELEASE ALL LIKE o*

* Make the following variables public for demonstration
* purposes, so you can inspect the objects when the
* program has finished. oSourceRange must be public
* if you're following along with the example in the book.
PUBLIC oExcel, oSourceRange

* Create an instance of Excel
oExcel = CreateObject("Excel.Application")

* Make Excel visible.
oExcel.Visible = .T.

oBook = oExcel.Workbooks.Add()
WITH oBook.Sheets[1]
  .Range("A1").Value = "Quarter"
  .Range("A2").Value = "First"
  .Range("A3").Value = "Second"
  .Range("A4").Value = "Third"
  .Range("A5").Value = "Fourth"

  .Range("B1").Value = "Sales Volume"
  .Range("B2").Value = "100000"
  .Range("B3").Value = "125000"
  .Range("B4").Value = "150000"
  .Range("B5").Value = "175000"

  oSourceRange = .Range("A1:B5")

ENDWITH
```

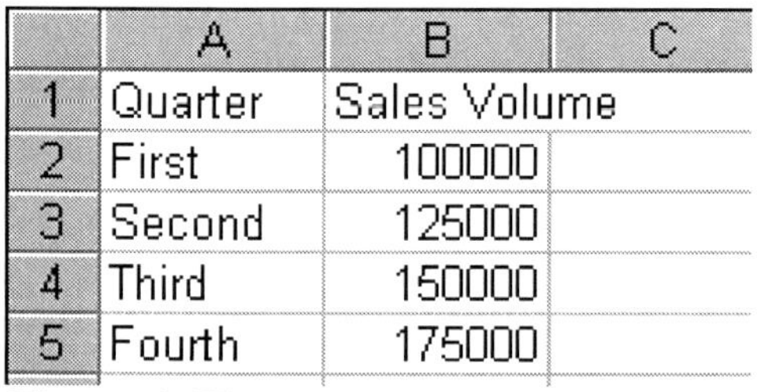

	A	B	C
1	Quarter	Sales Volume	
2	First	100000	
3	Second	125000	
4	Third	150000	
5	Fourth	175000	

Figure 1. *The example spreadsheet to copy into a Word document. While this is a simple spreadsheet, any of Excel's robust features can be used. Chapters 7, 8, and 9 cover Excel in detail (see "Excel Basics," "Advanced Excel Features," and "Excel's Graphing Engine," respectively).*

Notice that the next-to-last line of code sets a variable, oSourceRange. To make life a bit easier, it's worthwhile to set up a variable containing the data you want to copy while you still have the WITH...ENDWITH constructs open. We've made this one PUBLIC so that it's available to work along with the rest of the example. Normally, oSourceRange would be scoped more appropriately.

For Excel, this example shows the source data object to be a Range. It could also be a whole Worksheet or a Chart object. For Word, the source data is likely to be a range of text. For PowerPoint, the source data is likely to be a single slide. Be aware that you can use a whole multi-sheet Workbook, multi-slide Presentation, or multi-page Document as the source, but when copied to the target application, it may not view or print as you expect, since the target applications generally show only one worksheet, slide, or page.

Copy the data to the clipboard

Once you have the object reference, use the Copy method to get it to the clipboard. For Excel, the Range, Chart, and Worksheet objects have a Copy method. Using this method without parameters copies the object to the clipboard (parameters are available to allow you to copy the object to other locations within Excel). Issue the following command to place the source data on the clipboard:

```
oSourceRange.Copy()
```

Several Word objects, including the Range object, have a Copy method, which is used without parameters to copy to the clipboard. Likewise, the Copy method is available for a number of PowerPoint objects, including Slide, Shape, and TextRange objects.

Preparing the target application

 Preparing the target application consists of opening the application and positioning your insertion point at the proper location. The Basics chapters for each of the Office servers cover this. To illustrate this concept, the example opens a blank document and adds a line of text. The cursor is positioned at the point where the spreadsheet is to be entered. **Figure 2** shows the results of **Listing 2**, which is stored as TargetSetup.PRG in the Developer Download files available at www.hentzenwerke.com.

> *If you are working interactively along with us, be sure to use TargetSetup.PRG, or key in the following lines in the Command Window. Do not copy and paste these from the electronic version of the book, as you will overwrite the Excel spreadsheet in the clipboard buffer. Word then faithfully places this code into the document, instead of the spreadsheet.*
>
> *Happily, this only happens when working interactively; generally, nobody can change the clipboard buffer while Automation code runs. Just be careful when you're working in the Command Window and developing code that uses the clipboard that you're not creating problems unrelated to your code.*

Listing 2. *A sample Word document in which to place the spreadsheet from Listing 1.*
See Figure 2 for the results.

```
#DEFINE wdCollapseEnd 0

* Make oRange and oWord public to use during the exercise,
* while following along in the text.
RELEASE oWord, oRange
PUBLIC oWord, oRange

* Create an instance of Word.
oWord = CreateObject("Word.Application")

* Make Word visible.
oWord.Visible = .T.
oDocument = oWord.Documents.Add()

oRange = oDocument.Range()
oRange.InsertAfter("This is an example of copying a portion " + ;
                  "of a spreadsheet into Word." + CHR(13))
oRange.Collapse(wdCollapseEnd)
```

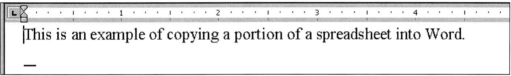

Figure 2. *The sample Word document, which can receive the spreadsheet. This is a*
simple Word document, but it could be as advanced as you want it to be. Chapters 4,
5, and 6 ("Word Basics," "Intermediate Word," and "Advanced Word," respectively)
describe the Word server in detail.

Because the range is collapsed to the end after inserting the text, oRange (declared
PUBLIC for this interactive example) is positioned properly. Pay no attention to the actual
cursor position in Figure 2—Ranges are independent of the cursor position. Be assured that
oRange is properly positioned to paste the spreadsheet.

Pasting the data from the clipboard

In Word, the Range object describes a position in the document, so it makes sense to have a
Paste method, which pastes the contents of the clipboard into the Range (so be sure to Collapse
your Range, unless you want the contents of the Range replaced). The syntax is simply:

```
oRange.Paste()
```

Figure 3 shows the resulting spreadsheet in the Word document. The Excel spreadsheet is
converted to a Word Table object.

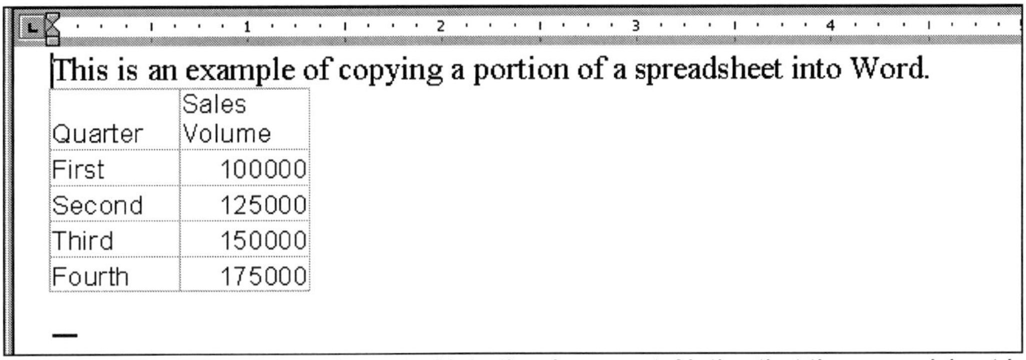
This is an example of copying a portion of a spreadsheet into Word.

Quarter	Sales Volume
First	100000
Second	125000
Third	150000
Fourth	175000

***Figure 3**. The spreadsheet is pasted into the document. Notice that the spreadsheet is converted to a table.*

Word is nice and easy—the Range object has a Paste command that takes no parameters. Excel is a bit different. The Worksheet's Paste command takes one of two parameters: the first is the Range object where the source data goes on the sheet, and the second is used if the first is not specified, and is a logical parameter describing whether to link to the source data (the default is false).

PowerPoint is a little different. First, you must ensure that you are in the Normal view, rather than the Slide Sorter, Notes, or Slideshow views. Then, you can use the Paste method of the Shapes collection object or the TextRange object (for text strings only). The Shapes collection is appropriate for pasting objects from other applications, as in:

```
oNewObj = oSlide.Shapes.Paste()
```

This pastes the spreadsheet (or other object) in the middle of the specified slide. Manipulate the Top and Left properties of the newly placed object, oNewObj, to put it where it needs to be. It is interesting to note that a Word Range pasted into the Shapes collection becomes a single text box. However, when a Range from Excel is pasted into the Shapes collection, it is placed as an embedded Excel object. Generally, pasting as an embedded or linked object requires other commands, such as PasteSpecial or AddOLEObject.

PasteSpecial

The Paste method generally places a converted copy of the source data. The source data is converted to the most similar kind of object in the target application. Once converted, the data loses the editing capabilities of the original application. While in some circumstances, it is a benefit that an Excel spreadsheet becomes a Word table, other circumstances may need the editing capabilities of the original application.

This is where the PasteSpecial method comes in. You may have used this interactively, clicking on Edit|Paste Special… from any of the Office applications' menus. It brings up the dialog shown in **Figure 4**, which displays the source of the data, identifying not just the name of the application, but the range (in the application's notation) as well. The option buttons at the left indicate how to paste the link, and the list box indicates the formats into which the source data can be converted.

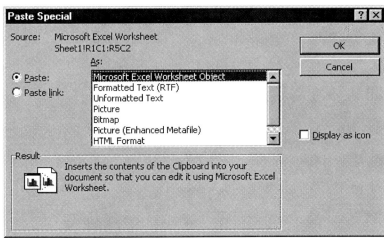

Figure 4. *The Paste Special dialog box, obtained interactively from Word. This shows the many options available when using the PasteSpecial method.*

Word's PasteSpecial method is available from the Range object. It takes a series of parameters, which parallel the options shown in Figure 4:

```
oRange.PasteSpecial( [nIconIndex], [lLink], [nPlacement],
                     [lDisplayAsIcon], [nDataType],
                     [cIconFileName], [cIconLabel])
```

nIconIndex	Numeric	If lDisplayAsIcon is .T., specifies the icon displayed for this object, instead of displaying the object itself (when lDisplayAsIcon is .F., the default). The number corresponds to the position of the icon in the icon filename specified by cIconFileName. If omitted, it defaults to the first icon in the specified file.
lLink	Logical	Indicates whether to link to the source file (.T.) or to embed it (.F.). The default is .F. See the text for more information on linking vs. embedding. This parameter corresponds to the Paste and Paste link option buttons in the dialog box shown in Figure 4.
nPlacement	Numeric	Determines how to place the object in relation to the existing text. Use one of the following constants:

		wdFloatOverText	1	The object floats over the text. The object can be formatted to have the text wrap to the right, the left, on both sides, through the object, or stop at the top and resume at the bottom. The object can also be positioned anywhere on the page.
		wdInLine	0	The object is positioned as if it were a character in the text. (Default)

| lDisplayAsIcon | Logical | Indicates whether to display this as an icon, which requires the user to click on the icon to open the object. When true, the object displays the icon chosen by nIconIndex in the cIconFileName, and displays the text label (passed in cIconLabel) underneath the icon. If false, the object is displayed in its native format (for example, it looks like a spreadsheet or slide). This corresponds to the Display as Icon check box in the dialog box shown in Figure 4. The default is false. |
| nDataType | Numeric | The format in which to paste the object. This corresponds to the As: list box in the dialog box shown in Figure 4. Some of the valid values are: |

wdPasteOLEObject	0	Retains link to source application (and optionally to the source file, if lLink is .T.).
wdPasteHTML	10	Converts to HTML.
wdPasteBitmap	4	Converts source data to a plain bitmap.
wdPasteText	2	Converts source data to text (similar to the Paste method).

The default varies, based on what is contained in the clipboard.

| cIconFileName | Character | The fully pathed filename containing the icon to be displayed, if lDisplayAsIcon is .T. |
| cIconLabel | Character | The text to display below the icon, if lDisplayAsIcon is .T. |

The most important parameter is the lLink parameter, which defines whether the source data object should be linked or not. A linked object is essentially a pointer back to its source file. Any changes made to the source file show up in the document (when the object is refreshed), and any changes made to the object within the document can be saved directly to the source file (assuming the user saves the changes). If the object is not linked, it is considered "embedded," which means that the object is edited in-place in its native fashion, just as if it were linked, but there is no connection to the original source file. The object is completely encapsulated within the Word document.

To illustrate the PasteSpecial method to embed an Excel spreadsheet object, we'll use the same sample files as previously. The only change is from a call to the Paste method to a call to the PasteSpecial method. **Figure 5** shows the results.

```
DO SourceSetup.PRG
oSourceRange.Copy()
DO TargetSetup.PRG

#DEFINE wdInLine            0
#DEFINE wdPasteOLEObject 0

oRange.PasteSpecial(,.F., wdInLine,  , wdPasteOLEObject)
```

The Excel object is added as a Shape object in the Shapes collection. Notice in Figure 5 that the "Sales Volume" label is cut off. If the width of column B was adjusted prior to cutting, or if the range included the blank column C, this would appear correctly. The default is to show exactly the range specified—no more and no less.

The user can edit any part of the spreadsheet by double-clicking on the newly added Shape object. The display changes to that shown in **Figure 6**. The user can complete the edits by clicking off the spreadsheet, anywhere within the document.

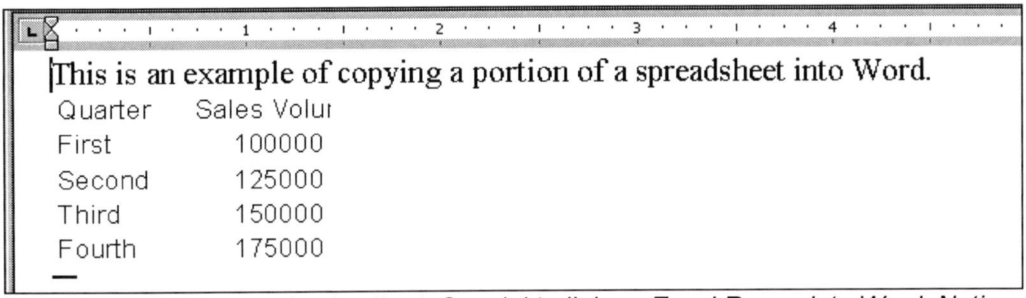

Figure 5. *An example of using PasteSpecial to link an Excel Range into Word. Notice that the "Sales Volume" label is cut off. A little work on formatting the column width before cutting to the clipboard would remedy the problem.*

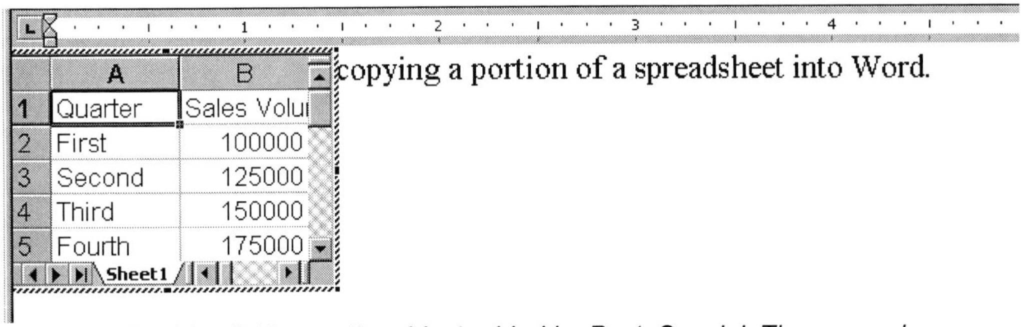

Figure 6. *Double-clicking on the object added by PasteSpecial. The menu changes to incorporate Excel's menu. When the user is finished editing (indicated by clicking off of the spreadsheet), the display returns to looking like Figure 5, along with reflecting any changes.*

If you are linking an object, the source object must be saved as a file. By explicitly saving the source document before copying it to the clipboard, the object on the clipboard will present that fact to the application doing the paste, and the clipboard object can supply the original filename. If the object is not saved, no error results when the PasteSpecial method's lLink parameter is .T.—but it doesn't get linked, either.

What about Excel's PasteSpecial command? Well, it's similar, but different. It uses most of the same parameters, but they are organized more coherently, as all the icon parameters are grouped together:

```
oExcel.ActiveSheet.PasteSpecial( [cFormat], [lLink],
                      [lDisplayAsIcon], [cIconFileName],
                      [nIconIndex], [cIconLabel] )
```

The cFormat parameter (which corresponds to the nDataType parameter for Word's method) is a major change from Word's syntax. It expects a string to identify the format of the data on the clipboard, such as "Microsoft Word 8.0 Document Object." Fortunately, this is only necessary if you want to change the format of the object to something other than what it already is, like changing it to a bitmap or any of the other supported formats. By default, lLink is false, which embeds the object. The remaining parameters are for the icon, and work just like in Word.

How about PowerPoint's PasteSpecial command? Surprisingly, there isn't one. Since the Paste method adds Word text as a Shape object with text, and adds an Excel spreadsheet as an embedded object anyway, we guess Microsoft felt it wasn't needed. But how does one add a linked object to PowerPoint? There is an alternative method to PasteSpecial, which does not require the use of the clipboard. It is the AddOLEObject method, and it's available in all Office servers.

Using AddOLEObject

Why would you use AddOLEObject, when PasteSpecial is available? There are a couple of reasons. First, if you're using PowerPoint, it's the only way to link an object (that's a pretty compelling reason). Second, AddOLEObject accesses a file, which doesn't have to be opened in your code (it can even be a user-generated file). You don't have to select the object and use the clipboard to transfer it.

We're going to use a different example here. Since PowerPoint doesn't have a PasteSpecial method to link to a file, we'll use PowerPoint as our target application. We'll use an Excel Chart as our source data. Charts are visual analysis tools and are very well suited to presentations. It's understandable that someone would want to come up with an automated method to generate PowerPoint slides with charts that reflect the most current data.

PowerPoint's AddOLEObject method is available only to the Shapes collection object. Its syntax is:

```
oSlide.Shapes.AddOLEObject([nLeft], [nTop], [nWidth], [nHeight],
                    [cClassName], [cFileName], [lDisplayAsIcon],
                    [cIconFileName], [nIconIndex], [cIconLabel],
                    [lLink])
```

The first two parameters are the position of the left and top edges of the object. These are in points, and the default is 0. The next two parameters define the width and height of the object, in points. Fortunately, these are optional in PowerPoint 2000 (they are not optional in PowerPoint 97).

You pass either cClassName or cFileName, leaving the other blank. Unless you're building blank objects, you won't need to pass a class name or ProgID as cClassName. More likely, you'll pass the filename containing the object to add.

The next four parameters (lDisplayAsIcon, cIconFileName, nIconIndex, and cIconLabel) determine whether the object is displayed as an icon, and are the same as the PasteSpecial parameters.

The last parameter, lLink, determines whether the object is linked or embedded. **Listing 3**, stored as AddOLEObject.PRG in the Developer Download files available at www.hentzenwerke.com, shows building and saving a simple chart in Excel, then opening PowerPoint and linking the chart.

Listing 3. Using AddOLEObject to link an Excel chart into a PowerPoint presentation.

```
* Clean out any existing references to servers.
* This prevents memory loss to leftover instances.
RELEASE ALL LIKE o*

#DEFINE xlColumn                    3
#DEFINE xlColumns                   2
#DEFINE autoColumnFormat            4
#DEFINE autoOneSeriesLabel          1
#DEFINE autoOneCategoryLabel        1
#DEFINE autoHasLegend              .T.
#DEFINE autoIn2Pt                   72
#DEFINE ppLayoutBlank               12

* Add a workbook, using default settings
oExcel = CreateObject("Excel.Application")
oExcel.Visible = .T.

oBook  = oExcel.Workbooks.Add()

* Add simple data to graph
WITH oBook.Sheets[1]
   .Range("A2").Value = "First"
   .Range("A3").Value = "Second"
   .Range("B1").Value = "Test"
   .Range("B2").Value = "10"
   .Range("B3").Value = "20"

   oChartSource = .Range("A1:B3")
ENDWITH

* Create the chart as a Chart Sheet
oChart = oExcel.Charts.ADD()
oChart.ACTIVATE()
oExcel.ActiveChart.ChartWizard(oChartSource, xlColumn, autoColumnFormat, ;
      xlColumns, autoOneCategoryLabel, autoOneSeriesLabel, autoHasLegend, ;
      "Sample Chart", "", "")

* Save the file, with the data sheet active
oExcel.Sheets["Sheet1"].Activate()
XLSFile = FULLPATH("SampleChart.XLS")
oExcel.ActiveWorkbook.SaveAs(XLSFile)
oExcel.Quit()

RELEASE oExcel, oBook, oChart, oChartSource

* Make variables for demonstration purposes, so
* you can inspect them after the program finishes
PUBLIC oPowerPoint, oOLEChart

* Create the PowerPoint object
oPowerPoint = CreateObject("PowerPoint.Application")

* Make it visible, and add the presentation and slides
oPowerPoint.Visible = .T.
oPresentation = oPowerPoint.Presentations.Add()
```

```
oSlide = oPresentation.Slides.Add(1, ppLayoutBlank)

* Add the worksheet
oOLEChart = oSlide.Shapes.AddOLEObject(;
          1.0 * autoIn2Pt, 1.5 * autoIn2Pt,;
          8.0 * autoIn2Pt, 5.0 * autoIn2Pt, ,;
          XLSFile, ,,,, .T.)
```

There's a little gotcha with adding Excel charts (and worksheets, too), because there are multiple worksheets in the workbook. How does PowerPoint know which worksheet to display? It displays the first worksheet. If your workbook is set up to have the chart on a sheet other than the first sheet, or if your workbook contains multiple chart sheets, then you can specify which sheet is displayed if the object is linked (this option is not available if the object is embedded). Use the Shape's LinkFormat object's SourceFullName property to specify the sheet name. Set this property to a concatenation of the filename, an exclamation point, and the sheet name, as in "C:\My Files\SampleChart.XLS!Chart1." Once this property is set, update the link by calling the Update method of the Shape's LinkFormat object.

The Excel and Word AddOLEObject methods work similarly, except their list of parameters is in a different order.

```
oObj.AddOLEObject( [cClassName], [cFileName], [lLink],
                   [lDisplayAsIcon], [cIconFileName], [nIconIndex],
                   [cIconLabel], [nLeft], [nTop], [nWidth], [nHeight] )
```

oObj must be one of the following: an Excel Sheet's Shapes collection object, a Word Document's Shapes collection object, or a Word Document's InlineShapes collection object.

As with PowerPoint, pass either cClassName or cFileName, and leave the other blank. The next parameter is the logical parameter determining whether to link or embed the object (it defaults to false to embed the object). Following that are the icon parameters. Last are the parameters defining the new object's location, in points. If they're not specified, Left and Top default to 0, and the height and width default to the dimensions of the object.

Adding a document to Excel, using syntax like:

```
oOLEDoc = oSheet.Shapes.AddOLEObject(, "C:\MyDocs\Test.DOC")
```

adds a document at 0,0 relative to the active cell. If cell B3 is selected, then the new object is placed relative to cell B3. The default size of the object is 468 points wide and 717.75 points high. On the spreadsheet, this takes approximately 10 columns by 57 rows (given the default column width and row height). The size calculates to 6.5 by 9.9 inches, which are the dimensions of the margins stored in the document. If the user double-clicks on the object, it activates in-place editing of the document.

Adding a presentation to Excel, using syntax like:

```
oOLEPpt = oSheet.Shapes.AddOLEObject(, "C:\MyDocs\Test.PPT")
```

adds the presentation at 0,0 relative to the active cell. The default size of a PowerPoint presentation is 360 points wide by 270 points high (7 columns by 22 rows). Double-clicking the object runs the slide show.

Add a Presentation to Word at the top, left corner within the margin of the currently selected page with syntax similar to the following:

```
oOLEPpt = oDoc.Shapes.AddOLEObject(,"C:\MyDocs\Test.PPT")
```

It adds a presentation that is 360 points wide by 270 points high, and runs the slide show when double-clicked by the user.

Add a workbook to Word at the top, left corner of the current page with a command similar to the following:

```
oOLEXls = oDoc.Shapes.AddOLEObject(,"C:\MyDocs\Test.XLS")
```

An Excel worksheet defaults to displaying only the first cell of the worksheet that was active when the file was last saved, regardless of how many cells are used in the worksheet (though we have seen differences, which may be related to page setup properties stored as Excel defaults). The default cell is 52.2 points wide by 13.8 points tall—not very big. However, if a chart sheet was the active sheet when the file was saved, then the chart comes in at a whopping 683 by 487 points—9.5 by 6.7 inches, too wide for the page! For Excel worksheets, it seems prudent to specify the height and width, and perhaps predetermine what's in the worksheet (either a chart or the extents of the cells in the worksheet) before adding the object.

In Word, when the object is linked, there is a LinkFormat object with a SourceFullName property, but it does not allow you to specify the sheet name, as PowerPoint does. Word appears to display only the first slide or worksheet, so consider this when designing your application.

Communicating between Office applications, whatever the method, can add significant functionality to your application. Wait until you see what we can do with events.

Communicating events with VFPCOM

Throughout this book, we've concentrated on telling the servers what to do. Communication to the server takes the form of calling methods and setting properties; communication from the server takes the form of VFP initiating a query of a property or getting a return value from method calls. Communication seems a bit lopsided, requiring VFP to start all the conversations. This seems strange when contrasted to COM (ActiveX) controls, which can communicate back to VFP through event code.

While FoxPro can see and act on events raised by ActiveX controls, it cannot see any events raised by objects created with the CreateObject() function. This can lead to some awkward kludges, like having VFP sit in a loop waiting for the status of a server to change, or invoking a server and leaving the VFP screen with a message displaying, "Press this button when you are done." In contrast, Visual Basic has a WITH EVENTS construct that allows events in the servers VB invokes to fire code within VB. Shortly after VFP 6.0 shipped, the wizards at Microsoft came up with a COM control called VFPCOM that solves this problem. VFPCOM binds the server's events to an event handler object you create, which has methods with the same names as the events of the server object. When Word raises its DocumentBeforeClose event, VFPCOM looks for a DocumentBeforeClose method in the event handler object you've crafted.

Obtaining VFPCOM.DLL

You'll need to go get VFPCOM from Microsoft's web site, at msdn.microsoft.com/vfoxpro. Follow the links to the Product Updates page (as of this writing, it's under Samples and Downloads on the main page). Then select the VFPCOM utility to download. It's approximately 156KB. Save the VFPCOM.EXE file to disk. While you're at the web site, be sure to save or print the ReadMe file, which is not included in the EXE.

When you run VFPCOM.EXE to install it, it places the DLL and its sample files in a \VFPCOM directory underneath VFP's main directory (unless you specify otherwise). It also registers the DLL.

Using VFPCOM.DLL

The first step in using VFPCOM is to create an object reference. Use the class name in the CreateObject() function, like this:

```
oVFPCOM = CreateObject("vfpcom.comutil")
```

To use VFPCOM, you also need a reference to an Office server. For the examples, we'll use Word (if you're trying this interactively, do yourself a favor and make it visible so you don't orphan an invisible instance of the server):

```
oWord = CreateObject("Word.Application")
oWord.Visible = .T.
```

The VFPCOM server has five methods, but only two are important to us: ExportEvents and BindEvents. The ExportEvents method provides the answer to the question, "But how do I find all the names of the events to write that event handler object?" ExportEvents not only extracts the names of the events, it creates a program file that holds the entire class definition! WOW! The method takes two parameters: the first is the object reference whose events you want to export, and the second is the filename to write all this to. Assuming you've created oVFPCOM and oWord (as shown previously), create the file WordEvents.PRG like this:

```
oVFPCOM.ExportEvents(oWord, "WordEvents.PRG")
```

And then, like magic, the file WordEvents.PRG contains this:

```
DEFINE CLASS ApplicationEvents2 AS custom

  PROCEDURE DocumentBeforeClose(Doc,Cancel)
  * Add user code here
  ENDPROC

  PROCEDURE DocumentBeforePrint(Doc,Cancel)
  * Add user code here
  ENDPROC

  PROCEDURE DocumentBeforeSave(Doc,SaveAsUI,Cancel)
  * Add user code here
  ENDPROC
```

```
PROCEDURE DocumentChange
* Add user code here
ENDPROC

PROCEDURE DocumentOpen(Doc)
* Add user code here
ENDPROC

PROCEDURE NewDocument(Doc)
* Add user code here
ENDPROC

PROCEDURE Quit
* Add user code here
ENDPROC

PROCEDURE WindowActivate(Doc,Wn)
* Add user code here
ENDPROC

PROCEDURE WindowBeforeDoubleClick(Sel,Cancel)
* Add user code here
ENDPROC

PROCEDURE WindowBeforeRightClick(Sel,Cancel)
* Add user code here
ENDPROC

PROCEDURE WindowDeactivate(Doc,Wn)
* Add user code here
ENDPROC

PROCEDURE WindowSelectionChange(Sel)
* Add user code here
ENDPROC

ENDDEFINE
```

Cool, no? Just change the name of the class from ApplicationEvents2 to WordEvents, change the parameter variable names to your own naming convention, then add your code, and you've got your class definition.

The next step is to use the BindEvents method to tell VFPCOM which object is the server and which object contains the methods that are mapped to the events. The first parameter is the object reference to the Office application; the second is the object reference to the object (the skeleton of which could be the output of ExportEvents).

```
oWordEvents = CreateObject("WordEvents")
oVFPCOM.BindEvents(oWord, oWordEvents)
```

Be sure you've scoped the variables for the VFPCOM utility and the event handler objects (oVFPCOM and oWordEvents) so they are available while the Office application reference is available.

Let's examine a small example that shows how VFPCOM works. **Listing 4** shows a very pared-down version of what's needed to handle Word's events. Listing 4 is available as VFPCOMandWord.PRG in the Developer Download files available at www.hentzenwerke.com.

Listing 4. *A simple example of how VFPCOM handles Word's events. This interactive example illustrates how VFPCOM handles Word's BeforeClose event.*

```
* Clean out any existing references to servers.
* This prevents memory loss to leftover instances.
RELEASE ALL LIKE o*

* Make the following variables public for demonstration
* purposes, so they are available after this PRG has run
* to demonstrate the VFPCOM functionality.
PUBLIC oWord, oWordEvents, oVFPCom

* Create the server application
oWord = CreateObject("Word.Application")

* Make it visible
oWord.Visible = .T.
oWord.Documents.Add()
oWord.Documents[1].Range.Text = "This is a test."

* Create the VFPCOM object
oVFPCom = CreateObject("vfpcom.comutil")

* Create the event handler
oWordEvents = CreateObject("WordEvents")

* Bind the server to the event handler
oVFPCom.BindEvents(oWord, oWordEvents)

* Bring VFP to the top and tell the user what to do next
_SCREEN.AlwaysOnTop = .T.
_SCREEN.AlwaysOnTop = .F.
MessageBox("When you close this box, you'll be put in Word." + CHR(13) + ;
           "Close down Word to see how VFPCOM handles it." + CHR(13) + ;
           "VFP should give 'BeforeClose' MessageBox, " + CHR(13) + ;
           "then Word should give its Save dialog." )
oWord.Activate() && Activate Word

* The definition for the pared-down event handler
DEFINE CLASS WordEvents AS Custom
  PROCEDURE DocumentBeforeClose(lCancel, oDoc)
    * Cheap way to bring VFP to the front.
    _SCREEN.AlwaysOnTop = .T.
    _SCREEN.AlwaysOnTop = .F.

    MessageBox("BeforeClose")

    * Go back to Word to see what it presents (prevent Alt-Tab)
    oWord.Activate()
  ENDPROC
ENDDEFINE
```

As you can see, the event handler has been trimmed to handle only one event; that's simply to save space in the book—run the ExportEvents method to get the full code. The code that is run is a simple MessageBox, to show you where your code would run. It also handles moving the proper windows on top, so you don't have to Alt-Tab between applications.

After this code runs, the PUBLIC variables are still in scope, so the event handler still works. When you close the message box, VFP activates the Word window. Close either the Document or the Application (both fire the DocumentBeforeClose event). When the DocumentBeforeClose event fires in the WordEvents object, VFP comes forward, gives a simple "BeforeClose" message box, then puts you back in Word to see that Word continues with its Save dialog.

Imagine the possibilities…there are many events to trap, and with total access to the document, you have lots of possibilities. Imagine letting the user edit the Word document, then passing the contents of the document back to VFP to put in a text control when they save the document. You can trap for a right-click, and run code based on where the user right-clicked in the document. You can trap for quitting Word, and remind the user that they can't close Word while the Automation code is running. Cool. Way cool.

VFPCOM with Excel
VFPCOM works well with Excel, with one minor difference: there are different events for the Application object, the Workbook object, and the Worksheet object. Run the ExportEvents with oExcel, oBook, and oSheet and compare the results. Make an event handler for each kind of object, then use BindEvents to bind each kind of object to its event handler.

VFPCOM with PowerPoint
VFPCOM works quite a bit differently with PowerPoint. An inconsistency in VFPCOM and/or in PowerPoint's object model means that VFPCOM doesn't work as advertised. One of the first indicators is that VFPCOM's ExportEvents results in an empty file; none of the events appear as if they're exposed. Also, if you try to BindEvents, you'll receive an error: "OLE Error code 0x80070002: The system cannot find the file specified."

 Fortunately, there is a workaround. Our thanks to John V. Petersen, who has written a DLL in Visual Basic, which takes care of the problem. The DLL, as well as its source, is available as a series of vbPowerPoint files (DLL, VBP, LIB, and EXP) in the Developer Download files available at www.hentzenwerke.com. The DLL uses VB to create a class, which is an instance of PowerPoint. This VB instance exposes the event interface. You need to register the DLL before you use it. Run the following command from the Start button's Run menu option:

```
REGSVR32 C:\YourDriveAndPathHere\vbPowerpoint.dll
```

Be sure that the path is appropriate for your machine. To uninstall this DLL, issue the same command, adding " /u" to the end.

 Listing 5, stored as VFPCOMandPPT.PRG in the Developer Download files available at www.hentzenwerke.com, shows how to use the DLL to get VFP to work. The main difference is that oVBPowerPoint is created from the VB class and contains the PowerPoint application in the oPowerPoint property.

Listing 5. *Using VFPCOM with PowerPoint. A workaround is required here involving vbPowerPoint.DLL.*

```
* Clean out any existing references to servers.
* This prevents memory loss to leftover instances.
RELEASE ALL LIKE o*

* Make the following variables public for demonstration
* purposes, so they are available after this PRG has run
* to demonstrate the VFPCOM functionality.
PUBLIC oVFPCom, oVBPowerPoint, oVFPPowerPoint

#DEFINE ppLayoutTitle 1

* Create an instance of VFPCOM
oVFPCom = CreateObject("vfpcom.comutil")

* Create the VB class, which, in turn, creates PowerPoint
oVBPowerPoint = CreateObject("vbPowerPoint.Class1")

* Add a small presentation
oVBPowerPoint.oPowerPoint.Visible = .T.
oPres = oVBPowerPoint.oPowerPoint.Presentations.Add()
oSlide = oPres.Slides.Add(1, ppLayoutTitle)
oSlide.Shapes[1].TextFrame.TextRange.Text = "This is a Test"
oSlide.Shapes[2].TextFrame.TextRange.Text = "It is ONLY a Test."

* Create an instance of the event handler object
oVFPPowerPoint = CreateObject("vfpPowerPoint")

* Bind PowerPoint to the error handler object
oVFPCom.BindEvents(oVBPowerPoint, oVFPPowerPoint)

* Let the user in on what to do
_SCREEN.AlwaysOnTop = .T.
_SCREEN.AlwaysOnTop = .F.

MessageBox("When you close this box, you'll be put in PowerPoint." + CHR(13) +;
           "Close down PowerPoint to see how VFPCOM handles it." + CHR(13) + ;
           "VFP should give 'BeforeClose' MessageBox, " + CHR(13) + ;
           "then PowerPoint should give its Save dialog." )
oVBPowerPoint.oPowerPoint.Activate() && Activate PowerPoint

DEFINE CLASS  vfpPowerPoint  AS custom

  PROCEDURE PresentationClose(Pres)
    * Cheap way to bring VFP to the front.
    _SCREEN.AlwaysOnTop = .T.
    _SCREEN.AlwaysOnTop = .F.

    MessageBox("PresentationClose")

    * Activate PowerPoint
    oVBPowerPoint.oPowerPoint.Activate()
  ENDPROC

ENDDEFINE
```

The last word

Communicating between Office applications takes many forms. One of the most common is reusing data: taking the chart created for one part of the application and embedding or linking it in a document or a presentation. Thanks to VFPCOM, the servers can send information back based on events, alerting the program that the user has completed modifications because they've closed the server (or are closing it prematurely). We've shown you some simple examples to illustrate these concepts; we know that you're brimming with ideas on how to scale these examples into complex applications.

Chapter 14
Handling Automation Errors

Automation programming is just like other kinds of programming—errors happen. However, the errors are a bit different from those you've dealt with in a stand-alone application. Your application must be prepared to handle errors that are specific to Automation.

Most developers deal with errors that occur only in their application environment. In FoxPro (or Basic, C, or any other programming language), you set up your environment, check to be sure that any support libraries are available, then let your application run. Once your program is running, you don't have to worry about what else is installed and running on the user's computer.

Automation is a bit different. CreateObject() won't work if the Office application isn't installed, or if it is properly installed in the registry but the executable no longer resides on the disk (some users still haven't gotten the hang of uninstall programs, preferring to delete directories to free up disk space, which doesn't remove the registry settings). Once you've created the instance and made it visible, users seem to want to close it down before your application is done with it. To make matters really annoying, none of the Office servers knows anything about the FoxPro environment, so you can't rely on SET PATH, SET DEFAULT, and other FoxPro settings.

Automation-specific errors

Fortunately for us, there are a limited number of VFP errors that are specific to Automation. **Table 1** shows a list of all the Automation-specific errors. As you can see from their descriptions, the error messages refer to Automation's roots in OLE.

Table 1. The Automation errors you'll need to get used to seeing.

Error number	Error description
1420	OLE object is invalid or corrupted.
1421	Cannot activate the OLE server.
1423	Error creating the OLE object.
1424	Error copying the OLE object to Clipboard.
1426	OLE error code 0x "name".
1427	OLE IDispatch exception code "name".
1428	OLE IDispatch exception code "number" from "server": "name".
1429	"OLE error".
1440	OLE exception error "name". OLE object may be corrupt.

The most common errors are 1426–1429, which generally indicate that the server has a problem with the property being set or the method being executed. The other errors indicate a problem with the server application itself, such as a problem finding the server. Errors 1420, 1421, and 1423 happen when the object is instantiated, when CreateObject() or GetObject() is called. Error 1424 happens only when copying to the clipboard; if you don't copy an object to the clipboard (as in Chapter 13, "Inter-Office Communication"), you don't have to worry about this error. Error 1440 is new to VFP 6.0 and indicates that the server has caused a general protection fault, and the instance is no longer available.

The war of 1426–1429

No, we're not talking about a centuries-old battle here, we're talking about a series of error numbers. But we're certain you'll battle these four errors frequently while writing Automation code. These four errors are raised by the Automation server sending back an error code. Which one you get depends on how much information the server is willing to provide. This is the frustrating part: there isn't any categorical difference between these errors, and each error has a variety of meanings. These four errors return every possible problem from every Automation server; in contrast, FoxPro has hundreds of error messages!

Before you think that this is an awful design, remember that FoxPro is receiving the errors in a standard COM/Automation interface. There isn't any way to assign a unique error number to every possible error in every possible server—even if we could ensure the errors are unique across servers, we'd have error numbers larger than GUIDs, which would cause other problems.

So why is it so frustrating to work with these four errors? You can't tell the difference between a fatal error (the server has disconnected), a syntax error, and an error that can be fixed (like a divide by zero error) by the number. Yes, it is possible to keep a meticulous database of the text and number of each error for each server, but because of the volume of errors, it's very hard to track every error you come across *and* stay on-track with your development efforts.

Subtle differences

As we said before, the difference between these errors is in the quantity of information the server is willing to provide. Error 1426, "OLE error code 0x,"is the most simplistic. It returns only a character string containing the hexadecimal number and a short message, for example: "OLE error code 0x800706ba: The RPC server is unavailable." In your error handler, ERROR() returns 1426, and MESSAGE() returns "OLE error code 0x800706ba: The RPC server is unavailable."

Errors 1427, 1428, and 1429 all appear to return similar information: an exception code followed by the message. While FoxPro sees them as different errors, their messages seem eerily similar. The differences may lie in what is returned in the AERROR() function.

Visual FoxPro's AERROR() function returns more information for an error. It builds an array with seven columns containing various information, depending on whether it is a FoxPro, OLE, or ODBC error. Help indicates that most FoxPro errors return nulls for most of the entries, with the exception of OLE errors 1427 and 1429, and ODBC error 1526. In fact, OLE errors 1426 and 1428 also make good use of AERROR().

Table 2 lists the contents of the resulting AERROR() array. Error 1426 sets only the first three values; the remaining four are set to null values. Errors 1427, 1428, and 1429 use up to seven columns of the array.

***Table 2**. The contents of the AERROR() array, using a 1429 error generated by Excel. The described positions reflect those for OLE errors only; not general FoxPro errors or ODBC errors, which have different descriptions.*

Position	Contents	Example
1	The error number. Same as ERROR().	1429
2	Text of the VFP error message. Same as MESSAGE(). Note that this is a concatenation of some of the other information in this array.	"OLE IDispatch exception code 0 from Microsoft Excel: Unable to set the Bold property of the Font class"
3	The text of the OLE message.	"Unable to set the Bold property of the Font class"
4	The application sending the message.	"Microsoft Excel"
5	The application's Help file, if available (.Null. if not).	"c:\Program Files\Microsoft Office\Office\1033\xlmain9.chm"
6	The Help context ID, if available (.Null. if not).	0
7	The OLE 2.0 exception number.	0

Error 1426 sets the first three columns. The first is the error number, which is the same as querying ERROR(). The second is the VFP error message—the one that's displayed in the error dialog box, as in: "OLE error code 0x80020026: Unknown name." This is the same string that is returned from the MESSAGE() function. The third column contains only a portion of the text string; it is the string returned from the OLE server. VFP adds some standard text to clarify the message; in the case of 1426, it's "OLE error code 0x." While you can parse that out of the string, it's probably easier just to check the third column of the array, which contains the error code followed by the message: "80020026: Unknown name." Actually, it's even easier to check SYS(2018), the most recent error message parameter function. The remaining AERROR() array columns are .Null., like any other VFP error.

Errors 1427–1429 fill all columns of the array (if the Help file and Help Context ID are available). As you can see from Table 1, the VFP message is a concatenation of a standard message ("OLE IDispatch exception code "), the exception number (column 7), the application name (column 4), and finally the text of the OLE message (column 3). The text of the message (column 3) is also the value returned by SYS(2018), the most recent error message parameter, which is different from error 1426, which returns just the text (as in column 3). Actually, SYS(2018) returns only the first 255 characters of the message, which can be significant in longer messages, as we'll see later on.

 As we wrote this chapter, it became evident that 1426 and 1429 are the most common errors. In fact, in our hunt for error examples, we couldn't even bag a live error 1427 or 1428. This does not mean that you will never see an error 1427 or 1428; instead, it means that we haven't encountered every Office Automation error (though it sure seems that we have!). While Office may not use these errors, other COM objects might, so we strongly recommend that you build your error handler to handle 1427 and 1428, just in case.

Some interesting error observations

To really see how frustrating handling these errors can be, a few examples are in order. The first example shows the range of how informative these errors can be. For example, imagine the following line of code (yes, it has a typo in it, to illustrate our point):

```
oChart.ChartWizrd(oExcel.Sheets(cSheetName).Range(cGraphRange), ;
    xlColumn, 6, xlColumns, 1, 1, 1, "", "", "Assets", "")
```

The resulting error message is shown in **Figure 1**.

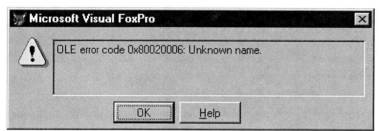

Figure 1. *A sample error, 1426, obtained by a misspelled method name. While its conciseness is admirable, a bit of help on exactly what the unknown name is would be helpful.*

Just a bit brief, no? Especially since our example has no fewer than five names in it: the references to oExcel, oChart, the ChartWizard method (which is the culprit here), the Sheets object, and the Range object. To be fair, VFP is reporting what it received from the server, so we can blame the server for its omission of one small, but very helpful, piece of information.

On the flip side, there's this error that comes from the following line of code. This line references a file that doesn't exist:

```
oWord.Documents.Open("Test.Doc")
```

This error, number 1429, is shown in **Figure 2**.

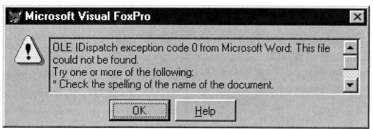

Figure 2. *Another error, 1429, offers a lot of information. There's so much information, it even has a scroll bar!*

This message is so unusually long and informative, the error message box actually has a scroll bar to allow you to read the full text of the message! The full text of the error message is as follows:

```
OLE IDispatch exception code 0 from Microsoft Word: This file could not be
found.
Try one or more of the following:
* Check the spelling of the name of the document.
* Try a different file name.
(Test.Doc).
```

It was while testing this error that we found that SYS(2018) contains only the first 255 characters.

Another situation is that the same error number gives different kinds of errors that need to be handled differently. One kind of error is the syntax error, those pesky typos that the compiler usually catches, or the run-time notification that informs you that you've reversed those two parameters. Another kind of error is when the user is notified that their system is improperly configured, or they've made a mistake. Almost all FoxPro errors fall into one category or the other, so it's much easier to handle each individual error.

Errors 1426–1429 return errors in both of these categories (and any other category you can think of). To illustrate, let's pick on error 1426. We've already talked about "OLE error code 0x80020026: Unknown name," shown in Figure 1, which generally means there's a misspelled method or property in the code and the developer needs to fix the code. The error handler can gracefully skip this line, shut down the module, or whatever action is appropriate (ideally, the developer fixes this before it gets to the user!). In contrast to that situation, **Figure 3** shows a different error: "OLE error code 0x800706ba: The RPC server is unavailable." This error can show up on two occasions: when you're opening the server and it doesn't start up correctly (or doesn't start up all), or later, after your program opens the server, and the user closes it before your program is finished with it. Another 1426 classic is "OLE error code 0x80080005: Server execution failed." This means that the server is registered, but the actual EXE file isn't found (usually due to the user uninstalling by deleting the folder instead of using the Uninstall routine). These last two errors are handled a bit differently than a syntax error! Who knows how many other errors are returned as 1426.

Figure 3. *Another error 1426, this one indicating the server is unavailable. Automation errors can return nearly any kind of error (including syntax errors, run-time errors, and configuration errors), which makes programming your error handler a bit tricky.*

Error-handling strategies

In any programming environment, there are two ways to handle errors: proactively and reactively. The proactive approach is to write your code so you prevent errors from happening. For example, you can avoid "Invalid Index" errors by checking oExcel.Workbooks.Count to ensure that oExcel.Workbooks[43] is available. The reactive approach is to let the ON ERROR procedure and/or the Form or Object's Error method handle the error. A solid error-handling strategy uses both methods to ensure errors are handled gracefully.

Exactly how much of the error-handling strategies should be proactive or reactive is a personal preference. In fact, "personal preference" should really be stated as "intensely held beliefs defended with the tenacity of a pit-bull." We've both had heated conversations with others about how to handle errors, and we're not going to go into a debate about the pros and cons of specific implementations of error handlers.

We will say, though, that because all Automation errors are funneled through just a few error numbers, this challenge requires some creative problem solving. There are some techniques that you can mull over and decide how to implement in your existing error handling scheme. We'll also insist on some proactive, preventive approaches.

ON ERROR and the Error method

Chances are, you are adding Automation code to an existing application, or using an existing application framework. You can choose to handle Automation errors in the procedure called by ON ERROR, which works just fine, especially if Automation code is sprinkled throughout your application.

If your application isolates the Automation code, then a localized error handler may be more appropriate. In the JFAST application, the Automation code is launched from one form, and nearly all the code launched there is Automation code (as opposed to VFP statements). The error handler works nicely in the form's Error method, which overrides the setting of ON ERROR. Another logical place for error handling is in the Error method of the wrapper class that you should use (see Chapter 15, "Wrapping Up the Servers"). Just remember that the wrapper class can't trap for errors in code that runs outside the wrapper class.

If you're working in a team of developers, before you go cobbling your application's ON ERROR routines with the latest and greatest Automation error handling, try isolating it and perfecting it in the form's Error method. That way, you can perfect the error handling routines while testing your form, then make one change to the application's error handler. That way, you can minimize the number of times you make changes to the application's error code (and the number of times your team members show up at your desk demanding to know why you've "fixed" it).

Listing 1 (ErrorMethod.PRG in the Developer Download files available at www.hentzenwerke.com) shows some sample code to use as a starting point.

Undoubtedly, you'll find other ways to handle certain flavors of 1426 and 1429 in your application. This is a good starting point on which to expand as you become more familiar with the kinds of errors your application experiences. This simple skeleton builds a string to indicate what has happened, and displays it to the user. The last bit of the method closes down the code that is running—you'll want to comment out that code during development, replacing it with a SUSPEND or returning you to your code (like an Ignore) to find the next error.

Listing 1. *A sample format for an Automation error handler, residing in the form's Error method. This method is available as ErrorMethod.PRG in the Developer Download files.*

```
* ErrorMethod.PRG
LPARAMETERS nError, cMethod, nLine
LOCAL ErrorArray[1], AppName, Instructions, oWkBk

m.ErrorMessage = MESSAGE()

#DEFINE CR   CHR(13)
#DEFINE wdDoNotSaveChanges 0

* Grab the info in the error array--useful only for OLE errors 1426-1429.
= AERROR(ErrorArray)

* Build a user-friendly error message.
DO CASE
  CASE nError = 1420  && OLE object is invalid or corrupted.
    m.Instructions = "Try reinstalling Office."

  CASE nError = 1421  && Cannot activate the OLE server.
    m.Instructions = "Try reinstalling Office"

  CASE nError = 1422  && Error saving the OLE object.
    m.Instructions = "Report this error."

  CASE nError = 1423  && Error creating the OLE object.
    m.Instructions = "Report this error."

  CASE nError = 1424  && Error copying the OLE object to Clipboard.
    m.Instructions = "Report this error."

  CASE nError = 1426  && OLE error code 0x"name".

    * This is a good place to check for ErrorArray[3], and determine what
    * to do based on LEFT(ErrorArray[3], 8), the error code. One example
    * is shown below.

    IF LEFT(ErrorArray[3], 8) = "800706ba" && The RPC server is unavailable
      m.Instructions = "The server was shut down."
    ELSE
      m.Instructions = "Report this error"
    ENDIF

  CASE INLIST(nError, 1427, 1428, 1429 )
    * 1427 = OLE IDispatch exception code "name".
    * 1428 = OLE IDispatch exception code "number"
    *                  && from "server": "name".
    * 1429 = "OLE error"

    * Don't forget that you can query the following:
    * ErrorArray[3], the text of the OLE message
    * ErrorArray[5], the application's Help File
    * ErrorArray[6], the Help context ID
    * ErrorArray[7], the OLE 2.0 exception number - this is particularly
    *                  useful for handling individual exceptions.
```

```
    IF NOT ISNULL(ErrorArray[4])
      m.AppName = "Problem with the application: " + ErrorArray[4] + CR
    ELSE
      m.AppName = ""
    ENDIF

    m.Instructions = AppName

  CASE nError =  1440 && OLE exception error "name". OLE object may be corrupt.
    m.Instructions = "Report this error."

  OTHERWISE
    m.Instructions = "Report this error."

ENDCASE

= MessageBox("UNEXPECTED AUTOMATION ERROR:" + CR + CR + ;
             m.ErrorMessage + CR + ;
             "Error #: " + TRANSFORM(nError, '9999') + " in " + cMethod + CR +;
             "at line " +  TRANSFORM(nLine, '9999999') + CR + CR + ;
             m.Instructions, "AUTOMATION ERROR")

* Our example shuts down open objects. Your application may need
* a different strategy, such as closing the module, closing the app, or
* issuing an Ignore, Retry, Resume message box. Modify this to fit your
* application

IF TYPE("oPowerPoint") = "O" AND NOT ISNULL(oPowerPoint)
  oPowerPoint.Quit()
ENDIF

IF TYPE("oWord") = "O" AND NOT ISNULL(oWord)
  oWord.Quit( wdDoNotSaveChanges )
ENDIF

IF TYPE("oExcel") = "O" AND NOT ISNULL(oExcel)
    FOR EACH oWkBk IN oExcel.Workbooks
      * Insert your favorite method of saving or closing
      * each workbook, so Excel quits without a message
    NEXT oWkBk

    oExcel.Quit()
ENDIF

* Remove the variables - modify to fit your application
RELEASE oPowerPoint, ;  && and any other references to PowerPoint objects
        oExcel, ;       && and any other references to Excel objects
        oWord           && and any other references to Word objects

ThisForm.Release()
RETURN TO MASTER
```

Why do we shut everything down in this error handler? With so many different kinds of errors funneled through 1426–1429, we don't know if this error will affect only the one line (for example, unable to set the bold property), or if it will cause a cascade of errors (as in the case of the server disconnecting). This is the safest method to prevent cascading errors. As you develop your application, you'll find specific OLE error numbers (1427–1429) or error codes

(1426) that you can handle within this framework. For example, in some situations such as batch processing, it may be sufficient to log certain errors and proceed.

Preventing errors

Instead of reacting to errors that occur, it makes sense to try to prevent them. Many of the errors can be prevented, such as checking the Count property of a collection before you specify an index, to ensure that the index isn't out of range.

Another frequently encountered error is to assume that the server application knows about the FoxPro environment. Most developers have relied on the settings of SET PATH and SET DEFAULT to find files. Anytime you find yourself specifying a filename that's in the default directory, be sure to prefix the filename with SYS(5) + SYS(2003), so the server can find it. If it's not in the default directory, be sure to specify the drive and path. Using FullPath() is a quick way to get the path to a file, although more than one same-named file in the path can caused some surprising results.

The server doesn't have a clue about the setting of SET SAFETY, either. Worse yet, if you automate all four Office applications, you'll find that each one behaves differently when you attempt to overwrite a file or exit the application with a document in an unsaved state. Check the "Basics" chapters for each server to ensure that your application does what you want it to do.

If your servers routinely don't open, check the status of SET OLEOBJECT, which must be ON. When SET OLEOBJECT is ON, it tells VFP to search the registry for the server. If it's set to OFF, it prevents VFP from searching the registry, which is where all the Automation servers are found.

Ensuring the server exists

Your application needs to make sure that the user has Office installed on their machine, and that it's properly registered. FoxPro locates COM (hence Automation) objects through the registry. A quick peek at the registry can tell you whether the server has been installed.

You can tell it's been installed. But what if the user is short on disk space, and decides to free up some space by deleting the whole series of Office directories, rather than uninstalling Office? The registry entries are intact, but they point to a non-existent file. You need to check that, too.

Did you know that a user can have the Office applications on their machines, and they work successfully from the desktop icons and the Start menu, but Automation can't find them? Yes, it can happen, and you'll spend weeks trying to figure this one out. The problem is in the registry. Della found out the hard way when a user decided he didn't like the default location of the Office files, and manually moved the directory, then changed the icons and the Start menu to reflect the new location. The problem was that he didn't change the registry (it wasn't his fault...he didn't even know what a registry was). The error message, "Excel is not properly installed on this machine; please reinstall it," was terribly confusing to him, since he was using Excel, so it must be properly installed. Another reason to check for the file that the registry thinks it's supposed to find.

One more gotcha: if you're using Office 97, you want SR-1 applied at a minimum (there is also SR-2 and SR-2B), because it fixes some problems with Automation. Check the version numbers to ensure your user has the proper version. The good news is that it isn't hard to check the registry. A few API functions are used that access the registry. If you're thinking APIs are hard to use, get over it! First, though, a few words about the registry.

Registry 101

The registry is a hierarchical list, made up of *keys*. **Figure 4** shows the Registry Editor, with the six basic keys (Windows 98 is shown). Opening a key reveals a series of *subkeys*. **Figure 5** shows the HKEY_CLASSES_ROOT key opened to reveal its first level of subkeys. If you look in the Registry Editor's Help file, you won't find a reference to the term "subkey." The distinction between key and subkey is helpful when passing parameters to the API functions.

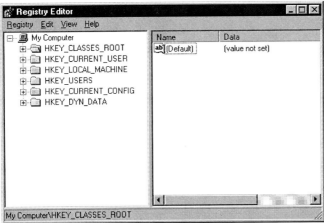

Figure 4. *The Registry Editor open to show the registry keys. The registry keys vary with each version of Windows; Windows 98 is shown here.*

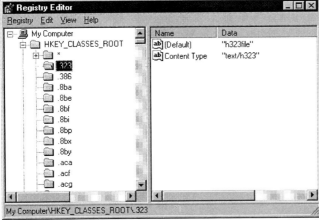

Figure 5. *The Registry Editor shows the HKEY_CLASSES_ROOT key opened, with the subkeys displayed. The pane on the right shows the values associated with the subkey.*

Each subkey has one or more *values* associated with it. A value is made up of two parts: the name and the data. The name is simply a character string describing the contents of the data. Figure 5 shows the .323 subkey with two values: the "(Default)" value of "h323file," and the "Content Type" value of "text/h323."

As we said before, the registry is a hierarchical list of keys. The main key contains subkeys, subkeys can have subkeys, and so on. Many programs have a series of keys sprinkled liberally throughout the registry. There is a series of keys for each Office application used in Automation tasks.

Automation uses the class name key to find the server information. Excel's class name, "Excel.Application," is shown in **Figure 6**. The class name key has a subkey, CLSID, that contains the GUID, or Globally Unique IDentifier. GUIDs, like Excel's, shown in the right pane of Figure 6, are generated by the application developer (in this case, Microsoft). The registry uses these GUIDs to track the programs. This number ensures each application is uniquely represented in the registry.

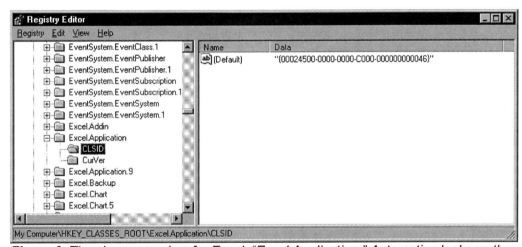

Figure 6. *The class name key for Excel, "Excel.Application." Automation looks up the class name key, finds its CLSID subkey, and looks for its default value, which contains the GUID. This is used for further registry lookups.*

Once we obtain the CLSID key's data value, we can use that to find the key that has a value containing the fully qualified filename. The hierarchy of keys is HKEY_CLASSES_ROOT, CLSID, the GUID (the globally unique identifier), and finally LocalServer32. Its one and only value is the fully qualified EXE name. **Figure 7** shows the Registry Editor opened to this key for Excel.

Now you know what to look for. Now you need to know how to do it. A quick primer on APIs is in order.

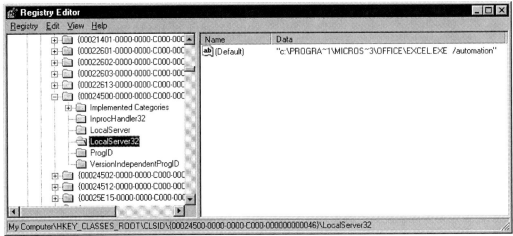

Figure 7. *Some registry keys for Excel. The left pane shows the hierarchy of the subkeys. The parent keys that are off the top of the display are HKEY_CLASSES_ROOT\CLSID. The default value for the LocalServer32 key is the executable called by Automation calls.*

API 101

API stands for Application Programming Interface. Windows comes with a number of DLLs, which contain functions that access all kinds of system-level information. This collection of functions comprises the Windows API.

To use one of these API functions, you must first register the function with the DECLARE command. The DECLARE command takes a number of arguments. The first is an optional argument that indicates the data type of the value returned by the function. The options are SHORT, INTEGER, SINGLE, DOUBLE, LONG, and STRING. The next argument is the function name to register. This argument is case-sensitive—if you're getting errors, be sure to check the case, as most of the Windows API calls are mixed case. The third argument tells the library name. You can specify the DLL, or, if it's a standard Win32API call (usually those in Kernel, User, and GDI DLLs) , you can specify the keyword WIN32API. Be sure to include the required keyword IN. In the event that the function name collides with an existing FoxPro keyword, you can add an optional phrase AS <aliasname>, so you can rename the function.

Lastly, you need to specify the data types of each of the function's parameters. Pass a comma-separated list of data types. Your choices are INTEGER, SINGLE, DOUBLE, LONG, and STRING. If the parameter is to be passed by reference (where the function will change the value of the variable), you must add an @ sign after the data type (and before the comma). You also have to use the @ when you call the function, to pass by reference, but if you omit the @ in the DECLARE, you won't be able to pass by reference. You may also add an optional name after the @; it's not used at all by FoxPro, except to document it, but that's a good enough reason to do it.

The RegOpenKey function is used to open a key. Once a key is opened, you can query its values. The DECLARE command for the RegOpenKey function is:

```
DECLARE RegOpenKey IN ADVAPI32.DLL ;
    INTEGER Key, STRING Subkey, INTEGER @ ReturnedHandle
```

You can now use this function like any other function, as in:

```
hOpenKey = 0
= RegOpenKey(2147483648, ;
    "CLSID\{000209FF-0000-0000-C000-000000000046}\LocalServer32", ;
    @hOpenKey)
```

Just be sure that you have a variable defined, of the proper type, before you pass a variable by reference. The variable, hOpenKey, should be initialized to 0 before calling, as in the preceding example.

API functions aren't all that difficult to use. The hard part is knowing how to find the functions that are available. Fortunately, the Visual FoxPro team provides wrapper classes (containing full source code) for the API functions used to access the registry. In VFP 6, a FoxPro Foundation Class called Registry.VCX is available. In VFP 5, you'll find a sample file called Registry.PRG, containing the same code as the VFP 6 VCX, except defined in code.

By instantiating the Registry class to a variable, oRegistry, you can take advantage of the wrapper classes. In VFP 6, use the NewObject() function, which works like CreateObject(), except you specify what VCX the class is in. The VCX does not have to be opened or in the path for NewObject() to create the instance of the object:

```
oRegistry = NewObject("Registry", HOME() + "FFC\Registry")
```

In VFP 5, you have to set the procedure file to Registry.PRG, then instantiate the class:

```
SET PROCEDURE TO \vfp5\samples\classes\registry.prg ADDITIVE
oRegistry = CreateObject("Registry")
```

The Registry class is a custom class with many methods to take the pain out of using the API functions. It performs the DECLAREs for all the functions (regardless of how many functions you intend to use), and then uses properties to store many of the values passed by reference. To open a key, you pass by reference a variable that has been initialized to 0. The API sets that variable to the handle. Then, you use that handle in the RegEnumValue() function, also passing it blank variables to fill. The Registry class OpenKey method stores that handle to a property for use by the EnumKeyValues method (or any other method that relies on the opened key). This lets you concentrate on getting the information out of the registry rather than trying to manage hordes of variables.

Digging in
We've established what to look for, where to look for it, and how to find it; now let's put it together. Once a key is opened with the Registry class's OpenKey method, you can obtain a list of the key's values with EnumKeyValues.

Once you have opened a key, you can list its values to an array. EnumKeyValues takes one parameter, a blank array passed by reference. The method populates your array with a list of all the values, putting the name in column 1 and the data in column 2. While a key can contain many values, in both the keys you want to check, only one value is returned. The first position of the array contains the key name "(Default)," and the second position contains the data you're looking for. These two Registry class functions are demonstrated in **Listing 2**, which is included as CheckServer.PRG in the Developer Download files available at www.hentzenwerke.com. It's set up to take one of the Office server class names as a parameter, as in:

```
? CheckServer("Word.Application")
```

The function returns a logical indicating whether the server is installed. Note that once we find the value of the key, we need to strip off some trailing characters (see Figure 7 for an example of the string). Then we check for the existence of the file.

Listing 2. *Pass the class name of the application to find out whether the Office application is registered and on the disk. Try changing the name of Word.EXE to test it; be sure to rename the EXE back when you're done testing.*

```
LPARAMETER cServerName

LOCAL oRegistry, cClassID, cEXEName, lEXEExists, ;
      aClassIDValues, aClassIDValues, aServerNameValues

IF VERSION() = "Visual FoxPro 06"
  oRegistry = NewObject("Registry", HOME() + "FFC\Registry")
ELSE
  SET PROCEDURE TO HOME() + "samples\classes\registry.prg" ADDITIVE
  oRegistry = CreateObject("Registry")
ENDIF

lEXEExists = .F.
DECLARE aClassIDValues[1], aServerNameValues[1]

WITH oRegistry

  * Find the CLSID of the server. First, look for
  * the Class's Key.
  IF .OpenKey(cServerName + "\CLSID") = 0

    * The Class's Key is open, now enumerate its values
    .EnumKeyValues(@aClassIDValues)

    * The data portion of the first (only) value returned
    * is the CLSID. Find the LocalServer32 key for the CLSID
    IF .OpenKey("CLSID\" + aClassIDValues[1,2] + "\LocalServer32") = 0

      * Enumerate the LocalServer32 values
      .EnumKeyValues(@aServerNameValues)

      * The EXE file is stored in the first (only) data value returned.
```

```
    cEXEName = aServerNameValues[2]

    * The value that's returned may have " -Automation" or " /Automation" or
    * " /AUTOMATION" & other trailing stuff at the end. Strip it off.
    IF "AUTO" $ UPPER(cEXEName)
      cEXEName = LEFT(cEXEName, ATC("AUTO", UPPER(cEXEName)) - 2)
    ENDIF

    * Verify that the file exists
    lEXEExists = FILE(cEXEName)

   ENDIF
  ENDIF
ENDWITH

RETURN lEXEExists
```

Office versions

Since both the 97 and 2000 versions of each Office application share the same GUID, the code only verifies that one of the versions exists; it doesn't tell you which one (unless you specifically check for a specific version in the class name, as in "Word.Application.9"). VFP 6 introduces the AGetFileVersion() function, which lets you check on the version information stamped into the file. It takes two parameters—the first is an array to populate with the version information, and the second is the filename from which to extract the version information. The function returns the number of rows in the resulting array, which is 15 if it's successful. Of the 15 elements in the array, we're interested in the fourth, the file version (see Help for the other 14 items). Element 4 is a character string, which looks something like "9.0.2719".

Listing 2 pulls out the filename into the variable cEXEName; you may want to append the following code segment to the end of the code, and pass a version parameter by reference to have the CheckServer() function check the server and version.

```
* Verify that this is the path to Excel on your machine, or use the
* variable of the same name in Listing 2.
cEXEName = "C:\Program Files\Microsoft Office\Office\Excel.EXE"

nRows = AGetFileVersion(aVersionInfo, cEXEName)
cVersion = aVersionInfo[4]
```

Now it's your choice what to do with the character string, whether to convert it to a number or leave it as a character for your comparisons. Keep in mind that version 9 is Office 2000, and version 8 is Office 97.

AGetFileVersion() is only available in VFP 6. VFP 5 has a GetFileVersion() function in FoxTools. It takes the same two parameters, but their order is reversed. Also, the array must already exist and be defined to at least 12 rows and one column before you pass it by reference. Here's the code rewritten for VFP 5:

```
cExeName = "C:\Program Files\Microsoft Office\Office\Excel.EXE"
SET LIBRARY TO FOXTOOLS.FLL
DECLARE aVersionInfo[12]
```

```
= GetFileVersion(cExeName, @aVersionInfo)
cVersion = aVersionInfo[4]
```

Wrapping it up

Handling Automation errors can be challenging, but it's not impossible. It's important to include a method for dealing with Automation errors in your overall error handling strategy. Better yet, see the next chapter on wrapper classes, and incorporate your Automation error handling strategy into a wrapper class.

Chapter 15
Wrapping Up the Servers

There's so much to the Office servers that it's hard to use them. Wrapper classes make it easier, as well as protect you from changes in future versions.

Each Office server provides a great deal of power, but their greatest strength is also their biggest weakness. To use them, you need to learn them. For each application you want to automate, you have to learn a lot. Despite the promise of polymorphism, working with more than one Office server means learning lots of exceptions.

To make matters worse, every time Microsoft releases a new version of Office, things change. New properties and methods are added, properties get additional values, and most important, methods take new parameters. In recent years, Microsoft has cleaned up its act considerably, so it's unusual for the order of parameters to change anymore, and it's not likely for a parameter to be required when it used to be optional, but once in a while, even those things still happen.

Sometimes, the changes in a new version are good ones and offer improved ways of performing an Automation task. But if you've used a particular technique all over your code, you won't want to go back and change it in dozens or hundreds of places.

So how can you use Automation without having it become a full-time chore? The answer is to wrap the operations you use in Visual FoxPro classes.

Why wrap the servers?

A *wrapper class*, as the name implies, goes around another class, or sometimes around code that isn't object-oriented (for example, something like FoxTools) to give it an object structure. The goal, generally, is to provide a cleaner interface and to offer the opportunity of subclassing. (If you're familiar with design patterns, you may recognize wrapper classes as an implementation of the Adaptor pattern. To learn about patterns, a very useful tool in class design, we recommend the classic *Design Patterns: Elements of Reusable Object-Oriented Software* by Gamma, Helm, Johnson, and Vlissides.)

When dealing with Automation, wrapper classes do several things for you.

First, they let you simplify. Many methods of the Office servers expect tons of parameters. In your wrapper classes, you can hide all those extra parameters. The methods you choose to expose accept only the parameters you really need—your code can deal with the rest internally. Alternatively, you can expose a set of properties to allow the calling program to set those parameters it needs, and then use your method call to set default values for any unspecified parameters.

Second, wrapper classes protect you from Microsoft's changes. If the order of parameters to a server method does change, you only have to fix it in one place—your wrapper class—not everywhere you've used that method.

Third, wrapper classes let you centralize error handling. For example, rather than writing all your application code to worry about whether you have an instance of the server available, your application code calls on methods of your wrapper class and those methods worry about whether the server is available. In the same way, your wrapper class methods can worry about whether there's an open document and what to do if a call to the server fails.

Structuring the wrapper classes

The rest of this chapter explores a set of wrapper classes for the Office servers. At the top of the class hierarchy, there's an abstract class called cusWrapServer based on the Visual FoxPro Custom class. It has several custom properties and methods, the details of which are explored in the following sections. (In fact, while Custom is technically the right class for this, since the wrapper classes don't need the container capabilities of Custom, consider starting with a simpler class like Line that doesn't use as many resources as Custom.)

The cusWrapServer class can be subclassed to create individual wrapper classes for Word, Excel, and PowerPoint (and probably for some other Automation servers, as well). Outlook's object model is so different from the other Office servers that this wrapper class structure isn't appropriate for it, but of course, you can develop a wrapper class for Outlook.

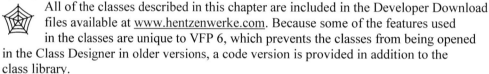 All of the classes described in this chapter are included in the Developer Download files available at www.hentzenwerke.com. Because some of the features used in the classes are unique to VFP 6, which prevents the classes from being opened in the Class Designer in older versions, a code version is provided in addition to the class library.

Fundamental operations

No matter which server you're dealing with, there are certain operations you need: opening the server, closing the server, opening and closing a document, checking whether the server is open, checking whether you have a document to work with, and so forth. Methods and properties to handle these operations are added to cusWrapServer, though some of the methods are abstract because they require server-specific code. **Table 1** shows the custom properties of cusWrapServer. **Table 2** shows the custom methods of the class.

Table 1. Properties of cusWrapServer. These properties are added to the abstract wrapper class.

Property	Type	Description
cServerName	Character	The name of the Automation server, for example, "Word.Application".
lOpenAsNeeded	Logical	Indicates whether to open the server when a method is called that requires its use. If this is .F., some methods may fail.
oDocument	Object	Object reference to the active document. "Document" here is used in the broad sense to refer to the primary type of object used by the application.
oServer	Object	Object reference to the server.

Table 2. *Methods of cusWrapServer. These custom methods are added to the abstract class so they're available to all wrapper classes. Many of them are abstract at this level; that is, the code to be executed must be specified in subclasses.*

Method	Description
CloseDocument	Close a document of the primary type for the server. Abstract.
CloseServer	Close the server instance. Abstract.
HideServer	Make the server instance invisible. Abstract
IsDocOpen	Indicates whether there's a document open. Abstract.
IsServerOpen	Indicates whether there's an instance of the server available. Abstract.
NewDocument	Creates a new document of the primary type for the server. Abstract.
oDocument_Access	Returns a reference to the active document.
OpenDocument	Opens a document of the primary type for the server.
OpenServer	Opens an instance of the server.
OpenServerDocument	Server-specific portion of OpenDocument. Handles server-specific details. Abstract.
SaveDocument	Saves a document of the primary type for the server.
ShowServer	Makes the server visible. Abstract.
TellUser	Displays a message to the user.
zReadme	Documentation method.

Talking to the user

All communication with the user is sent through a single method, TellUser. This provides centralized message services for the wrapper class. In the version of cusWrapServer provided, TellUser is quite simple (and is really aimed more at the developers using the wrapper class than at end users). It uses either a WAIT WINDOW or a basic message box and doesn't accept any input. While this version is fine for simple testing, you'll probably want to replace this method with one that ties into the message services already in use in your applications.

```
* cusWrapServer.TellUser
* Pass a message along to the user. By sending all messages through this
* method, it's easy to change the mechanism used for messages.
* This is just a very basic message handler.

LPARAMETER cMessageText, lDontWait

IF SYS(2335) = 1 ; && Not in unattended mode
   AND This.Application.StartMode = 0  && Normal VFP interactive session.

   IF lDontWait
      WAIT WINDOW cMessageText NOWAIT
   ELSE
      MessageBox( cMessageText )
   ENDIF

ELSE  && Can't generate a UI dialog
  ERROR cMessageText  && generates error 1098
  * You may prefer to use COMReturnError() here instead.
ENDIF


RETURN
```

Because every method that communicates with the user calls on TellUser, it would be quite easy to substitute a more sophisticated messaging mechanism. One obvious change is to offer the option of "silent messaging," returning error codes rather than displaying messages.

Creating a server instance

Probably the hardest, most error-prone part of Automation is getting a server started. The server might be missing or not registered, or Windows may be unable to start it for some reason. To deal with all these possibilities, cusWrapServer uses a separate class whose sole purpose is to instantiate an Automation server. This class, called cusOpenServer, is also derived from Custom. Although the methods in cusOpenServer could be included in cusWrapServer, it makes sense to keep them in a separate class because many processes need to open an Automation server. Rather than forcing them all to load the entire abstract wrapper class, which has many methods unrelated to the task of opening a server, they can use just cusOpenServer.

cusOpenServer has two custom properties and two custom methods. The cServerName property holds the name of the server to be instantiated; the oServer property holds the reference to the newly-created server. The OpenServer method does the actual work of creating the server. The zReadMe method of the class is a documentation method (as in all the classes presented here).

The Init method of cusOpenServer accepts two parameters, the name of the server to instantiate and a logical value indicating whether to instantiate it right away or wait until OpenServer is called explicitly. It then uses the Registry class (provided as a VCX with VFP 6 and as a PRG with VFP 5) to make sure the server is registered. If not, Init returns .F., which prevents this object (cusOpenServer) from being created. Here's the code for cusOpenServer.Init:

```
* cusOpenServer.Init
* Check whether the specified server name is valid and,
* if the user specified, create the server
LPARAMETERS cServerName, lCreateAtInit

LOCAL oRegistry

IF VarType(cServerName) = "C"
   * Check to see if this is a valid server name
   * In development/testing, you may need to add the
   * Registry.VCX from HOME()+"\FFC\" to your path
   oRegistry = NewObject("Registry","Registry")
   IF oRegistry.IsKey(cServerName)
      This.cServerName = cServerName
   ELSE
      RETURN .F.
   ENDIF
   RELEASE oRegistry
ELSE
   * No point in creating this object
   RETURN .F.
ENDIF

IF VarType(lCreateAtInit) = "L" AND lCreateAtInit
   This.OpenServer()
```

```
ENDIF

RETURN
```

The OpenServer method of cusOpenServer instantiates the server and preserves the reference. Here's the code:

```
* cusOpenServer.OpenServer
* Open the server specified by This.cServerName
* Store the new instance to This.oServer

IF VARTYPE(This.cServerName) = "C"
   This.oServer = CreateObject(This.cServerName)
ENDIF

RETURN This.oServer
```

There are actually some other problems that can occur when you attempt to instantiate the server. They're discussed in Chapter 14, "Handling Automation Errors." In an attempt to keep this code easy to read, we haven't dealt with all of them here. If you use this class as a basis for your own wrapper class, be sure to integrate the code from Chapter 14 into this Init method.

The OpenServer method of cusWrapServer instantiates cusOpenServer, passing .F. for the lCreateAtInit parameter. If cusOpenServer is successfully instantiated, OpenServer retrieves the reference to the new server and stores it in the oServer property. If not, the user is informed that the server couldn't be started.

```
* cusWrapServer.OpenServer
* Create an instance of the Automation server
* and store a reference to it in This.oServer

LOCAL oGetServ

IF EMPTY(This.cServerName)
   This.TellUser("No server specified")
   RETURN .F.
ENDIF

oGetServ = NewObject("cusOpenServer","Automation","",This.cServerName,.F.)
IF VarType(oGetServ) = "O"
   This.oServer = oGetServ.OpenServer()
   IF VarType(This.oServer)<>"O"
      This.TellUser("Can't create automation server")
      RETURN .F.
   ENDIF
ENDIF

RETURN
```

Closing the server

Unlike creating instances of servers, the method for shutting down the different servers varies. In particular, you need to take different actions to be sure that the user doesn't see a dialog when you attempt to close the server application. So, the CloseServer method is left empty (abstract) at the cusWrapServer level and must be coded in each concrete subclass.

However, we want to be sure not to leave server applications running when we shut down our wrapper class. So, the Destroy method contains this code:

```
* cusWrapServer.Destroy
* Close the server on the way out, if necessary,
* so we don't leave it running in the background.

IF This.IsServerOpen()
   This.CloseServer()
ENDIF

RETURN
```

Opening a document

The term "document" in Windows is used to mean the primary type of file on which an application operates. In Excel, it's a workbook, and in PowerPoint, it's a presentation. Word confuses the issue, because its primary file type is also called a document. The remainder of this chapter uses the term "document" in the Windows sense, rather than meaning a Word file.

Much of what you need to do to open a document is the same regardless of the application. You need to make sure the user specified a document to open, make sure the document exists, and make sure the server is open or, if appropriate, open the server. However, the actual process of opening a document varies for the individual servers. The wrapper class divides the code into these two parts. The OpenDocument method does everything it can, then calls the OpenServerDocument method, which is coded at the subclass level. Here's the code for OpenDocument:

```
* cusWrapServer.OpenDocument
* Open a specified document and make it the active document.
* Return a logical value indicating whether the document
* was successfully opened.

LPARAMETER cDocument
   * cDocument = name of document to be opened including FULL PATH

LOCAL lIsServerOpen, lSuccess

* Check whether parameter was passed and is valid
IF VarType(cDocument)<>"C"
   This.TellUser("Must specify document to open")
   RETURN .F.
ENDIF

IF NOT FILE(cDocument)
   This.TellUser("Can't find " + cDocument)
   RETURN .F.
ENDIF

* Make sure server is open
lIsServerOpen = This.IsServerOpen()
```

```
DO CASE
CASE NOT lIsServerOpen AND NOT This.lOpenAsNeeded
   This.TellUser("Program is not available")
   RETURN .F.

CASE NOT lIsServerOpen
   * Open server
   This.OpenServer()

OTHERWISE
   * Server is open and all is well
ENDCASE

* Attempt to open document
* Call server specified method
lSuccess = This.OpenServerDocument( cDocument )

RETURN lSuccess
```

Saving a document

The techniques for saving documents are similar enough in the Office servers that the
SaveDocument method can be defined in the abstract class. This method accepts two
parameters, an object reference to the document to be saved and the filename, including the full
path, where it's to be saved. Both parameters are optional. If the document reference is omitted,
the active document is saved. If the filename is omitted, the file is re-saved to its current
location. As written, the method overwrites existing files without informing the user.

```
* cusWrapServer.SaveDocument
* Save the specified document. If a filename is passed,
* save it with that filename. Otherwise, use the name it
* already has. If it's a new document and no name is
* specified, fail.
* DOES NOT CHECK FOR OVERWRITE OF FILE

* If no document is passed, use the active document.

LPARAMETERS oDocument, cFileName

LOCAL lReturn, cOldCentury


IF VarType(oDocument) <> "O"
   oDocument = This.oDocument
ENDIF

DO CASE
CASE IsNull(oDocument)
   * No document to save
   * Tell the user and get out
   This.TellUser("No document to save.")
   lReturn = .F.

CASE VarType(cFileName) = "C"
   * Just save it with the specified name
```

```
   lReturn  = .T.
   oDocument.SaveAs( cFileName )
   tFDateTime = This.GetFileDateTime( cFileName)
   IF NOT FILE(cFileName) OR NOT (tFDateTime + 1 > DATETIME())
      * If file doesn't exist or wasn't updated in the last second
      This.TellUser("Couldn't save document as " + cFileName)
      lReturn = .F.
   ENDIF

CASE VarType(cFileName) = "L" AND NOT (oDocument.Name == oDocument.FullName)

   * No name, but previously saved, so save with current name
   lReturn = .T.
   oDocument.Save()

   cFileName = oDocument.FullName
   tFDateTime = This.GetFileDateTime( cFileName)
   IF NOT (tFDateTime + 1 > DATETIME())
      * If file wasn't updated in the last second
      This.TellUser("Couldn't save document")
      lReturn = .F.
   ENDIF

OTHERWISE
   This.TellUser("Specify filename")
   lReturn = .F.

ENDCASE


RETURN lReturn
```

This method works for Word and PowerPoint. Excel doesn't let you use SaveAs to overwrite an existing file without prompting the user, so the Excel-specific subclass contains its own version of SaveDocument that works around this annoyance.

The GetFileDateTime method used here returns the time the file was last saved as a datetime value. We were surprised to have to resort to this round-about method of checking for a successful save, but surprisingly, the Save and SaveAs methods don't return a value to indicate whether they were able to save the file. In a network situation, this test can fail even though the file was saved if the clock on the server is out of synch with the clock on the local machine.

Other basic operations

Although there are other methods that are clearly needed for every server, such as printing or closing the server application, they have to be defined in subclasses because they depend on specific properties and methods of the servers, or the way of doing them is too different from one server to the next.

Creating subclasses

The next step in creating wrapper classes is to create concrete subclasses of cusWrapServer. We want one subclass for each application server to be wrapped. For Office, we'll look at three subclasses: cusWord, cusExcel, and cusPowerPoint. All three inherit the custom properties and methods of cusWrapServer, as well as the code added at the abstract level.

At the subclass level, we can deal with the peculiarities of the individual products, as well as the normal differences among them. The first step is to finish defining the basic operations.

Each of the subclasses has an include file that #DEFINEs appropriate constants. Unlike other code in this book, the code that follows does not show constant definitions each time a constant is used.

The Excel and PowerPoint classes each have one additional property to add in basic operations. It's called lShouldBeVisible, and it tracks the visibility of the server. It's used in figuring out whether there's a reference to a server or not. See the section "Checking the server" later in this chapter.

Closing servers

The biggest issue in shutting down Automation servers is keeping them from displaying any messages to the user because files are unsaved. There are various ways to solve the problem—the versions presented here close the files without saving them. Other alternatives are to automatically save all open documents or let you pass a parameter to CloseServer to decide whether to save open documents or prompt the user for each open document, but do it on the VFP side rather than the server side.

A couple of different approaches are needed in order to shut down without saving open documents. Word's is the easiest—Quit takes a parameter that tells it to close without saving changes. Here's the CloseServer method for the cusWord class:

```
* cusWord.CloseServer
* Close the Word Automation server.

LOCAL lReturn

IF This.IsServerOpen()
   This.oServer.Quit( wdDoNotSaveChanges )
   This.oServer = .NULL.
   This.oDocument = .NULL.
   lReturn = .T.
ELSE
*    Could tell user, but why?
*    This.TellUser("Word is not open")
   lReturn = .F.
ENDIF

RETURN lReturn
```

Excel and PowerPoint both make you do it the hard way—you have to go through all the open documents and close them before you can call Quit. Here's the code for Excel's CloseServer method. PowerPoint's is pretty much the same—just mentally substitute Presentation wherever you see Workbook.

```
* cusExcel.CloseServer
* Close the Excel Automation server.
```

```
LOCAL lReturn, oWorkbook

IF This.IsServerOpen()
   * Close open workbooks first
   FOR EACH oWorkbook IN This.oServer.Workbooks
      This.CloseDocument( oWorkbook.Name )
   ENDFOR
   This.oServer.Quit()
   This.oServer = .NULL.
   This.oDocument = .NULL.
   This.lShouldBeVisible = .F.
   lReturn = .T.
ELSE
*    Could tell user, but why?
*    This.TellUser("Excel is not open")
   lReturn = .F.
ENDIF

RETURN lReturn
```

Note the use of the CloseDocument method here. Without that call, CloseServer would be much longer and more complex—among other things, CloseDocument is hiding the details of closing workbooks without saving changes or prompting the user.

Opening a document, part 2

The OpenDocument method (described in "Opening a document" earlier in this chapter) handles the common aspects of getting a specified document. It then calls the OpenServerDocument method to perform the server-specific portion of the task. Each subclass has code in that method. The code is pretty similar among the three classes, differing primarily in the names of the objects it deals with. Here's the PowerPoint version:

```
* cusPowerPoint.OpenServerDocument
* This method performs the PowerPoint-specific portion
* of opening a document. It's called by OpenDocument
* after that method checks for a valid server,
* a valid filename, and so forth.

LPARAMETER cDocument

* Attempt to open document
This.oDocument = This.oServer.Presentations.Open(cDocument)
IF UPPER(This.oDocument.FullName) <> UPPER(cDocument)
   This.TellUser("Unable to open " + cDocument)
   RETURN .F.
ENDIF

RETURN .T.
```

Closing a document

When we're ready to close a document, all kinds of questions present themselves. Which document should we close? Has the document been saved? Should it be saved? The Close methods of the Office servers have a different willingness to deal with unsaved changes without prompting the user. Regardless of the application's willingness, however, the goal of our CloseDocument methods is to avoid all prompts and carry out the user's wishes.

The CloseDocument methods we've implemented accept three parameters, all optional. The first is the name of the document to be closed; if more than one open document could have the same name, the path should be included. The second parameter is logical and indicates whether the document is to be saved before closing it; if not, changes are discarded. The third parameter is the filename, including path, to give the document when it's saved. (You can pass the third parameter to save an existing document to a new location before closing it.)

As with many of the methods defined at this level, much of the difference between the classes is simply that you're dealing with different objects. Here's the Word version of CloseDocument:

```
* cusWord.CloseDocument
* Close a document in Word. If a document name is passed,
* close that one; otherwise, close the active document.
* Save the document before closing if lSaveFirst is .t.

LPARAMETERS cDocument, lSaveFirst, cFileName
   * cDocument = name of document to close. Include path if more than one
   *             document could have the same stem.
   * lSaveFirst = save document before closing?
   * cFileName = filename to assign on save

LOCAL oDocToClose && the document to be closed

* Check parameters
IF NOT INLIST(VarType(cDocument), "C", "L")
   This.TellUser("Specify document name or leave empty for active document")
   RETURN .F.
ENDIF

IF VarType(lSaveFirst)<>"L"
   This.TellUser("Specify .T. to save before closing; " + ;
                 ".F. or omit to close without saving")
   RETURN .F.
ENDIF

* Make sure Word is open and that there's at least one document.
IF NOT This.IsServerOpen()
   This.TellUser("Word is not available.")
   RETURN .F.
ENDIF

IF NOT This.IsDocOpen()
   This.TellUser("No documents open.")
   RETURN .F.
ENDIF

* Did the user specify a document?
IF VarType(cDocument) = "C"
   * Check for a matching document - must use TYPE() here instead of
   * VARTYPE() to avoid having the expression evaluated.
   IF TYPE("This.oServer.Documents[cDocument]") = "O"
      oDocToClose = This.oServer.Documents[cDocument]
   ELSE
```

```
      This.TellUser(cDocument + " is not open.")
      RETURN .F.
   ENDIF
ELSE
   oDocToClose = This.oDocument
ENDIF

lSuccess = .T.
IF lSaveFirst
   lSuccess = This.SaveDocument( oDocToClose, cFileName)
ENDIF

IF lSuccess
   * Don't close if requested save failed
   oDocToClose.Close(wdDoNotSaveChanges)
ENDIF

RETURN lSuccess
```

 The Excel and PowerPoint versions are quite similar; for the details, see the Developer Download files available at www.hentzenwerke.com.

Creating new documents

One of the most common operations is creating a new document of whatever type the server uses. Like the final steps in opening a document, this has to be done in the subclasses because the details depend on the object hierarchy.

 Both Word and Excel let you specify a template on which to base the new document, so the methods in those subclasses accept a single, optional, parameter containing the name of the template to use. If it's omitted, the default template is used. The code for the NewDocument method for those two classes is complex because it searches for the specified template to be sure it's available before attempting to create the new document. To do so, it uses a class called cusDirectoryHandler from a library named Utilities.VCX (which is included in the Developer Download files available at www.hentzenwerke.com). Here's the Excel version:

```
* cusExcel.NewDocument
* Create a new Excel workbook. Use a template if specified.
LPARAMETERS cTemplate
   * cTemplate - the name of a template for the new workbook

LOCAL lFoundIt, cTemplatePath, oDirectoryHandler, cPath
LOCAL lSuccess, lIsServerOpen
   * lFoundIt = was the specified template found somewhere?
   * cTemplatePath = path to directory specified by Excel for templates
   * oDirectoryHandler = object reference to directory handling object
   * cPath = path to test for template
   * lSuccess = return value indicating whether new document was created
   * lIsServerOpen = is Excel open already?

* Check parameter
IF NOT INLIST(VarType(cTemplate), "C", "L")
   This.TellUser("Specify template name or omit to use default template")
   RETURN .F.
```

```
ENDIF

* Make sure Excel is open
lIsServerOpen = This.IsServerOpen()

DO CASE
CASE NOT lIsServerOpen AND NOT This.lOpenAsNeeded
   This.TellUser("Excel is not available")
   RETURN .F.

CASE NOT lIsServerOpen
   * Open Excel
   This.OpenServer()

OTHERWISE
   * Excel is open and all is well
ENDCASE

IF EMPTY(cTemplate)
   * If no template was specified, use the default template
   * and set the flag that says we're done.

   This.oDocument = This.oServer.Workbooks.Add()
   lSuccess = .T.
ELSE
   * Does the specified template exist?
   * There are several possibilities.
   *    1) If the caller provided a complete path and file,
   *       check it and no more.
   *    2) The caller provided a relative path and file.
   *       We need to clean it up and check it.
   *    3) The caller provided just a filename. We need to
   *       check for it in the appropriate template
   *       directories of Excel.
   * The first two can be combined.

   IF NOT EMPTY(JustPath(cTemplate))
      * Some path was provided, so we can just go there.
      cTemplate = FULLPATH(cTemplate)
      lFoundIt = FILE(cTemplate)

   ELSE
      * First, try the user's template directory (and its subdirectories)
      oDirectoryHandler = NewObject("cusDirectoryHandler","Utilities")
      cTemplatePath = This.oServer.TemplatesPath
      IF EMPTY(cTemplatePath)
         lFoundIt = .F.
      ELSE
         IF FILE(ForcePath(cTemplate, cTemplatePath))
            lFoundIt = .T.
            cTemplate=ForcePath(cTemplate, cTemplatePath)
         ELSE
            * Need to go down through directory tree below here
            nDirectoryCount = ;
               oDirectoryHandler.BuildDirectoryTree(cTemplatePath)
            nDir = 1
            DO WHILE NOT lFoundIt AND nDir <= nDirectoryCount
```

```
            cPath = oDirectoryHandler.GetDirectory(nDir)
            IF FILE(ForcePath(cTemplate, cPath))
                lFoundIt = .T.
                cTemplate = ForcePath(cTemplate, cPath)
            ENDIF
            nDir = nDir + 1
        ENDDO
        oDirectoryHandler.ClearDirectoryTree()
    ENDIF


    * If still not found, try group template path
    IF NOT lFoundIt
        cTemplatePath = This.oServer.NetworkTemplatesPath
        IF EMPTY(cTemplatePath)
            lFoundIt = .F.
        ELSE
            IF FILE(ForcePath(cTemplate, cTemplatePath))
                lFoundIt = .T.
                cTemplate=ForcePath(cTemplate, cTemplatePath)
            ELSE
                * Need to go down through directory tree below here
                nDirectoryCount = ;
                    oDirectoryHandler.BuildDirectoryTree(cTemplatePath)
                nDir = 1
                DO WHILE NOT lFoundIt AND nDir <= nDirectoryCount
                    cPath = oDirectoryHandler.GetDirectory(nDir)
                    IF FILE(ForcePath(cTemplate, cPath))
                        lFoundIt = .T.
                        cTemplate = ForcePath(cTemplate, cPath)
                    ENDIF
                    nDir = nDir + 1
                ENDDO
            ENDIF


        ENDIF
      ENDIF
    ENDIF

    * Release the directory handler. We're done with it.
    RELEASE oDirectoryHandler
ENDIF

* So, did we find the template somewhere?
IF lFoundIt
    * Create the new document
    This.oDocument = This.oServer.Workbooks.Add( cTemplate )
    lSuccess = .T.
ELSE
    This.TellUser("Can't find specified template")
    lSuccess = .F.
ENDIF

ENDIF

RETURN lSuccess
```

The Word version of NewDocument is very similar to the one shown here. The PowerPoint version is much simpler because PowerPoint doesn't offer the ability to specify a template, so it simply creates a new presentation and returns a success indicator.

Checking the server

Many of the wrapper's methods need to make sure that the server is available. The IsServerOpen method checks the server's status and returns .T. if it's open and .F. if it's not.

Two very different strategies are needed for testing the server's status because Word behaves quite differently from Excel and PowerPoint on shut down. When Word closes either by calling the Quit method or because a user shuts it down interactively, it disappears from the Task Manager and references to the Word application object generate errors. So, to determine whether the oServer property refers to a valid Word instance, we can use this code:

```
* cusWord.IsServerOpen
* Check whether Word is open


RETURN VarType(This.oServer)<>"O" OR TYPE("This.oServer.Name")<>"C"
```

PowerPoint and Excel, however, keep the Application object available until every reference to them is destroyed. In addition, even though the server has been closed, you can continue to refer to its properties and methods through the reference variable (the oServer property, in this case) without getting an error. So another strategy is called for.

Our approach has two parts. First, the CloseServer method sets oServer to .NULL. after issuing Quit, so that the server application actually closes. That handles cases where the server is closed through the wrapper class. The harder case is the one where a user closes the application interactively. To deal with that situation, the lShouldBeVisible property tracks the expected visibility of the server. It's set to .F. when the server is opened, and then set to match the server's visibility in the ShowServer and HideServer methods (see "Displaying the server" later in this chapter). When the user closes the server through the interface, the server's Visible property changes, but lShouldBeVisible does not. So IsServerOpen can check for a mismatch between those two properties. The code for Excel and PowerPoint is slightly different, due to the way they handle logical values, but the idea is identical. Here's the Excel version:

```
* cusExcel.IsServerOpen
* Check whether server is open.
* This method compares the custom lShouldBeVisible property to
* the server's own Visible property. If they match, the
* server is open. If not, then a user must have closed
* the server interactively. The reason this technique is needed
* is that Excel keeps the server in memory
* even after it's shut down.

LOCAL lReturn

IF IsNull(This.oServer)
   * No instantiated server
   lReturn = .F.
ELSE
   * Compare actual Visible value to tracked visibility
```

```
   IF This.oServer.Visible = This.lShouldBeVisible
      * They match, so the server is open and good
      lReturn = .T.
   ELSE
      * Visibility doesn't match. User must have shut server down
      lReturn = .F.
   ENDIF
ENDIF

RETURN lReturn
```

In order to make this work, one additional step is needed in the OpenServer method—the lShouldBeVisible property must be set to .F. So, for the Excel and PowerPoint subclasses, OpenServer contains this code:

```
* cusExcel.OpenServer/cusPowerPoint.OpenServer
DoDefault()

* If open of server was successful,
* set tracked visibility.
IF NOT IsNull(This.oServer)
   This.lShouldBeVisible = .F.
ENDIF
```

Checking open documents

Just as we need to know whether there's a reference to a server, many methods need to know whether there's a document open. The IsDocOpen method serves that purpose. It's coded at the subclass level because of differences in the object hierarchy, but is essentially identical in each case. Here's the PowerPoint version:

```
* cusPowerPoint.IsDocOpen
* Check whether there's a presentation open in PowerPoint.
* This method should always be preceded by a call to IsServerOpen

RETURN This.oServer.Presentations.Count > 1
```

Keeping track of the active document

A number of the methods in the wrapper class operate on the active document (whether "document" means workbook, presentation, or document for the server). It's important that the wrapper class always have a way to reference the server's active document, whichever type it is. Because the name of the server's property for that object varies depending on which server you're using, having to refer to that server property each time you need it is inconvenient.

Instead of accessing the active document through the server's property, cusWrapper has an oDocument property. To keep it up-to-date, that property's Access method contains code at the subclass level. (Since Access methods were introduced in VFP 6, this method does not easily translate to VFP 5. If you're using that version, you must keep track of the active document yourself. Though cumbersome, doing so is no problem unless the user is also allowed to interact with the Automation server instance.)

The code for oDocument_Access is quite similar for each subclass, varying only in which server property it references. Here's the Excel version of oDocument_Access:

```
* oDocument_Access
* Make sure the property points to the currently active document.
IF This.IsServerOpen() AND This.IsDocOpen()
   This.oDocument = This.oServer.ActiveWorkbook
ELSE
   This.oDocument = .NULL.
ENDIF

RETURN This.oDocument
```

> *PowerPoint only recognizes active objects if PowerPoint itself is visible, so code analogous to that shown here fails when PowerPoint.Visible = .F. This annoying little difference can really impact your code. See "Wrapping PowerPoint—standardizing text" later in this chapter for more information.*

Displaying the server

The ShowServer and HideServer methods let you display and hide the server. There are small variations between the Excel and Word versions of the two, and PowerPoint's version of ShowServer is identical to Excel's. However, when it comes to HideServer and PowerPoint, there's a big difference. That's because once you make PowerPoint visible, you can't hide it again. PowerPoint doesn't allow that.

The only difference between the Word and Excel versions of these methods is that the Excel version tracks the custom lShouldBeVisible property that it needs for the IsServerOpen method. Here are the Excel versions of both methods:

```
* cusExcel.ShowServer
* Show the Excel Automation session.

LOCAL lReturn
   * lReturn = return value - .T. if Excel is open; .F. otherwise

* Is Excel open?
IF This.IsServerOpen()
   This.oServer.Visible = .T.
   This.lShouldBeVisible = .T.
   lReturn = .T.
ELSE
   lReturn = .F.
ENDIF

RETURN lReturn

* cusExcel.HideServer
* Hide the Excel Automation session.

* Is Excel open?
IF This.IsServerOpen()
```

```
   This.oServer.Visible = .F.
   This.lShouldBeVisible = .F.
ENDIF

RETURN
```

Using the fundamental operations

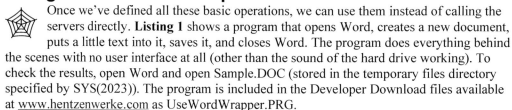 Once we've defined all these basic operations, we can use them instead of calling the servers directly. **Listing 1** shows a program that opens Word, creates a new document, puts a little text into it, saves it, and closes Word. The program does everything behind the scenes with no user interface at all (other than the sound of the hard drive working). To check the results, open Word and open Sample.DOC (stored in the temporary files directory specified by SYS(2023)). The program is included in the Developer Download files available at www.hentzenwerke.com as UseWordWrapper.PRG.

Listing 1. Using a wrapper class. This program uses the Word wrapper class to open Word, create a document, and save it. The only code in this program that talks directly to Word is the two lines that actually put text in the document. Everything else goes through the wrapper class.

```
* Demonstrate the Word wrapper class
#DEFINE CR CHR(13)

LOCAL oWord

* Open Word
oWord = NewObject("cusWord","automation")

WITH oWord
   .OpenServer()

   IF NOT .IsServerOpen()
      WAIT WINDOW "Couldn't open Word."
      RETURN .F.
   ENDIF

   * Create a document
   .NewDocument()

   * Check whether document is open
   IF .IsDocOpen()

      * Put some text in the new document
      WITH .oDocument.Range()
         .InsertAfter("This is our new Word document." + CR)
         .InsertAfter("Only these lines directly reference Word methods." + CR)
      ENDWITH

      * Save the new document
      .SaveDocument(,SYS(2023) + "\sample.doc")

   ELSE
      WAIT WINDOW "Couldn't create new document"
```

```
    ENDIF

    * Close Word
    .CloseServer()
ENDWITH

RETURN
```

Because OpenServer and NewDocument both return logical values to indicate success or failure, this code could actually be condensed somewhat. The whole process of opening the server and creating a new document could be reduced to a single line:

```
IF .OpenServer() and .NewDocument()
```

We didn't do it that way, for two reasons. First, we wanted to demonstrate more of the methods. In fact, in a longer example, you're likely to use IsServerOpen and, especially, IsDocOpen quite a bit. Second, combining those two methods into one line prevents you from providing specific error messages. All you know is that the process failed. Since the wrapper class generates error messages, that may be sufficient. (In fact, if your version of the wrapper class provides messages from TellUser, you may not want to include any error messages in the program that uses the class.)

Notice that the oWord variable here refers not to the Word Automation object itself as in the examples in previous chapters, but to the cusWord wrapper object.

While this example doesn't seem that much shorter than those in earlier chapters, realize that the big difference is that this version includes a lot of error handling behind the scenes.

Adding server-specific operations

So far, all the methods we've defined have been common to all the servers. While they do make it easier to write Automation code, they're just the beginning. The next step is to wrap the operations specific to the individual servers.

But the Office servers have dozens of methods. How do you know which ones to wrap? That's easy—wrap the ones you use. As you write Automation code, pay attention. Keep in mind that the goal of wrapping the servers is to make your life simpler. Think in terms of what you're trying to accomplish when you use a particular method of the server.

The second time you find yourself performing a particular task, it's time to put a wrapper on it. But just because you've wrapped it, don't assume you're done with it. As you see how you really use it, you'll probably have to clean it up. Among the questions you need to ask are what parameters it ought to have, whether the wrapper class needs some properties to support this method, whether the method really needs to be broken into multiple methods, and whether several of the server's methods should be grouped into a single wrapper method because you're always going to use them together. What you want to end up with is a set of methods with meaningful names and not too many parameters, each of which accomplishes a single task, but which you can put together to perform complex operations.

To make your job a little bit harder, it turns out that your wrapper classes will probably need to work differently for different applications. We hinted at that earlier when we talked about the CloseServer method—in some applications, it's appropriate to close all open documents without saving them; in others, you need to save every open document; and in others, the user has to make that choice. It's the same way with other server-specific tasks—both the set of operations you need and the way they work vary based on what you're trying to accomplish.

Fortunately, in an object-oriented environment like VFP, it's easy to deal with such variations. Subclassing provides one technique for doing so, though it can lead to maintenance headaches, if you need too many variations. An alternative is to use properties and parameters to handle application-specific needs. If a particular operation needs to be implemented in several very different ways, you may even want to use a separate class to handle it. Then, the server-specific subclass can determine the appropriate implementation at run-time and instantiate the class it needs. (This is the Strategy pattern—for details, see *Design Patterns: Elements of Reusable Object-Oriented Software* by Gamma, Helm, Johnson, and Vlissides.)

To get you started, here are wrapper methods for one common operation in each of the Office servers.

Wrapping Word—from table to table

As we discussed in Chapter 5, "Intermediate Word," Word tables are handy for displaying FoxPro data. One of the things you're most likely to do when sending VFP data to Word is convert a VFP cursor of some sort into a Word table. The method here, DBFToTable, takes the data in a workarea, whether it represents a cursor, table, or view, and creates and populates a Word table containing that data. The method accepts four parameters, all optional: the range where the table is to be placed, the alias for the cursor, and two logical flags. The first flag indicates whether to leave an empty row at the top of the table for headings, and the second determines whether the AutoFit method is used to resize the table once it's been filled. Here's the code:

```
* cusWord.DBFToTable
* This method puts the data in a cursor, view, or table
* into a Word table. It creates one table row per record
* with one column for each field. Returns a reference to
* newly created table; .null. if the table can't be
* created

LPARAMETERS oRange, cAlias, lAddHeader, lAutoFit
    * oRange - where to put the new table. If omitted,
    *          add at current insertion point.
    * cAlias - the alias for the workarea containing
    *          the cursor/view/table. If omitted,
    *          use current workarea.
    * lAddHeader - include a header row in the table?
    * lAutoFit - automatically resize columns?

LOCAL nOldSelect, nRows, nCols, oTable, nCurRow, nCol, nActualCol
    * nOldSelect = workarea selected when called
    * nRows = number of rows to add
    * nCols = number of columns to add
    * oTable = holds a reference to the newly created table
    * nCurRow = the current row receiving data
    * nCol = column counter
    * nActualCol = indicates which column to insert into table

* Check parameters
```

```
nOldSelect = SELECT()
IF EMPTY( cAlias )
   cAlias = ALIAS()
   IF EMPTY( cAlias )
      This.TellUser("Must specify cursor")
      RETURN .NULL.
   ENDIF
ELSE
   IF USED( cAlias )
      SELECT (cAlias)
   ELSE
      This.TellUser("No such cursor is in use")
      RETURN .NULL.
   ENDIF
ENDIF

IF VarType( lAddHeader ) <> "L"
   This.TellUser("Use a logical value to indicate whether or not " + ;
                 "to add a header row")
   SELECT (nOldSelect)
   RETURN .NULL.
ENDIF

IF VarType( lAutoFit ) <> "L"
   This.TellUser("Use a logical value to indicate whether or not " + ;
                 "to resize columns")
   SELECT (nOldSelect)
   RETURN .NULL.
ENDIF

* Now make sure there's a document.
IF NOT (This.IsServerOpen() AND This.IsDocOpen())
   This.TellUser("Word must be open with a document ready.")
   SELECT (nOldSelect)
   RETURN .NULL.
ENDIF

* Check oRange parameter
IF VarType( oRange ) <> "O"
   oRange = This.oServer.Selection.Range()
ENDIF

* Ready to go. Add the table at the current insertion point
WITH This.oDocument
   nRows = RECCOUNT()
   IF lAddHeader
      nRows = nRows + 1
   ENDIF

   * Determine the number of columns to create.
   * Omit any General fields
   nColumns = 0
   FOR nCol = 1 TO FCOUNT()
      IF TYPE(FIELD(nCol)) <> "G"
         nColumns = nColumns + 1
      ENDIF
   ENDFOR
   oTable = .Tables.Add(oRange,nRows,nColumns)
ENDWITH
```

```
WITH oTable
   IF lAddHeader
      * Set the first row as a header row to be repeated on subsequent pages
      .Rows(1).HeadingFormat = .T.
      nCurRow = 2
   ELSE
      nCurRow = 1
   ENDIF

   * Now add data to rows, skipping any general fields
   SCAN
      nActualCol = 1
      FOR nCol = 1 TO .Columns.Count
         * Eliminate general fields
         DO WHILE TYPE(FIELD(nActualCol)) = "G"
            nActualCol = nActualCol + 1
         ENDDO

         .Cell[ nCurRow, nCol ].Range.InsertAfter( ;
            TRANSFORM(EVAL(FIELD(nActualCol))))
         nActualCol = nActualCol + 1
      ENDFOR

      nCurRow = nCurRow + 1
   ENDSCAN

   IF lAutoFit
      .Columns.AutoFit()
   ENDIF

ENDWITH

RETURN oTable
```

The code itself is pretty straightforward. What makes the method worth writing is that it takes a task we're likely to perform pretty frequently and turns it into a single call.

Listing 2 is another program that uses the Word wrapper class. Like the program in Listing 1, it creates an Automation server, and opens a new document. Then, it creates a cursor based on the Supplier table from TasTrade, sends that data to the new document, then saves the document and closes the server. This program is included as BuildSupplierTable.PRG in the Developer Download files available at www.hentzenwerke.com. **Figure 1** shows part of the resulting document.

Listing 2. *Using a Word-specific method. This program creates a Word table with one method call from the Word wrapper class.*

```
* Build a Word table using the wrapper class
#DEFINE CR CHR(13)

LOCAL oWord

* Open Word
oWord = NewObject("cusWord","automation")

WITH oWord
```

```
   .OpenServer()

   IF NOT .IsServerOpen()
      WAIT WINDOW "Couldn't open Word."
      RETURN .F.
   ENDIF

   * Create a document
   .NewDocument()

   * Check whether document is open
   IF .IsDocOpen()
      * Put some text in the new document
      OPEN DATABASE _SAMPLES + "TasTrade\Data\TasTrade"
      SELECT Company_Name, Contact_Name, Contact_Title, Phone ;
         FROM Supplier ;
         ORDER BY 1 ;
         INTO CURSOR SupplierList

      oRange = .oDocument.Range()
      .DBFToTable(oRange, ,.F., .T.)

      USE IN Supplier
      USE IN SupplierList
   ENDIF

   * Save the new document
   .SaveDocument(, SYS(2023) + "\suppliers.doc")

   * Close Word
   .CloseServer()
ENDWITH

RETURN
```

Aux joyeux ecclésiastiques	Guylène Nodier	Sales Manager	(1) 03.83.00.68
Bigfoot Breweries	Cheryl Saylor	Regional Account Rep.	(503) 555-9931
Cooperativa de Quesos 'Las Cabras'	Antonio del Valle Saavedra	Export Administrator	(98) 598 76 54
Escargots Nouveaux	Marie Delamare	Sales Manager	85.57.00.07
Exotic Liquids	Charlotte Cooper	Purchasing Manager	(71) 555-2222
Formaggi Fortini s.r.l.	Elio Rossi	Sales Representative	(0544) 60323
Forêts d'érables	Chantal Goulet	Accounting Manager	(514) 555-2955
G'day, Mate	Wendy Mackenzie	Sales Representative	(02) 555-5914
Gai pâturage	Eliane Noz	Sales Representative	38.76.98.06
Grandma Kelly's Homestead	Regina Murphy	Sales Representative	(313) 555-5735

Figure 1. *List of suppliers. This table was generated by Listing 2, which uses the Word wrapper class. The DBFToTable method handles all the details of moving data from a cursor to a Word table.*

Wrapping Excel—from table to graph

As we saw in Chapter 9, "Excel's Graphing Engine," Excel has a wonderful graphing engine. The ChartWizard method has many parameters, most of which don't change over the course of your application. The method here, MakeGraph, takes a range of data and creates a chart sheet displaying the data. It accepts three parameters: one required, the range of data as an object, and two optional, a string to name the chart sheet, and the title of the graph.

A series of custom properties hold the defaults for the chart. The property oChart stores an object reference to the chart, in the event that you want to directly edit the chart. nChartType determines the type of chart (bar, column, and so on), and nChartFormat determines which of Excel's predefined formats is used (for a complete description, see "Chart types" in Chapter 9). The default for those two is column type, using the first predefined format. Your program can easily change these properties to generate different kinds of charts (or add optional parameters to override the property settings). The nChartPlotBy property determines whether the series are in rows or columns; the default is columns. Several other parameters in the call to ChartWizard are hard-coded, but these, too, could be switched to refer to properties of the cusExcel object, or to parameters passed into the MakeGraph method. Here's the code:

```
* cusExcel.MakeGraph
* This method wraps Excel's ChartWizard method.
* It creates a graph from a range of data.

LPARAMETERS oGraphRange, cSheetName, cTitle


* Verify oGraphRange
IF VarType(oGraphRange) <> "O"
  This.TellUser("The graph range must be an object.")
  RETURN .F.
ENDIF

* Check cSheetName
IF VarType(cSheetName) <> "C"
  cSheetName = .NULL.
ENDIF

* Check cTitle
IF VarType(cTitle) <> "C"
  cTitle = ""
ENDIF

WITH This.oServer

  * Generate the chart
  .Charts.Add()
  IF NOT ISNULL(cSheetName)
    .ActiveChart.Name = cSheetName
  ENDIF

  * The only constants are that there is one row and one column
  * for series and category labels, and it has a legend
  * (corresponds to the three 1's)
```

```
This.oChart = .ActiveChart.ChartWizard(oGraphRange, ;
    This.nChartType, This.nChartFormat,  This.nChartPlotBy, ;
    1,  1,  1, cTitle,  "", "", "")

ENDWITH
```

The first part of the code performs a series of checks to ensure that you've passed good data. Then it adds the chart sheet, renames it (if a valid name is passed), and then formats the chart using the ChartWizard method. What makes this so special is that you now need to remember three parameters—the range to graph, what to call the resulting chart, and what to title the chart—instead of a long series of ChartWizard parameters. If your graphs need special formatting (such as incorporating the corporate colors into the background, or changing the axes' font face, size, and color), you can include it here. Imagine how much time you save as a developer writing this code once.

Listing 3 is a program that uses the Excel wrapper class with the Excel-specific MakeGraph method. It instantiates an Automation server and opens a new document (a Workbook, in Excel's case). Then, it creates a cursor based on the Product table from TasTrade, choosing only the Confections records. It sends that data to the new workbook, creates the graph, saves the document, and closes the server. This program is included as BuildGraph.PRG in the Developer Download files available at www.hentzenwerke.com. **Figure 2** shows part of the resulting document.

Listing 3. Using an Excel-specific method. This program creates an Excel graph with one method call from the Excel wrapper class.

```
* BuildGraph.PRG

* Demonstrate the Excel wrapper class with
* Excel-specific MakeGraph method.

LOCAL oExcel, oRange, cRow

* Open Excel
oExcel = NewObject("cusExcel","automation")

WITH oExcel
   .OpenServer()

   IF NOT .IsServerOpen()
      WAIT WINDOW "Couldn't open Excel."
      RETURN .F.
   ENDIF

   * Create a workbook
   .NewDocument()

   * Check whether workbook is open
   IF .IsDocOpen()

      * Get the product data cursor
      IF NOT DBUSED("TasTrade")
```

```
        OPEN DATABASE (_SAMPLES + "TASTRADE\DATA\Tastrade")
     ENDIF
     IF NOT USED("Products")
       USE Products IN 0
     ENDIF

     SELECT English_Name, ;
            Unit_Price, ;
            Unit_Cost ;
       FROM Products ;
      WHERE Category_ID = "     3" ;
        AND NOT Discontinued ;
        INTO CURSOR GraphProduct

     WITH .oDocument.Sheets[1]
       * Put in data headings
       .Range("A1").Value = "Product Name"
       .Range("B1").Value = "Unit Price"
       .Range("C1").Value = "Unit Cost"

       * Put the cursor's data into the spreadsheet
       SELECT GraphProduct
       SCAN
         cRow = ALLTRIM(STR(RECNO() + 1))
         .Range("A" + cRow).Value = GraphProduct.English_Name
         .Range("B" + cRow).Value = GraphProduct.Unit_Price
         .Range("C" + cRow).Value = GraphProduct.Unit_Cost
       ENDSCAN

       * Set up the range
       oRange = .Range("A1:C" + cRow)

     ENDWITH

       * Build the graph.
       .MakeGraph(oRange, "Confections", "Price vs. Cost of Confections")

   ENDIF

  RELEASE oRange

   * Save the new workbook
   .SaveDocument(, SYS(2023) + "\sample.xls")

   * Close Excel
   .CloseServer()
ENDWITH

* Clean up the data
CLOSE DATA ALL

RETURN
```

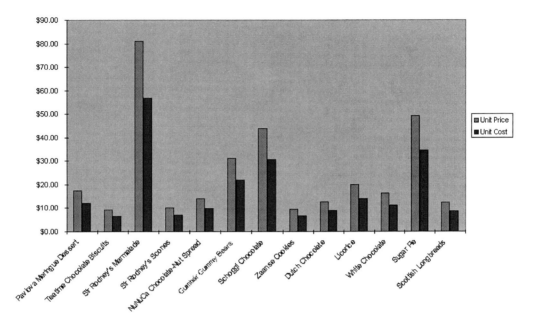

Figure 2. *A graph showing the price vs. the cost of confections. This graph was generated by Listing 3, which uses the Excel wrapper class. The MakeGraph method handles all the details of generating the graph.*

The example points out another Excel-specific method you're likely to want—a method to send data from a VFP cursor to a Worksheet. With such a method, the code in Listing 3 would be simplified even further.

Wrapping PowerPoint—standardizing text

In Chapter 10, "PowerPoint Basics," we discuss the many properties available for text frames. Good presentation design dictates that font face, size, and color should remain constant throughout your presentation, to avoid the ransom-note effect. Of course, there are times when changing one or more of the properties is necessary to call attention to the phrase. We've created an AddTextFrame method to standardize the text properties, yet allow for quick changes.

Before we get into the AddTextFrame method, we must discuss a serious inconsistency between PowerPoint and the other servers. The other servers always have an active document of some sort (ActiveDocument in Word, ActiveWorkbook, ActiveSheet, and ActiveChart in Excel) that's always available. PowerPoint works a bit differently. When PowerPoint isn't visible, the ActivePresentation property isn't available (in fact, accessing it generates an error). In addition, while there isn't an ActiveSlide property, you can query the View for the SlideIndex property. However, when PowerPoint isn't visible, Views aren't available (accessing Views generates an error in this case). We suspect that PowerPoint likes to be visible (since it is a very visual product), and when it's not visible, it just doesn't accept that there are active views or presentations, since nobody can view them.

To make things work properly, we need to make a few changes. The first is to the oDocument_Access method, which verifies that oDocument still points to a valid document (see "Keeping track of the active document" earlier in this chapter). We've added a check to see whether the server is visible before setting oDocument to ActivePresentation, to prevent invisible instances from raising an error. There's a side effect here: if you run PowerPoint nonvisually, you must keep oDocument current on your own (by updating it whenever you change presentations). Here's the changed code for the oDocument_Access method:

```
* Make sure the property points to the currently active document.
IF This.IsServerOpen() AND This.IsDocOpen()

  * PowerPoint has no Active properties when it is not Visible.
  * Be sure that you don't change the active Presentation when
  * PowerPoint is not visible (if you do, manually update oDocument).
  IF This.oServer.Visible <> 0
    This.oDocument = This.oServer.ActivePresentation
    * Else, assume that the developer's kept up oDocument, and assume
    * whatever it's pointing to is valid.
  ENDIF

ELSE
   This.oDocument = .NULL.
ENDIF

RETURN THIS.oDocument
```

The other change we need to make is to track the current slide. This requires a custom oCurrentSlide property and a custom AddSlide method. oCurrentSlide, as its name implies, tracks the current slide. The new AddSlide method is used to add new slides and update oCurrentSlide. It takes two parameters: the slide layout value (see "Using the slide layouts" in Chapter 10 for a list of the values) and the index of the new slide in the slide show. Here's the code:

```
* cusPowerPoint.AddSlide
* Wrap the Slides.Add method in order to
* keep track of the current slide.

LPARAMETER nSlideLayout, nNewIndex
      * nSlideLayout = The number of the slide layout. Optional.
      *                (Corresponds to ppLayout constants.)
      *                If omitted, ppLayoutBlank is used.
      * nNewIndex = The Index of the new slide. Optional.
      *             If omitted, the index of the slide in oCurrentSlide
      *             is used. If no slide in oCurrentSlide, 1 is used.
WITH This

  * Check Parameters
  IF PARAMETERS() = 0
    nSlideLayout = ppLayoutBlank
  ENDIF
```

```
  IF PARAMETERS() <= 1
    IF TYPE(".oCurrentSlide") = "O"
      nNewIndex = .oCurrentSlide.SlideIndex
    ELSE
      nNewIndex = 1
    ENDIF
  ENDIF

  * Add the slide
  .oCurrentSlide = .oDocument.Slides.Add(nNewIndex, nSlideLayout)
ENDWITH
```

The AddTextFrame method places a text box in the current presentation (referenced by the oDocument property) on the current slide (referenced by the oCurrentSlide property). AddTextFrame uses the custom TextFrameFont, TextFrameFontSize, and TextFrameTextColor properties to set the look of the text. The idea is that you set these properties once, and change them only when needed (remembering to set them back when you're done). The same concept holds for TextFrameHeight and TextFrameWidth, which set the default height and width for the text frame. By storing all these properties, you can concentrate on the items you need, which are passed as parameters: the text, the distance from the top of the slide, in points, and the distance from the left of the slide, in points. Optionally, you can pass the height and width of the frame (in points) to override the default properties. The method returns a reference to the new frame, in case you need to further manipulate the text frame. Here's the code for the AddTextFrame method:

```
* cusPowerPoint.AddTextFrame
* Add a text box to the current slide of the current presentation.

LPARAMETERS cTextString, nLeftPoints, nTopPoints, ;
            nWidthPoints, nHeightPoints
    * cTextString   = String to place in text frame
    * nLeftPoints   = The left edge, in points
    * nTopPoints    = The top edge, in points
    * nWidthPoints  = The width of the text frame, in points.
    *                 Optional; uses TextFrameWidth property if not passed.
    * nHeightPoints = The height of the text frame, in points.
    *                 Optional; uses TextFrameHeight property if not passed.

LOCAL oNewFrame, nCurrentSlide
    * oNewFrame = The object reference to the new TextFrame
    * nCurrentSlide = Index of the current slide

* If there's no text string, just return
IF EMPTY(cTextString)
  RETURN .F.
ENDIF

* Check the left and top, to be sure they're numeric
IF TYPE("nLeftPoints") <> "N"
  This.TellUser("Must specify the left edge in points.")
  RETURN .F.
ENDIF

IF TYPE("nTopPoints") <> "N"
```

```
   This.TellUser("Must specify the top edge in points.")
   RETURN .F.
ENDIF

* Check the width and height -- if not passed, set them
* to the default; if passed, ensure they're numeric
IF TYPE("nWidthPoints") <> "N"
  nWidthPoints =  This.TextFrameWidth
ENDIF

IF TYPE("nHeightPoints") <> "N"
  nHeightPoints =  This.TextFrameHeight
ENDIF

* Check the status of oCurrentSlide
IF TYPE("This.oCurrentSlide") <> "O"
  This.TellUser("oCurrentSlide property must be set.")
  RETURN .F.
ENDIF

* Place the text frame
oNewFrame = This.oCurrentSlide.Shapes.AddTextBox(1, ;
            nLeftPoints, nTopPoints, ;
            nWidthPoints, nHeightPoints)

WITH oNewFrame
  * Set it invisible, to maximize performance
  .Visible = .F.

  * Add the text to the text frame, and set the
  * rest of the properties
  WITH oNewFrame.TextFrame
    WITH .TextRange
      .Text = cTextString

      .Font.Name = This.TextFrameFont
      .Font.Size = This.TextFrameFontSize
      .Font.Color.RGB = This.TextFrameTextColor
    ENDWITH

    .MarginLeft    = 0
    .MarginTop     = 0
    .MarginRight   = 0
    .MarginBottom  = 0

  ENDWITH

  .Visible = .T.
ENDWITH

RETURN oNewFrame
```

 Listing 4 is a program that uses the PowerPoint wrapper class. It instantiates an Automation server and opens a new document (a Presentation, in PowerPoint's case). Then it adds a new slide with the AddSlide method, and uses the AddTextFrame method to add three text frames. This program is included as BuildPptSlide.PRG in the

Developer Download files available at www.hentzenwerke.com. **Figure 3** shows part of the
resulting document.

Listing 4. *Using a PowerPoint-specific subclass. This program creates a PowerPoint
slide with one call to the PowerPoint wrapper class.*

```
* BuildPptSlide.PRG

* Demonstrate the PowerPoint wrapper class with
* PowerPoint-specific methods

#DEFINE CR   CHR(13)
#DEFINE ppLayoutTitle  1
#DEFINE msoIn2Pts      72

LOCAL oPowerPoint, OrigTextColor

* Open PowerPoint
oPowerPoint = NewObject("cusPowerPoint","automation")

WITH oPowerPoint
   .OpenServer()

   IF NOT .IsServerOpen()
      WAIT WINDOW "Couldn't open PowerPoint."
      RETURN .F.
   ENDIF

   * Create a document
   .NewDocument()

   * Check whether document is open
   IF .IsDocOpen()

      * Add a slide using the wrapper class. No parameters
      * means it will add a blank slide as the first slide.
      .AddSlide()

      * Put some text frames on the new slide
      .AddTextFrame("First text box.", 2 * msoIn2Pts, 2 * msoIn2Pts)
      .AddTextFrame("Second text box.", 6 * msoIn2Pts, 2 * msoIn2Pts)

      OrigTextColor = .TextFrameTextColor
      .TextFrameTextColor = RGB(0, 255, 255) && Cyan
      .AddTextFrame("Third text box.", 4 * msoIn2Pts, 4 * msoIn2Pts)
      .TextFrameTextColor = OrigTextColor

   ENDIF

   * Save the new document
   .SaveDocument(, SYS(2023) + "\sample.ppt")

   * Close PowerPoint
   .CloseServer()
ENDWITH

RETURN
```

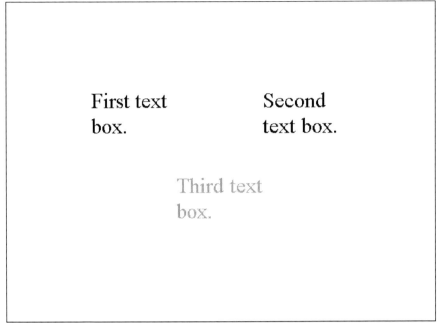

Figure 3. *A slide showing simple text frames added with the AddTextFrame PowerPoint-specific method. This slide was generated by Listing 4, which uses the PowerPoint wrapper class.*

Wrapping it up

Creating your own wrapper classes may seem like an overwhelming task. Just remember that you don't have to do it all at once. The secret is to stay alert and, as soon as you find yourself thinking, "I've written this code before," stop and take the time to wrap it up.

In an ideal world, of course, you would wrap every server method before you use it so that you wouldn't get caught short when the next version of the server application introduces a change. But we don't write code in an ideal world. Wrap the methods you use regularly, and put the most effort into the code you use most often. If you find that a method is becoming overly complicated or seems to need a lot of parameters, consider breaking it up into multiple methods.

Whatever you wrap, document it carefully. You're likely to remember how to use the methods you use every day, but you won't necessarily remember the names and parameters for methods you only use once a month.

Appendices

Appendix A
On-line User Communities

When you're really stuck, the best place to get help is usually an on-line user group of some sort.

The two of us first met on-line. Before we actually saw each other face-to-face, we'd been corresponding in CompuServe's FoxForum for quite a while. We met the Technical Editor of this book and the Publisher the same way. In fact, most of our best opportunities in the FoxPro community came from relationships that began on-line. So we're big believers that the place you go to get help with your programming problems is on-line.

The thing that distinguishes one resource from another is the quality of the help you get. For the most part, all the help that's available comes from volunteers who enjoy answering questions as a way of honing their own skills or to thank the people who helped them along the way. Many of the people (including Tamar) who answer questions in the places we list are Microsoft Most Valuable Professionals, recipients of an annual award given to those who spend inordinate amounts of time helping others on-line.

The tricky part about listing on-line resources is that the particulars can change. Some places stay put for a long time, but others seem to move around regularly. Even those that we'd consider permanent sometimes undergo revision. While we were writing this book, CompuServe made major changes in its forum structure. So, while this list is accurate as of the date we're writing it (and this is the last part of the book we're writing), we're sadly aware that the minute we commit it to paper, something may change. So search around the links we list, or use search engines to find similarly named sites if the exact locations we supply are no longer valid.

We're dividing this list into two parts, FoxPro resources and Office resources. As FoxPro developers, we're far more familiar with the former, but we've done our best to root out the latter for you, as well. Also, before we get started listing user communities, we should remind you that Microsoft offers considerable on-line resources at its MSDN web site, **msdn.microsoft.com**. That site provides access to the Microsoft Knowledge Base, tons of documentation and technical articles, and lots of other support documents. It's often a good place to start your search for help.

FoxPro resources

The granddaddy of them all, the place where it all started, is CompuServe. There's been a Fox presence there for nearly as long as there have been Fox products. Starting as a single section in a multi-vendor forum, like Topsy, Fox Software's FoxForum "grew and grew" so that it needed an entire forum. A second, less technical, forum (FoxUsers) was added in the early '90s. Both weathered the migration to Microsoft's sponsorship, then finally to a third party when Microsoft left CompuServe for the Internet. For a brief, glorious period when Visual FoxPro first came out, there were even three FoxPro forums. That quickly settled back down to two forums, divided roughly into one for Visual FoxPro, and one for FoxPro 2.x and general discussions. Then, in December 1999, the two FoxPro forums were merged with several other forums devoted to Microsoft software to form the MSDevApps forum. Four of its sections are devoted specifically to FoxPro and Visual FoxPro, while a number of other sections address more general development issues and topics related to Microsoft-centric development (like HTML Help). CompuServe forums are a pleasure to use because of their rich threaded messaging model—each original message is followed by the replies to that message, as well as the replies to the replies and so on. In addition to being threaded, it's easy to find replies to messages you posted, something that's hard to do in many web-based messaging systems, even those that are threaded. In addition, CompuServe does a tremendous job of keeping out spam—you won't find abusive messages or ads for get rich quick schemes or porno sites. As of April 2000, many CompuServe forums are open to the general public, so you can participate in them, even if you're not a CompuServe member. Point your browser to **go.compuserve.com/msdevapps?loc=US**.

Microsoft sponsors newsgroups for FoxPro and Visual FoxPro on its public server, **msnews.microsoft.com** (Microsoft has assured us that if there are any changes to the addresses of any of their FoxPro sites, there will be information on **msdn.microsoft.com/vfoxpro**—or at least that address will be redirected to the new address). Look for groups with names beginning with "microsoft.public.fox". Although Microsoft tries to keep out solicitations and other way off-topic posts, there's more of that stuff here than in any of the other FoxPro sites we list.

One of the busiest places to talk FoxPro on the Internet is the Universal Thread at **www.universalthread.com**. Like CompuServe, it offers threaded messaging with a way to find replies to your own postings. It's privately owned, and offers free access to all messages with a limited user interface. A reasonable monthly fee gets you a Premier Membership that gives access to some more advanced tools for using it.

A newer site that's gotten a lot of attention is **www.foxforum.com**, which has a different approach to looking at a message and its replies. It puts them all into a single message so that you don't have to keep clicking on Next, Next, Next to see the whole thread.

Unique in the FoxPro community is the forum's sister, the FoxForum wiki, **fox.wikis.com**. Rather than a discussion group or forum, it's an evolving knowledge base where anyone can post information on a topic and others can add to it or edit it. You can find entries there on everything from object-oriented frameworks to naming conventions and just about anything else to do with FoxPro and the Fox community you can think of. If it's not there, you can add it yourself.

Advisor Media sponsors forums for a variety of products, including FoxPro, on its web site, **www.advisor.com**. Choose Advisor forums from the home page.

Brand-new as we were putting this list together is **www.vfpguru.com**. The site is impressive-looking, featuring forums and a chat area, as well as space for downloads and articles. It remains to be seen whether it will attract enough users to make it worth stopping by.

Also a new addition is a discussion group for Visual FoxPro sponsored by Fawcette Technical Publications. Unlike vfpguru.com, however, devx.com is well-known in the developer community for its other discussion groups, so we expect this one to quickly become active. You'll find it at **news.devx.com**.

In addition to all this, a number of companies and individuals working with Visual FoxPro provide useful information and downloads on their web sites. You'll find links to them either as advertising at some of the sites listed here or in the messages themselves.

Office resources

As with FoxPro, you can find help for the Office products on CompuServe. Also like FoxPro, the forums that support Office were consolidated in late 1999. The new home for Office is MSOForum, and it includes sections for Word, Excel, PowerPoint, Outlook, Access, and several other related products. Best of all, as with FoxPro, the people who hang out there are warm, friendly, and helpful. To get there on the web, point to **go.compuserve.com/msofficeforum?loc=US**.

The Microsoft public newsgroups on msnews.microsoft.com include groups for all the Office products. They're spread out all over the server, but look for groups with the various product names in their names plus strings like "vba" or "programming" or "automation." Don't be too choosy, though—it appears that there's a single group for all PowerPoint questions called microsoft.public.powerpoint.

Woody Leonhard has been writing about Word and the other Office products practically since before we even heard of them. His web site, **www.wopr.com**, offers discussion groups for the Office products, as well as a pair of newsletters, *Woody's Office Watch* and *Woody's Windows Watch*, and more.

Many of the Microsoft MVPs have web sites that provide tips, tricks, and code. Rather than trying to provide a comprehensive list here of the Office-related sites, we're pointing you to a site that contains such a list and gets updated occasionally. Our thanks to Karl Petersen for maintaining this list. Check out **www.mvps.org/links.html** for links to sites about not just Office, but pretty much any Microsoft product you can think of.

Finally, if all else fails, don't forget to try the search engines, particularly those that archive newsgroup postings. With the worldwide distribution of the tools we're working with, it is a rare day that you encounter a problem someone has not seen, if not solved.

On-line etiquette

In closing, we present some comments on how to behave in forums and newsgroups. The key is to remember the word we used in the title of this appendix—"community." Act as you would in your neighborhood and you'll get along just fine.

What does that mean? First, almost everyone who answers questions on-line is a volunteer who does it because he or she enjoys it. It's not his or her job, so don't go in with the expectation that someone "owes" you an answer. The person who answers your question is doing you a favor. Acknowledge that favor by your attitude.

In the same vein, the reason on-line communities work is that people take the time to answer other people's questions. If you can, return the favor and answer someone else's question.

Within a given forum or set of newsgroups, post your question only once. The regulars read all the sections of the forum or all the groups for their subject, so they'll see it. Posting the same question to many groups (called "cross-posting") is considered rude.

When you've solved your problem, posting a brief "thanks, that did the trick" note is fine, though not strictly necessary. Don't post a "thank you" to everyone who answered you. A single "thanks to all who helped" is sufficient. If the problem was particularly hairy, do post a single message explaining how you finally solved it, so that others can learn from your experience.

Don't send e-mail to someone who answers your question unless he or she specifically asks you to do so. One of the advantages of public forums and newsgroups is that many people learn from the exchanges there. When you switch to private e-mail, others can't learn from your discussion. In addition, many of the people who answer questions are just plain too busy to answer questions in e-mail, as well.

Use your real name. Technical forums are no place for cute handles.

Most of the on-line communities have a set of rules. The rules of conduct for the Microsoft newsgroups, for example, are pretty basic—you'll find them at **support.microsoft.com/support/news/rules.asp**. On the Universal Thread, the list is much more extensive—the rules are accessed from a link on the home page. Wherever you go, you should be able to find the rules; if you can't find them, ask. Observing local customs is just as much of a good idea when you visit an on-line community as it is when you travel in the physical world.

Appendix B
ChartWizard Values

Excel's ChartWizard method takes two parameters, and uses the combination to set the ChartType property (and potentially other properties).

In Chapter 9, "Excel's Graphing Engine," Table 1 shows a few of the values for the nChartFormat and nChartType variables for the ChartWizard method. This appendix shows the complete series of values.

The ChartWizard method takes two parameters, nChartType and nChartFormat, and the combination of the two sets the Chart's ChartType property. The value to pass as the nChartType parameter is shown in the bolded heading, along with its constant. For example, the first line shows "For Chart Type: xlArea (1)." Use the value 1 or the constant xlArea for the nChartType property, to select an area chart. For the nChartFormat parameter, select a value from the second column (Chart Format Parameter) based on the description shown.

The ChartWizard method fills the ChartType property with the value shown in the Chart Type Property column. The Chart Type Constant column lists the corresponding constant name.

Note that the ChartWizard sets more properties than just the ChartType; grid lines, labels, and the like are also set as a part of the nChartFormat parameter.

Those items marked with an asterisk (*) are extremely similar to their same-named items higher up in the table, so much so as to be virtually indistinguishable (though there must be some difference, perhaps a single property that isn't readily apparent).

Chart Format Description	Chart Format Parameter	Chart Type Property	Chart Type Constant
For Chart Type: xlArea (1)			
Stacked Area	1	76	xlAreaStacked
100% Stacked Area	2	77	xlAreaStacked100
Stacked Area with vertical block lines	3	76	xlAreaStacked
Stacked Area with black grid lines	4	76	xlAreaStacked
Stacked Area with series labels	5	76	xlAreaStacked
For Chart Type: xlBar (2)			
Clustered Bar	1	57	xlBarClustered
Clustered Bar*	2	57	xlBarClustered
Stacked Bar	3	58	xlBarStacked
Clustered Bar with overlap set to 30	4	57	xlBarClustered
100% Stacked Bar	5	59	xlBarStacked100
Clustered Bar with black vertical grid lines	6	57	xlBarClustered
Clustered Bar with data labels	7	57	xlBarClustered
Clustered Bar with 0 overlap and 0 gap width	8	57	xlBarClustered
Stacked Bar with series lines	9	58	xlBarStacked
100% Stacked Bar with series lines	10	59	xlBarStacked100

Chart Format Description	Chart Format Parameter	Chart Type Property	Chart Type Constant
For Chart Type: xlColumn (3)			
Clustered Column with gap width set to 150	1	51	xlColumnClustered
Clustered Column with gap width set to 150*	2	51	xlColumnClustered
Stacked Column	3	52	xlColumnStacked
Clustered Column with overlap set to 30	4	51	xlColumnClustered
100% Stacked Column	5	53	xlColumnStacked100
Clustered Column with horizontal grid lines	6	51	xlColumnClustered
Clustered Column with data labels	7	51	xlColumnClustered
Clustered Column with 0 overlap and 0 gap width	8	51	xlColumnClustered
Stacked Column with series lines	9	52	xlColumnStacked
100% Stacked Column with series lines	10	53	xlColumnStacked100
For Chart Type: xlLine (4)			
Line with markers	1	65	xlLineMarkers
Line with no data markers	2	4	xlLine
Data markers only (no connecting lines)	3	65	xlLineMarkers
Lines with markers and dashed horizontal grid	4	65	xlLineMarkers
Lines with markers and dashed grid lines	5	65	xlLineMarkers
Lines with markers and logarithmic scale	6	65	xlLineMarkers
Data markers only with high-low lines	7	65	xlLineMarkers
Stock Chart	8	88	xlStockHLC
Stock Chart*	9	88	xlStockHLC
Smoothed line with no markers	10	4	xlLine
For Chart Type: xlPie (5)			
Pie with no labels	1	5	xlPie
Pie with labels, highlighting first wedge	2	5	xlPie
Pie with no labels*	3	5	xlPie
Exploded pie	4	69	xlPieExploded
Pie with label data labels	5	5	xlPie
Pie with percent data labels	6	5	xlPie
Pie with label and percent data labels	7	5	xlPie
For Chart Type: xlRadar (-4151)			
Radar with markers and category labels	1	81	xlRadarMarkers
Radar with category labels	2	-4111	xlCombination
Radar with no axes, with category labels	3	-4111	xlCombination
Radar with category labels and grid lines	4	-4111	xlCombination
Radar with logarithmic axis	5	-4111	xlCombination
Filled Radar with category labels	6	82	xlRadarFilled
For Chart Type: xlXYScatter (-4169)			
Scatter	1	-4111	xlCombination
Scatter with connecting lines	2	74	xlXYScatterLines
Scatter with black grid lines	3	-4111	xlCombination
Scatter on logarithmic axis, horizontal lines	4	-4111	xlCombination
Scatter on logarithmic axis, both grid lines	5	-4111	xlCombination
Smoothed line with markers	6	-4111	xlCombination

Chart Format Description	Chart Format Parameter	Chart Type Property	Chart Type Constant
For Chart Type: xl3DArea (-4098)			
Stacked 3D area	1	78	xl3DAreaStacked
Stacked 3D area with series labels	2	78	xl3DAreaStacked
Stacked 3D area with vertical block lines, no grid	3	78	xl3DAreaStacked
Stacked 3D area with data label	4	78	xl3DAreaStacked
Area 3D elevated, no grid lines	5	-4098	xl3DArea
Area 3D elevated, both grid lines	6	-4098	xl3DArea
Area 3D elevated, vertical grid lines	7	-4098	xl3DArea
Stacked 3D area with data label, no walls	8	78	xl3DAreaStacked
For Chart Type: xl3DBar (-4099)			
Clustered 3D	1	60	xl3DBarColumn
Stacked 3D	2	61	xl3DBarStacked
100% Stacked 3D	3	62	xl3DBarStacked
Clustered 3D with walls	4	60	xl3DBarColumn
Clustered 3D, no walls	5	60	xl3DBarColumn
For Chart Type: xl3DColumn (-4100)			
Clustered 3D	1	54	xl3DColumnClustered
Stacked 3D	2	55	xl3DColumnStacked
100% Stacked 3D	3	56	xl3DColumnStacked100
Clustered 3D, no elevation or rotation	4	54	xl3DColumnClustered
Clustered 3D elevated, no grids	5	-4100	xl3DColumn
Clustered 3D elevated, both grids	6	-4100	xl3DColumn
Clustered 3D elevated, vertical grids	7	-4100	xl3DColumn
Clustered 3D, no walls	8	54	xl3DColumnClustered
For Chart Type: xl3DLine (-4101)			
3D Line, no grid	1	-4101	xl3DLine
3D Line with both grid lines	2	-4101	xl3DLine
3D Line with vertical grid lines	3	-4101	xl3DLine
3D Line, logarithmic axis	4	-4101	xl3DLine
For Chart Type: xl3DPie (-4102)			
3D Pie with no labels	1	-4102	xl3DPie
3D Pie with labels, highlight wedge	2	-4102	xl3DPie
3D Pie with no labels*	3	-4102	xl3DPie
3D Exploded pie	4	70	xl3DPieExploded
3D Pie with label data labels	5	-4102	xl3DPie
3D Pie with percent data labels	6	-4102	xl3DPie
3D Pie with label and percent data labels	7	-4102	xl3DPie
For Chart Type: xl3DSurface (-4103)			
3D Surface (with color)	1	83	xlSurface
Wireframe 3D surface (no color)	2	84	xlSurfaceWireFrame
Contour (with color)	3	85	xlSurfaceTopView
Wireframe contour (no color)	4	86	xlSurfaceTopViewWireframe
For Chart Type: xlDoughnut (-4120)			
Doughnut	1	-4120	xlDoughnut
Exploded doughnut, highlight data point	2	-4120	xlDoughnut
Exploded doughnut	3	-4120	xlDoughnut
Exploded doughnut*	4	80	xlDoughnutExploded
Doughnut with label data labels	5	-4120	xlDoughnut

Chart Format Description	Chart Format Parameter	Chart Type Property	Chart Type Constant
Doughnut with percent data labels	6	-4120	xlDoughnut
Doughnut with label and percent data labels	7	-4120	xlDoughnut
For Chart Type: xlCombination (-4111)			
Column and line	1	-4111	xlCombination
Column and line, second axis is currency	2	-4111	xlCombination
Line, second axis is currency	3	-4111	xlCombination
Column and area	4	-4111	xlCombination
Stock	5	88	xlStockHLC
Column and high-low	6	-4111	xlCombination

Index